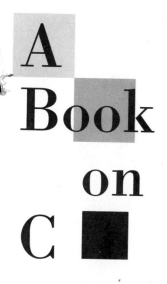

A Book on C

D1123418

Al Kelley / Ira Pohl

PROGRAMMING IN C

THIRD EDITION

The Benjamin Cummings Publishing Company, Inc.
Redwood City, California ● Menlo Park, California ● Reading, Massachusetts
New York ● Don Mills, Ontario ● Wokingham, U.K.
Amsterdam ● Bonn ● Sydney ● Singapore ● Tokyo ● Madrid ● San Juan

Acquisitions Editor: J. Carter Shanklin
Executive Editor: Dan Joraanstad
Production Editor: Adam Ray
Editorial Assistant: Melissa Standen
Marketing Manager: Mary Tudor
Manufacturing Coordinator: Janet Weaver
Composition: ETP
Cover Designer: Annabelle Ison
Text Designer: Peter Vacek
Copyeditor: Carol Dondrea
Proofreader: Joe Ruddick
Indexer: Joan Dickey

Library of Congress Cataloging-in-Publication Data
Kelley, Al.
    A book on C : programming in C / Al Kelley and Ira Pohl.–3rd ed.
      p. cm.
    Includes index.
    ISBN 0-8053-1677-9
    1. C (Computer program language) I. Pohl, Ira. II. Title.
QA76.73.C15K44 1995
005.13\3–dc20   94-32576
                                      CIP

ISBN 0-8053-1677-9

2 3 4 5 6 7 8 9 10 DOC 98 97 96 95

The Benjamin/Cummings Publishing Company, Inc.
390 Bridge Parkway
Redwood City, California 94065

For additional information on programming with C and C++, the Benjamin/Cummings Publishing Company offers the following titles by noted authors Al Kelley and Ira Pohl.

C by Dissection, Al Kelley and Ira Pohl, 1992 / 450 pp. ISBN: (0-8053-3140-9)
  • Introduces beginning students to the powerful C language and features a step-by-step guide to ANSI C programs. New edition coming in Fall 1995.

C++ for C Programmers, 2/e, Ira Pohl, 1994 / 368 pp. ISBN: (0-8053-3159-x)
  • By building on the programmer's knowledge of C, this text provides a fast and easy transition to C++.

C++ for Pascal Programmers, 2/e, Ira Pohl, 1995 / 385 pp. ISBN: (0-8053-3158-1)
  • This new edition teaches Pascal programmers C++, by first introducing them to C and then focusing on this powerful object-oriented language.

Object-Oriented Programming Using C++, Ira Pohl, 1993 / 496 pp. ISBN: (0-8053-5382-8)
  • This best-selling book provides a clear and thorough introduction to object-oriented programming using C++ and includes extensive exercises making the book ideal for self-study. New edition coming in Fall 1995.

Turbo C++, Ira Pohl, 1991 / 300 pp. ISBN: (0-8053-6017-4)
  • This tutorial-based book provides a quick, practical introduction to the powerful features of Turbo C++.

To purchase these titles contact your local bookstores or call the Benjamin/Cummings Publishing Company at 1-800-950-2665.

To Our Parents

CONTENTS

Appendix A: The Standard Library   568

Appendix B: C Language Syntax   610

Appendix C: Differences: ANSI C Compared to Traditional C   615

PREFACE

A Book on C conveys an appreciation for both the elegant simplicity and the power of this general-purpose programming language. By presenting interactive running programs from many application areas, this book describes the ANSI version of the C language. The complete language is presented step by step, along with many complete working programs. Where appropriate, we discuss the differences between traditional C and ANSI C, and differences between ANSI C and C++. Dozens of example programs are used to illustrate each important language feature, and many tables summarize key information and provide easy access for later reference. Each chapter ends with a summary and exercises. The summary reviews key elements presented in the chapter, and the exercises augment and extend the text.

This book assumes a general-purpose use of the C language, and as such, both students and professionals will find it helpful. For students, it is intended for use in either a first or second programming course. However, it can be readily used in conjunction with courses on topics such as comparative programming languages, computational linguistics, data structures, database systems, fractal geometry, graphics, numerical analysis, operating systems, programming methodology, and scientific applications. Applications from each of these domains are suitable to C and all features of C needed to code such applications are explained. It is appropriate for a data structures course because advanced data structuring features such as enumeration types, unions, self-referential structures, and ragged arrays are discussed. For operating systems courses concerned with UNIX or MS-DOS, the book explores the file structure and systems routines that enable the C programmer to add to existing systems libraries and understand the C code underlying the operating system. For applications programming and scientific programming, it discusses how to write sample function libraries. Statistics, root finding, sorting, text manipulation, file handling, and game playing are all represented with working code.

NEW C++ SECTION

In Chapter 13, "Moving from C to C++," we discuss how the C programmer can very naturally and easily begin programming in C++. This chapter allows ready migration to a complete understanding of the C++ language as presented in *C++ for C Programmers*, Second Edition, (ISBN 0–8053–3159–X), by Ira Pohl. Much of the material on arrays and structures is the basis for the data-centered view that underlies object-oriented programming in C and C++.

ENHANCED FEATURES

Complete ANSI C Language

Computer professionals will find a complete treatment of the language, including enumeration types, list processing, and the operating system interface. An overview of the language is presented in Chapter 1. After reading this chapter, the professional will already be able to write C code. Because the chapters are self-contained, the knowledgeable reader can skip to particular sections as needed. The professional systems programmer who needs to use C to work within an MS-DOS or UNIX environment is given a thorough introduction in Chapter 11 to the connections to the operating system.

Interactive Environment

This book is written entirely with the modern interactive environment in mind. Experimentation is encouraged throughout. Keyboard and screen input/output is taken as the norm, and its attendant concerns are explained. Thus the book is useful to users of small home and business computers as well as to users of workstations on a network. We assume that the reader will have access to an interactive ANSI C system. During the writing of this book, we used a number of different systems and compilers: the GNU *gcc* compiler on a variety of UNIX workstations from DEC, SGI, Sun, and others; the C/C++ compilers from Borland and from Microsoft, running on various 386 and 486 PCs; and the C compiler running on the Cray C90 at the San Diego Supercomputer Center in San Diego, California (via the Internet).

Working Code

Our approach to describing the language is to use examples, explanation, and syntax. Working code is employed throughout. Small but useful examples are used to describe important technical points: Small because small is comprehensible; useful because programming is based on a hierarchy of building blocks and ultimately is pragmatic. The programs and functions described in the book can be used in actual systems. The authors' philosophy is that one should enjoy and experiment.

Flexible Organization—Dissections

This book is constructed to be very flexible in its use.

In Chapter 1, a specially developed technique, program "dissection," is introduced to explain new language features. We use highlighted dissections throughout the book; they help both beginning and experienced programmers alike to understand details about the C programming language. Chapter 1 is in two parts. The first part explains the crucial programming techniques needed for interactive terminal input/output, material that must be understood by all. The second part surveys the entire language and will be comprehensible to experienced programmers familiar with comparable features in other languages. *Caution:* Beginning programmers should postpone the second part of Chapter 1.

Chapter 2 describes the lexical level of the language and syntactic rules, which are selectively employed to illustrate C language constructs. The instructor may decide to teach Backus-Naur-Form (BNF) notation as described in Chapter 2 or may omit it without any loss of continuity. The book uses BNF-style syntactic descriptions so the student can learn this standard form of programming language description. In addition, language components are thoroughly described by example and ordinary explanation.

Reference Work

This book is designed to be a valuable reference to the C language. Throughout, many tables concisely illustrate key areas of the language. The complete ANSI C standard library, along with its associated header files, is described in Appendix A. Sections in this appendix are devoted to explaining each of the standard header files such as *stdio.h*, *ctype.h*, *string.h*, and *signal.h*. Where appropriate, example code is given to illustrate the use of a particular construct or function.

In Appendix B we provide the complete syntax of the C language. In Appendix C we list the major differences between ANSI C and traditional C. Finally, special care has been taken to make the index easy to use and suitable for a reference work.

The Complete ANSI C Language

Chapters 3 through 10 cover the complete ANSI C language feature by feature. Many advanced topics are discussed that may be omitted on first reading without loss of comprehension, if so desired. For example, enumeration types are relatively new to the language, and their use can be omitted in a first course. Machine-dependent features such as word size considerations and floating-point representation are discussed. However, these details need not concern the beginner.

The Preprocessor

Chapter 8 is devoted entirely to the preprocessor, which is used to extend the power and notation of the C language. Macros can be used to generate in-line code, which takes the place of a function call. Their use can reduce program execution time. The chapter presents a detailed discussion of the preprocessor, including new features added by the ANSI committee. In traditional C, the preprocessor varies considerably from one compiler to another. In ANSI C, the functionality of the preprocessor has been completely specified.

Recursion and List Processing

Chapter 5 has a careful discussion of recursion, which is often a mystifying topic for the beginner. The use of recursion is illustrated again in Chapter 8, with the quicksort algorithm, and in Chapter 10 with basic list processing techniques. A thorough knowledge of list processing techniques is necessary in advanced programming and data structure courses.

Operating System Connection

Chapter 11 makes the operating system connection. In this chapter we explain how to do file processing and discuss at length the various input/output functions in the standard library. How to execute a system command from within a C program is explained. Setting file permissions and the use of environment variables is explained. Explicit examples are given showing the use of the profiler, the librarian, and the *make* facility.

Advanced Applications

A number of advanced applications is discussed in Chapter 12. Topics such as creating concurrent processes, overlaying a process, interprocess communication, and signals are presented, along with working code. The dynamic allocation of vectors and matrices for engineers and scientists is also discussed. These advanced topics can be used selectively according to the needs of the audience. They could form the basis for an excellent second course in programming practice. This book can be used, too, as an auxiliary text in advanced computer science courses that employ C as their implementation language.

Tables, Summaries, and Exercises

Throughout the book are many tables and lists that succinctly summarize key ideas. These tables aid and test language comprehension. For example, C is very rich in operators and allows almost any useful combination of operator mix. It is crucial to understand the order of evaluation and association of each of these operators separately and in combination. These points are illustrated in tables throughout the text. As a reference tool, the tables and code are easily looked up.

The exercises test elementary features of the language and discuss advanced and system-dependent features. Many exercises are oriented to problem solving; others test the reader's syntactic or semantic understanding of C. Some exercises include a tutorial discussion that is tangential to the text but may be of special interest to certain readers. The exercises offer the instructor all levels of questions, so as to allow assignments suitable to the audience.

ACKNOWLEDGMENTS

Our special thanks go to Robert Field, ParcPlace Systems, Mountain View, California, who acted as the chief technical reviewer for the first edition of this book. We found his expertise and suggestions extremely valuable. The "Dining Philosophers" picture in Chapter 12 is due to John de Pillis, University of California, Riverside. Our special thanks go to him, too.

We also want to thank other people who provided us with helpful suggestions:

Paul Andersen	Purdue University, Indiana
Murray Baumgarten	University of California, Santa Cruz
Michael Beeson	San Jose State University, San Jose, California
Randolph Bentson	Colorado State University, Ft. Collins
John Berry	Foothill College, California
Jim Bloom	University of California, Berkeley
John Bowie	Hewlett-Packard Co., Inc.
Skona Brittain	University of California, Santa Barbara
Timothy Budd	University of Arizona, Tucson
Nick Burgoyne	University of California, Santa Cruz
Bill Burke	University of California, Santa Cruz
John Carroll	San Diego State University, California
Jim Chrislock	Private consultant, Bonny Doon, California
Al Conrad	Keck Telescope, Mauna Kea, Hawaii
Albert Crawford	Southern Illinois University, Carbondale
Debra Dolsberry	Cottage Consulting, Aptos, California
Jeff Donnelly	University of Illinois, Urbana
Dan Drew	Texas A & M University, College Station
Daniel Edelson	IA Corporation, Emeryville, California
Peter Farkas	Sun Microsystems, Mountain View, California
Dick Fritz	AT&T Bell Laboratories, Naperville, Illinois
Rex Gantenbein	University of Wyoming, Laramie
Buz Gaver	SRI International, Augusta, Georgia
Leonard Garrett	Temple University, Philadelphia
Arthur Geis	College of DuPage, Illinois
William Giles	San Jose State University, San Jose, California
Susan Graham	University of California, Berkeley
Jorge Hankamer	University of California, Santa Cruz
Bob Haxo	University of California, Davis
Paul Higbee	University of North Florida
Rex Hurst	Utah State University, Logan
Mike Johnson	Oregon State University, Corvallis
Keith Jolly	Chabot College, San Leandro, California
Carole Kelley	Cabrillo College, Aptos, California
Stephen Kelley	Harbor High School, Santa Cruz, California
Donald Knuth	Stanford University, California
Clifford Layton	Rogers State University
Darrell Long	University of California, Santa Cruz

Dean Long	Sun Microsystems, Mountain View, California
Charlie McDowell	University of California, Santa Cruz
Ann Mitchell	Purdue University, Indiana
William Muellner	Elmhurst College, Elmhurst, Illinois
Jay Munyer	University of California, Santa Cruz
Andrew Pleszkun	University of Colorado, Boulder
Tim Poston	Centre for Information-Enhanced Medicine, Singapore
Patrick Powell	San Diego State University, California
Geoffrey Pullum	University of California, Santa Cruz
Peter Rosencrantz	The Santa Cruz Operation, Inc., California
Mike Schoonover	Hewlett-Packard Co., Inc., Oklahoma
Peter Scott	University of California, Santa Cruz
Alan Shaw	University of Washington, Seattle
Tilly Shaw	University of California, Santa Cruz
Dain Smith	Mt. Hood Community College, Oregon
Matt Stallmann	University of Denver, Colorado
Dennie Van Tassel	University of California, Santa Cruz

In addition, we would like to thank J. Carter Shanklin, Acquisitions Editor, and Dan Joraanstad, Executive Editor, for their enthusiasm, support, and encouragement; and we would like to thank Adam Ray, Production Editor, and Melissa Standen, Editorial Assistant, for their careful attention to the production of this book on C.

Al Kelley   Ira Pohl
University of California, Santa Cruz

STARTING FROM ZERO

Zero is the natural starting point in the C programming language. C counts from 0. C uses 0 to mean false and not 0 to mean true. C array subscripts have 0 as a lower bound. C strings use 0 as an end-of-string sentinel. C pointers use 0 to designate a null value. C external and static variables are initialized to 0 by default. This book explains these ideas and initiates you into the pleasures of programming in C.

C is a general-purpose programming language that was originally designed by Dennis Ritchie of Bell Laboratories and implemented there on a PDP11 in 1972. It was first used as the systems language for the UNIX operating system. Ken Thompson, the developer of UNIX, had been using both an assembler and a language named B to produce initial versions of UNIX in 1970. C was invented to overcome the limitations of B.

B was a programming language based on BCPL, a language developed by Martin Richards in 1967 as a typeless systems programming language. Its basic data type was the machine word, and it made heavy use of pointers and address arithmetic. This is contrary to the spirit of structured programming, which is characterized by the use of strongly typed languages, such as the ALGOL-like languages. C evolved from B and BCPL, and incorporated typing.

By the early 1980s, the original C language had evolved into what is now known as "traditional C" by adding the void type, enumeration types, and some other improvements. In the late 1980s, the American National Standards Institute (ANSI) Committee X3J11 created draft standards for what is known as "ANSI C" or "standard C." The committee added the void * type, function prototypes, a new function definition syntax, and more functionality for the preprocessor, and in general made the language definition more precise. Today, ANSI C is a mature, general-purpose language that is widely available on many machines and in many operating systems. It is one of the chief industrial programming languages of the world, and it is commonly found in colleges and universities everywhere. Also, ANSI C is the foundation for C++, a programming language that incorporates object-oriented constructs. This book describes the ANSI version of the C language, along with some topics in C++.

0.1   WHY C?

C is a small language. And small is beautiful in programming. C has fewer keywords than Pascal, where they are known as reserved words, yet it is arguably the more powerful language. C gets its power by carefully including the right control structures and data types, and allowing their uses to be nearly unrestricted where meaningfully used. The language is readily learned as a consequence of its functional minimality.

C is the native language of UNIX, and UNIX is a major interactive operating system on workstations, servers, and mainframes. Also, C is the standard development language for personal computers. Much of MS-DOS and OS/2 is written in C. Many windowing packages, database programs, graphics libraries, and other large-application packages are written in C.

C is portable. Code written on one machine can be easily moved to another. C provides the programmer with a standard library of functions that work the same on all machines. Also, C has a built-in preprocessor that helps the programmer isolate any system-dependent code.

C is terse. C has a very powerful set of operators, and some of these operators allow the programmer to access the machine at the bit level. The increment operator ++ has a direct analogue in machine language on many machines, making this an efficient operator. Indirection and address arithmetic can be combined within expressions to accomplish in one statement or expression what would require many statements in another language. For many programmers this is both elegant and efficient. Software productivity studies show that programmers produce, on average, only a small amount of working code each day. A language that is terse explicitly magnifies the underlying productivity of the programmer.

C is modular. C supports one style of routine, the external function, for which arguments are passed "call by value." The nesting of functions is not allowed. A limited form of privacy is provided by using the storage class static within files. These features, along with tools provided by the operating system, readily support user-defined libraries of functions and modular programming.

C is the basis for C++. This means that many of the constructs and methodologies that are routinely used by the C programmer are also used by the C++ programmer. Thus learning C can be considered a first step in learning C++.

C is efficient on most machines. Because certain constructs in the language are explicitly machine-dependent, C can be implemented in a manner that is natural with respect to the machine's architecture. Because a machine can do what comes naturally, compiled C code can be very efficient. Of course, the programmer must be aware of any code that is machine-dependent.

C is not without criticism. It has a complicated syntax. It has no automatic array bounds checking. It makes multiple use of such symbols as * and =. For example, a common programming error is to use the operator = in place of the operator ==. Nevertheless, C is an elegant language. It places no straitjacket on the programmer's access to the machine. Its imperfections are easier to live with than a perfected restrictiveness.

C is appealing because of its powerful operators and its unfettered nature. A C programmer strives for functional modularity and effective minimalism. A C programmer welcomes experimentation and interaction. Indeed, experimentation and interaction are the hallmarks of this book.

0.2   ANSI C STANDARD

The acronym ANSI stands for "American National Standards Institute." This institute is involved in setting standards for many kinds of systems, including programming languages. In particular, ANSI Committee X3J11 is responsible for setting the standard for the programming language C. In the late 1980s, as noted, the committee created draft standards for what is known as "ANSI C" or "standard C." By 1990, the committee had finished its work, and the International Standardization Organization (ISO) approved the standard for ANSI C as well. Thus ANSI C, or ANSI/ISO C, is an internationally recognized standard.

The standard specifies the form of programs written in C and establishes how these programs are to be interpreted. The purpose of the standard is to promote portability, reliability, maintainability, and efficient execution of C language programs on a variety of machines. Almost all C compilers now follow the ANSI C standard.

0.3   FROM C TO C++

C is widely available on PCs, workstations, and mainframes throughout the world. At the same time, machines and operating systems continue to evolve. To expand the C language or to restrain the use of its constructs in order to conform to a particular discipline is not in the spirit of C.

Although the C language itself is not being expanded, it often serves as the kernel for other more advanced or more specialized languages. Concurrent C extends the language by incorporating concurrency primitives. Objective C extends the language by providing Smalltalk style objects. Other forms of C are used on supercomputers to take advantage of different forms of parallelism.

Most important is C++, an object-oriented language already in widespread use. Because it is an extension of C, it allows both C and C++ code to be used on large software projects. C++ is readily learned by the C programmer (see Chapter 13).

## CHAPTER 1

AN OVERVIEW OF C

This chapter gives an overview of the C programming language. A series of programs is presented, and the elements of each program are carefully explained. Experimentation and interaction are emphasized throughout the text. In this chapter we emphasize how to use the basic input/output functions of C. Note carefully that all our C code also serves as C++ code and that all the ideas we discuss hold for C++ as well as for C. Of course, the C++ programmer has available a richer set of tools and techniques out of which programs can be constructed (see Chapter 13).

Except for Section 1.8, "Arrays, Strings, and Pointers," and Section 1.9, "Files," everyone should read all the material in this chapter. Any reader who has had experience with arrays, pointers, and files in some other language can read all the sections of this chapter to get a more complete overview of C. Others can come back to the material when they feel they are ready. Everyone should read this chapter with the understanding that technical details and further explanations will come in later chapters.

1.1 PROGRAMMING AND PREPARATION

Resident on the machine is a collection of special programs called the *operating system*. Commonly available operating systems include MS-DOS, OS/2, and UNIX. An operating system manages machine resources, provides software for the user, and acts as an interface between the user and the hardware. Among the many software packages provided by the operating system are the C compiler and various text editors. The principal text editor on the UNIX system is called *vi*. Some systems, such as Borland C++, integrate the text editor and the compiler. We assume that the reader is able to use some text editor to create files containing C code. Such files are called source files, and they are compiled on most UNIX systems with the *cc* command, which invokes the C compiler. Roughly speaking, a compiler translates source code to object code that is executable. On UNIX systems this compiled code is automatically created in a file named *a.out*. On MS-DOS systems this compiled code is automatically created in a file with the same name as the *.c* file, but with the *.exe* extension replacing the *.c* extension. At the end of this chapter, in Section 1.10, "Operating System Considerations," we present in detail the steps necessary to edit, compile, and execute a program.

1.2 PROGRAM OUTPUT

Programs must communicate to be useful. Our first example is a program that prints on the screen the phrase "from sea to shining C." The complete program is

```
#include <stdio.h>

int main(void)
{
    printf("from sea to shining C\n");
    return 0;
}
```

Using a text editor, we type this into a file whose name ends in *.c*. The choice of a file name should be mnemonic. Let us suppose the program has been written in the file *sea.c*. To compile the program, we give the command

```
cc sea.c
```

If there are no errors in the code, the executable file *a.out* is created by this command. Now the command

a.out

executes the program and prints on the screen

```
from sea to shining C
```

DISSECTION OF THE *sea* PROGRAM

■ `#include <stdio.h>`
A preprocessor is built into the C compiler. When the command to compile a program is given, the code is first preprocessed, and then compiled. Lines that begin with a # communicate with the preprocessor. This `#include` line causes the preprocessor to include a copy of the header file *stdio.h* at this point in the code. This header file is provided by the C system. The angle brackets around `<stdio.h>` indicate that the file is to be found in the "usual place," which is system-dependent. We have included this file because it contains information about the `printf()` function.

■ `int main(void)`
This is the first line of the function definition for `main()`. (We write parentheses after the name `main` to remind the reader that `main()` is a function.) The two words `int` and `void` are keywords, also called reserved words. They have special meaning to the compiler. In Chapter 2 we will see that there are 32 keywords in C, including `int` and `void`.

■ `int main(void)`
  `{`
     `.....`

Every program has a function named `main()`. Program execution always starts with this function. The top line should be read as "`main()` is a function that takes no arguments and returns an `int` value." Here, the keyword `int` tells the compiler that this function returns a value of type `int`. The word `int` stands for "integer," but the word *integer* itself cannot be used. The parentheses following `main` indicate to the compiler that `main` is a function. This idea is confusing at first because what you see following `main` is `(void)`, but only the parentheses `()` constitute an operator telling the compiler that `main` is a function. The keyword `void` indicates to the compiler that this function takes no arguments.

When we write about functions such as `main()` and `printf()`, we usually follow the name in print with parentheses. This indicates to the reader that we are discussing a function. (Many programming books follow this practice.)

■ `{`
Braces surround the body of a function definition. They are also used to group statements together.

■ `printf()`
The C system contains a standard library of functions that can be used in programs. This is a function from the library that prints on the screen. We included the header file *stdio.h* because it provides certain information to the compiler about the function `printf()` (see Exercise 14).

■ `"from sea to shining C\n"`
A string constant in C is a series of characters surrounded by double quotes. This string is an argument to the function `printf()`, and it controls what gets printed. The two characters `\n` at the end of the string (read "backslash n") represent a single character called *newline*. It is a nonprinting character. It advances the cursor on the screen to the beginning of the next line.

■ `printf("from sea to shining C\n")`
This is a call to the `printf()` function. In a program, the name of a function followed by parentheses causes the function to be called, or invoked. If appropriate, the parentheses may contain arguments. Here, when the `printf()` function is invoked, it prints its argument, a string constant, on the screen.

■ `printf("from sea to shining C\n");`
This is a statement. Many statements in C end with a semicolon.

■ `return 0;`
This is a `return` statement. It causes the value zero to be returned to the operating system, which in turn may use the value in some way, but is not required to do so. (See Section 12.7, "Returning the Status," in Chapter 12 for further discussion.) Our use of this `return` statement keeps the compiler happy. If we do not use it, the compiler will complain (see Exercise 4). One of the principal rules of programming is "keep your compiler happy."

■ `}`
This right brace matches the left brace above and ends the function definition for `main()`.

The function `printf()` acts to print continuously across the screen. It moves the cursor to the start of a new line when a newline character is read. The screen is a two-dimensional display that prints from left to right and top to bottom. To be readable, output must appear properly spaced on the screen.

We can rewrite our first program as follows:

```
#include <stdio.h>

int main(void)
{
    printf("from sea to ");
    printf("shining C");
    printf("\n");
    return 0;
}
```

Although it is different from the first version, it will produce the same output. Each time `printf()` is called, printing begins at the position where the previous call to `printf()` left off. If we want to print our phrase on three lines, we can use newline characters.

```
#include <stdio.h>

int main(void)
{
    printf("from sea\n");
    printf("to shining\nC\n");
    return 0;
}
```

When executed, this program will print

```
from sea
to shining
C
```

Let us write one additional variation on this program, one that will box the phrase in a rectangle of asterisks. It will show how each character, including blanks and newline characters, is significant, and when it is executed, it will give some sense of the screen proportions.

```
#include <stdio.h>

int main(void)
{
    printf("\n\n\n\n\n\n\n\n\n\n");
    printf("          ************************\n");
    printf("          *  from sea           *\n");
    printf("          *  to shining C       *\n");
    printf("          ************************\n");
    printf("\n\n\n\n\n\n\n\n\n\n");
    return 0;
}
```

1.3   VARIABLES, EXPRESSIONS, AND ASSIGNMENT

We will write a program to convert the distance of a marathon in miles and yards to kilometers. In English units a marathon is defined to be 26 miles and 385 yards. These numbers are integers. To convert miles to kilometers, we multiply by the conversion factor 1.609, a real number. In memory, computers represent integers differently from reals. To convert yards to miles, we divide by 1760.0, and, as we shall see, it is essential to represent this number as a real rather than as an integer.

Our conversion program will use variables capable of storing integer values and real values. In C, all variables must be declared, or named, at the beginning of the program. A variable name, also called an identifier, consists of a sequence of letters, digits, and underscores, but may not start with a digit. Identifiers should be chosen to reflect their use in the program. In this way they serve as documentation, making the program more readable.

```
/* The distance of a marathon in kilometers. */

#include <stdio.h>

int main(void)
{
    int     miles, yards;
    float   kilometers;

    miles = 26;
    yards = 385;
    kilometers = 1.609 * (miles + yards / 1760.0);
    printf("\nA marathon is %f kilometers.\n\n", kilometers);
    return 0;
}
```

The output of the program is

```
A marathon is 42.185970 kilometers.
```

DISSECTION OF THE *marathon* PROGRAM

■ /* The distance of a marathon in kilometers. */
Anything written between the characters /* and */ is a comment and is ignored by the compiler. All programs in this book that start with a comment are listed in the index.

■ int   miles, yards;
This is a declaration. Declarations and statements end with a semicolon. int is a keyword and is one of the fundamental types of the language. It informs the compiler that the variables following it are of type int and are to take on integer values. Thus the variables miles and yards in this program are of type int.

■ float   kilometers;
This is a declaration. float is a keyword and is one of the fundamental types of the language. It informs the compiler that the variables following it are of type float and are to take on real values. Thus the variable kilometers in this program is of type float.

■ miles = 26;
yards = 385;
These are assignment statements. The equal sign is an assignment operator. The two numbers 26 and 385 are integer constants. The value 26 is assigned to the variable miles. The value 385 is assigned to the variable yards.

■ `kilometers = 1.609 * (miles + yards / 1760.0);`
This is an assignment statement. The value of the expression on the right side of the equal sign is assigned to the variable `kilometers`. The operators `*`, `+`, and `/` stand for multiplication, addition, and division, respectively. Operations inside parentheses are performed first. Because division has higher precedence than addition (see Chapter 3), the value of the subexpression

```
yards / 1760.0
```

is calculated first. That value is added to the value of the variable `miles` to produce a value that is then multiplied by `1.609`. This final value is assigned to the variable `kilometers`.

■ `printf("\nA marathon is %f kilometers.\n\n", kilometers);`
This is a statement that invokes, or calls, the `printf()` function. The function `printf()` can have a variable number of arguments. The first argument is always a string, called the *control string*. The control string in this example is

```
"\nA marathon is %f kilometers.\n\n"
```

It is the first argument to the function `printf()`. Inside this string is the conversion specification, or format, `%f`. The formats in a control string, if any, are matched with the remaining arguments in the `printf()` function. In this case, `%f` is matched with the argument `kilometers`. It means that the value of the variable `kilometers` is to be printed as a floating-point number and inserted into the print stream where the format `%f` occurs.

Certain words, called *keywords*, are reserved and cannot be used by the programmer as names of variables. For example, `int`, `float`, and `double` are keywords. A table of keywords is given in Chapter 2. Other names are known to the C system and normally would not be redefined by the programmer. The name `printf` is an example. Because `printf` is the name of a function in the standard library, it usually is not used as the name of a variable.

A decimal point in a number indicates that it is a floating-point constant rather than an integer constant. Thus the numbers 37 and 37.0 would be treated differently in a program. Although there are three floating types—`float`, `double`, and `long double`—and variables can be declared to be of any of these types, floating constants are automatically of type `double`.

Expressions typically are found on the right side of assignment operators and as arguments to functions. The simplest expressions are just constants, such as 385 and 1760.0, which were used in the previous program. The name of a variable itself can be considered an expression, and meaningful combinations of operators with variables and constants are also expressions.

The evaluation of expressions can involve conversion rules. This is an important point. The division of two integers results in an integer value, and any remainder is discarded. Thus, for example, the expression 7/2 has the int value 3. The expression 7.0/2, however, is a double divided by an int. When the expression 7.0/2 is evaluated, the value of the expression 2 is automatically converted to a double, causing 7.0/2 to have the value 3.5. In the previous program, suppose that the statement

```
kilometers = 1.609 * (miles + yards / 1760.0);
```

is changed to

```
kilometers = 1.609 * (miles + yards / 1760);
```

This leads to a program bug. Because the variable yards is of type int and has value 385, the expression

```
yards / 1760
```

has the int value 0. This is not what is wanted. Use of the constant 1760.0, which is of type double, corrects the bug.

1.4   THE USE OF #define AND #include

The C compiler has a preprocessor built into it. Lines that begin with a # are called *preprocessing directives*. If the lines

```
#define   LIMIT   100
#define   PI      3.14159
```

occur in a file that is being compiled, the preprocessor first changes all occurrences of the identifier LIMIT to 100 and all occurrences of the identifier PI to 3.14159, except in quoted strings and in comments. The identifiers LIMIT and PI are called *symbolic constants.* A #define line can occur anywhere in a program. It affects only the lines in the file that come after it.

Normally, all #define lines are placed at the beginning of the file. By convention, all identifiers that are to be changed by the preprocessor are written in capital letters. The contents of quoted strings are never changed by the preprocessor. For example, in the statement

```
printf("PI = %f\n", PI);
```

only the second PI will be changed by the above #define directives to the preprocessor. The use of symbolic constants in a program make it more readable. More importantly, if a constant has been defined symbolically by means of the #define facility and used throughout a program, it is easy to change it later, if necessary. For example, in physics the letter *c* is often used to designate the speed of light. Historically, the value for *c* was measured experimentally, but now the value is defined to be precisely 299792.458 km/sec. If we write

```
#define   C   299792.458      /* speed of light in km/sec */
```

and then use C throughout thousands of lines of code to represent symbolically the constant 299792.458, it will be easy to change the code at some later time if physicists should redefine the value. All the code is updated by simply changing the constant in the #define line.

In a program, a line such as

```
#include "my_file.h"
```

is a preprocessing directive that causes a copy of the file *my_file.h* to be included at this point in the file when compilation occurs. A #include line can occur anywhere in a file, though it is typically at the head of the file. The quotes surrounding the name of the file are necessary. An include file, also called a "header file," can contain #define lines and other #include lines. By convention, the names of header files end in *.h*.

The C system provides a number of standard header files. Some examples are *stdio.h*, *string.h*, and *math.h*. These files contain the declarations of functions in the standard library, macros, structure templates, and other programming elements that are commonly used. As we have already seen, the preprocessing directive

```
#include <stdio.h>
```

causes a copy of the standard header file *stdio.h* to be included in the code when compilation occurs. In ANSI C, whenever the functions printf() or scanf() are used, the standard header file *stdio.h* should be included. This file contains the declarations, or more specifically, the function prototypes, of these functions. (See Section 1.7, "Functions," for further discussion.)

The Santa Cruz campus of the University of California overlooks the Monterey Bay on the Pacific Ocean and some of the ocean just to the northwest of the bay. We like to call this part of the ocean that is visible from the campus the "Pacific Sea." To illustrate how the #include facility works, we will write a program that prints the area of the Pacific Sea in various units of measure. First we create a header file and put in the following lines:

In file pacific_sea.h:

```
#include <stdio.h>

#define    AREA                        2337
#define    SQ_MILES_PER_SQ_KILOMETER   0.3861021585424458
#define    SQ_FEET_PER_SQ_MILE         (5280 * 5280)
#define    SQ_INCHES_PER_SQ_FOOT       144
#define    ACRES_PER_SQ_MILE           640
```

Next we write the function main( ) in a *.c* file.

In file pacific_sea.c:

```
/* Measuring the Pacific Sea. */

#include "pacific_sea.h"

int main(void)

{
    const int   pacific_sea = AREA;      /* in sq kilometers */
    double      acres, sq_miles, sq_feet, sq_inches;

    printf("\nThe Pacific Sea covers an area");
    printf(" of %d square kilometers.\n", pacific_sea);
    sq_miles = SQ_MILES_PER_SQ_KILOMETER * pacific_sea;
    sq_feet = SQ_FEET_PER_SQ_MILE * sq_miles;
    sq_inches = SQ_INCHES_PER_SQ_FOOT * sq_feet;
    acres = ACRES_PER_SQ_MILE * sq_miles;
    printf("In other units of measure this is:\n\n");
    printf("%22.7e acres\n", acres);
    printf("%22.7e square miles\n", sq_miles);
    printf("%22.7e square feet\n", sq_feet);
    printf("%22.7e square inches\n\n", sq_inches);
    return 0;
}
```

Now our program is written in two files, a *.h* file and a *.c* file. The output of this program is

```
The Pacific Sea covers an area of 2337 square kilometers.
In other units of measure this is:

        5.7748528e+05 acres
        9.0232074e+02 square miles
        2.5155259e+10 square feet
        3.6223572e+12 square inches
```

The new programming ideas are described in the following dissection table.

DISSECTION OF THE *pacific_sea* PROGRAM

■ `#include "pacific_sea.h"`
This `#include` line is a preprocessing directive. It causes a copy of the file *pacific_sea.h* to be included when the program is compiled. Because this file contains the line

```
#include <stdio.h>
```

the preprocessor expands the line in turn and includes a copy of the standard header file *stdio.h* in the code as well. We have included *stdio.h* because we are using `printf()`. Five symbolic constants are defined in *pacific_sea.h*.

■ `#define    AREA                    2337`
This `#define` line is a preprocessing directive. It causes the preprocessor to replace all occurrences of the identifier `AREA` by 2337 in the rest of the file. By convention, capital letters are used for identifiers that will be changed by the preprocessor. If at some future time a new map is made and a new figure for the area of the Pacific Sea is computed, only this line needs to be changed to update the program.

■ `#define    SQ_MILES_PER_SQ_KILOMETER    0.3861021585424458`
The floating constant `0.3861021585424458` is a conversion factor. The use of a symbolic name for the constant makes the program more readable.

■ `#define    SQ_FEET_PER_SQ_MILE          (5280 * 5280)`

The preprocessor changes occurrences of the first sequence of characters into the second. If a reader of this program knows that there are 5280 feet in a mile, then that reader will quickly recognize that this line of code is correct. Instead of (5280 * 5280), we could have written 27878400. Notice that although the parentheses are not necessary, they do not do any harm either. For technical reasons parentheses are often needed around symbolic expressions (see Chapter 8). Hence it is considered good programming practice to use them. Because C compilers expand constant expressions during compilation, the use of (5280 * 5280) instead of 27878400 does not lessen runtime efficiency.

■ `const int    pacific_sea = AREA;      /* in sq kilometers */`

When the code is compiled, the preprocessor first changes AREA to 2337. The compiler then interprets this line as a declaration of the identifier `pacific_sea`. The variable is declared as type `int` and initialized to the value 2337. The keyword `const` is a type qualifier that has been newly introduced by ANSI C. It means that the associated variable can be initialized, but cannot thereafter have its value changed (see Exercise 18).

■ `double    acres, sq_miles, sq_feet, sq_inches;`

In traditional C the floating types are `float` and `double`. ANSI C has added `long double` as a new floating type. Each of these types is used to store real values. Typically a `float` will store 6 significant digits and a `double` will store 16 significant digits. A `long double` will store at least as many significant digits as a `double` (see Chapter 3).

■ `printf("%22.7e acres\n", acres);`

This statement causes the line

        `5.7748528e+05 acres`

to be printed. The number is written in scientific notation and is interpreted to mean 5.7748528×10^5. Numbers written this way are also said to be written in an e-format. The conversion specification %e causes the system to print a floating expression in an e-format with default spacing. A format of the form %m.ne, where m and n are positive integers, causes the system to print a floating expression in an e-format in m spaces total, with n digits to the right of the decimal point (see Chapter 11).

1.5   THE USE OF printf() AND scanf()

The function printf() is used for output. In an analogous fashion the function scanf() is used for input. (The f in printf and scanf stands for "formatted.") Technically, these functions are not part of the C language, but rather are part of the C system. They exist in a library and are available for use wherever a C system resides. Although the object code for functions in the library is supplied by the C system, it is the responsibility of the programmer to declare the functions being used. ANSI C has introduced a new and improved kind of function declaration called a *function prototype*. This is one of the most important changes introduced into the language by ANSI C. The function prototypes of functions in the standard library are available in the standard header files. In particular, the function prototypes for printf() and scanf() are in *stdio.h*. Thus this header file should be included whenever the function printf() or scanf() is used. (For further discussion of function prototypes, see Section 1.7, "Functions.")

Both printf() and scanf() are passed a list of arguments that can be thought of as

   control_string   and   *other_arguments*

where *control_string* is a string and may contain conversion specifications, or formats. A conversion specification begins with a % character and ends with a conversion character. For example, in the format %d the letter d is the conversion character. As we have already seen, this format is used to print the value of an expression as a decimal integer. To print the letters *abc* on the screen, we could use the statement

```
printf("abc");
```

Another way to do this is with the statement

```
printf("%s", "abc");
```

The format %s causes the argument "abc" to be printed in the format of a string. Yet another way to do this is with the statement

```
printf("%c%c%c", 'a', 'b', 'c');
```

Single quotes are used to designate character constants. Thus `'a'` is the character constant corresponding to the lowercase letter *a*. The format %c prints the value of an expression as a character. Notice that a constant by itself is considered an expression.

printf()

Conversion character	How the corresponding argument is printed
c	as a character
d	as a decimal integer
e	as a floating point number in scientific notation
f	as a floating point number
g	in the e-format or f-format, whichever is shorter
s	as a string

When an argument is printed, the place where it is printed is called its *field* and the number of characters in its field is called its *field width*. The field width can be specified in a format as an integer occurring between the % and the conversion character. Thus the statement

```
printf("%c%3c%5c\n", 'A', 'B', 'C');
```

will print

```
A  B    C
```

The function `scanf()` is analogous to the function `printf()` but is used for input rather than output. Its first argument is a control string having formats that correspond to the various ways the characters in the input stream are to be interpreted. The other arguments are *addresses*. Consider, for example, the statement

```
scanf("%d", &x);
```

The format %d is matched with the expression &x, causing `scanf()` to interpret characters in the input stream as a decimal integer and to store the result at the address of x. Because the symbol & is the address operator, the expression &x is read "the address of x."

When the keyboard is used to input values into a program, a sequence of characters is typed, and it is this sequence of characters, called the input stream, that is received by the program. If 1337 is typed, the person typing it may think of it as a decimal integer, but the program receives it as a sequence of characters. The scanf() function can be used to convert a string of decimal digits into an integer value and to store the value at an appropriate place in memory.

The function `scanf()` returns as an `int` the number of successful conversions accomplished (see Exercise 19).   The function `printf()` returns as an `int` the number of characters printed, or a negative value in case of an error (see Exercise 20).

scanf()

Conversion character	What characters in the input stream are converted to
c	to a character
d	to a decimal integer
f	to a floating point number (`float`)
lf	to a floating point number (`double`)
LF	to a floating point number (`long double`)
s	to a string

The details concerning `printf()` and `scanf()` are found in Chapter 11. Here we only want to present enough information to get data into and out of the machine in a minimally acceptable way. The following program reads in three characters and some numbers, and then prints them out. Notice that variables of type `char` are used to store character values.

```
#include <stdio.h>

int main(void)
{
    char      c1, c2, c3;
    int       i;
    float     x;
    double    y;

    printf("\n%s\n%s",
        "Input three characters,"
        "an int, a float, and a double:   ");
    scanf("%c%c%c%d%f%lf", &c1, &c2, &c3, &i, &x, &y);
    printf("\nHere is the data that you typed in:\n");
    printf("%3c%3c%3c%5d%17e%17ebs|n\n", c1, c2, c3, i, x, y);
    return 0;
}
```

If we compile the program, run it, and type in ABC 3 55 77.7. This is what appears on the screen:

```
Input three characters,
an int, a float, and a double:  ABC  3  55  77.7

Here is the data that you typed in:
  A  B  C    3      5.500000e+01      7.770000e+01
```

When reading in numbers, scanf() will skip white space (blanks, newlines, and tabs), but when reading in a character, white space is not skipped. Thus the program will not run correctly with the input AB C 3 55 77.1. The third character read is a blank, which is a perfectly good character; but then scanf() attempts to read C as a decimal integer, which causes difficulties.

1.6 FLOW OF CONTROL

Statements in a program are normally executed in sequence. However, most programs require alteration of the normal sequential flow of control. The if and if-else statements provide alternative actions, and the while and for statements provide looping mechanisms. These constructs typically require the evaluation of logical expressions, expressions that the programmer thinks of as being either *true* or *false*. In C, any nonzero value is considered to represent *true*, and any zero value is considered to represent *false*.

The general form of an if statement is

> if (*expr*)
>   *statement*

If *expr* is nonzero (*true*), then *statement* is executed; otherwise it is skipped. It is important to recognize that an if statement, even though it contains a statement part, is itself a single statement. Consider as an example the code

```
a = 1;
if (b == 3)
    a = 5;
printf("%d", a);
```

The symbols == represent the "is equal to" operator. A test is made to see if the value of b is equal to 3. If it is, then a is assigned the value 5 and control passes to the printf() statement, causing 5 to be printed. If, however, the value of b is not 3, then the statement

```
a = 5;
```

is skipped and control passes directly to the `printf()` statement, causing 1 to be printed. In C, logical expressions have either the `int` value 1 or the `int` value 0. Consider the logical expression

```
b == 3
```

This expression has the `int` value 1 (*true*) if b has the value 3; otherwise it has the `int` value 0 (*false*).

A group of statements surrounded by braces constitutes a *compound statement*. Syntactically, a compound statement is itself a statement; a compound statement can be used anywhere that a statement can be used. The next example uses a compound statement in place of a simple statement to control more than one action:

```
if (a == 3) {
    b = 5;
    c = 7;
}
```

Here, if a has value 3, then two assignment statements are executed; if a does not have value 3, then the two statements are skipped.

An `if-else` statement is of the form

```
if (expr)
    statement1
else
    statement2
```

It is important to recognize that the whole construct, even though it contains statements, is itself a single statement. If *expr* is nonzero (*true*), then *statement1* is executed; otherwise *statement2* is executed. As an example, consider the code

```
if (cnt == 0) {
    a = 2;
    b = 3;
    c = 5;
}
else {
    a = -1;
    b = -2;
    c = -3;
}
printf("%d", a + b + c);
```

This causes 10 to be printed if cnt has value 0, and causes -6 to be printed otherwise.

Looping mechanisms are very important because they allow repetitive actions. The following program illustrates the use of a while loop:

```c
#include <stdio.h>

int main(void)
{
    int   i = 1, sum = 0;

    while (i <= 5) {
        sum += i;
        ++i;
    }
    printf("sum = %d\n", sum);
    return 0;
}
```

DISSECTION OF THE *consecutive_sum* PROGRAM

■ while (i <= 5) {
    sum += i;
    ++i;
}

This construct is a while statement, or while loop. The symbols <= represent the "less than or equal to" operator. A test is made to see if i is less than or equal to 5. If it is, the group of statements enclosed by the braces { and } is executed, and control is passed back to the beginning of the while loop for the process to start over again. The while loop is repeatedly executed until the test fails—that is, until i is not less than or equal to 5. When the test fails, control passes to the statement immediately following the while statement, which in this program is a printf() statement.

■   `sum += i;`

This is a new kind of assignment statement. It causes the stored value of `sum` to be incremented by the value of `i`. An equivalent statement is

    `sum = sum + i;`

The variable `sum` is assigned the old value of `sum` plus the value of `i`. A construct of the form

    variable op= expr

where *op* is an operator such as +, -, *, or /   is equivalent to

    variable = variable op (expr)

■   `++i;`

C uses ++ and -- to increment and decrement, respectively, the stored values of variables. The statement

    `++i;`   is equivalent to   `i = i + 1;`

In a similar fashion, `--i` will cause the stored value of `i` to be decremented. (See Chapter 2 for further discussion of these operators.)

    A hand simulation of the program shows that the `while` loop is executed five times, with `i` taking on the values 1, 2, 3, 4, 5 successively. When control passes beyond the `while` statement, the value of `i` is 6, and the value of `sum` is

    $1 + 2 + 3 + 4 + 5$ which is equal to   15

This is the value printed by the `printf()` statement.

    The general form of a `while` statement is

    `while` *(expr)*
        statement

where *statement* is either a simple statement or a compound statement. When the `while` statement is executed, *expr* is evaluated. If it is nonzero (*true*), then *statement* is executed and control passes back to the beginning of the `while` loop. This process continues until *expr* has value 0 (*false*). At this point control passes on to the next statement. In C, a logical expression such as `i <= 5` has `int` value 1 (*true*) if `i` is less than or equal to 5, and has `int` value 0 (*false*) otherwise.

Another looping construct is the for statement. (See Section 4.9, "The for Statement," in Chapter 4 for a more complete discussion.) It has the form

```
for (expr1; expr2; expr3)
    statement
```

If all three expressions are present, then this is equivalent to

```
expr1;
while (expr2) {
    statement
    expr3;
}
```

Typically, *expr1* performs an initial assignment, *expr2* performs a test, and *expr3* increments a stored value. Note that *expr3* is the last thing done in the body of the loop. The for loop is repeatedly executed as long as *expr2* is nonzero (*true*). As an example, consider

```
for (i = 1; i <= 5; ++i)
    sum += i;
```

This for loop is equivalent to the while loop used in the last program.

Our next program illustrates the use of an if-else statement within a for loop. Numbers are read in one after another. On each line of the output we print the count and the number, along with the minimum, maximum, sum, and average of all the numbers seen up to that point. (For further discussion concerning the computation of the average, see Exercises 15, 16, and 17.)

```
/* Compute the minimum, maximum, sum, and average. */

#include <stdio.h>
#include <stdlib.h>

int main(void)
{
    int      i;
    double   x, min, max, sum, avg;

    if (scanf("%lf", &x) != 1) {
        printf("No data found - bye!\n");
        exit(1);
    }
    min = max = sum = avg = x;
    printf("%5s%9s%9s%9s%12s%12s\n%5s%9s%9s%9s%12s%12s\n\n",
        "Count", "Item", "Min", "Max", "Sum", "Average",
        "-----", "----", "---", "---", "---", "-------");
    printf("%5d%9.1f%9.1f%9.1f%12.3f%12.3f\n",
        1, x, min, max, sum, avg);
    for (i = 2; scanf("%lf", &x) == 1; ++i) {
        if (x < min)
            min = x;
        else if (x > max)
            max = x;
        sum += x;
        avg = sum / i;
        printf("%5d%9.1f%9.1f%9.1f%12.3f%12.3f\n",
            i, x, min, max, sum, avg);
    }
    return 0;
}
```

This program has been designed to read numbers from a file. We can type them in from the keyboard, but if we do this, then what appears on the screen will not be formatted correctly. To test this program, we compile it and put the executable code in *running_sum*. Then we create a file called *data* and put the following numbers in it:

3   -5   7   -9   11   -13   15   -17   19   -21

Now, when we give the command

running_sum < *data*

the following appears on the screen:

Count	Item	Min	Max	Sum	Average
-----	----	---	---	---	-------
1	3.0	3.0	3.0	3.000	3.000
2	-5.0	-5.0	3.0	-2.000	-1.000
3	7.0	-5.0	7.0	5.000	1.667
.....					

The use of the symbol < in the command

running_sum < *data*

causes the input to be redirected. The program *running_sum* takes its input from the standard input file, which is normally connected to the keyboard. The operating system, however, has redirected the input to the file *data*. In this context the symbol < is thought of as a left pointing arrow. (See Section 1.10, "Operating System Considerations," for further discussion.)

DISSECTION OF THE *running_sum* PROGRAM

■ ```
if (scanf("%lf", &x) != 1) {
    printf("No data found - bye!\n");
    exit(1);
}
```
Recall that scanf() returns as an int the number of successful conversions performed. If scanf() is unable to make a conversion, then we print a message and exit the program. The function exit() is in the standard library, and its function prototype is in *stdlib.h*. When exit() is invoked, certain housekeeping tasks are performed and the program is terminated. This function takes a single argument of type int that, by convention, is zero if the programmer considers the exit to be normal, and is nonzero otherwise.

■ ```
printf("%5s%9s%9s%9s%12s%12s\n%5s%9s%9s%9s%12s%12s\n\n",
    "Count", "Item", "Min", "Max", "Sum", "Average",
    "-----", "----", "---", "---", "---", "-------");
```
This statement prints headings. The field widths in the formats have been chosen to put headings over columns.

■   `printf("%5d%9.1f%9.1f%9.1f%12.3f%12.3f\n",`
    `        1, x, min, max, sum, avg);`
    After the headings, this is the first line to be printed. Notice that the field widths here match the field widths in the previous `printf()` statement.

■   `for (i = 2; scanf("%lf", &x) == 1; ++i) {`
    The variable `i` is initially assigned the value 2. Then a test is made to see if the logical expression

    `    scanf("%lf", &x) == 1`

    is true. If `scanf()` can read characters from the standard input stream, interpret them as a `double` (read `lf` as "long float"), and place the value at the address of `x`, then a successful conversion has been made. This causes `scanf()` to return the `int` value 1, which in turn makes the logical expression true. As long as `scanf()` can continue to read characters and convert them, the body of the `for` loop will be executed repeatedly. The variable `i` is incremented at the end of the body of the loop.

■   `if (x < min)`
    `    min = x;`
    `else if (x > max)`
    `    max = x;`
    This construct is a single `if-else` statement. Notice that the statement part following the `else` is itself an `if` statement. Each time through the loop this `if-else` statement causes the values for `min` and `max` to be updated, if necessary.

1.7   FUNCTIONS

The heart and soul of C programming is the function. A function represents a piece of code that is a building block in the problem-solving process. All functions are on the same external level; they cannot be nested one inside another. A C program consists of one or more functions in one or more files (see Chapter 5). Precisely one of the functions is a `main()` function, where execution of the program begins. Other functions are called from within `main()` and from within each other.

   Functions should be declared before they are used. Suppose, for example, that we want to use the function `pow()`, called the power function, one of many functions in the mathematics library available for use by the programmer. A function call such as `pow(x, y)` returns the value of `x` raised to the `y` power. To give an explicit example, `pow(2.0, 3.0)` yields the value 8.0. The declaration of the function is given by

```
double   pow(double x, double y);
```

Function declarations of this type are called *function prototypes*. An equivalent function prototype is given by

```
double    pow(double, double);
```

Identifiers such as x and y that occur in parameter type lists in function prototypes are not used by the compiler. Their purpose is to provide documentation to the programmer and other readers of the code.

A function prototype tells the compiler the number and type of arguments that are to be passed to the function and the type of the value that is to be returned by the function.

ANSI C has added the concept of function prototype to the C language. This is an important change. In traditional C, the function declaration of pow( ) is given by

```
double    pow();        /* traditional style */
```

Parameter type lists are not allowed. Most ANSI C compilers will still accept this style, but function prototypes, because they greatly reduce the chance for errors, are much preferred (see Exercise 5 in Chapter 5).

A function prototype has the following general form:

type   function_name (parameter type list);

The *parameter type list* is typically a list of types separated by commas. Identifiers are optional; they do not affect the prototype. The keyword void is used if a function takes no arguments. Also, the keyword void is used if no value is returned by the function. If a function takes a variable number of arguments, then an ellipsis . . . is used. For example, the function prototype

```
int    printf(const char *format, ...);
```

can be found in *stdio.h* (see Exercise 14).

To illustrate the use of functions, we set for ourselves the following task:

1 Print information about the program (this list).
2 Read an integer value for *n*.
3 Read in *n* real numbers.
4 Find minimum and maximum values.

Let us write a program called *maxmin* that accomplishes the task. It consists of three functions written in the file *maxmin.c*.

```
#include <stdio.h>

float    maximum(float x, float y);
float    minimum(float x, float y);
void     prn_info(void);

int main(void)
{
    int      i, n;
    float    max, min, x;

    prn_info();
    printf("Input n:   ");
    scanf("%d", &n);
    printf("\nInput %d real numbers:   ", n);
    scanf("%f", &x);
    max = min = x;
    for (i = 2; i <= n; ++i) {
        scanf("%f", &x);
        max = maximum(max, x);
        min = minimum(min, x);
    }
    printf("\n%s%11.3f\n%s%11.3f\n\n",
        "Maximum value:", max,
        "Minimum value:", min);
    return 0;
}

float maximum(float x, float y)
{
    if (x > y)
        return x;
    else
        return y;
}

float minimum(float x, float y)
{
    if (x < y)
        return x;
    else
        return y;
}

void prn_info(void)
{
    printf("\n%s\n%s\n\n",
        "This program reads an integer value for n, and then",
        "processes n real numbers to find max and min values.");
}
```

To test the program, we give the command

maxmin

Suppose, when prompted, we type in 5 followed by the line

```
737.7799   -11.2e+3   -777   0.001   3.14159
```

Here is what appears on the screen:

```
This program reads an integer value for n, and then
processes n real numbers to find max and min values.

Input n:   5

Input 5 real numbers:  737.7799   -11.2e+3   -777   0.001   3.14159

Maximum value:      737.780
Minimum value: -11200.000
```

DISSECTION OF THE *maxmin* PROGRAM

■ `#include <stdio.h>`

```
float    maximum(float x, float y);
float    minimum(float x, float y);
void     prn_info(void);

int main(void)
{
    . . . . .
```

The function prototypes for the functions `maximum()`, `minimum()`, and `prn_info()` occur at the top of the file after any `#include` lines and `#define` lines. The first two function prototypes tell the compiler that the functions `maximum()` and `minimum()` each take two arguments of type `float` and each return a value of type `float`. The third function prototype tells the compiler that `prn_info()` takes no arguments and returns no value. Note that for the first two function prototypes we could just as well have written

```
float    maximum(float, float);
float    minimum(float, float);
```

The compiler does not make any use of parameters such as x and y in function prototypes. The parameters serve only as documentation for the reader of the code.

```
■   int main(void)
    {
        int      i, n;
        float    max, min, x;

        prn_info();
        printf("Input n:   ");
        scanf("%d", &n);
        .....
```

Variables are declared at the beginning of main(). The first executable statement in main() is

```
    prn_info();
```

This statement invokes the function prn_info(). The function contains a single printf() statement that prints information about the program on the screen. The user responds to the prompt by typing characters on the keyboard. We use scanf() to interpret these characters as a decimal integer and to place the value of this integer at the address of n.

```
■   printf("\nInput %d real numbers:   ", n);
    scanf("%f", &x);
    max = min = x;
```

The user is asked to input n real numbers. The first real number is read in, and its value is placed at the address of x. Because the assignment operator associates from right to left (see Chapter 2),

```
    max = min = x;       is equivalent to       max = (min = x);
```

Thus the value x is assigned first to min and then to max.

```
■   for (i = 2; i <= n; ++i) {
        scanf("%f", &x);
        max = maximum(max, x);
        min = minimum(min, x);
    }
```

Each time through the loop a new value for x is read in. Then the current values of max and x are passed as arguments to the function maximum(), and the larger of the two values is returned and assigned to max. Similarly, the current values of min and x are passed as arguments to the function minimum(), and the smaller of the two values is returned and assigned to min. In C, arguments to functions are *always* passed "by value." This means that a copy of the value of each argument is made, and it is these copies that are processed by the function. The effect is that variables passed as arguments to functions are *not changed* in the calling environment.

■
```
float maximum(float x, float y)
{
   if (x > y)
      return x;
   else
      return y;
}
```
This is the function definition for the function maximum(). It specifies explicitly how the function will act when it is called, or invoked. A function definition consists of a header and a body. The header is the code that occurs before the first left brace {. The body consists of the declarations and statements between the braces { and }. For this function definition the header is the line

```
float maximum(float x, float y)
```

The first keyword float in the header tells the compiler that this function is to return a value of type float. The parameter list consists of the comma-separated list of identifier declarations within the parentheses (and) that occur in the header to the function definition. Here, the parameter list is given by

```
float x, float y
```

The identifiers x and y are formal parameters. Although we have used the identifiers x and y both here and in the function main(), there is no need to do so. There is no relationship, other than a mnemonic one, between the x and y used in maximum() and the x and y used in main().

Parameters in a function definition can be thought of as placeholders. When expressions are passed as arguments to a function, the values of the expressions are associated with these parameters. The values are then manipulated according to the code in the body of the function definition. Here, the body of the function definition consists of a single if-else statement. The effect of this statement is to return the larger of the two values x and y that are passed in as arguments.

■ `return x;`
This is a return statement. The general form of a return statement is

```
return;        or        return expr;
```

A return statement causes control to be passed back to the calling environment. If an expression follows the keyword return, then the value of the expression is passed back as well.

■ ```
   float minimum(float x, float y)
   {
      if (x < y)
         return x;
      else
         return y;
   }
   ```
   The function definition for `minimum()` comes next. Note that the header to the function definition matches the function prototype that occurs at the top of the file. This is a common programming style.

■  ```
   void prn_info(void)
   {

      . . . . .
   ```
   This is the function definition for `prn_info()`. The first `void` tells the compiler that this function returns no value. The second `void` tells the compiler that this function takes no arguments.

Call by Value

In C, arguments to functions are *always* passed "by value." This means that when an expression is passed as an argument to a function, the expression is evaluated, and it is this value that is passed to the function. The variables passed as arguments to functions are *not changed* in the calling environment. Here is a program that illustrates this:

```
#include <stdio.h>

    void    try_to_change_it(int);

int main(void)
{
   int    a = 1;

   printf("%d\n", a);        /* 1 is printed */
   try_to_change_it(a);
   printf("%d\n", a);        /* 1 is printed again! */
   return 0;
}

void try_to_change_it(int a)
{
   a = 777;
}
```

When a is passed as an argument, the expression a is evaluated to produce a value that we can think of as a copy of a. It is this copy, rather than a itself, that is passed to the function. Hence, in the calling environment the variable a does not get changed.

This argument-passing convention is known as "call by value." To change the value of a variable in the calling environment, other languages provide "call by reference." In C, to get the effect of "call by reference," pointers must be used (see Chapter 6).

1.8 ARRAYS, STRINGS, AND POINTERS

In C, a string is an array of characters, and an array name by itself is a pointer. Because of this, the concepts of arrays, strings, and pointers are intimately related. A pointer is just an address of an object in memory. C, unlike most languages, provides for pointer arithmetic. Because pointer expressions of great utility are possible, pointer arithmetic is one of the strong points of the language.

Arrays

Arrays are used when many variables, all of the same type, are desired. For example, the declaration

```
int    a[3];
```

allocates space for the three-element array a. The elements of the array are of type int and are accessed as a[0], a[1], and a[2]. The index, or subscript, of an array always starts at 0. The next program illustrates the use of an array. The program reads in five scores, sorts them, and prints them out in order.

```
#include <stdio.h>

#define    CLASS_SIZE    5

int main(void)
{
   int    i, j, score[CLASS_SIZE], sum = 0, tmp;

   printf("Input %d scores:  ", CLASS_SIZE);
   for (i = 0; i < CLASS_SIZE; ++i) {
      scanf("%d", &score[i]);
      sum += score[i];
   }
   for (i = 0; i < CLASS_SIZE - 1; ++i)          /* bubble sort */
      for (j = CLASS_SIZE - 1; j > i; --j)
         if (score[j-1] < score[j]) {      /* check the order */
            tmp = score[j-1];
            score[j-1] = score[j];
            score[j] = tmp;
         }
   printf("\nOrdered scores:\n\n");
   for (i = 0; i < CLASS_SIZE; ++i)
      printf("   score[%d] =%5d\n", i, score[i]);
   printf("\n%18d%s\n%18.1f%s\n\n",
      sum, " is the sum of all the scores",
      (double) sum / CLASS_SIZE, " is the class average");
   return 0;
}
```

If we execute the program and enter the scores 63, 88, 97, 53, 77 when prompted, we will see on the screen

```
Input 5 scores:  63  88  97  53  77

Ordered scores:

   score[0] =   97
   score[1] =   88
   score[2] =   77
   score[3] =   63
   score[4] =   53

           378 is the sum of all the scores
          75.6 is the class average
```

A bubble sort is used in the program to sort the scores. This construction is typically done with nested for loops, with a test being made in the body of the inner loop to check on the order of a pair of elements. If the elements being compared are out of order, their values are interchanged. Here, this interchange is accomplished by the code

```
tmp = score[j-1];
score[j-1] = score[j];
score[j] = tmp;
```

In the first statement, the variable tmp is used to temporarily store the value of score[j-1]. In the next statement, the value of score[j-1] stored in memory is being overwritten with the value of score[j]. In the last statement, the value of score[j] is being overwritten with the original value of score[i], which is now in tmp. Hand simulation of the program with the given data will show the reader why this bubble sort construct of two nested for loops achieves an array with sorted elements. The name "bubble sort" comes from the fact that at each step of the outer loop the desired value among those left to be worked over is "bubbled" into position. Although bubble sorts are easy to code, they are relatively inefficient. Other sorting techniques execute much faster. This is of no concern when sorting a small number of items infrequently, but if the number of items is large or the code is used repeatedly, then efficiency is, indeed, an important consideration. The expression

```
(double) sum / CLASS_SIZE
```

which occurs as an argument in the final printf() statement uses a cast operator. The effect of (double) sum is to cast, or convert, the int value of sum to a double. Because the precedence of a cast operator is higher than that of the division operator (see Chapter 3), the cast is done before division occurs. When a double is divided by an int, we have what is called a "mixed expression." Automatic conversion now takes place. The int is promoted to a double, and the result to the operation is a double. If a cast had not been used, then integer division would have occurred and any fractional part would have been discarded. Moreover, the result would have been an int, which would have caused the format in the printf() statement to be in error.

Strings

In C, a string is an array of characters. In this section, in addition to illustrating the use of strings, we want to introduce the use of getchar() and putchar(). These are macros defined in *stdio.h*. Although there are technical differences (see Chapter 8), a macro is used in the same way a function is used. The macros getchar() and putchar() are used to read characters from the keyboard and to print characters on the screen, respectively.

Our next program stores a line typed in by the user in an array of characters (a string), and then prints the line backwards on the screen. The program illustrates how characters in C can be treated as small integers.

```c
/* Have a nice day! */

#include <ctype.h>
#include <stdio.h>

#define    MAXSTRING    100

int main(void)
{
    char    c, name[MAXSTRING];
    int     i, sum = 0;

    printf("\nHi!  What is your name?  ");
    for (i = 0; (c = getchar()) != '\n'; ++i) {
        name[i] = c;
        if (isalpha(c))
            sum += c;
    }
    name[i] = '\0';
    printf("\n%s%s%s\n%s",
        "Nice to meet you ", name, ".",
        "Your name spelled backwards is ");
    for (--i; i >= 0; --i)
        putchar(name[i]);
    printf("\n%s%d%s\n\n%s\n",
        "and the letters in your name sum to ", sum, ".",
        "Have a nice day!");
    return 0;
}
```

If we run the program and enter the name `Alice B. Carole` when prompted, the following appears on the screen:

```
Hi!  What is your name?  Alice B. Carole

Nice to meet you Alice B. Carole.
Your name spelled backwards is eloraC .B ecilA
and the letters in your name sum to 1142.

Have a nice day!
```

DISSECTION OF THE *nice_day* PROGRAM

■ `#include <ctype.h>`
`#include <stdio.h>`
The standard header file *stdio.h* contains the function prototype for `printf()`. It also contains the macro definitions for `getchar()` and `putchar()`, which will be used to read characters from the keyboard and to write characters to the screen, respectively. The standard header file *ctype.h* contains the macro definition for `isalpha()`, which will be used to determine if a character "is alphabetic"—that is, if it is a lower- or uppercase letter.

■ `#define    MAXSTRING    100`
The symbolic constant `MAXSTRING` will be used to set the size of the character array name. We are making the assumption that the user of this program will not type in more than 100 characters.

■ `char    c, name[MAXSTRING];`
`int     i, sum = 0;`
The variable `c` is of type `char`. The identifier `name` is of type "array of char," and its size is `MAXSTRING`. In C, all array subscripts start at 0. Thus `name[0]`, `name[1]`,..., `name[MAXSTRING - 1]` are the elements of the array. The variables `i` and `sum` are of type `int`; `sum` is initialized to 0.

■ `printf("\nHi!  What is your name?  ");`
This is a prompt to the user. The program now expects a name to be typed in followed by a carriage return.

■   `(c = getchar()) != '\n'`
This expression consists of two parts. On the left we have

```
(c = getchar())
```

Unlike other languages, assignment in C is an operator (see Chapter 2). Here, `getchar()` is being used to read a character from the keyboard and to assign it to `c`. The value of the expression as a whole is the value of whatever is assigned to `c`. Parentheses are necessary because the order of precedence of the `=` operator is less than that of the `!=` operator. Thus

   `c = getchar() != '\n'`   is equivalent to   `c = (getchar() != '\n')`

which is syntactically correct, but not what we want.

■
```
for (i = 0; (c = getchar()) != '\n'; ++i) {
    name[i] = c;
    if (isalpha(c))
        sum += c;
}
```
The variable `i` is initially assigned the value 0. Then `getchar()` gets a character from the keyboard, assigns it to `c`, and tests to see if it is a newline character. If it is not, the body of the `for` loop is executed. First, the value of `c` is assigned to the array element `name[i]`. Next, the macro `isalpha()` is used to determine whether `c` is a lower- or uppercase letter. If it is, `sum` is incremented by the value of `c`. As we will see in Chapter 3, a character in C has the integer value corresponding to its ASCII encoding. For example, `'a'` has value 97, `'b'` has value 98, and so forth. Finally, the variable `i` is incremented at the end of the `for` loop. The `for` loop is executed repeatedly until a newline character is received.

■ `name[i] = '\0';`
After the `for` loop is finished, the null character \0 is assigned to the element `name[i]`. By convention, all strings end with a null character. Functions that process strings, such as `printf()`, use the null character \0 as an end-of-string sentinel. We now can think of the array `name` in memory as

A	l	i	c	e		B	.		C	a	r	o	l	e	\0	*	· · ·	*
0	1	2	3	4	5	6	7	8	9	10	11	12	13	14	15	16		99

■ `printf("\n%s%s%s\n%s",`
    `"Nice to meet you ", name, ".",`
    `"Your name spelled backwards is ");`
Notice that the format `%s` is used to print the character array `name`. The elements of the array are printed one after another until the end-of-string sentinel \0 is encountered.

■ `for (--i; i >= 0; --i)`
    `putchar(name[i]);`
If we assume that `Alice B. Carole` followed by a carriage return was typed in, then `i` has value 15 at the beginning of this `for` loop. (Do not forget to count from 0, not 1.) After `i` has been decremented, the subscript corresponds to the last character of the name that was typed in. Thus the effect of this `for` loop is to print the name on the screen backwards.

■ `printf("\n%s%d%s\n\n%s\n",`
    `"and the letters in your name sum to ", sum, ".",`
    `"Have a nice day!");`
We print the sum of the letters in the name typed in by the user, and then we print a final message.

Pointers

A pointer is an address of an object in memory. Because an array name is itself a pointer, the uses of arrays and pointers are intimately related. The following program is designed to illustrate some of these relationships:

```c
#include <stdio.h>
#include <string.h>

#define    MAXSTRING    100

int main(void)
{
   char    c = 'a', *p, s[MAXSTRING];

   p = &c;
   printf("%c%c%c   ", *p, *p + 1, *p + 2);
   strcpy(s, "ABC");
   printf("%s  %c%c%s\n", s, *s + 6, *s + 7, s + 1);
   strcpy(s, "she sells sea shells by the seashore");
   p = s + 14;
   for ( ; *p != '\0'; ++p) {
      if (*p == 'e')
         *p = 'E';
      if (*p == ' ')
         *p = '\n';
   }
   printf("%s\n", s);
   return 0;
}
```

The output of this program is

```
abc   ABC   GHBC
she sells sea shElls
by
thE
sEashorE
```

DISSECTION OF THE *abc* PROGRAM

- ■ `#include <string.h>`
  The standard library contains many string-handling functions (see Chapter 6). The standard header file *string.h* contains the function prototypes for these functions. In this program we will use `strcpy()` to copy a string.

- ■ `char   c = 'a', *p, s[MAXSTRING];`
  The variable c is of type char. It is initialized with the value 'a'. The variable p is of type pointer to char. The string s has size MAXSTRING.

- ■ `p = &c;`
  The symbol & is the address operator. The value of the expression &c is the address in memory of the variable c. The address of c is assigned to p. We now think of p as "pointing to c."

- ■ `printf("%c%c%c   ", *p, *p + 1, *p + 2);`
  The format %c is used to print the value of an expression as a character. The symbol * is the dereferencing, or indirection, operator. The expression *p has the value of whatever p is pointing to. Because p is pointing to c and c has the value 'a', this is the value of the expression *p and an a is printed. The value of the expression *p + 1 is one more than the value of *p and this causes a b to be printed. The value of the expression *p + 2 is two more than the value of *p and this causes a c to be printed.

- ■ `"ABC"`
  A string constant is stored in memory as an array of characters, the last of which is the null character \0. Thus the size of the string constant "ABC" is 4, not 3. Even the null string "" contains one character, namely \0. It is important to realize that string constants are of type "array of char". An array name by itself is treated as a pointer, and this is true of string constants as well.

- ■ `strcpy(s, "ABC");`
  The function `strcpy()` takes two arguments, both of type pointer to char, which we can think of as strings. The string pointed to by its second argument is copied into memory beginning at the location pointed to by its first argument. All characters up to and including a null character are copied. The effect is to copy one string into another. It is the responsibility of the programmer to ensure that the first argument points to enough space to hold all the characters being copied. After this statement has been executed, we can think of s in memory as

```
┌───┬───┬───┬────┬───┐           ┌───┐
│ A │ B │ C │ \0 │ * │  ·  ·  ·  │ * │
└───┴───┴───┴────┴───┘           └───┘
  0   1   2   3    4               99
```

- ```
  printf("%s  %c%c%s\n", s, *s + 6, *s + 7, s + 1);
  ```
  The array name s by itself is a pointer. We can think of s as pointing to s[0], or we can think of s as being the base address of the array, which is the address of s[0]. Printing s in the format of a string causes ABC to be printed. The expression *s has the value of what s is pointing to, which is s[0]. This is the character A. Because six letters more than A is G and seven letters more than A is H, the expressions *s + 6 and *s + 7, printed in the format of a character, cause G and H to be printed, respectively. The expression s + 1 is an example of pointer arithmetic. The value of the expression is a pointer that points to s[1], the next character in the array. Thus s + 1 printed in the format of a string causes BC to be printed.

- ```
  strcpy(s, "she sells sea shells by the seashore");
  ```
  This copies a new string into s. Whatever was in s before gets overwritten.

- ```
  p = s + 14;
  ```
  The pointer value s + 14 is assigned to p. An equivalent statement is

  ```
  p = &s[14];
  ```

  If you count carefully, you will see that p now points to the first letter in the word "shells." Note carefully that even though s is a pointer, it is not a pointer variable, but rather a pointer constant. A statement such as

  ```
  p = s;
  ```

  is legal because p is a pointer variable, but the statement

  ```
  s = p;
  ```

  would result in a syntax error. Although the value of what s points to may be changed, the value of s itself may *not* be changed.

- ```
  for ( ; *p != '\0'; ++p) {
      if (*p == 'e')
          *p = 'E';
      if (*p == ' ')
          *p = '\n';
  }
  ```
  As long as the value of what p is pointing to is not equal to the null character, the body of the for loop is executed. If the value of what p is pointing to is equal to 'e', then that value in memory is changed to 'E'. If the value of what p is pointing to is equal to ' ', then that value in memory is changed to '\n'. The variable p is incremented at the end of the for loop. This causes p to point to the next character in the string.

■ `printf("%s\n", s);`
The variable s is printed in the format of a string followed by a newline character. Because the previous for loop changed the values of some of the elements of s, the following is printed:

```
she sells sea shElls
by
thE
sEashorE
```

In C, arrays, strings, and pointers are closely related. To illustrate consider the declaration

```
char    *p, s[100];
```

This creates the identifier p as a pointer to char and the identifier s as an array of 100 elements of type char. Because an array name by itself is a pointer, both p and s are pointers to char. However, p is a variable pointer whereas s is a constant pointer that points to s[0]. Note that the expression ++p can be used to increment p, but because s is a constant pointer, the expression ++s is wrong. The value of s cannot be changed. Of fundamental importance is the fact that the two expressions

```
s[i]        and        *(s + i)
```

are equivalent. The expression s[i] has the value of the *i*th element of the array (counting from 0), whereas *(s + i) is the dereferencing of the expression s + i, a pointer expression that points i character positions past s. In a similar fashion, the two expressions

```
p[i]        and        *(p + i)
```

are equivalent.

1.9   FILES

Files are easy to use in C. To open the file named *my_file*, the following code can
be used:

```
#include <stdio.h>

int main(void)
{
    int     c;
    FILE    *ifp;

    ifp = fopen("my_file", "r");
    .....
```

The second line in the body of main() declares ifp (which stands for "infile
pointer") to be a pointer to FILE. The function fopen() is in the standard library,
and its function prototype is in *stdio.h*. The type FILE is defined in *stdio.h* as a
particular structure. To use the construct, a user need not know any details about it.
However, the header file must be made available by means of a #include directive
before any reference to FILE is made. The function fopen() takes two strings as
arguments, and it returns a pointer to FILE. The first argument is the name of the
file, and the second argument is the mode in which the file is to be opened.

Three modes for a file
"r"   for read
"w"   for write
"a"   for append

When a file is opened for writing and it does not exist, it is created. If it already
exists, its contents are destroyed and the writing starts at the beginning of the file.
If for some reason a file cannot be accessed, the pointer value NULL is returned by
fopen(). After a file has been opened, all references to it are via its file pointer.
Upon the completion of a program, the C system automatically closes all open files.
All C systems put a limit on the number of files that can be open simultaneously.
Typically, this limit is either 20 or 64. When using many files, the programmer
should explicitly close any files not currently in use. The library function fclose()
is used to close files.

Let us now examine the use of files. With text, it is easy to make a frequency analysis of the occurrence of the characters and words making up the text. Such analyses have proven useful in many disciplines, from the study of hieroglyphics to the study of Shakespeare. To keep things simple, we will write a program that counts the occurrences of just uppercase letters. Among our files is one named *chapter1*, which is the current version of this chapter. We will write a program called *cnt_letters* that will open files for reading and writing to do the analysis on this chapter. We give the command

   cnt_letters chapter1 data1

to do this. However, before we present our program, let us describe how command line arguments can be accessed from within a program.

The C language provides a connection to the arguments on the command line. Typically, to use the connection one would code

```
#include <stdio.h>

int main(int argc, char *argv[])
{
    .....
```

Up until now we have always invoked `main()` as a function with no arguments. In fact, it is a function that takes a variable number of arguments. The parameter `argc` stands for "argument count." Its value is the number of arguments in the command line that was used to execute the program. The parameter `argv` stands for "argument variable." It is an array of pointers to `char`. Such an array can be thought of as an array of strings. The successive elements of the array point to successive words in the command line that was used to execute the program. Thus `argv[0]` is a pointer to the name of the command itself. As an example of how this facility is used, suppose that we have written our program and have put the executable code in the file *cnt_letters*. The intent of the command line

   cnt_letters chapter1 data1

is to invoke the program *cnt_letters* with the two file names *chapter1* and *data1* as command line arguments. The program should read file *chapter1* and write to file *data1*. If we give a different command, say

   cnt_letters chapter2 data2

then the program should read file *chapter2* and write to file *data2*. In our program the three words on the command line will be accessible through the three pointers `argv[0]`, `argv[1]`, and `argv[2]`.

Here is our program:

```
/* Count uppercase letters in a file. */

#include <stdio.h>
#include <stdlib.h>

int main(int argc, char *argv[])
{
   int    c, i, letter[26];
   FILE   *ifp, *ofp;

   if (argc != 3) {
      printf("\n%s%s%s\n\n%s\n%s\n\n",
         "Usage:  ", argv[0], "  infile  outfile",
         "The uppercase letters in infile will be counted.",
         "The results will be written in outfile.");
      exit(1);
   }
   ifp = fopen(argv[1], "r");
   ofp = fopen(argv[2], "w");
   for (i = 0; i < 26; ++i)          /* initialize array to zero */
      letter[i] = 0;
   while ((c = getc(ifp)) != EOF)
      if (c >= 'A' && c <= 'Z')       /* find uppercase letters */
         ++letter[c - 'A'];
   for (i = 0; i < 26; ++i) {                    /* print results */
      if (i % 6 == 0)
         putc('\n', ofp);
      fprintf(ofp, "%c:%5d      ", 'A' + i, letter[i]);
   }
   putc('\n', ofp);
   return 0;
}
```

After we have given the command

>   *cnt_letters chapter1 data1*

this is what we find in the file *data1*:

A:	248	B:	240	C:	1292	D:	100	E:	461	F:	79
G:	33	H:	51	I:	569	J:	1	K:	3	L:	202
M:	71	N:	108	O:	164	P:	1222	Q:	19	R:	182
S:	215	T:	455	U:	33	V:	27	W:	63	X:	87
Y:	14	Z:	17								

Observe that the frequency of the letters in *chapter1* is not what one expects in ordinary text.

DISSECTION OF THE *cnt_letters* PROGRAM

■
```
int     c, i, letter[26];
FILE    *ifp, *ofp;
```
The array `letter` will be used to count the occurrences of the uppercase letters. The variables `ifp` and `ofp` are of type "pointer to `FILE`." We often use the identifiers `ifp` and `ofp`, which stand for "infile pointer" and "outfile pointer," respectively.

■
```
if (argc != 3) {
    printf("\n%s%s%s\n\n%s\n%s\n\n",
        "Usage:  ", argv[0], "  infile  outfile",
        "The uppercase letters in infile will be counted.",
        "The results will be written in outfile.");
    exit(1);
}
```
If the number of words on the command line is not three, then the program is being used incorrectly. This causes a message to be printed and the program to be exited. Suppose the following command line is typed:

>   *cnt_letters chapter1 abc abc*

Because the line contains four words, `argc` will have value 4, and this will cause the message

```
Usage:  cnt_letters  infile  outfile

The uppercase letters in infile will be counted.
The results will be written in outfile.
```

to appear on the screen.

■ `ifp = fopen(argv[1], "r");`
   `ofp = fopen(argv[2], "w");`

   If we assume that we have typed the command line

   cnt_letters   chapter1   data1

   to execute this program, then `argv[0]` points to the string `"cnt_letters"`, `argv[1]` points to the string `"chapter1"`, and `argv[2]` points to the string `"data1"`. The C system does this automatically. Thus the file *chapter1* is opened for reading with file pointer `ifp` referring to it, and the file *data1* is opened for writing with file pointer `ofp` referring to it.

■ `for (i = 0; i < 26; ++i)          /* initialize array to zero */`
   `    letter[i] = 0;`

   Many C systems will automatically initialize elements of an array to zero, but ANSI C does not require this. To be sure, the programmer should do it.

■ `(c = getc(ifp)) != EOF`

   The function `getc()` is a macro defined in *stdio.h*. It is similar to `getchar()` except that it takes as an argument a pointer to `FILE`. When `getc(ifp)` is invoked, it gets the next character from the file pointed to by `ifp`. The identifier `EOF` stands for "end-of-file." It is a symbolic constant defined in *stdio.h*, typically by the line

   `#define   EOF   (-1)`

   The value `EOF` is returned by `getc()` when there are no more characters in the file. In C, characters have the integer value corresponding to their ASCII encoding (see Chapter 3). For example, `'a'` has value 97, `'b'` has value 98, and so forth. A `char` is stored in 1 byte, and an `int` is typically stored in either 2 or 4 bytes. Thus a `char` can be considered a small integer type. Conversely, an `int` can be considered a large character type. In particular, an `int` can hold all the values of a `char` and other values as well, such as `EOF`, which is not an ordinary character value. The variable `c` was declared to be an `int` rather than a `char` because it eventually would be assigned the value `EOF`.

■ `while ((c = getc(ifp)) != EOF)`
   `    if (c >= 'A' && c <= 'Z')       /* find uppercase letters */`
   `        ++letter[c - 'A'];`

   A character is read and assigned to `c`. If the value of the character is not `EOF`, then the body of the `while` loop is executed.

■ c >= 'A' && c <= 'Z'
The expression c >= 'A' is true if c is greater than or equal to 'A'. Similarly, the expression c <= 'Z' is true if c is less than or equal to 'Z'. The symbols && represent the "logical and" operator. An expression of the form

expr1 && *expr2*

is true if and only if both *expr1* and *expr2* are true. Because of operator precedence (see Chapter 3),

c >= 'A' && c <= 'Z'   is equivalent to   (c >= 'A') && (c <= 'Z')

Thus the expression c >= 'A' && c <= 'Z' is true if and only if c has the value of an uppercase letter.

■ ++letter[c - 'A'];
If c has the value 'A', then c - 'A' has the value 0. Thus the array element letter[0] gets incremented when c has the value 'A'. Similarly, if c has the value 'B', then c - 'A' has the value 1. Thus the array element letter[1] gets incremented when c has the value 'B'. In this way a count of the uppercase letters is kept in the elements of the array letter with letter[0] corresponding to the letter A, letter[1] corresponding to the letter B, and so forth.

■ for (i = 0; i < 26; ++i) {   /* print results */
      if (i % 6 == 0)
         putc('\n', ofp);
      . . . . .

The symbol % is the modulus operator. An expression such as a % b yields the remainder of a divided by b. For example, 5 % 3 has the value 2. In the body of the for loop we have used the expression , which has the value 0 whenever the value of i is a multiple of 6. Because of operator precedence, the expression

i % 6 == 0   is equivalent to   (i % 6) == 0

Thus the expression i % 6 == 0 is true every sixth time through the loop; at these times a newline character is printed. If you look at the output of the program, you will see that it is printed in six columns. The macro putc() is defined in *stdio.h*. It is similar to putchar() except that its second argument is a pointer to FILE. The value of its first argument is written to the indicated file in the format of a character.

- `fprintf(ofp, "%c:%5d    ", 'A' + i, letter[i]);`
  The function `fprintf()` is similar to `printf()` except that it takes as its first argument a pointer to `FILE`. When the function is invoked, it writes to the indicated file rather than to the screen. Observe that `'A' + i` is being printed in the format of a character. When i is 0, the expression `'A' + i` has the value `'A'`, causing the letter A to be printed; when i is 1, the expression `'A' + i` has the value `'B'`, causing the letter B to be printed; and so forth.

- `fclose(ifp);`
  `fclose(ofp);`
  Although we did not do so, we could have explicitly closed the open files just before we exited from `main()`. Instead, we relied on the C system to close the files.

1.10 OPERATING SYSTEM CONSIDERATIONS

In this section we discuss a number of topics that are system-dependent. We begin with the mechanics of writing and running a C program.

Writing and Running a C Program

The precise steps that have to be followed to create a file containing C code and to compile and execute it depend on three things: the operating system, the text editor, and the compiler. However, in all cases the general procedure is the same. We first describe in some detail how it is done in a UNIX environment. Then we discuss how it is done in an MS-DOS environment.

In the discussion that follows we will be using the *cc* command to invoke the C compiler. In reality, however, the command depends on the compiler that is being used. For example, if we were using the command line version of the Turbo C compiler from Borland, then we would use the command *tcc* instead of *cc*. (For a list of C compilers, see the table in Section 11.13, "The C Compiler," in Chapter 11.)

Steps to be followed in writing and running a C program

1   Using an editor, create a text file, say *pgm.c*, that contains a C program. The name of the file must end with *.c*, indicating that the file contains C source code. For example, to use the *vi* editor on a UNIX system, we would give the command

    vi pgm.c

To use an editor, the programmer must know the appropriate commands for inserting and modifying text.

2 Compile the program. This can be done with the command

    cc pgm.c

The *cc* command invokes in turn the preprocessor, the compiler, and the loader. The preprocessor modifies a copy of the source code according to the preprocessing directives and produces what is called a *translation unit*. The compiler translates the translation unit into object code. If there are errors, then the programmer must start again at step 1 with the editing of the source file. Errors that occur at this stage are called *syntax errors* or *compile-time errors*. If there are no errors, then the loader uses the object code produced by the compiler, along with object code obtained from various libraries provided by the system, to create the executable file *a.out*. The program is now ready to be executed.

3 Execute the program. This is done with the command

    a.out

Typically, the program will complete execution, and a system prompt will reappear on the screen. Any errors that occur during execution are called *runtime errors*. If for some reason the program needs to be changed, the programmer must start again at step 1.

If we compile a different program, then the file *a.out* will be overwritten, and its previous contents lost. If the contents of the executable file *a.out* are to be saved, then the file must be moved, or renamed. Suppose that we give the command

    cc sea.c

This causes executable code to be written automatically into *a.out*. To save this file, we can give the command

    mv a.out sea

This causes *a.out* to be moved to *sea*. Now the program can be executed by giving the command

    sea

In UNIX, it is common practice to give the executable file the same name as the corresponding source file, except to drop the *.c* suffix. If we wish, we can use the *−o* option to direct the output of the *cc* command. For example, the command

    cc −o sea sea.c

causes the executable output from *cc* to be written directly into *sea*, leaving intact whatever is in *a.out*.

Different kinds of errors can occur in a program. Syntax errors are caught by the compiler, whereas run-time errors manifest themselves only during program execution. For example, if an attempt to divide by zero is encoded into a program, a run-time error may occur when the program is executed (see Exercises 5 and 6). Usually, an error message produced by a run-time error is not very helpful in finding the trouble.

Let us now consider an MS-DOS environment. Here, some other text editor would most likely be used. Some C systems, such as Turbo C, have both a command line environment and an integrated environment. The integrated environment includes both the text editor and the compiler. (Consult Turbo C manuals for details.) In MS-DOS, the executable output produced by a C compiler is written to a file having the same name as the source file, but with the extension *.exe* instead of *.c*. Suppose, for example, that we are using the command line environment in Turbo C. If we give the command

> *tcc   sea.c*

then the executable code will be written to *sea.exe*. To execute the program, we give the command

> *sea.exe*   or equivalently   *sea*

To invoke the program, we do not need to type the *.exe* extension. If we wish to rename this file, we can use the *rename* command.

Interrupting a Program

When running a program, the user may want to interrupt, or kill, the program. For example, the program may be in an infinite loop. (In an interactive environment it is not necessarily wrong to use an infinite loop in a program.) Throughout this text we assume that the user knows how to interrupt a program. In MS-DOS and in UNIX, a control-c is commonly used to effect an interrupt. On some systems a special key, such as *delete* or *rubout* is used. Make sure that you know how to interrupt a program on your system.

Typing an End-of-File Signal

When a program is taking its input from the keyboard, it may be necessary to generate an end-of-file signal for the program to work properly. In UNIX, a carriage return followed by a control-d is the typical way to effect an end-of-file signal. In MS-DOS a control-z must be typed instead. (For further discussion, see Exercise 26.)

Redirection of the Input and the Output

Many operating systems, including MS-DOS and UNIX, can redirect the input and the output. To understand how this works, first consider the UNIX command

> *ls*

This command causes a list of files and directories to be written to the screen. (The comparable command in MS-DOS is *dir*.) Now consider the command

   ls > tmp

The symbol > causes the operating system to redirect the output of the command to the file *tmp*. (In MS-DOS, the file name needs an extension.) What was written to the screen before is now written to the file *tmp*.

   Our next program is called *dbl_out*. It can be used with redirection of both the input and the output. The program reads characters from the standard input file, which is normally connected to the keyboard, and writes each character twice to the standard output file, which is normally connected to the screen.

```
#include <stdio.h>

int main(void)
{
    char    c;

    while (scanf("%c", &c) == 1) {
        printf("%c", c);
        printf("%c", c);
    }
    return 0;
}
```

If we compile the program and put the executable code in the file *dbl_out*, then, using redirection, we can invoke the program in four ways:

   dbl_out
   dbl_out < infile
   dbl_out > outfile
   dbl_out < infile > outfile

Used in this context, the symbols < and > can be thought of as arrows. (See Exercise 26 for further discussion.)

   Some commands are not meant to be used with redirection. For example, the *ls* command does not read characters from the keyboard. Therefore, it makes no sense to redirect the input to the *ls* command; because it does not take keyboard input, there is nothing to redirect.

1.11   SUMMARY

1   Programming is the art of communicating algorithms to computers. An algorithm is a computational procedure whose steps are completely specified and elementary.

2   The C system provides a standard library of functions that can be used by the programmer. Two functions from the library are printf() and scanf(). They are used for output and input, respectively. The function printf() can print out explicit text and can use conversion specifications that begin with the character % to print the values of the arguments that follow the control string. The use of scanf() is somewhat analogous, but conversion specifications in the control string are matched with the other arguments, all of which must be addresses (pointers).

3   The C compiler has a preprocessor built into it. Lines that begin with a # are preprocessing directives. A #define directive can be used to define symbolic constants. A #include directive can be used to copy the contents of a file into the code.

4   Statements are ordinarily executed sequentially. Special statements such as if, if-else, for, and while statements can alter the sequential flow of control during execution of a program.

5   A program consists of one or more functions written in one or more files. Execution begins with the function main(). Other functions may be called from within main() and from within each other.

6   A function definition is of the form

    type   function_name(parameter type list)
    {
        declarations

        statements
    }

    A function definition consists of two parts, a header and a body. The header consists of the code before the first left brace, and the body consists of the declarations and statements between the braces.

7   In a function definition all declarations must occur before any statements. All variables must be declared. Compound statements are surrounded by the braces { and }. Syntactically, a compound statement is itself a statement. A compound statement can be used anywhere that a simple statement can be used.

8 All arguments to functions are passed "call by value." This means that when an expression is passed as an argument, the value of the expression is computed, and it is this value that is passed to the function. Thus, when a variable is passed as an argument to a function, the value of the variable is computed, which we may think of as a copy of the variable, and it is this copy that is passed to the function. Hence, the value of the variable is not changed in the calling environment.

9 When a return statement is encountered in a function, control is passed back to the calling environment. If an expression is present, then its value is passed back as well.

10 The use of many small functions as a programming style aids modularity and documentation of programs. Moreover, programs composed of many small functions are easier to debug.

11 Arrays, strings, and pointers are intimately related. A string is an array of characters, and an array name by itself a pointer that points to its first element. By convention, the character \0 is used as an end-of-string sentinel. A constant string such as "abc" can be considered a pointer to type char. This string has four characters in it, the last one being \0.

1.12 EXERCISES

1 On the screen write the words

```
she sells sea shells by the seashore
```

(a) all on one line, (b) on three lines, (c) inside a box.

2 Use a hand calculator to verify that the output of the *marathon* program is correct. Create another version of the program by changing the floating constant 1760.0 to an integer constant 1760. Compile and execute the program and notice that the output is not the same as before. This is because integer division discards any fractional part.

3 Write a version of the *marathon* program in which all constants and variables are of type double. Is the output of the program exactly the same as that of the original program?

4 Take one of your working programs and alter it by deleting the keyword void
in the line

```
int main(void)
```

When you compile your program does your compiler complain? Probably not.
(See Chapter 5 for further discussion.) Next, remove the keyword void and
remove the following line from the body of main():

```
return 0;
```

When you compile the program, does your compiler complain? This time it
should. If your compiler does not complain, learn how to set a higher warning
level for your compiler. Generally speaking, programmers should always use
the highest warning level possible. One of the principal rules of programming is
"keep your compiler happy," but not at the expense of turning off all the warnings. Programmers should rework their code repeatedly until all the warnings
have vanished.

5 The following program may have a runtime error in it:

```
#include <stdio.h>

int main(void)
{
    int   x, y = 0;

    x = 1 / y;
    printf("x = %d\n", x);
    return 0;
}
```

Check to see that the program compiles without any error messages. Run the
program to see the effect of integer division by zero. On most systems this
program will exhibit a run-time error. If this happens on your system, try to
rewrite the program without the variable y, but keep the error in the program.
That is, divide by zero directly. Now what happens?

6 Most C systems provide for logically infinite floating values. Modify the program
given in Exercise 5 by changing int to double and, in the printf() statement,
%d to %f. Does the program still exhibit a runtime error? On most systems the
answer is no. What happens on your system?

7 Any #include lines in a program normally occur at the top of the file. But do they have to be at the top? Rewrite the *pacific_sea* program so that the #include line is not at the top of the file. For example, try

```
int main(void)
{
    #include "pacific_sea.h"
    .....
```

8 Take one of your files containing a working program, say *sea.c*, and rename the file as *sea*. Now try to compile it. Some C compilers will complain; others will not. On UNIX systems, the complaint may be quite cryptic, with words such as "bad magic number" or "unable to process using elf libraries." What happens on your system?

9 The following program writes a large letter *I* on the screen:

```
#include <stdio.h>

#define    BOTTOM_SPACE    "\n\n\n\n\n"
#define    HEIGHT          17
#define    OFFSET          "                 "    /* 17 blanks */
#define    TOP_SPACE       "\n\n\n\n\n"

int main(void)
{
    int    i;

    printf(TOP_SPACE);
    printf(OFFSET "IIIIIII\n");
    for (i = 0; i < HEIGHT; ++i)
        printf(OFFSET "   III\n");
    printf(OFFSET "IIIIIII\n");
    printf(BOTTOM_SPACE);
    return 0;
}
```

Compile and run this program so you understand its effect. Write a similar program that prints a large letter *C* on the screen.

10 Take a working program and omit each line in turn and run it through the
compiler. Record the error messages each such-deletion causes. As an example,
consider the following code in the file *nonsense.c*:

```
#include <stdio.h>

/* forgot main */
{
    printf("nonsense\n");
}
```

11 Write a program that asks interactively for your *name* and *age* and responds with

Hello *name,* next year you will be *next_age.*

where *next_age* is *age* + 1.

12 Write a program that neatly prints a table of powers. The first few lines of the
table might look like this:

```
:::::  A TABLE OF POWERS  :::::

Integer     Square     3rd power     4th power     5th power
-------     ------     ---------     ---------     ---------
      1          1             1             1             1
      2          4             8            16            32
      3          9            27            81           243
```

13 A for loop has the form

```
for (expr1; expr2; expr3)
    statement
```

If all three expressions are present, then this is equivalent to

```
expr1;
while (expr2) {
    statement
    expr3;
}
```

Why is there no semicolon following *statement*? Of course, it may well happen
that *statement* itself contains a semicolon at the end, but it does not have to.
In C, a compound statement consists of braces surrounding zero or more other
statements, and a compound statement is itself a statement. Thus both {} and

{ ; ; ; } are statements. Try the following code:

```
int   i;

for (i = 0; i < 3; ++i)
    { }                          /* no semicolon */
for (i = 0; i < 3; ++i)
    { ; ; ; }                    /* three semicolons,
                                    but none after the statement */
```

Is your compiler happy with this? (It should be.) Compilers care about legality. If what you write is legal but otherwise nonsense, your compiler will be happy.

14 The standard header files supplied by the C system can be found in one or more system-dependent directories. For example, on UNIX systems these header files might be in */usr/include*. On Turbo C systems they might be in *turboc**include* or *tc**include* or *bc**include*. Find the location of the standard header file *stdio.h* on your system. Read this file and find the line that pertains to printf(). The line will look something like

```
int   printf(const char *format, ...);
```

This line is an example of a function prototype. Function prototypes tell the compiler the number and type of arguments that are expected to be passed to the function and the type of the value that is returned by the function. As we will see in later chapters, strings are of type "pointer to char," which is specified by char *. The identifier format is provided only for its mnemonic value to the programmer. The compiler disregards it. The function prototype for printf() could just as well have been written

```
int   printf(const char *, ...);
```

The keyword const tells the compiler that the string that gets passed as an argument should not be changed. The ellipses ... indicate to the compiler that the number and type of the remaining arguments vary. The printf() function returns as an int the number of characters transmitted, or a negative value if an error occurs. Recall that the first program in this chapter prints the phrase "from sea to shining C" on the screen. Rewrite the program by replacing the #include line with the function prototype for printf() that we have given above. *Caution:* You can try to use verbatim the line that you found in *stdio.h*, but your program may fail. (For more information about the preprocessor, see Chapter 8.)

15 (Suggested to us by Donald Knuth at Stanford University.) In the *running_sum* program we first computed a sum and then divided by the number of summands to compute an average. The following program illustrates a better way to compute the average:

```
/* Compute a better average. */

#include <stdio.h>

int main(void)
{
    int       i;
    double    x;
    double    avg = 0.0;      /* a better average */
    double    navg;           /* a naive average */
    double    sum = 0.0;

    printf("%5s%17s%17s%17s\n%5s%17s%17s%17s\n\n",
        "Count", "Item", "Average", "Naive avg",
        "-----", "----", "--------", "---------");
    for (i = 1; scanf("%lf", &x) == 1; ++i) {
        avg += (x - avg) / i;
        sum += x;
        navg = sum / i;
        printf("%5d%17e%17e%17e\n", i, x, avg, navg);
    }
    return 0;
}
```

Run this program so that you understand its effects. Note that the better algorithm for computing the average is embodied in the line

```
avg += (x - avg) / i;
```

Explain why this algorithm does, in fact, compute the running average. *Hint:* Do some simple hand calculations first.

16 In Exercise 15 we used the algorithm suggested to us by Donald Knuth to write
    a program that computes running averages. In this exercise we want to use that
    program to see what happens when sum gets too large to be represented in the
    machine (see Section 3.6, "The Floating Types," in Chapter 3 for details about
    the values a double can hold). Create a file, say *data*, and put the following
    numbers into it:

```
1e308  1  1e308  1  1e308
```

Run the program, redirecting the input so that the numbers in your file *data* get
read in. Do you see the advantage of the better algorithm?

17 (Advanced) In this exercise you are to continue the work you did in Exercise 16.
    If you run the *better_average* program taking the input from a file that contains
    some "ordinary" numbers, then the average and the naive average seem to be
    identical. Find a situation where this is not the case. That is, demonstrate
    experimentally that the better average really is better, even when sum does not
    overflow.

18 Experiment with the type qualifier const. How does your compiler treat the
    following code?

```
const int   a = 0;

a = 333;
printf("%d\n", a);
```

19 Put the following lines into a program and run it so that you understand its
    effects:

```
int   a1, a2, a3, cnt;

printf("Input three integers:  ");
cnt = scanf("%d%d%d", &a1, &a2, &a3);
printf("Number of successful conversions: %d\n", cnt);
```

What happens if you type the letter *x* when prompted by your program? What
numbers can be printed by your program? *Hint:* If scanf() encounters an
end-of-file mark before any conversions have occurred, then the value EOF is
returned, where EOF is defined in *stdio.h* as a symbolic constant, typically with
the value −1. You should be able to get your program to print this number.

20   In ANSI C the `printf()` function returns as an `int` the number of characters printed. To see how this works, write a small program containing the following lines:

```
int    cnt;

cnt = printf("abc abc");
printf("\nNo. of characters printed: %d\n", cnt);
```

What gets printed if the control string is replaced by

     "abc\nabc \n"   or   "abc\0abc\0"

21   In Exercise 19 you were able to get different numbers printed, depending on the input you provided. Put the following lines into a program:

```
char    c1, c2, c3;
int     cnt;

printf("Input three characters:   ");
cnt = scanf("%c%c%c", &c1, &c2, &c3);
printf("Number of successful conversions: %d\n", cnt);
```

By varying the input, what numbers can you cause to be printed? *Hint:* The numbers printed by the program you wrote for Exercise 19 can be printed here, but you have to work much harder to do it.

22   Use the ideas presented in the *nice_day* program to write a program that counts the total number of letters. Use redirection to test your program. If *infile* is a file containing text, then the command

     nletters < *infile*

should cause something like

```
Number of letters:   179
```

to be printed on the screen.

23   In the *abc* program in Section 1.8 we used the loop

```
for ( ; *p != '\0'; ++p) {
    if (*p == 'e')
        *p = 'E';
    if (*p == ' ')
        *p = '\n';
}
```

The braces are needed because the body of the for loop consists of two if statements. Change the code to

```
for ( ; *p != '\0'; ++p)
   if (*p == 'e')
      *p = 'E';
   else if (*p == ' ')
      *p = '\n';
```

Explain why braces are not needed now. Check to see that the runtime behavior of the program is the same as before. Explain why this is so.

24 Suppose that a is an array of some type and that i is an int. There is a fundamental equivalence between the expression a[i] and a certain corresponding pointer expression. What is the corresponding pointer expression?

25 Complete the following program by writing a prn_string() function that uses putchar() to print a string passed as an argument. Remember that strings are terminated by the null character \0. The program uses the strcat() function from the standard library. Its function prototype is given in the header file *string.h*. The function takes two strings as arguments. It concatenates the two strings and puts the results in the first argument.

```
#include <stdio.h>
#include <string.h>

#define    MAXSTRING    100

void    prn_string(char *);

int main(void)

{
    char    s1[MAXSTRING], s2[MAXSTRING];

    strcpy(s1, "Mary, Mary, quite contrary,\n");
    strcpy(s2, "how does your garden grow?\n");
    prn_string(s1);
    prn_string(s2);
    strcat(s1, s2);          /* concatenate the strings */
    prn_string(s1);
    return 0;
}

.....
```

26 Redirection, like many new ideas, is best understood with experimentation. In
    Section 1.10, "Operating System Considerations," we presented the *dbl_out* pro-
    gram. Create a file, say *my_file*, that contains a few lines of text. Try the
    following commands, so that you understand the effects of using redirection
    with *dbl_out*.

> *dbl_out < my_file*
> *dbl_out < my_file > tmp*

The following command is of special interest:

> *dbl_out > tmp*

This command causes *dbl_out* to take its input from the keyboard and to write
its output in the file *tmp*, provided that you effect an end-of-file signal when you
are finished. What happens if instead of typing a carriage return followed by
a control-d (a control-z in MS-DOS), you type a control-c to kill the program?
Does anything at all get written into *tmp*?

CHAPTER **2**

LEXICAL ELEMENTS, OPERATORS, AND THE C SYSTEM

In this chapter we explain the lexical elements of the C programming language. C is a language. Like other languages, it has an alphabet and rules for putting together words and punctuation to make correct, or legal, programs. These rules are the *syntax* of the language. The program that checks on the legality of C code is called the *compiler*. If there is an error, the compiler will print an error message and stop. If there are no errors, then the source code is legal, and the compiler translates it into object code, which in turn gets used by the loader to produce an executable file.

When the compiler is invoked, the preprocessor does its work first. For that reason we can think of the preprocessor as being built into the compiler. On some systems this is actually the case, whereas on others the preprocessor is separate. This is not of concern to us in this chapter. We have to be aware, however, that we can get error messages from the preprocessor as well as from the compiler (see Exercise 29). Throughout this chapter, we use the term *compiler* in the sense that, conceptually, the preprocessor is built into the compiler.

A C program is a sequence of characters that will be converted by a C compiler to object code, which in turn gets converted to a target language on a particular machine. On most systems the target language will be a form of machine language that can be run or interpreted. For this to happen, the program must be syntactically correct. The compiler first collects the characters of the program into *tokens*, which can be thought of as the basic vocabulary of the language.

In ANSI C there are six kinds of tokens: keywords, identifiers, constants, string constants, operators, and punctuators. The compiler checks that the tokens can be formed into legal strings according to the syntax of the language. Most compilers are very precise in their requirements. Unlike human readers of English, who are able to understand the meaning of a sentence with an extra punctuation mark or a misspelled word, a C compiler will fail to provide a translation of a syntactically incorrect program, no matter how trivial the error. Hence the programmer must learn to be precise in writing code.

The programmer should strive to write understandable code. A key part of doing this is producing well-commented code with meaningful identifier names. In this chapter we illustrate these important concepts.

C program   →   group characters into tokens

→   translate to target code

2.1   CHARACTERS AND LEXICAL ELEMENTS

A C program is first constructed by the programmer as a sequence of characters. Among the characters that can be used in a program are the following:

```
lowercase letters    a  b  c...z
uppercase letters    A  B  C...Z
digits               0  1  2  3  4  5  6  7  8  9
other characters     +  -  *  /  =  ( )    [ ] < > ' "
                     !  @  #  $  %  &  _|    \  .  ,  ;  :  ?
white space characters such as blank, newline, and tab
```

These characters are collected by the compiler into syntactic units called *tokens*. Let us look at a simple program and informally pick out some of its tokens before we go on to a strict definition of C syntax.

```c
/* Read in two integers and print their sum. */

#include <stdio.h>

int main(void)
{
    int    a, b, sum;

    printf("Input two integers:  ");
    scanf("%d%d", &a, &b);
    sum = a + b;
    printf("%d + %d = %d\n", a, b, sum);
    return 0;
}
```

LEXICAL DISSECTION OF THE *sum* PROGRAM

■ `/* Read in two integers and print their sum. */`
Comments are delimited by `/*` and `*/`. The compiler first replaces each comment by a single blank. Thereafter, the compiler either disregards white space or uses it to separate tokens.

■ `#include <stdio.h>`
This is a preprocessing directive that causes the standard header file *stdio.h* to be included. We have included it because it contains the function prototypes for `printf()` and `scanf()`. A function prototype is a kind of declaration. The compiler needs function prototypes to do its work.

■ `int main(void)`
`{`
`    int    a, b, sum;`
The compiler groups these characters into four kinds of tokens. The function name `main` is an identifier, and the parentheses `( )` immediately following `main` is an operator. This idea is confusing at first, because what you see following `main` is `(void)`, but it is only the parentheses `( )` themselves that constitute the operator. This operator tells the compiler that `main` is a function. The characters "{", ",", and ";" are punctuators; `int` is a keyword; a, b, and sum are identifiers.

■ `int    a, b, sum;`
The compiler uses the white space between `int` and `a` to distinguish the two tokens. We cannot write

`    int a, b, sum;        /* wrong: white space is necessary */`

On the other hand, the white space following a comma is superfluous. We could have written

`    int  a,b,sum;`   but not   `int  absum;`

The compiler would consider `absum` to be an identifier.

■ `printf("Input two integers:   ");`
`scanf("%d%d", &a, &b);`
The names `printf` and `scanf` are identifiers, and the parentheses following them tell the compiler that they are functions. After the compiler has translated the C code, the loader will attempt to create an executable file. If the code for `printf()` and `scanf()` has not been supplied by the programmer, it will be taken from the standard library. A programmer would not normally redefine these identifiers.

■ `"Input two integers:   "`
A series of characters enclosed in double quotes is a string constant. The compiler treats this as a single token. The compiler also provides space in memory to store the string.

■ `&a, &b`
The character & is the address operator. The compiler treats it as a token. Even though the characters & and a are adjacent to each other, the compiler treats each of them as a separate token. We could have written

> `&  a  ,  &  b`   or   `&a,&b`

but not

> `&a &b`   `/* the comma is missing */`
> `a&, &b`   `/* & requires its operand to be on the right */`

The comma is a punctuator.

■ `sum = a + b;`
The characters = and + are operators. White space here will be ignored, so we could have written

> `sum=a+b;`   or   `sum  =  a  +  b  ;`

but not

> `s    u    m  =  a  +  b;`

If we had written the latter, then each letter on this line would be treated by the compiler as a separate identifier. Because not all of these identifiers have been declared, the compiler would complain—and even if they had been declared, the expression s u is not legal.

The compiler either ignores white space or uses it to separate elements of the language. The programmer uses white space to provide more legible code. To the compiler, program text is implicitly a single stream of characters, but to the human reader it is a two-dimensional tableau.

2.2   SYNTAX RULES

The syntax of C will be described using a rule system derived from Backus-Naur Form (BNF). These schemes were first used in 1960 to describe ALGOL 60. Although they are not adequate by themselves to describe the legal strings of C, in conjunction with some explanatory remarks they are a standard form of describing modern high-level languages.

A syntactic category will be written in italics and defined by productions, also called rewriting rules, such as

digit ::= 0 | 1 | 2 | 3 | 4 | 5 | 6 | 7 | 8 | 9

This should be read as

The syntactic category *digit* is rewritten as either symbol 0, the symbol 1, . . ., or the symbol 9.

The vertical bar separates alternate choices. Symbols not in italics are taken to be terminal symbols of the language to which no further productions are applied.

Symbols to be used in productions

italics	indicate syntactic categories
::=	"to be rewritten as" symbol
|	vertical bar to separate choices
{}$_1$	choose 1 of the enclosed items
{}$_{0+}$	repeat the enclosed items 0 or more times
{}$_{1+}$	repeat the enclosed items 1 or more times
{}$_{opt}$	optional items

Other items are terminal symbols of the language.

Let us define a category *letter_or_digit* to mean any lower- or uppercase letter of the alphabet or any decimal digit. Here is one way we can do this:

letter_or_digit ::= *letter* | *digit*
letter ::= *lowercase_letter* | *uppercase_letter*
lowercase_letter ::= a | b | c | . . . | z
uppercase_letter ::= A | B | C | . . . | Z
digit ::= 0 | 1 | 2 | 3 | 4 | 5 | 6 | 7 | 8 | 9

Now let us create a category *alphanumeric_string* to be an arbitrary sequence of letters or digits.

alphanumeric_string ::= {*letter_or_digit*}$_{0+}$

Using these productions, we see that strings of one character such as "3" and strings of many characters such as "ab777c" as well as the null string "" are all alphanumeric strings. Note that in each of our examples double quote characters were used to delimit the alphanumeric string. The double quote characters themselves are not part of the string.

If we wish to guarantee that a string has at least one character, we must define a new syntactic category, such as

alpha_string_1 ::= {*letter_or_digit*}$_{1+}$

and if we want strings that start with an uppercase letter, we could define

> *u_alpha_string* ::= *uppercase_letter* { *letter_or_digit* }$_{0+}$

or equivalently,

> *u_alpha_string* ::= *uppercase_letter alphanumeric_string*

To illustrate the {}$_{opt}$ notation, we can define a syntactic category called *conditional_statement* as follows:

> *conditional_statement* ::= if *(expression) statement*
> {else *statement*}$_{opt}$

Because *expression* and *statement* have not yet been supplied with rewriting rules, this category is not defined completely. Those rewriting rules are complicated, and we are not ready to present them here. In any case, some examples of this syntactic category are

```
if (big_big_big > 999)
    huge = giant + a_lot;     /* no else part immediately follows */

if (normalized_score >= 65)
    pass = 1;
else                /* else part associated with preceding if part */
    pass = 0;
```

2.3 COMMENTS

Comments are arbitrary strings of symbols placed between the delimiters /* and */. Comments are not tokens. The compiler changes each comment into a single blank character. Thus comments are not part of the executable program. We have already seen examples such as

```
/* a comment */        /*** another comment ***/        /*****/
```

Another example is

```
/*
 *    A comment can be written in this fashion
 *    to set it off from the surrounding code.
 */
```

The following illustrates one of many styles that can be used to highlight comments:

```
/****************************
*    If you wish, you can    *
*    put comments in a box.  *
****************************/
```

Comments are used by the programmer as a documentation aid. The aim of documentation is to explain clearly how the program works and how it is to be used. Sometimes a comment contains an informal argument demonstrating the correctness of the program.

Comments should be written simultaneously with program text. Although some programmers insert comments as a last step, there are two problems with this approach. The first is that once the program is running, the tendency is to either omit or abbreviate the comments. The second is that ideally the comments should serve as running commentary, indicating program structure and contributing to program clarity and correctness. They cannot serve this purpose if they are inserted after the coding is finished.

In C++, the C style of comment is still valid. But in addition, C++ provides for comments that begin with // and run to the end of the line.

```
// This is a comment in C++.

//
// This is one common way of writing
// a comment in C++ that consists
// of many lines.
//

/*
// This C comment style mimics the
// previous C++ comment style.
*/
```

2.4   KEYWORDS

Keywords are explicitly reserved words that have a strict meaning as individual tokens in C. They cannot be redefined or used in other contexts.

Keywords				
auto	do	goto	signed	unsigned
break	double	if	sizeof	void
case	else	int	static	volatile
char	enum	long	struct	while
const	extern	register	switch	
continue	float	return	typedef	
default	for	short	union	

Some implementations may have additional keywords. These will vary from one implementation, or system, to another. As an example, here are some of the additional keywords in Turbo C:

```
asm     cdecl     far     huge     interrupt     near     pascal
```

Compared to other major languages, C has only a small number of keywords. Ada, for example, has 62 keywords. It is a characteristic of C that it does a lot with relatively few special symbols and keywords.

2.5   IDENTIFIERS

An identifier is a token that is composed of a sequence of letters, digits, and the special character _, which is called an *underscore*. A letter or underscore must be the first character of an identifier. In most implementations of C the lower- and uppercase letters are treated as distinct. It is good programming practice to choose identifiers that have mnemonic significance so that they contribute to the readability and documentation of the program.

identifier ::= {*letter* | *underscore* }$_1$ {*letter* | *underscore* | *digit*}$_{0+}$
underscore ::= _

Some examples of identifiers are

```
k
_id
iamanidentifier2
so_am_i
```

but not

```
not#me         /* special character # not allowed */
101_south      /* must not start with a digit */
-plus          /* do not mistake - for _ */
```

Identifiers are created to give unique names to various objects in a program. Keywords can be thought of as identifiers that are reserved to have special meaning in the C language. Identifiers such as scanf and printf are already known to the C system as input/output functions in the standard library. These names would not normally be redefined. The identifier main is special, in that C programs always begin execution at the function called main.

One major difference among operating systems and C compilers is the length of discriminated identifiers. On some older systems, an identifier with more than 8 characters will be accepted, but only the first 8 characters will be used. The remaining characters are simply disregarded. On such a system, for example, the variable names

```
i_am_an_identifier     and       i_am_an_elephant
```

would be considered the same.

In ANSI C, at least the first 31 characters of an identifier are discriminated. Many C systems discriminate more.

Good programming style requires the programmer to choose names that are meaningful. If you were to write a program to figure out various taxes, you might have identifiers such as tax_rate, price, and tax, so that the statement

```
tax = price * tax_rate;
```

would have an obvious meaning. The underscore is used to create a single identifier from what would normally be a string of words separated by spaces. Meaningfulness and avoiding confusion go hand in hand with readability to constitute the main guidelines for a good programming style.

Caution: Identifiers that begin with an underscore can conflict with system names. Only systems programmers should use such identifiers. As an example, consider the identifier _iob, which is often defined as the name of an array of structures in *stdio.h*. If a programmer tries to use _iob for some other purpose, the compiler may complain, or the program may misbehave. Applications programmers are best advised to use identifiers that do not begin with an underscore.

2.6   CONSTANTS

As we have seen in some simple introductory programs, C manipulates various kinds of values. Numbers such as 0 and 17 are examples of integer constants, and numbers such as 1.0 and 3.14159 are examples of floating constants. Like most languages, C treats integer and floating constants differently. In Chapter 3 we will discuss in detail how C understands numbers. There are also character constants in C, such as 'a', 'b', and '+'. Character constants are written between single quotes, and as we shall see in Chapter 3, they are closely related to integers. Some character constants are special, such as the newline character, written '\n'. The backslash is the escape character, and we think of \n as "escaping the usual meaning of n." Even though \n is written with the two characters \ and n, it represents a single character called *newline*.

In addition to the constants that we have already discussed, there are enumeration constants in C. We will discuss these along with the keyword enum in Chapter 7. Integer constants, floating constants, character constants, and enumeration constants are all collected by the compiler as tokens. Because of implementation limits, constants that are syntactically expressible may not be available on a particular machine. For example, an integer may be too large to be stored in a machine word.

Decimal integers are finite strings of decimal digits. Because C provides octal and hexadecimal integers as well as decimal integers, we have to be careful to distinguish between the different kinds of integers. For example, 17 is a decimal integer constant, 017 is an octal integer constant, and 0x17 is a hexadecimal integer constant. (See Chapter 3 for further discussion.) Also, negative constant integers such as -33 are considered constant expressions.

> *decimal_integer* ::= 0 | *positive_decimal_integer*
> *positive_decimal_integer* ::= *positive_digit* {*digit*}$_{0+}$
> *positive_digit* ::= 1 | 2 | 3 | 4 | 5 | 6 | 7 | 8 | 9

Some examples of constant decimal integers are

```
0
77
123456789000        /* too large for the machine? */
```

but not

```
0123                /* an octal integer */
-49                 /* a constant expression */
123.0               /* a floating constant */
```

Although we have already used integer constants such as 144 and floating constants such as 39.7, their meaning in terms of type, along with details concerning memory requirements and machine accuracy, is complicated enough to require a thorough discussion. We do this in Chapter 3.

2.7 STRING CONSTANTS

A sequence of characters enclosed in a pair of double quote marks, such as "abc", is a string constant, or a string literal. It is collected by the compiler as a single token. In Chapter 6 we will see that string constants are stored by the compiler as arrays of characters. String constants are always treated differently from character constants. For example, "a" and 'a' are not the same.

Note that a double quote mark " is just one character, not two. If the character " itself is to occur in a string constant, it must be preceded by a backslash character \. If the character \ is to occur in a string constant, it too must be preceded by a backslash. Some examples of string constants are

```
"a string of text"
""                                        /* the null string */
"      "                                   /* a string of blanks */
"   a = b + c;    "                        /* nothing is executed */
"   /* this is not a comment */    "
"a string with double quotes \" within"
"a single backslash \\ is in this string"
```

but not

```
/* "this is not a string" */
"and
neither is this"
```

Character sequences that would have meaning if outside a string constant are just a sequence of characters when surrounded by double quotes. In the previous examples one string contains what appears to be the statement a = b + c;, but since it occurs surrounded by double quotes, it is explicitly this sequence of characters.

Two string constants that are separated only by white space are concatenated by the compiler into a single string. Thus

```
"abc" "def"        is equivalent to        "abcdef"
```

This is a new feature of the language available in ANSI C. It is not available in traditional C.

String constants are treated by the compiler as tokens. As with other constants, the compiler provides the space in memory to store string constants. We will emphasize this point again in Chapter 6 when we discuss strings and pointers.

2.8   OPERATORS AND PUNCTUATORS

In C, there are many special characters with particular meanings. Examples include the arithmetic operators

$$+ \qquad - \qquad * \qquad / \qquad \%$$

which stand for the usual arithmetic operations of addition, subtraction, multiplication, division, and modulus, respectively. Recall that in mathematics the value of a modulus b is obtained by taking the remainder after dividing a by b. Thus, for example, 5 % 3 has the value 2, and 7 % 2 has the value 1.

In a program, operators can be used to separate identifiers. Although typically we put white space around binary operators to heighten readability, this is not required.

```
a+b          /* this is the expression a plus b */
a_b          /* this is a 3-character identifier */
```

Some symbols have meanings that depend on context. As an example of this, consider the % symbol in the two statements

```
printf("%d", a);      and      a = b % 7;
```

The first % symbol is the start of a conversion specification, or format, whereas the second % symbol represents the modulus operator.

Examples of punctuators include parentheses, braces, commas, and semicolons. Consider the following code:

```
int main(void)
{
    int    a, b = 2, c = 3;

    a = 17 * (b + c);
    .....
```

The parentheses immediately following main are treated as an operator. They tell the compiler that main is the name of a function. After this, the symbols "{", ",", ";", "(", and ")" are punctuators. Both operators and punctuators are collected by the compiler as tokens, and along with white space, they serve to separate language elements.

Some special characters are used in many different contexts, and the context itself can determine which use is intended. For example, parentheses are sometimes used to indicate a function name; at other times they are used as punctuators. Another example is given by the expressions

```
a + b          ++a          a += b
```

They all use + as a character, but ++ is a single operator, as is +=. Having the meaning of a symbol depend on context makes for a small symbol set and a terse language.

2.9 PRECEDENCE AND ASSOCIATIVITY OF OPERATORS

Operators have rules of *precedence* and *associativity* that determine precisely how expressions are evaluated. Because expressions inside parentheses are evaluated first, parentheses can be used to clarify or change the order in which operations are performed. Consider the expression

```
1 + 2 * 3
```

In C, the operator * has higher precedence than +, causing the multiplication to be performed first, then the addition. Hence the value of the expression is 7. An equivalent expression is

```
1 + (2 * 3)
```

On the other hand, because expressions inside parentheses are evaluated first, the expression

```
(1 + 2) * 3
```

is different; its value is 9. Now consider the expression

```
1 + 2 - 3 + 4 - 5
```

Because the binary operators + and - have the same precedence, the associativity rule "left to right" is used to determine how it is evaluated. The "left to right" rule means that the operations are performed from left to right. Thus

```
(((1 + 2) - 3) + 4) - 5
```

is an equivalent expression.

The following table gives the rules of precedence and associativity for some of the operators of C. In addition to the operators we have already seen, the table includes operators that will be discussed later in this chapter.

Operators	Associativity
() ++ (*postfix*) -- (*postfix*)	left to right
+ (*unary*) - (*unary*) ++ (*prefix*) -- (*prefix*)	right to left
* / %	left to right
+ -	left to right
= += -= *= /= *etc*	right to left

All the operators on a given line, such as *, /, and %, have equal precedence with respect to each other, but have higher precedence than all the operators that occur on the lines below them. The associativity rule for all the operators on a given line appears at the right side of the table. Whenever we introduce new operators, we will give their rules of precedence and associativity, and often we will encapsulate the information by augmenting the above table. These rules are essential information for every C programmer.

In addition to the binary plus, which represents addition, there is a unary plus, and both these operators are represented by a plus sign. The minus sign also has binary and unary meanings. Note carefully that the unary plus was introduced with ANSI C. There is no unary plus in traditional C, only unary minus.

From the preceding table we see that the unary operators have higher precedence than the binary plus and minus. In the expression

```
- a * b - c
```

the first minus sign is unary and the second binary. Using the rules of precedence, we see that

```
((- a) * b) - c
```

is an equivalent expression.

2.10 INCREMENT AND DECREMENT OPERATORS

The increment operator ++ and decrement operator -- are unary operators with the same precedence as the unary plus and minus, and they associate from right to left. Both ++ and -- can be applied to variables, but not to constants or ordinary expressions. Moreover, the operators can occur in either prefix or postfix position, and different effects may occur. Some examples are

```
++i
cnt--
```

but not

```
777++              /* constants cannot be incremented */
++(a * b - 1)      /* ordinary expressions cannot be incremented */
```

Each of the expressions ++i and i++ has a value; moreover, each causes the stored value of i in memory to be incremented by 1. The expression ++i causes the stored value of i to be incremented first, with the expression then taking as its value the new stored value of i. In contrast, the expression i++ has as its value the current value of i; then, the expression causes the stored value of i to be incremented. The following code illustrates the situation:

```
int    a, b, c = 0;

a = ++c;
b = c++;
printf("%d %d %d\n", a, b, ++c);      /* 1 1 3 is printed */
```

In a similar fashion --i causes the stored value of i in memory to be decremented by 1 first, with the expression then taking this new stored value as its value. With i-- the value of the expression is the current value of i; then the expression causes the stored value of i in memory to be decremented by 1.

Note carefully that ++ and -- cause the value of a variable in memory to be changed. Other operators do not do this. For example, an expression such as a + b leaves the values of the variables a and b unchanged. These ideas are expressed by saying that the operators ++ and -- have a *side effect*; not only do these operators yield a value, they also change the stored value of a variable in memory (see Exercise 11).

In some cases we can use ++ in either prefix or postfix position, with both uses producing equivalent results. For example, each of the two statements

```
++i;        and        i++;
```

is equivalent to

```
i = i + 1;
```

In simple situations one can consider ++ and -- as operators that provide concise notation for the incrementing and decrementing of a variable. In other situations, careful attention must be paid as to whether prefix or postfix position is desired.

Declarations and initializations		
int a = 1, b = 2, c = 3, d = 4;		
Expression	**Equivalent expression**	**Value**
a * b / c	(a * b) / c	0
a * b % c + 1	((a * b) % c) + 1	3
++ a * b - c --	((++ a) * b) - (c --)	1
7 - - b * ++ d	7 - ((- b) * (++ d))	17

2.11   ASSIGNMENT OPERATORS

To change the value of a variable, we have already made use of assignment statements such as

    a = b + c;

Unlike other languages, C treats = as an operator. Its precedence is lower than all the operators we have discussed so far, and its associativity is right to left. In this section we explain in detail the significance of this.

To understand = as an operator, let us first consider + for the sake of comparison. The binary operator + takes two operands, as in the expression a + b. The value of the expression is the sum of the values of a and b. By comparison, a simple assignment expression is of the form

   variable = right_side

where *right_side* is itself an expression. Notice that a semicolon placed at the end would have made this an assignment statement. The assignment operator = has the two operands *variable* and *right_side*. The value of *right_side* is assigned to *variable*, and that value becomes the value of the assignment expression as a whole. To illustrate this, consider the statements

    b = 2;
    c = 3;
    a = b + c;

where the variables are all of type int. By making use of assignment expressions, we can condense this to

```
a = (b = 2) + (c = 3);
```

The assignment expression b = 2 assigns the value 2 to the variable b, and the assignment expression itself takes on this value. Similarly, the assignment expression c = 3 assigns the value 3 to the variable c, and the assignment expression itself takes on this value. Finally, the values of the two assignment expressions are added, and the resulting value is assigned to a.

Although this example is artificial, there are many situations where assignment occurs naturally as part of an expression. A frequently occurring situation is multiple assignment. Consider the statement

```
a = b = c = 0;
```

Because the operator = associates from right to left, an equivalent statement is

```
a = (b = (c = 0));
```

First, c is assigned the value 0, and the expression c = 0 has value 0. Then b is assigned the value 0, and the expression b = (c = 0) has value 0. Finally, a is assigned the value 0, and the expression a = (b = (c = 0)) has value 0. Many languages do not use assignment in such an elaborate way. In this respect C is different.

In addition to =, there are other assignment operators, such as += and -=. An expression such as

```
k = k + 2
```

will add 2 to the old value of k and assign the result to k, and the expression as a whole will have that value. The expression

```
k += 2
```

accomplishes the same task. The following list contains all the assignment operators.

Assignment operators

$$= \quad += \quad -= \quad *= \quad /= \quad \%= \quad >>= \quad <<= \quad \&= \quad \wedge= \quad |=$$

All these operators have the same precedence, and they all have right-to-left associativity. The semantics is specified by

  variable op= expression

which is equivalent to

  variable =variable op (expression)

with the exception that if *variable* is itself an expression, it is evaluated only once. When dealing with arrays, this is an important technical point. Note carefully that an assignment expression such as

  j *= k + 3   is equivalent to   j = j * (k + 3)

rather than

  j = j * k + 3

The following table illustrates how assignment expressions are evaluated.

Declarations and initializations
int   i = 1, j = 2, k = 3, m = 4;

Expression	Equivalent expression	Equivalent expression	Value
i += j + k	i += (j + k)	i = (i+ (j + k))	6
j *= k = m + 5	j *= (k = (m +5))	j = (j * (k = (m +5)))	18

2.12 AN EXAMPLE: COMPUTING POWERS OF 2

To illustrate some of the ideas presented in this chapter, we will write a program that prints on a line some powers of 2. Here is the program:

```
/* Some powers of 2 are printed. */

#include <stdio.h>

int main(void)
{
   int   i = 0, power = 1;

   while (++i <= 10)
      printf("%6d", power *= 2);
   printf("\n");
   return 0;
}
```

The output of the program is

```
   2     4     8    16    32    64   128   256   512  1024
```

DISSECTION OF THE *pow_of_2* PROGRAM

■ **/* Some powers of 2 are printed. */**
Programs often begin with a comment that explains the intent or use of the program. If the program is large, the comment may be extensive. The compiler treats comments as white space.

■ **#include <stdio.h>**
The header file *stdio.h* contains the function prototype for the printf() function. This is a kind of declaration for printf(). The compiler needs it to do its work correctly. (See Section 2.13, "The C System," for further details.)

■ **int   i = 0, power = 1;**
The variables i and power are declared to be of type int. They are initialized to 0 and 1, respectively.

■ **while (++i <= 10)**
As long as the value of the expression ++i is less than or equal to 10, the body of the while loop is executed. The first time through the loop the expression ++i has the value 1; the second time through the loop ++i has the value 2; and so forth. Thus the body of the loop is executed 10 times.

- ■ `printf("%6d", power *= 2);`
  The body of the `while` loop consists of this statement. The string constant `"%6d"` is passed as the first argument to the `printf()` function. The string contains the format %6d, which indicates that the value of the expression `power *= 2` is to be printed as a decimal with field length 6.

- ■ `power *= 2`
  This assignment expression is equivalent to

  ```
  power = power * 2
  ```

  which causes the old value of `power` to be multiplied by 2 and the resulting value to be assigned to `power`. The value assigned to `power` is the value of the assignment expression as a whole. The first time through the loop, the old value of `power` is 1, and the new value is 2; the second time through the loop, the old value of `power` is 2, and the new value is 4, and so forth.

2.13   THE C SYSTEM

The C system consists of the C language, the preprocessor, the compiler, the library, and other tools useful to the programmer, such as editors and debuggers. In this section we discuss the preprocessor and the library. For further details about the preprocessor, see Chapter 8. For details about functions in the standard library, see Appendix A.

The Preprocessor

Lines that begin with a # are called *preprocessing directives*. These lines communicate with the preprocessor. In traditional C, preprocessing directives were required to begin in column 1. In ANSI C this restriction has been removed. Although a # may be preceded on a line by white space, it is still a common programming style to start preprocessing directives in column 1.

We have already used preprocessing directives such as

```
#include <stdio.h>        and        #define PI 3.14159
```

Another form of the #include facility is given by

```
#include "filename"
```

This causes the preprocessor to replace the line with a copy of the contents of the named file. A search for the file is made first in the current directory and then in other system-dependent places. With a preprocessing directive of the form

```
#include <filename>
```

the preprocessor looks for the file only in the "other places" and not in the current directory.

Because #include directives commonly occur at the beginning of the program, the include files they refer to are called *header files*, and a .h is used to end the file name. This is a convention; the preprocessor does not require this. There is no restriction on what an include file can contain. In particular, it can contain other preprocessing directives that will be expanded by the preprocessor in turn. Although files of any type may be included, it is considered poor programming style to include files that contain the code for function definitions (see Chapter 5).

On UNIX systems the standard header files such as *stdio.h* are typically found in the directory */usr/include*. On Turbo C systems they might be found in the directory *bc\include* or *tc\include*. In general, the location of the standard #include files is system-dependent. All of these files are readable, and programmers, for a variety of reasons, have occasion to read them.

One of the primary uses of header files is to provide function prototypes. For example, the file *stdio.h* contains the following lines:

```
int    printf(const char *format, ...);
int    scanf(const char *format, ...);
```

These are the function prototypes for the printf() and scanf() functions in the standard library. Roughly speaking, a function prototype tells the compiler the types of the arguments that get passed to the function and the type of the value that gets returned by the function. Before we can understand the function prototypes for printf() and scanf(), we need to learn about the function definition mechanism, pointers, and type qualifiers. These ideas are presented in later chapters. The point we are making here is that when the programmer uses a function from the standard library, then the corresponding standard header file should be included. The header file will provide the appropriate function prototype. The compiler needs the function prototype to do its work correctly.

The Standard Library

The standard library contains many useful functions that add considerable power and flexibility to the C system. Many of the functions are used extensively by all C programmers, whereas other functions are used more selectively. Most programmers become acquainted with functions in the standard library on a need-to-know basis.

Programmers are not usually concerned about the location on the system of the standard library because it contains compiled code that is unreadable to humans. The standard library may comprise more than one file. The mathematics library, for example, is conceptually part of the standard library, but it often exists in a separate file (see Exercise 25 and 26). Whatever the case, the system knows where to find the code that corresponds to functions from the standard library, such as `printf()` and `scanf()`, that the programmer has used. However, even though the system provides the code, *it is the responsibility of the programmer to provide the function prototype.* This is usually accomplished by including appropriate header files.

Caution: Do not mistake header files for the libraries themselves. The standard library contains object code of functions that have already been compiled. The standard header files do not contain compiled code.

As an illustration of the use of a function in the standard library, let us show how `rand()` can be used to generate some randomly distributed integers. In later chapters we will have occasion to use `rand()` to fill arrays and strings for testing purposes. Here, we use it to print some integers on the screen.

```c
#include <stdio.h>
#include <stdlib.h>

int main(void)
{
   int   i, n;

   printf("\n%s\n%s",
      "Some randomly distributed integers will be printed.",
      "How many do you want to see?   ");
   scanf("%d", &n);
   for (i = 0; i < n; ++i) {
      if (i % 10 == 0)
         putchar('\n');
      printf("%7d", rand());
   }
   printf("\n\n");
   return 0;
}
```

Suppose that we execute the program and type 19 when prompted. Here is what appears on the screen:

```
Some randomly distributed integers will be printed.
How many do you want to see?  19

  16838   5758 10113 17515 31051   5627 23010   7419 16212   4086
   2749 12767   9084 12060 32225 17543 25089 21183 25137
```

DISSECTION OF THE *prn_rand* PROGRAM

■ `#include <stdio.h>`
  `#include <stdlib.h>`
  These header files are included because of the function prototypes they contain. In particular, the function prototype

```
int    rand(void);
```

is in *stdlib.h*. It tells the compiler that rand() is a function that takes no arguments and returns an int value. Rather than include *stdlib.h*, we could just as well supply this line ourselves at the top of the file just before main().

■ `printf("\n%s\n%s",`
  `    "Some randomly distributed integers will be printed.",`
  `    "How many do you want to see?   ");`
  `scanf("%d", &n);`
  A prompt to the user is printed on the screen. The characters typed in by the user are received by scanf(), converted in the format of a decimal integer, and placed at the address of n.

■ `for (i = 0; i < n; ++i) {`
  `    .....`
  `}`
  This is a for loop. It is equivalent to

```
i = 0;
while (i < n) {
    .....
    ++i;
}
```

Another way to write this program would be to initialize i to zero and then use the construct

```
while (i++ < n) {
    .....
}
```

Note carefully that i++ < n is different from ++i < n (see Exercise 16).

■   ```
    if (i % 10 == 0)
        putchar('\n');
    printf("%7d", rand());
    ```
    The operator == is the "is equal to" operator. If *expr1* and *expr2* are two expressions having the same value, then the expression *expr1*== *expr2* will be *true*; otherwise it will be *false*. In Chapter 4 we will see that == has lower precedence than %. Thus

    `i % 10 == 0`        is equivalent to        `(i % 10) == 0`

    The first time through the loop and every tenth time thereafter, the expression as a whole is *true*. Whenever the expression is *true*, a newline character gets printed.

■   ```
    printf("%7d", rand());
    ```
    Every time through the loop, the value returned by the call to rand( ) is printed in the format of a decimal integer. The width of the field where the integer gets printed is 7.

For most uses of rand( ), the programmer needs to seed the random number generator before it gets used. This can be done with the following line:

```
srand(time(NULL));
```

(See Exercise 19 for further discussion. Also, see Exercise 23 for the use of other random number generators.)

2.14   SUMMARY

1   Tokens are the basic syntactic units of C. They include keywords, identifiers, constants, string constants, operators, and punctuators. White space, along with operators and punctuators, can serve to separate tokens. For this reason, white space, operators, and punctuators are collectively called *separators*. White space, other than serving to separate tokens, is ignored by the compiler.

2   Comments are enclosed by the bracket pair /* and */ and are treated as white space by the compiler. They are critical for good program documentation. Comments should assist the reader to both use and understand the program.

3   A keyword, also called a *reserved word*, has a strict meaning. There are 32 keywords in C. They cannot be redefined.

4   Identifiers are tokens that the programmer uses chiefly to name variables and functions. They begin with a letter or underscore and are chosen to be meaningful to the human reader.

5 Some identifiers are already known to the system because they are the names of functions in the standard library. These include the input/output functions scanf() and printf(), and mathematical functions such as sqrt(), sin(), cos(), and tan().

6 Constants include various kinds of integer and floating constants, character constants such as 'a' and '#', and string constants such as "abc". All constants are collected by the compiler as tokens.

7 String constants such as "deep blue sea" are arbitrary sequences of characters, including white space characters, that are placed inside double quotes. A string constant is stored as an array of characters, but it is collected by the compiler as a single token. The compiler provides the space in memory needed to store a string constant. Character constants and string constants are treated differently. For example, 'x' and "x" are not the same.

8 Operators and punctuators are numerous in C. The parentheses that follow main in the code

```
int main(void)
{
    .....
```

are an operator; they tell the compiler that main is a function. The parentheses in the expression a * (b + c) are punctuators. The operations inside the parentheses are done first.

9 In C, the rules of precedence and associativity for operators determine how an expression gets evaluated. The programmer needs to know them.

10 The increment operator ++ and the decrement operator -- have a side effect. In addition to having a value, an expression such as ++i causes the stored value of i in memory to be incremented by 1.

11 The operators ++ and -- can be used in both prefix and postfix position, possibly with different effects. The expression ++i causes i to be incremented in memory, and the new value of i is the value of the expression. The expression i++ has as its value the current value of i, and then the expression causes i to be incremented in memory.

12 In C, the assignment symbol is an operator. An expression such as a = b + c assigns the value of b + c to a, and the expression as a whole takes on this value. Although the assignment operator in C and the equals sign in mathematics look alike, they are not comparable.

13 The standard library contains many useful functions. If the programmer uses a function from the standard library, then the corresponding standard header file should be included. The standard header file provides the appropriate function prototype.

2.15   EXERCISES

1 Is main a keyword? Explain.

2 List five keywords and explain their use.

3 Give examples of three types of tokens.

4 Which of the following are not identifiers and why?

```
3id       __yes        o_no_o_no    00_go       star*it
1_i_am   one_i_aren't  me_to-2      xYshouldI   int
```

5 Design a standard form of introductory comment that will give a reader information about who wrote the program and why.

6 Take a symbol such as + and illustrate the different ways it can be used in a
program.

7 ANSI C does not provide for the nesting of comments, although many compilers
provide an option for this. Try the following line on your compiler and see what
happens.

```
/* This is an attempt /* to nest */ a comment. */
```

8 Write an interactive program that converts pounds and ounces to kilograms and
grams. Use symbolic constants that are defined at the top of the file outside of
main().

9 This exercise illustrates one place where white space around operators is important. Because both + and ++ are operators, the expression a+++b can be
interpreted as either

```
a++ + b        or        a + ++b
```

depending on how the plus symbols are grouped. Normally, the first two plusses
would be grouped and passed to the compiler to see if this were syntactically
correct. Write a short program to see which interpretation is made by your
compiler.

10 For the *pow_of_2* program, explain what the effect would be if the expression
++i were changed to i++.

11 Study the following code and write down what you think gets printed. Then write a test program to check your answers.

```
int    a, b = 0, c = 0;

a = ++b + ++c;
printf("%d %d %d\n", a, b, c);
a = b++ + c++;
printf("%d %d %d\n", a, b, c);
a = ++b + c++;
printf("%d %d %d\n", a, b, c);
a = b-- + --c;
printf("%d %d %d\n", a, b, c);
```

12 What is the effect in the following statement if some, or all, of the parentheses are removed? Explain.

```
x = (y = 2) + (z = 3);
```

13 First complete the entries in the table that follows. After you have done this, write a program to check that the values you entered are correct.

Declarations and initializations		
int a = 2, b = -3, c = 5, d = -7, e = 11;		
Expression	Equivalent expression	Value
a / b / c	(a / b) / c	0
7 + c * -- d / e	7 + ((c * (-- d)) / e)	
2 * a % - b + c + 1		
39 / - ++ e - + 29 % c		
a += b += c += 1 + 2		
7 - + ++ a % (3 + b)		/* error, why? */

14 Consider the following code:

```
int    a = 1, b = 2, c = 3;

a += b += c += 7;
```

Write an equivalent statement that is fully parenthesized. What are the values of the variables a, b, and c? First write down your answer. Then write a test program to check your answer.

15 A good programming style is crucial to the human reader, even though the compiler sees only a stream of characters. Consider the following program:

```
int main(void
){float qx,
zz,
tt;printf("gimme 3"
);scanf
(   "%f%f      %f",&qx,&zz

,&tt);printf("averageis=%f",
(qx+tt+zz)/3.0);return
0
;}
```

Although the code is not very readable, it should compile and execute. Test it to see if that is true. Then completely rewrite the program. Use white space and comments to make it more readable and well documented. *Hint:* Include a header file and choose new identifiers to replace qx, zz, and tt.

16 Rewrite the *prn_rand* program, replacing the for loop with the following while loop:

```
while (i++ < n) {
   .....
}
```

After you get your program running and understand its effects, rewrite the program, changing

```
i++ < n        to        ++i < n
```

Now the program will behave differently. To compensate for this, rewrite the body of the while loop so that the program behaves exactly as it did in the beginning.

17 The integers produced by the function rand() all fall within the interval [0, *n*], where *n* is system-dependent. In ANSI C, the value for *n* is given by the symbolic constant RAND_MAX, which is defined in the standard header file *stdlib.h*. Write a program that prints out the value of RAND_MAX on your system. *Hint:* Include the header file *stdlib.h* and use the line

```
printf("RAND_MAX = %d\n", RAND_MAX);
```

If possible, run your program on a number of different C systems. You will probably find that RAND_MAX has the same value on all systems. The reason for this is that the ANSI C committee suggested how the function rand() could be implemented, and most compiler writers followed the committee's suggestions verbatim. It has been our experience that C systems on PCs, UNIX workstations, and even the Cray supercomputer in San Diego all use the same value for RAND_MAX and that on all of these systems rand() produces the same output values. (See Exercise 23 for further discussion.)

18 Run the *prn_rand* program three times to print out, say, 100 randomly distributed integers. Observe that the same list of numbers gets printed each time. For many applications, this is not desirable. Modify the *prn_rand* program by using srand() to seed the random number generator. The first few lines of your program should look like

```
#include <stdio.h>
#include <stdlib.h>
#include <time.h>

int main(void)
{
    int    i, n, seed;

    seed = time(NULL);
    srand(seed);
    printf("\n%s\n%s",
        "Some randomly distributed integers will be printed.",
        "How many do you want to see?   ");
    .....
```

The function call time(NULL) returns the number of elapsed seconds since 1 January 1970 (see Appendix A). We store this value in the variable seed, and then we use the function call srand(seed) to seed the random number generator. Repeated calls to rand() will generate all the integers in the interval [0, RAND_MAX], but in a mixed-up order. The value used to seed the random number generator determines where in the mixed-up order rand() will start to generate numbers. If we use the value produced by time() as a seed, then each time we run the program, the seed will be different, causing a different set of numbers to be produced. Run this program repeatedly. You should see a different set of numbers printed each time. Do you?

19 In Exercise 18, we suggested the code

```
seed = time(NULL);
srand(seed);
```

In place of these lines, most programmers would write

```
srand(time(NULL));
```

Make this change to your program, and then compile and execute it to see that
it behaves the same as before.

20 In Exercise 18 and 19 we used the value returned by `time()` to seed the random
number generator. In this exercise we want to use the value returned by `time()`
to measure the time it takes to call `rand()`. Here is one way this can be done:

```
#include <stdio.h>
#include <stdlib.h>
#include <time.h>

#define    NCALLS    1000000    /* number of fct calls */
#define    NCOLS     9          /* number of columns   */
#define    NLINES    5          /* number of lines     */

int main(void)
{
    int    i, val;
    long   begin, diff, end;

    begin = time(NULL);
    srand(time(NULL));
    printf("TIMING TEST: %d calls to rand()\n", NCALLS);
    for (i = 0; i < NCALLS; ++i) {
        val ≠ rand();
        if (i < NCOLS * NLINES) {
            if (i % NCOLS == 0)
                putchar('\n');
            printf("%7d", val);
        }
        if (i == NCOLS * NLINES)
            printf("\n%7s\n\n", ".....");
    }
    end = time(NULL);
    diff = end - begin;
    printf("%s%ld\n%s%ld\n%s%ld\n%s%.7f\n",
        "           end time: ", end,
        "         begin time: ", begin,
        "       elapsed time: ", diff,
        "time for each call: ", (double) diff / NCALLS);
    return 0;
{
```

Here is the output on our system:

```
TIMING TEST: 1000000 calls to rand()

    19178  23762  20820    2694  31811  31972    5119    8740  12857
    28989   8964  13727    1334  12078  13657    4028  32750  19952
    16310  12897  23099    7756  28878   1064    1465    4365  13646
    19109  26657   6181   32658  32120  24422   28321  20266  15889
    27538  29518  13327      70   6749    553   18853  12182   4242
    . . . . .

              end time: 777834844
            begin time: 777834842
          elapsed time: 2
    time for each call: 0.0000020
```

The intent of this program is to print out some of the values produced by the call to rand() but not all of them. After all, looking at a million numbers on the screen is not too interesting. Experiment with this program by modifying some of the #defines so that you can see what their effects are. For example, try making the following changes:

```
#define    NCALLS    1000      /* number of fct calls */
#define    NCOLS     7         /* number of columns   */
#define    NLINES    7         /* number of lines     */
```

In this program, note the use of the type long and the corresponding %ld formats in the printf() statements. On some machines a variable of type long can hold bigger values than a variable of type int (see Chapter 3). We have used the type long here because we want this program to run on both MS-DOS and UNIX machines. If a C system on an MS-DOS machine is available to you, run this program on that system. Then change long to int and %ld to %d and run the program again. Is the behavior of the program any different? *Caution:* If you are on a time-shared machine, then the use of values returned by time() to time things can be misleading. Between your calls to time(), the machine may be servicing other requests, making your timing results inaccurate. The proper way to time C code is with the use of the clock() function (see Chapter 11).

21 The function rand() returns values in the interval [0, RAND_MAX] (see Exercise 17). If we declare the variable median of type double and initialize it to have the value RAND_MAX / 2.0, then rand() will return a value that is sometimes larger than median and sometimes smaller. On average, however, there should be as many values that are larger as there are values that are smaller.

Test this hypothesis. Write a program that calls rand(), say 500 times, inside a for loop, increments the variable above_cnt every time rand() returns a value larger than median, and increments the variable below_cnt every time rand() returns a value less than median. Each time through the for loop, print out the value of the difference of above_cnt and below_cnt. This difference should oscillate about 0. Does it?

22 Rewrite the *prn_rand* program so that the integers printed are in the interval [0, 100]. *Hint:* Use the modulus operator. How many numbers do you have to print before you see the value 100? (If you do not see it, you have done something wrong.)

23 In this exercise we continue with the discussion started in Exercise 17. A call to rand() produces values in the interval [0, RAND_MAX], and RAND_MAX typically has the value 32767. Since this value is rather small, rand() is not useful for many scientific problems. Most C systems on UNIX machines provide the programmer with the rand48 family of random number generators, so called because 48-bit arithmetic gets used to generate the numbers. The function drand48(), for example, can be used to produce randomly distributed doubles in the range[0, 1), and the function lrand48() can be used to produce randomly distributed integers in the range $[0, 2^{31} - 1]$. Typically, the function prototypes for this family of functions is in *stdlib.h*. Modify the program that you wrote in Exercise 17 to use lrand48() in place of rand() and srand48() in place of srand(). You will see that on average larger numbers are generated. Whether the numbers are better depends on the application. To find out more about pseudo random number generators, consult the text *Numerical Recipes in C* by William Press et al. (Cambridge, England: Cambridge University Press, 1992), pages 274–328.

24 The value of an expression such as ++a + a++ is system-dependent because the side effects of the increment operator ++ can take place at different times. This is both a strength and a weakness of C. On the one hand, compilers can do what is natural at the machine level. On the other hand, because such an expression is system-dependent, the expression will have different values on different machines. Experienced C programmers recognize expressions such as this to be potentially dangerous and do not use them. Experiment with your machine to see what value is produced by ++a + a++ after a has been initialized to zero. Does your compiler warn you that the expression is dangerous?

25 Libraries on a UNIX system typically end in .*a*, which is mnemonic for "archive." Libraries in MS-DOS typically end in .*lib*. See if you can find the standard C libraries on your system. These libraries are not readable. On a UNIX system you can give a command such as

    ar t /usr/lib/libc.a

to see all the titles (names) of the objects in the library.

26 If UNIX is available to you, try the command

    ar t /usr/lib/libc.a

Among the names that get printed, do you see the names of mathematical functions such as cos( ), exp( ), and sqrt( )? If not, then the mathematics library, although conceptually part of the standard library, is separate. Try the command

    ar t /usr/lib/libm.a

27 In both ANSI C and traditional C, a backslash at the end of a line in a string constant has the effect of continuing it to the next line. Here is an example of this:

```
"by using a backslash at the end of the line \
a string can be extended from one line to the next"
```

Write a program that uses this construct. Many screens have 80 characters per line. What happens if you try to print a string with more than 80 characters?

28 In ANSI C, a backslash at the end of *any* line is supposed to have the effect of continuing it to the next line. This can be expected to work in string constants and macro definitions on any C compiler, either ANSI or traditional (see Exercise 27). However, not all ANSI C compilers support this in a more general way. After all, except in macro definitions, this construct gets little use. Does your C compiler support this in a general way? Try the following:

```
#\
include  <stdio.h>

int
mai\
n(
vo\
id)
{
    print\
f("Will this \
work?\n");
ret\
urn 0
;}
```

29 When you invoke the compiler, the system first invokes the preprocessor. In this
    exercise we want to deliberately make a preprocessing error, just to see what
    happens. Try the following program:

```
#incl <stdixx.h>          /* two errors on this line */

int main(void)
{
    printf("Try me.\n");
    return 0;
}
```

What happens if you change #incl to #include?

30 If Turbo C is available to you, try the following program:

```
#include <stdio.h>

int main(void)
{
    int   _ss = 1;          /* leading underscore, danger! */

    printf("_ss = %d\n", _ss);
    return 0;
}
```

It so happens that _ss is an additional keyword in Turbo C, and this program
misuses it. Do you find the error message produced by the compiler helpful?
Remember: The programmer can avoid problems by not using variable names
that begin with an underscore.

CHAPTER **3**

THE FUNDAMENTAL DATA TYPES

We begin this chapter with a brief look at declarations, expressions, and assignment. Then we give a detailed explanation for each of the fundamental data types, paying particular attention to how C treats characters as small integers. In expressions with operands of different types, certain implicit conversions occur. We explain the rules for conversion, and examine the cast operator, which forces explicit conversion.

3.1 DECLARATIONS, EXPRESSIONS, AND ASSIGNMENT

Variables and constants are the objects that a program manipulates. In C, all variables must be declared before they can be used. The beginning of a program might look like this:

```
#include <stdio.h>

int main(void)
{
    int     a, b, c;                   /* declaration */
    float   x, y = 3.3, z = -7.7;      /* declaration
                                          with initializations */

    printf("Input two integers:  ");   /* function call */
    scanf("%d%d", &b, &c);             /* function call */
    a = b + c;                         /* assignment statement */
    x = y + z;                         /* assignment statement */
    .....
```

Declarations serve two purposes. First, they tell the compiler to set aside an appropriate amount of space in memory to hold values associated with variables, and second, they enable the compiler to instruct the machine to perform specified operations correctly. In the expression b + c, the operator + is being applied to two variables of type int, which at the machine level is a different operation than + applied to variables of type float, as occurs in the expression y + z. Of course, the programmer need not be concerned that the two + operations are mechanically different, but the C compiler has to recognize the difference and give the appropriate machine instructions. The braces { and } surround a block. They are used to enclose declarations and statements. The declarations, if any, must occur before the statements.

Expressions are meaningful combinations of constants, variables, operators, and function calls. A constant, variable, or function call by itself can also be considered an expression. Some examples of expressions are

```
a + b
sqrt(7.333)
5.0 * x - tan(9.0 / x)
```

Most expressions have a value. For example, the expression a + b has an obvious value, depending on the values of the variables a and b. If a has value 1 and b has value 2, then a + b has value 3.

The equals sign = is the basic assignment operator in C. An example of an assignment *expression* is

```
i = 7
```

The variable i is assigned the value 7, and the expression as a whole takes that value as well. When followed by a semicolon, an expression becomes a statement. Some examples of statements are

```
i = 7;
printf("The plot thickens!\n");
```

The following two statements are perfectly legal, but they do no useful work.

```
3.777;
a + b;
```

A simple assignment statement is of the form

$variable = expr;$

This can be thought of as an assignment expression followed by a semicolon. The value of the expression on the right side of the equal sign is computed and then assigned to the variable on the left side of the equal sign. Note that the value of the assignment expression as a whole is not used. That is perfectly all right. The programmer is not required to use the value produced by an expression.

Even though assignment statements sometimes resemble mathematical equations, the two notions are distinct and should not be confused. The mathematical equation

$$x + 2 = 0$$

does not become an assignment statement by typing

```
x + 2 = 0;      /* wrong */
```

The left side of the equals sign is an expression, not a variable, and this expression may not be assigned a value. Now consider the assignment statement

```
x = x + 1;
```

The current value of x is assigned the old value of x plus 1. If the old value of x is 2, then the value of x after execution of the statement will be 3. Observe that as a mathematical equation

$$x = x + 1$$

is meaningless; after subtracting x from both sides of the equation, we obtain

$$0 = 1$$

Caution: Although they look alike, the assignment operator in C and the equals sign in mathematics are not comparable.

3.2 THE FUNDAMENTAL DATA TYPES

C provides several fundamental types. Many of them we have already seen. For all of them we need to discuss limitations on what can be stored.

Fundamental data types: long form		
char	signed char	unsigned char
signed short int	signed int	signed long int
unsigned short int	unsigned int	unsigned long int
float	double	long double

These are all keywords. They may not be used as names of variables. Of course, char stands for "character" and int stands for "integer," but only char and int can be used as keywords. Other data types such as arrays, pointers, and structures are derived from the fundamental types. They are presented in later chapters.

Usually, the keyword signed is not used. For example, signed int is equivalent to int, and because shorter names are easier to type, int is typically used. The type char, however, is special in this regard (see the next section). Also, the keywords short int, long int, and unsigned int may be, and usually are, shortened to just short, long, and unsigned, respectively. The keyword signed by itself is equivalent to int, but it is seldom used in this context. With all these conventions we obtain a new list.

Fundamental data types		
char	signed char	unsigned char
short	int	long
unsigned short	unsigned	unsigned long
float	double	long double

Let us assume that the category *type* is defined to be any one of the fundamental types given in the preceding table. Using this category, we can provide the syntax of a simple declaration:

> *declaration* ::= *type* *identifier* { , *identifier* }$_{0+}$;

The fundamental types can be grouped according to functionality. The integral types are those types that can be used to hold integer values; the floating types are those that can be used to hold real values. They are all arithmetic types.

Fundamental types grouped by functionality			
Integral types:	char	signed char	unsigned char
	short	int	long
	unsigned short	unsigned	unsigned long
Floating types:	float	double	long double
Arithmetic types:	*Integral types + Floating types*		

These collective names are a convenience. In Chapter 6, for example, when we discuss arrays, we will explain that only integral expressions are allowed as subscripts, meaning only expressions involving integral types are allowed.

3.3   CHARACTERS AND THE DATA TYPE char

In C, variables of any integral type can be used to represent characters. In particular, both char and int variables are used for this purpose. In some situations an int may be required for technical reasons (see Section 3.9, "The Use of getchar() and putchar()"). Constants such as 'a' and '+' that we think of as characters are of type int, not of type char. There are no constants of type char in C. This is one of the few places where C++ differs from C. In C++, character constants are of type char (see Exercise 15).

In addition to representing characters, a variable of type char can be used to hold small integer values. Each char is stored in memory in 1 byte. Other than being large enough to hold all the characters in the character set, the size of a byte is not specified in C. However, on most machines a byte is composed of 8 bits and is capable, therefore, of storing 2^8, or 256, distinct values. Only a subset of these values represents actual printing characters. These include the lower- and uppercase letters, digits, punctuation, and special characters such as % and +. The character set also includes the white space characters blank, tab, and newline.

Most machines use either ASCII or EBCDIC character codes. In the discussion that follows we will be using the ASCII code. A table for this code is given in an appendix. For any other code the numbers will be different, but the ideas are analogous. The following table illustrates the correspondence between some character and integer values on an ASCII machine.

Some character constants and their corresponding integer values					
Character constants:	'a'	'b'	'c'	. . .	'z'
Corresponding values:	97	98	99	. . .	112
Character constants:	'A'	'B'	'C'	. . .	'Z'
Corresponding values:	65	66	67	. . .	90
Character constants:	'0'	'1'	'2'	. . .	'9'
Corresponding values:	48	49	50	. . .	57
Character constants:	'&'	'*'	'+'		
Corresponding values:	38	42	43		

Observe that there is no particular relationship between the value of the character constant representing a digit and the digit's intrinsic integer value. That is, the value of '2' is *not* 2. The property that the values for 'a', 'b', 'c', and so on occur in order is important. It makes convenient the sorting of characters, words, and lines into lexicographical order. Character arrays are needed for this kind of work (see Chapter 6).

Some nonprinting and hard-to-print characters require an escape sequence. The horizontal tab character, for example, is written as \t in character constants and in strings. Even though it is being described by the two characters \ and t, it represents a single character. The backslash character \ is called the *escape character* and is used to escape the usual meaning of the character that follows it. The following table contains some nonprinting and hard-to-print characters.

Name of character	Written in C	Integer value
alert	\a	7
backslash	\\	92
backspace	\b	8
carriage return	\r	13
double quote	\"	34
formfeed	\f	12
horizontal tab	\t	9
newline	\n	10
null character	\0	0
single quote	\'	39
vertical tab	\v	11

The alert character \a is special; it causes the bell to ring. To hear the bell, try executing a program that contains the line

```
printf("%c", '\a');
```

The double quote character " has to be escaped if it is used as a character in a string. An example is

```
printf("\"abc\"");     /* "abc" is printed */
```

However, inside single quotes we can write '"', although '\"' is also accepted. In general, escaping an ordinary character has no effect. Inside a string the single quote is just an ordinary character.

```
printf("'abc'");     /* 'abc' is printed */
```

Another way to write a character constant is by means of a one-, two-, or three-octal-digit escape sequence, as in '\007'. This is the alert character, or the audible bell. It can be written also as '\07' or '\7', but it cannot be written as '7'. ANSI C has added hexadecimal escape sequences. An example is '\x1a', which is control-z.

Next, we want to understand how characters are treated as small integers, and, conversely, how small integers are treated as characters. Consider the declaration

```
char   c = 'a';
```

The variable c can be printed either as a character or as an integer.

```
printf("%c", c);     /*  a is printed */
printf("%d", c);     /* 97 is printed */
```

Because c has an integer value, we may use it in arithmetic expressions.

```
printf("%c%c%c", c, c + 1, c + 2);      /* abc is printed */
```

Actually, in this regard there is nothing special about the type char. Any integral expression can be printed either in the format of a character or in the format of an integer.

```
char    c;
int     i;

for (i = 'a'; i <= 'z'; ++i)
    printf("%c", i);                    /* abc ... z is printed */
for (c = 65; c <= 90; ++c)
    printf("%c", c);                    /* ABC ... Z is printed */
for (c = '0'; c <= '9'; ++c)
    printf("%d ", c);                   /* 48 49 ... 57 is printed */
```

We now want to look at how a char is stored in memory at the bit level. Consider the declaration

```
char    c = 'a';
```

We can think of c stored in memory in 1 byte as

$$\boxed{0 \mid 1 \mid 1 \mid 0 \mid 0 \mid 0 \mid 0 \mid 1}$$
$$7\ \ 6\ \ 5\ \ 4\ \ 3\ \ 2\ \ 1\ \ 0$$

Here, each box represents a bit, and the bits are numbered beginning with the least significant bit. The bits making up a byte are either on or off, and these states are represented by 1 and 0, respectively. Thus each byte in memory can be considered as a string of 8 binary digits. More generally, each machine word can be considered as a string of binary digits grouped into bytes. A string of binary digits can be interpreted as a binary number. Before we describe this, recall how strings of decimal digits are interpreted as decimal numbers. Consider, for example, the decimal number 10753. Its value is given by

$$1 \times 10^4 + 0 \times 10^3 + 7 \times 10^2 + 5 \times 10^1 + 3 \times 10^0$$

More generally, a decimal positional number is written in the form

$$d_n d_{n-1} \ldots d_2 d_1 d_0$$

where each d_i is a decimal digit. It has the value

$$d_{n\times 10} + d_{n-1} \times 10^{n-1} + \cdots + d_{10} \times 10^2 + d_1 \times 10^1 + d_0 \times 10^0$$

A binary, or base 2, positional number is written in the form

$$b_n b_{n-1} \ldots b_2 b_1 b_0$$

where each b_i is a binary digit, either 0 or 1. It has the value

$$b_n \times 2^n + b_{n-1} \times 2^{n-1} + \cdots + b_2 \times 2^2 + b_1 \times 2^1 + b_0 \times 2^0$$

Now let us consider the value for c again. It was stored in a byte as 01100001. This binary number has the value

$$1 \times 2^6 + 1 \times 2^5 + 0 \times 2^4 + 0 \times 2^3 + 0 \times 2^2 + 0 \times 2^1 + 1 \times 2^0$$

which is 64 + 32 + 1, or 97, in decimal notation.

ANSI C provides the three types char, signed char, and unsigned char. Typically, the type char is equivalent to either signed char or unsigned char, depending on the compiler. Each of the three char types is stored in 1 byte, which can hold 256 distinct values. For a signed char the values go from –128 to 127. For an unsigned char the values go from 0 to 255. To determine the values that are appropriate for a plain char on your system, see Exercise 11.

3.4 THE DATA TYPE int

The data type int is the principal working type of the C language. This type, along with the other integral types such as char, short, and long, is designed for working with the integer values that are representable on a machine.

In mathematics, the natural numbers are 0, 1, 2, 3, ..., and these numbers, along with their negatives, comprise the integers. On a machine, only a finite portion of these integers are representable for a given integral type.

Typically, an int is stored in a machine word. Some computers use a machine word of 2 bytes (= 16 bits), others use a machine word of 4 bytes (= 32 bits). There are other possibilities, but many machines fall within these two classes. Examples of machines with 2-byte words are personal computers. Examples of machines with 4-byte words are high-end personal computers, workstations made by Apollo, Hewlett-Packard, Next, Silicon Graphics, Sun, and others, and many different brands of mainframes. Because word size varies from one machine to another, the number of distinct values that an int can hold is machine-dependent. Suppose that we are on a computer that has 4-byte words. This implies that an int, because it is stored in a word with 32 bits, can take on 2^{32} distinct states. Half of these states are used to represent negative integers and half are used to represent nonnegative integers:

$$-2^{31}, -2^{31} + 1, \ldots - 3, -2, -1, 0, 1, 2, 3, \ldots, 2^{31} - 1$$

If, however, we are on a computer that has 2-byte words, then an int can take on only 2^{16} distinct states. Again, half of these states are used to represent negative integers and half are used to represent nonnegative integers:

$$-2^{15}, -2^{15} + 1, \ldots, -3, -2, -1, 0, 1, 2, 3, \ldots, 2^{15} - 1$$

Let N_{min_int} represent the smallest integer that can be stored in an int, and let N_{max_int} represent the largest integer that can be stored in an int. If i is a variable of type int, then the range of values that i can take on is given by

$$N_{min\_int} \leq i \leq N_{max\_int}$$

with the end points of the range being machine-dependent. The typical situation is

On machines with 4-byte words:

$$N_{min\_int} = -2^{31} \quad = -2147483648 \approx -2 \; billion$$
$$N_{max\_int} = +2^{31} - 1 = +2147483647 \approx +2 \; billion$$

On machines with 2-byte words:

$$N_{min\_int} = -2^{15} \quad = -32768 \approx -32 \; thousand$$
$$N_{max\_int} = +2^{15} - 1 = +32767 \approx +32 \; thousand$$

On any machine, the following code is syntactically correct:

```
#define   BIG   2000000000      /* 2 billion */

int main(void)
{
   int   a, b = BIG, c = BIG;

   a = b + c;      /* out of range? */
   .....
```

However, at run-time the variable a may be assigned an incorrect value. The logical value of the expression b + c is 4 billion, which is greater than N_{max_int}. This condition is called an *integer overflow*. Typically, when an integer overflow occurs, the program continues to run, but with logically incorrect results. For this reason the programmer must strive at all times to keep the values of integer expressions within the proper range.

In addition to decimal integer constants, there are hexadecimal integer constants such as 0x1a and octal integer constants such as 0377 (see Section 3.12). Many C programmers have no particular need for hexadecimal and octal numbers, but all programmers have to know that integers that begin with a leading 0 are not decimal integers. For example, 11 and 011 do not have the same value.

3.5   THE INTEGRAL TYPES short, long, AND unsigned

In C, the data type int is considered the "natural" or "usual" type for working with integers. The other integral types, such as char, short, and long, are intended for more specialized use. The data type short, for example, might be used in situations where storage is of concern. The compiler may provide less storage for a short than for an int, although it is not required to do so. In a similar fashion the type long might be used in situations where large integer values are needed. The compiler may provide more storage for a long than for an int, although it is not required to do so. Typically, a short is stored in 2 bytes and a long is stored in 4 bytes. Thus, on machines with 4-byte words, the size of an int is the same as the size of a long, and on machines with 2-byte words, the size of an int is the same as the size of a short. If s is a variable of type short, then the range of values that s can take on is given by

$$N_{min\_short} \leq s \leq N_{max\_short}$$

where typically

$$N_{min\_short} = -2^{15} \quad = -32768 \approx -32 \; thousand$$
$$N_{max\_short} = +2^{15} - 1 = +32767 \approx +32 \; thousand$$

If l is a variable of type long, then the range of values that l can take on is given by

$$N_{min\_long} \leq l \leq N_{max\_long}$$

where typically

$$N_{min\_long} = -2^{31} \quad = -2147483648 \approx -2 \; billion$$
$$N_{max\_long} = +2^{31} - 1 = +2147483647 \approx +2 \; billion$$

A variable of type unsigned is stored in the same number of bytes as an int. However, as the name implies, the integer values stored have no sign. Typically, variables of type int and unsigned are stored in a machine word. If u is a variable of type unsigned, then the range of values that u can take on is given by

$$0 \leq u \leq 2^{wordsize} - 1$$

The typical situation is

On machines with 4-byte words:

$$N_{max\_unsigned} = +2^{32} - 1 = +4294967295 \approx +4 \; billion$$

On machines with 2-byte words:

$$N_{max\_unsigned} = +2^{16} - 1 = +65535 \approx +64 \; billion$$

Arithmetic on unsigned variables is performed modulo $2^{wordsize}$ (see Exercise 18).

Suffixes can be appended to an integer constant to specify its type. The type of an unsuffixed integer constant is either int, long, or unsigned long. The system chooses the first of these types that can represent the value. For example, on machines with 2-byte words, the constant 32000 is of type int, but 33000 is of type long.

Suffix	Type	Example
u or U	unsigned	37U
l or L	long	37L
ul or UL	unsigned long	37UL

3.6 THE FLOATING TYPES

ANSI C provides the three floating types float, double, and long double to deal with real numbers such as 0.001 and 3.14159. A suffix can be appended to a floating constant to specify its type. Any unsuffixed floating constant is of type double. Unlike other languages, the working floating type in C is double, not float.

Suffix	Type	Example
f or F	float	3.7F
l or L	long double	3.7L

Integers are representable as floating constants, but they must be written with a decimal point. For example, the constants 1.0 and 2.0 are both of type double, whereas the constant 3 is an int.

In addition to the ordinary decimal notation for floating constants, there is an exponential notation, as in the example 1.234567e5. This corresponds to the scientific notation 1.234567×10^5. Recall that

$$1.234567 \times 10^5 = 1.234567 \times 10 \times 10 \times 10 \times 10 \times 10$$

$$= 1.234567 \times 100000$$

$$= 123456.7 \quad (decimal\ point\ shifted\ 5\ places)$$

In a similar fashion, the number 1.234567e-3 calls for shifting the decimal point 3 places to the left to obtain the equivalent constant 0.001234567.

Now we want to carefully describe exponential notation. After we give the precise rules, we will show some examples. A floating constant such as `333.77777e-22` may not contain any embedded blanks or special characters. Each part of the constant is given a name:

> 333   is the integer part
> 77777 is the fractional part
> e-22   is the exponential part

A floating constant may contain an integer part, a decimal point, a fractional part, and an exponential part. A floating constant *must* contain either a decimal point or an exponential part or both. If a decimal point is present, either an integer part or fractional part or both *must* be present. If no decimal point is present, then there must be an integer part along with an exponential part.

> *floating_constant* ::= *f_constant* {*f_suffix*}$_{opt}$
> *f_constant*   ::=   *i_part* . *f_part* *e_part*
> | *i_part* . *f_part*
> | *i_part* .
> | . *f_part*
> | . *f_part* *e_part*
> | *i_part*   *e_part*
> *i_part* ::= *integer_part* ::= {*digit*}$_{1+}$
> *f_part* ::= *fractional_part* ::= {*digit*}$_{1+}$
> *e_part* ::= *exponential_part* ::= {e|E}$_1${+|-}$_{opt}${*digit*}$_{1+}$
> *f_suffix* ::= *floating_suffix* ::= f|F|l|L

Some examples of floating constants are

```
3.14159
314.159e-2F      /* of type float */
0e0              /* equivalent to 0.0 */
1.               /* equivalent to 1.0, but harder to read */
```

but not

```
3.14,159         /* comma not allowed */
314159           /* decimal point or exponential part needed */
.e0              /* integer part or fractional part needed */
-3.14159         /* this is a floating constant expression */
```

Typically, a C compiler will provide more storage for a variable of type `double` than for one of type `float`, although it is not required to do so. On most machines a `float` is stored in 4 bytes and a `double` is stored in 8 bytes. The effect of this is that a `float` stores about 6 decimal places of accuracy, and a `double` stores about

15 decimal places of accuracy. An ANSI C compiler may provide more storage for a variable of type long double than for one of type double, although it is not required to do so (see Exercise 14).

The possible values that a floating type can be assigned are described in terms of attributes called *precision* and *range*. The precision describes the number of significant decimal places that a floating value carries. The range describes the limits of the largest and smallest positive floating values that can be represented in a variable of that type. A float on many machines has an approximate precision of 6 significant figures and an approximate range of 10^{-38} to 10^{+38}. This means that a positive float value is represented in the machine in the form (only approximately true)

$$0.d_1 d_2 d_3 d_4 d_5 d_6 \times 10^n$$

where each d_i is a decimal digit, the first digit d_1 is positive, and $-38 \leq n \leq +38$. The representation of a float value in a machine is actually in base 2, not base 10, but the ideas as we presented them give the correct flavor.

A double on many machines has an approximate precision of 15 significant figures and an approximate range of 10^{-308} to 10^{+308}. This means that a positive double value is represented in the machine in the form (only approximately true)

$$0.d_1 d_2 \ldots d_{15} \times 10^n$$

where each d_i is a decimal digit, the first digit d_1 is positive, and $-308 \leq n \leq +308$. Suppose that x is a variable of type double. Then the statement

```
x = 123.45123451234512345;    /* 20 significant digits */
```

will result in x being assigned a value that is stored in the form (only approximately true)

$0.123451234512345 \times 10^{+3}$ (*15 significant digits*)

The main points that one must be aware of are (1) that not all real numbers are representable, and (2) that floating arithmetic operations, unlike the integer arithmetic operations, need not be exact. For small computations this is usually of no concern. For very large computations, such as numerically solving a large system of ordinary differential equations, a good understanding of rounding effects, scaling, and so on may be necessary. This is the domain of numerical analysis.

3.7   THE USE OF typedef

The C language provides the typedef mechanism, which allows the programmer to explicitly associate a type with an identifier. Some examples are

```
typedef   char          uppercase;
typedef   int           INCHES, FEET;
typedef   unsigned long  size_t;        /* found in stddef.h */
```

In each of these type definitions, the named identifiers can be used later to declare variables or functions in the same way ordinary types can be used. Thus

```
uppercase   u;
INCHES      length, width;
```

declares the variable u to be of type uppercase, which is synonymous with the type char, and it declares the variables length and width to be of type INCHES, which is synonymous with the type int.

What is gained by allowing the programmer to create a new nomenclature for an existing type? One gain is in abbreviating long declarations. Another is having type names that reflect the intended use. Furthermore, if there are system-sensitive declarations, such as an int that is 4 bytes on one system and 2 bytes on another, and these differences are critical to the program, then the use of typedef may make the porting of the software easier. In later chapters, after we introduce enumeration types and structure types, we will see that the typedef facility gets used routinely.

3.8   THE sizeof OPERATOR

C provides the unary operator sizeof to find the number of bytes needed to store an object. It has the same precedence and associativity as all the other unary operators. An expression of the form

    sizeof(*object*)

returns an integer that represents the number of bytes needed to store the object in memory. An object can be a type such as int or float, or it can be an expression such as a + b, or it can be an array or structure type. The following program uses this operator. On a given machine it provides precise information about the storage requirements for the fundamental types.

```
/* Compute the size of some fundamental types. */

#include <stdio.h>

int main(void)
{
    printf("The size of some fundamental types is computed.\n\n");
    printf("        char:%3d byte \n", sizeof(char));
    printf("       short:%3d bytes\n", sizeof(short));
    printf("         int:%3d bytes\n", sizeof(int));
    printf("        long:%3d bytes\n", sizeof(long));
    printf("    unsigned:%3d bytes\n", sizeof(unsigned));
    printf("       float:%3d bytes\n", sizeof(float));
    printf("      double:%3d bytes\n", sizeof(double));
    printf("long double:%3d bytes\n", sizeof(long double));
    return 0;
}
```

Because the C language is flexible in its storage requirements for the fundamental types, the situation can vary from one machine to another. However, it is guaranteed that

sizeof(char) = 1

sizeof(short) ≤ sizeof(int) ≤ sizeof(long)

sizeof(signed) = sizeof(unsigned) = sizeof(int)

sizeof(float) ≤ sizeof(double) ≤ sizeof(long double)

All the signed and unsigned versions of each of the integral types are guaranteed to have the same size.

Notice that we wrote sizeof(...) as if it were a function. It is not, however—it is an operator. If sizeof is being applied to a type, then parentheses are required; otherwise they are optional. The type returned by the operator is typically unsigned.

3.9   THE USE OF getchar() AND putchar()

In this section we illustrate the use of getchar() and putchar(). These are macros defined in *stdio.h* that are used to read characters from the keyboard and to print characters on the screen, respectively. Although there are technical differences (see Chapter 8), a macro is used as a function is used. These macros, as well as others, are often used when manipulating character data.

In memory, a char is stored in 1 byte, and an int is stored typically in either 2 or 4 bytes. Because of this, an int can hold all the values that can be stored in a char, and more. We can think of a char as a small integer type, and, conversely, we can think of an int as a large character type. This is a fundamental idea, and, unfortunately, a difficult one for beginning C programmers.

Our next program is called *double*$_{out}$. It reads characters one after another from the standard input file, which is normally connected to the keyboard, and writes each character twice to the standard output file, which is normally connected to the screen.

```
#include <stdio.h>

int main(void)
{
    int   c;

    while ((c = getchar()) != EOF) {
        putchar(c);
        putchar(c);
    }
    return 0;
}
```

DISSECTION OF THE *double_out* PROGRAM

■ `#include <stdio.h>`
One line of this header file is

```
#define   EOF   (-1)
```

The identifier EOF is mnemonic for "end-of-file." What is actually used to signal an end-of-file mark is system-dependent. Although the int value −1 is often used, different systems can have different values. By including the file *stdio.h* and using the symbolic constant EOF, we have made the program portable. This means that the source file can be moved to a different system and run with no changes. The header file *stdio.h* also contains the macro definitions of getchar( ) and putchar( ).

■ `int   c;`
The variable c has been declared in the program as an int rather than a char. Whatever is used to signal the end of a file, it cannot be a value that represents a character. Because c is an int, it can hold all possible character values as well as the special value EOF.

■ while ((c = getchar()) != EOF) {
. . . . .

The expression

(c = getchar()) != EOF

is composed of two parts. The subexpression

c = getchar()

gets a value from the keyboard and assigns it to the variable c, and the value of the subexpression takes on that value as well. The symbols != represent the "not equal" operator. As long as the value of the subexpression c = getchar() is not equal to EOF, the body of the while loop is executed. The parentheses around the subexpression c = getchar() are necessary. Suppose we had left out the parentheses and had typed

c = getchar() != EOF

Because of operator precedence this is equivalent to

c = (getchar() != EOF)

which is syntactically correct, but not what we want.

■ putchar(c);
The value of c is written to the standard output stream in the format of a character.

Characters have an underlying integer-valued representation that on most C systems is the numeric value of their ASCII representation. For example, the character constant 'a' has the value 97. The values of both the lower and uppercase letters occur in order. Because of this, the expression 'a' + 1 has the value 'b', the expression 'b' + 1 has the value 'c', and so on. Also, because there are 26 letters in the alphabet, the expression 'z' - 'a' has the value 25. Now consider the expression 'A' - 'a'. It has a value that is the same as 'B' - 'b', which is the same as 'C' - 'c', and so on. Because of this, if the variable c has the value of a lowercase letter, then the expression c + 'A' - 'a' has the value of the corresponding uppercase letter. These ideas are incorporated into the next program, which capitalizes all lowercase letters.

```c
#include <stdio.h>

int main(void)
{
   int   c;

   while ((c = getchar()) != EOF)
      if (c >= 'a' && c <= 'z')
         putchar(c + 'A' - 'a');
      else
         putchar(c);
   return 0;
}
```

Because of operator precedence, the expressions

```
c >= 'a' && c <= 'z'          and        (c >= 'a') && (c <= 'z')
```

are equivalent. The symbols <= represent the operator "less than or equal." The subexpression c >= 'a' tests to see if the value c is greater than or equal to the value of 'a'. The subexpression c <= 'z' tests to see if the value of c is less than or equal to the value 'z'. The symbols && represent the operator "logical and." If both subexpressions are true, then the expression

```
c >= 'a' && c <= 'z'
```

is true; otherwise it is false. Thus the expression is true if and only if c is a lowercase letter. If the expression is true, then the statement

```
putchar(c + 'A' - 'a');
```

is executed, causing the corresponding uppercase letter to be printed.

3.10   MATHEMATICAL FUNCTIONS

There are no built-in mathematical functions in C. Functions such as

```
sqrt()     pow()     exp()     log()     sin()     cos()     tan()
```

are available in the mathematics library, which is conceptually part of the standard library. All of these functions, except the power function pow(), take a single argument of type double and return a value of type double. The power function takes two arguments of type double and returns a value of type double. Our next program illustrates the use of sqrt() and pow(). It asks the user to input a value for *x*, and then prints it out, along with the square root of *x* and the value of *x* raised to the *x* power.

```
#include <math.h>
#include <stdio.h>

int main(void)
{
   double   x;

   printf("\n%s\n%s\n%s\n\n",
       "The square root of x and x raised",
       "to the x power will be computed.",
       "---");
   while (1) {                      /* do it forever */
      printf("Input x:   ");
      scanf("%lf", &x);
      if (x >= 0.0)
         printf("\n%15s%22.15e\n%15s%22.15e\n%15s%22.15e\n\n",
            "x = ", x,
            "sqrt(x) = ", sqrt(x),
            "pow(x, x) = ", pow(x, x));
      else
         printf("\nSorry, your number must be nonnegative.\n\n");
   }
   return 0;
}
```

If we execute the program and enter 2 when prompted, here is what appears on the screen:

```
The square root of x and x raised
to the x power will be computed.
---

Input x:   2

          x = 2.000000000000000e+000
    sqrt(x) = 1.414213562373095e+000
  pow(x, x) = 4.000000000000000e+000

Input x:
```

DISSECTION OF THE *sqrt_pow* PROGRAM

■ `#include <math.h>`
  `#include <stdio.h>`
  These header files contain function prototypes. In particular, *math.h* contains the prototypes for the functions in the mathematics library. As an alternative to including *math.h*, we can supply our own function prototypes:

  ```
  double   sqrt(double), pow(double, double);
  ```

  This declaration should be placed in the file just above `main()`. (Some compilers will complain if the function prototype is placed in the body of `main()` itself.)

■ `while (1) {`   `/* do it forever */`
  `  .....`
  Because any nonzero value is considered to be true, the expression 1 creates an infinite `while` loop. The user is expected to input values repeatedly and to interrupt the program when finished.

■ `scanf("%lf", &x);`
  The format `%lf` is used in the control string because x is a `double`. A common error is to use `%f` instead of `%lf`. Notice that we typed 2 when we illustrated the use of this program. Equivalently, we could have typed `2.0` or `2e0` or `0.2e1`. The function call `scanf("%lf", &x)` would have converted each of these to the same `double`. In C source code, 2 and 2.0 are different. The first is of type `int`, and the second is of type `double`. The input stream that is read by `scanf()` is *not* source code, so the rules for source code do not apply. When `scanf()` reads in a `double`, the number 2 is just as good as the number 2.0. (For details about `scanf()` see Chapter 11.)

■ `if (x >= 0.0)`

   `. . . . .`

Because the square root function is defined only for nonnegative numbers, a test is made to ensure that the value of x is nonnegative. A call such as `sqrt(-1.0)` can cause a run-time error (see Exercise 21).

■
```
printf("\n%15s%22.15e\n%15s%22.15e\n%15s%22.15e\n\n",
    "x = ", x,
    "sqrt(x) = ", sqrt(x),
    "pow(x, x) = ", pow(x, x));
```
Notice that we are printing `double` values in the format `%22.15e`. This results in 1 place to the left of the decimal point and 15 places to the right, 16 significant places in all. On our machine, only n places are valid, where n is between 15 and 16. (The fraction comes about because of the translation from binary to decimal.) You can ask for lots of decimal places to be printed, but you should not believe all that you read.

The Use of abs() and fabs()

In many languages, the function `abs()` returns the absolute value of its real argument. In this respect C is different. In C, the function `abs()` takes an argument of type `int` and returns its absolute value as an `int`. Its function prototype is in *stdlib.h*. For mathematical code, the C programmer should use `fabs()`, which takes an argument of type `double` and returns its absolute value as a `double` (see Exercise 25). Its function prototype is in *math.h*. The name `fabs` stands for floating absolute value.

Unix and the Mathematics Library

In ANSI C, the mathematics library is conceptually part of the standard library. This means that you should not have to do anything special to get access to mathematical functions. However, on older UNIX systems this is often not the case. Suppose you write a program in a file, say *pgm.c*, that uses the `sqrt()` function. The following command should then compile your program:

   cc pgm.c

If, however, the ANSI C system is not properly connected, you will see something like the following printed on the screen:

   `ld: Undefined symbol: _sqrt`

This means that the loader looked through the libraries that were made available to it, but was unable to find a *.o* file that contained the object code for the sqrt() function. (See Section 11.15 in Chapter 11 for further discussion of libraries.) If you give the command

   cc pgm.c   –lm

the mathematics library will be attached, which will allow the loader to find the necessary *.o* file. In *–lm* the letter *l* stands for "library" and the letter *m* stands for "mathematics." As older versions of UNIX give way to newer versions, the necessity of using the *–lm* option disappears.

3.11   CONVERSIONS AND CASTS

An arithmetic expression such as x + y has both a value and a type. If both x and y have type int, then the expression x + y also has type int. But if both x and y have type short, then x + y is of type int, not short. This is because in any expression, a short always gets promoted, or converted, to an int. In this section we want to give the precise rules for conversions.

The Integral Promotions

A char or short, either signed or unsigned, or an enumeration type (see Chapter 7) can be used in any expression where an int or unsigned int may be used. If all the values of the original type can be represented by an int, then the value is converted to an int; otherwise it is converted to an unsigned int. This is called an *integral promotion*. Here is an example:

```
char    c = 'A';

printf("%c\n", c);
```

The char variable c occurs by itself as an argument to printf(). However, because an integral promotion takes place, the type of the expression c is int, not char.

The Usual Arithmetic Conversions

Arithmetic conversions can occur when the operands of a binary operator are evaluated. Suppose, for example, that i is an int and f is a float. In the expression i + f, the operand i gets promoted to a float and the expression i + f as a whole has type float. The rules governing this are called the *usual arithmetic conversions*:

> If either operand is of type long double, the other operand is converted to long double.

Otherwise, if either operand is of type `double`, the other operand is converted to `double`.

Otherwise, if either operand is of type `float`, the other operand is converted to `float`.

Otherwise, the integral promotions are performed on both operands, and the following rules are applied:

If either operand is of type `unsigned long`, the other operand is converted to `unsigned long`.

Otherwise, if one operand has type `long` and the other has type `unsigned`, then one of two possibilities occurs:

If a `long` can represent all the values of an `unsigned`, then the operand of type `unsigned` is converted to `long`.

If a `long` cannot represent all the values of an `unsigned`, then both of the operands are converted to `unsigned long`.

Otherwise, if either operand has type `long`, the other operand is converted to `long`.

Otherwise, if either operand has type `unsigned`, the other operand is converted to `unsigned`.

Otherwise, both operands have type `int`.

This process goes under various names:

automatic conversion

implicit conversion

coercion

promotion

widening

To illustrate the idea of automatic conversion, we first make the following declarations:

```
char c;   short s;   int i;          unsigned u;   unsigned long ul;
float f;  double d;  long double ld;
```

Now we can list a variety of mixed expressions, along with their corresponding types.

Expression	Type
c - s / i	int
u * 2.0 - i	double
c + 3	int
c + 5.0	double
d + s	double
2 * i / l	long

Expression	Type
u * 7 - i	unsigned
f * 7 - i	float
7 * s * ul	unsigned long
ld + c	long double
u - ul	unsigned long
u - l	*system-dependent*

In addition to automatic conversions in mixed expressions, an automatic conversion can also occur across an assignment. For example,

```
d = i
```

causes the value of i, which is an int, to be converted to a double and then assigned to d, and double is the type of the expression as a whole. A promotion or widening such as d = i will usually be well behaved, but a narrowing or demotion such as i = d can lose information. Here, the fractional part of d will be discarded. Precisely what happens in each case is system-dependent.

Casts

In addition to implicit conversions, which can occur across assignments and in mixed expressions, there are explicit conversions called *casts*. If i is an int, then

```
(double) i
```

will cast the value of i so that the expression has type double. The variable i itself remains unchanged. Casts can be applied to expressions. Some examples are

```
(long) ('A' + 1.0)
x = (float) ((int) y + 1)
(double) (x = 77)
```

but not

```
(double) x = 77      /* equivalent to ((double) x) = 77, error */
```

The cast operator (*type*) is a unary operator having the same precedence and right to left associativity as other unary operators. Thus the expression

`(float) i + 3`   is equivalent to   `((float) i) + 3`

because the cast operator (*type*) has higher precedence than +.

3.12   HEXADECIMAL AND OCTAL CONSTANTS

A number represented by a positional notation in base 16 is called a hexadecimal number. There are 16 hexadecimal digits.

Hexadecimal digits and their corresponding decimal values										
Hexadecimal digit:	0	1	...	9	A	B	C	D	E	F
Decimal value:	0	1	...	9	10	11	12	13	14	15

A positive integer written in hexadecimal notation is a string of hexadecimal digits of the form

$$h_n h_{n-1} \ldots h_2 h_1 h_0$$

where each h_i is a hexadecimal digit. The value of such an integer is

$$h_n \times 16^n + h_{n-1} \times 16^{n-1} + \cdots + h_{16} \times 16^2 + h_1 \times 16^1 + h_0 \times 16^0$$

For example,

$$\begin{aligned}
A0F3C &= A \times 16^4 + 0 \times 16^3 + F \times 16^2 + 3 \times 16^1 + C \times 16^0 \\
&= 10 \times 16^4 + 0 \times 16^3 + 15 \times 16^2 + 3 \times 16^1 + 12 \times 16^0 \\
&= 659260
\end{aligned}$$

Some hexadecimal numbers and their decimal equivalents are given in the following table.

Hexadecimal number	Conversion to decimal
2A	$2 \times 16 + A = 2 \times 16 + 10 = 42$
B3	$B \times 16 + 3 = 11 \times 16 + 3 = 179$
113	$1 \times 16^2 + 1 \times 16 + 3 = 275$

On machines that have 8-bit bytes, a byte is conveniently represented as two hexadecimal digits. Moreover, the representation has two simultaneously valid interpretations. First, one may consider the 8 bits in a byte as representing a number in base 2 notation. That number can be expressed uniquely as a hexadecimal number with two hexadecimal digits. The following table lists 8-bit bytes and corresponding two-digit hexadecimal numbers. For convenience, decimal numbers are listed, and for later reference octal numbers are also listed.

Decimal	Binary	Hexadecimal	Octal
0	00000000	00	000
1	00000001	01	001
2	00000010	02	002
3	00000011	03	003
. . . . .			
31	00011111	1F	037
32	00100000	20	040
. . . . .			
188	10111100	BC	274
. . . . .			
254	11111110	FE	376
255	11111111	FF	377

Another interpretation of this correspondence is also useful. By definition, a *nibble* consists of 4 bits, so that a byte is made up of 2 nibbles. Each nibble has a unique representation as a single hexadecimal digit, and 2 nibbles, making up a byte, are representable as 2 hexadecimal digits. For example,

   1011 1100   corresponds to   BC

Note that this same correspondence occurs in the table. All of this is useful when manipulating the values of variables in bit form.

The octal digits are 0, 1, 2, ..., 7. A positive integer written in octal notation is a string of digits of the form

$$o_n o_{n-1} \ldots o_2 o_1 o_0$$

where each o_i is an octal digit. The value of such an integer is

$$o_n \times 8^n + o_{n-1} \times 8^{n-1} + \cdots + o_2 \times 8^2 + o_1 \times 8^1 + o_0 \times 8^0$$

For example,

$$75301 = 7 \times 8^4 + 5 \times 8^3 + 3 \times 8^2 + 0 \times 8^1 + 1 \times 8^0$$

On machines that have words consisting of 24 or 48 bits, it is natural to have words consisting of "bytes" with 6 bits, each "byte" made up of 2 "nibbles" of 3 bits each. In this case a "nibble" has a unique representation as a single octal digit, and a "byte" has a unique representation as two octal digits.

In C source code, positive integer constants prefaced with 0 represent integers in octal notation, and positive integer constants prefaced with 0x or 0X represent integers in hexadecimal notation. Just as with decimal integer constants, octal and hexadecimal constants may have suffixes appended to specify the type. The letters A through F and a through f are used to code hexadecimal digits.

hexadecimal_integer_constant ::= *h_integer_constant* { *i_suffix* }*opt*
h_integer_constant ::= { 0x | 0X }₁ { *hexadecimal_digit* }₁₊
hexadecimal_digit ::= 0 | 1 | ... | 9 | a | A | ... | f | F
octal_integer_constant ::= *o_integer_constant* { *i_suffix* }*opt*
o_integer_constant ::= 0 { *octal_digit* }₁₊
octal_digit ::= 0 | 1 | ... | 7
i_suffix ::= *integer_suffix* ::= { u | U }*opt* { l | L }*opt*

Let us write a program to illustrate these ideas. We will show the output of each printf() statement as a comment.

```
/* Decimal, hexadecimal, octal conversions. */

#include <stdio.h>

int main(void)
{
    printf("%d  %x  %o\n", 19, 19, 19);          /* 19   13   23 */
    printf("%d  %x  %o\n", 0x1c, 0x1c, 0x1c);    /* 28   1c   34 */
    printf("%d  %x  %o\n", 017, 017, 017);       /* 15    f   17 */
    printf("%d\n", 11 + 0x11 + 011);             /* 37          */
    printf("%x\n", 2097151);                     /* 1fffff      */
    printf("%d\n", 0x1FfFFf);                     /* 2097151     */
    return 0;
}
```

On machines with 2-byte words the last two formats must be changed to %lx and %ld, respectively. The functions printf() and scanf() use the conversion characters and d, x, and o in conversion specifications for decimal, hexadecimal, and octal, respectively. With printf(), formats of the form %x and %o cause integers to be printed out in hexadecimal and octal notation, but not prefaced with 0x or 0. The formats %#x and %#o can be used to get the prefixes (see Chapter 11 for further discussion).

3.13 SUMMARY

1 The fundamental data types are char, short, int, long, unsigned versions of these, and three floating types. The type char is a 1-byte integral type mostly used for representing characters.

2 The type int is designed to be the "natural" or "working" integral type. The other integral types such as short, long, and unsigned are provided for more specialized situations.

3 Three floating types, float, double, and long double, are provided to represent real numbers. Typically, a float is stored in 4 bytes and a double in 8 bytes. The number of bytes used to store a long double varies from one compiler to another. However, as compilers get updated, the trend is to store a long double in 16 bytes. The type double, not float, is the "working" type.

4 Unlike integer arithmetic, floating arithmetic is not always exact. Engineers and numerical analysts often have to take rounding effects into account when doing extensive calculations with floating-point numbers.

5 The unary operator sizeof can be used to find the number of bytes needed to store a type or the value of an expression. For example, sizeof(int) is 2 on most small machines and is 4 on most large machines.

6 The usual mathematical functions, such as sin( ), cos( ), and tan( ), are available in the mathematics library. Most of the functions in the library take a single argument of type double and return a value of type double. The standard header file *math.h* should be included when using these functions.

7 Automatic conversions occur in mixed expressions and across an equals sign. Casts can be used to force explicit conversions.

8 Integer constants beginning with 0x and 0 designate hexadecimal and octal integers, respectively.

9 Suffixes can be used to explicitly specify the type of a constant. For example, 3U is of type unsigned and 7.0F is of type float.

10 A character constant such as 'A' is of type int in C, but it is of type char in C++. This is one of the few places where C++ differs from C.

3.14 EXERCISES

1 Not all real numbers are machine-representable; there are too many of them. Thus the numbers that are available on a machine have a "graininess" to them. As an example of this, the code

```
double   x = 123.45123451234512345;
double   y = 123.45123451234512300;   /* last two digits
     are different */

printf("%.17f  %.17f\n", x, y);
```

causes two identical numbers to be printed. How many zeros must the initializer for y end with to get different numbers printed? Explain your answer.

2 If you use a library function and do not declare it, the compiler assumes it is to return an `int` value by default. (These ideas will be discussed further in Chapter 5.) Consider the following code:

```
double   cos(double), x, y;      /* sin() is not declared */

while (1) {
    printf("Input a number:   ");
    scanf("%1f", &x);
    y = sin(x) * sin(x) + cos(x) * cos(x);
    printf("\n%s%.15g\n%s%.15e\n\n",
        "x = ", x,
        "sin(x) * sin(x) + cos(x) * cos(x) = ", y);
}
```

This code, when correctly written, illustrates the mathematical fact that

$$\sin^2(x) + \cos^2(x) = 1 \qquad \text{for all } x \text{ real}$$

Note that the declaration for `sin()` is missing. Put this code into a program, first with the correct declaration so that you understand its proper effects. Then experiment to see what the effect is when the `sin()` function is not declared. Does your compiler complain? It should.

3 Write a program that prints a table of trigonometric values for `sin()`, `cos()`, and `tan()`. The angles in your table should go from 0 to π in 20 steps.

4 Write a test program to find out whether the `printf()` function truncates or rounds when writing a `float` or `double` with a fractional part.

5 Use the following code to print out a list of powers of 2 in decimal, hexadecimal, and octal:

```
int    a = 1, i;

for (i = 0; i < 35; ++i) {
    printf("%15u%15d%15x%15o\n", a, a, a, a);
    a *= 2;
}
```

What gets printed? Explain. Powers of 2 have a special property when written in hexadecimal and octal notation. What is the property?

6 Try the following code on your system:

```
int    big_big = 2000000000 + 2000000000;

printf("%d    %u\n", big_big, big_big);
```

If you are working on a machine with a 2-byte word, change 2000000000 to 32000. What gets printed? Explain. Does the output change if `big_big` is declared to be `unsigned` instead of `int`?

7 The program in this exercise needs to be studied carefully.

```
/*
// Mystery?
*/

#include <stdio.h>

int main(void)
{
    printf("Why is 21 + 31 equal to %d?\n", 21 + 31);
    return 0;
}
```

Here is the output from the program:

```
Why is 21 + 31 equal to 5?
```

Can you deduce the moral?

8 In mathematics the Greek letter ϵ, called "epsilon," is often used to represent a small positive number. Although it can be arbitrarily small in mathematics, on a machine there is no such concept as "arbitrarily small." In numerical analysis it is convenient sometimes to declare `eps` (for "epsilon") as a variable of type `double`, and to assign to `eps` the smallest positive number with the property that

```
1.0 < 1.0 + eps
```

is *true*. This number is machine-dependent. See if you can find `eps` on your machine. Begin by assigning the value `1e-37` to `eps`. You will find that for this value the expression is *false*.

9 In traditional C, the types `long float` and `double` are synonymous. However, because `long float` is harder to type, it was not popular and was rarely used. In ANSI C, the type `long float` has been eliminated. Nonetheless, many ANSI C compilers still accept it. Check to see if this is true on your compiler.

10 If you expand the two functions *tan(sin(x))* and *sin(tan(x))* in a Taylor series about the origin, the two expansions agree for the first seven terms. (If you have access to a computer algebra system such as Maple or Mathematica, you can see this easily.) This means that the difference of the two functions is very flat at the origin. Try the following program:

```
#include <math.h>
#include <stdio.h>

double    f(double x);

int main(void)
{
    double    x;

    for (x = -0.25; x <= +0.25; x += .01)
        printf("f(%+.2f) = %+.15f\n", x, f(x));
    return 0;
}

double f(double x)
{
    return (tan(sin(x)) - sin(tan(x)));
}
```

The output of this program illustrates the flatness of f() near the origin. Do you see it?

11 Most machines use the two's complement representation to store integers. On these machines, the value −1 stored in an integral type turns all bits on. Assuming that your system does this, here is one way to determine whether a char is equivalent to a signed char or to an unsigned char. Write a program that contains the lines

```
char              c = -1;
signed char       s = -1;
unsigned char     u = -1;

printf("c = %d    s = %d    u = %d\n", c, s, u);
```

Each of the variables c, s, and u is stored in memory with the bit pattern 11111111. What gets printed on your system? Can you tell from this what a char is equivalent to? Does your ANSI C compiler provide an option to change this? If so, invoke the option, recompile your program, and run it again.

12 Explain why the code

```
unsigned long    a = -1;

printf("The biggest number: %lu\n", a);
```

prints the largest integral value on your system.

13 A variable of type char can be used to store small integer values. What happens
if a large value is assigned to a char variable? Consider the code

```
char    c = 256;      /* too big! */

printf("c = %d\n", c);
```

Does your machine complain? If it does not complain, can you guess what gets
printed?

14 The following table shows how many bytes are required on most machines to
store some of the fundamental types. What are the appropriate values for your
machine? Write and execute a program that allows you to complete the table.

Fundamental type	Memory required on machines with 4-byte words	Memory required on machines with 2-byte words	Memory required on your machine
char	1 byte	1 byte	
short	2 bytes	2 bytes	
int	4 bytes	2 bytes	
unsigned	4 bytes	2 bytes	
long	4 bytes	4 bytes	
float	4 bytes	4 bytes	
double	8 bytes	8 bytes	
long double	?	?	

15 The type of a character constant such as 'A' is different in C and C++. In C its
type is int, but in C++ its type is char. Compile the following program first
in C and then in C++. In each case, what gets printed?

```
#include <stdio.h>

int main(void)
{
    printf("sizeof('A') = %d\n", sizeof('A'));
    return 0;
}
```

16 Consider the following code:

```
char    c;

printf("sizeof(c)        = %d\n", sizeof(c));
printf("sizeof('a')      = %d\n", sizeof('a'));
printf("sizeof(c + c)    = %d\n", sizeof(c + c));
printf("sizeof(c = 'a')  = %d\n", sizeof(c = 'a'));
```

Write down what you think gets printed; then write a small program to check your answer. How many lines of the output change if you compile the program in C++?

17 Let $N_{min\_u\_long}$ and $N_{max\_u\_long}$ represent the minimum and maximum values that can be stored in an unsigned long on your system. What are those values? *Hint:* Read the standard header file *limits.h*.

18 On a 24-hour clock the zero hour is midnight and the 23rd hour is 11 o'clock at night, one hour before midnight. On such a clock, when 1 is added to 23, we do not get 24, but instead we get 0. There is no 24. In a similar fashion 22 plus 5 yields 3, because 22 plus 2 is 0 and 3 more is 3. This is an example of modular arithmetic, or more precisely, of arithmetic modulo 24. Most machines do modular arithmetic on all the integral types. This is most easily illustrated with the unsigned types. Run the following program and explain what gets printed:

```
#include <limits.h>              /* for UINT_MAX */
#include <stdio.h>

int main(void)
{
    int         i;
    unsigned    u = UINT_MAX;    /* typically 4294967295 */

    for (i = 0; i < 10; ++i)
        printf("%u + %d = %u\n", u, i, u + i);
    for (i = 0; i < 10; ++i)
        printf("%u * %d = %u\n", u, i, u * i);
    return 0;
}
```

If you are working on a machine that has 2-byte words, first change 4294967295 to 65535 in the comment.

19 The computing world has been slowly coming to agreement (more or less) on how floating values should be represented in machines. In this regard, ANSI C suggests that the recommendations of a certain IEEE committee be followed. Does your system follow these recommendations? Well, one test is to try to see what happens when you assign a value to a floating variable that is out of its range. Write a small program containing the lines

```
float   x = 1e+999;      /* too big! */

printf("x = %e\n", x);
```

You may be surprised at what happens.

20 In mathematics the numbers e and π are well known. The number e is the base of the natural logarithms and the number π is the ratio of the diameter of a circle to its circumference. Which of the two numbers, e^{π} and π^{e}, is larger? This is a standard problem for students in an honors calculus course. However, even if you have never heard of e and π and know nothing about calculus, you should be able to answer this question. *Hint:*

$$e \approx 2.71828182845904524 \qquad \text{and} \qquad \pi \approx 3.14159265358979324$$

21 What happens when the argument to the `sqrt()` function is negative? In some compilers a call such as `sqrt(-1.0)` causes a run-time error to occur, whereas in other compilers the special value NaN gets returned. The value NaN is called "not a number." What happens on your system? To find out, write a test program that contains the line

```
printf("sqrt(-1.0) = %f\n", sqrt(-1.0));
```

22 If the value of x is too large, the call `pow(x, x)` may cause a run-time error or may cause the word `Inf` or `Infinity` to appear on the screen when a `printf()` statement is used to print the value produced by `pow(x, x)`. What is the largest integer value for x such that the statement

```
printf("pow(%.1f, %.1f) = %.7e\n", x, x, pow(x, x));
```

does not cause a run-time error and does not cause `Inf` or `Infinity` to be printed? *Hint:* Put the statement in a `for` loop.

23 Write a program called *try_me* that contains the following lines:

```
int   c;

while ((c = getchar()) != EOF)
    putchar(c);
```

Give the command

try_me < infile > outfile

to copy the contents of *infile* to *outfile*. (Make sure that you actually look at what is in *outfile*.) Now change the declaration of c from an int to a char. If your compiler produces executable code, try the command again. On some systems it will work; on others it will not. What happens on your system?

24 Change the *pacific_sea* program given in Chapter 1 to the *pacific_ocean* program. Begin by changing the first #define directive to

```
#define   AREA   179680425   /* Pacific Ocean */
```

On machines that have 4-byte words, the program should now run without errors. However, on machines that have 2-byte words, the program runs incorrectly. Explain why. What must you do to the program to exhibit the trouble, even though your machine has 4-byte words? Try it and see. What must you do to the program so that it will run with the same results on most machines, irrespective of whether they have 4-byte or 2-byte words?

25 In mathematical code, the use of abs() instead of fabs() can be disastrous. Try the following code on your machine:

```
double   x = 3.357;

printf("abs(%.3f) = %.3f\n", x, abs(x));      /* wrong! */
```

Does your compiler give you a warning? (It should.) Here, the programmer can easily spot that something is wrong. But sometimes the use of abs() is deeply embedded in lots of other code, making its misuse difficult to spot.

26 Which of the following are valid constants?

```
-0xabc          -0xaBc          -0xABC
```

Find the decimal value of the constants that are valid. Which one is the largest?

27 The following code is machine-dependent. If it does the unexpected, see if you can explain what is happening.

```
char   c = 0xff;

if (c == 0xff)
    printf("Truth!\n");
else
    printf("This needs to be explained!\n");
```

CHAPTER

FLOW OF CONTROL

Statements in a program are normally executed one after another. This is called *sequential flow of control*. Often it is desirable to alter the sequential flow of control to provide for a choice of action, or a repetition of action. By means of `if`, `if-else`, and `switch` statements, a selection among alternative actions can be made. By means of `while`, `for`, and do statements, iterative actions can be taken. We explain these flow of control constructs in this chapter.

Because the relational, equality, and logical operators are heavily used in flow of control constructs, we begin with a thorough discussion of these operators. They are used in expressions that we think of as being *true* or *false*. We explain how *true* and *false* are implemented in C. We also discuss the compound statement, which is used to group together statements that are to be treated as a unit.

4.1 RELATIONAL, EQUALITY, AND LOGICAL OPERATORS

The following table contains the operators that are most often used to affect flow of control:

Relational, Equality, and Logical Operators		
Relational operators:	less than:	`<`
	greater than:	`>`
	less than or equal:	`<=`
	greater than or equal:	`>=`
Equality operators:	equal:	`==`
	not equal:	`!=`
Logical operators:	(unary) negation:	`!`
	logical and:	`&&`
	logical or:	`||`

Just as with other operators, the relational, equality, and logical operators have rules of precedence and associativity that determine precisely how expressions involving these operators are evaluated.

134

Operators	Associativity
+ *(unary)* – *(unary)* ++ -- !	right to left
* / %	left to right
+ –	left to right
< <= > >=	left to right
== !=	left to right
&&	left to right
||	left to right
= += -= *= /= *etc*	right to left

The ! operator is unary. All the other relational, equality, and logical operators are binary. They operate on expressions and yield either the int value 0 or the int value 1. The reason for this is that in the C language *false* is represented by the value zero and *true* is represented by any nonzero value. The value for *false* can be any zero value; it can be a 0 or 0.0 or the null character '\0' or the NULL pointer value. The value for *true* can be any nonzero value. Intuitively, an expression such as a < b is either *true* or *false*. In C, this expression will yield the int value 1 if it is *true* and the int value 0 if it is *false*.

4.2 RELATIONAL OPERATORS AND EXPRESSIONS

The relational operators

     <   >   <=   >=

are all binary. They each take two expressions as operands and yield either the int value 0 or the int value 1.

     relational_expression   ::=   *expr* < *expr*
                           | *expr* > *expr*
                           | *expr* <= *expr*
                           | *expr* >= *expr*

Some examples are

```
a < 3
a > b
-1.3 >= (2.0 * x + 3.3)
a < b < c                      /* syntactically correct, but confusing */
```

but not

```
a =< b          /* out of order */
a < = b         /* space not allowed */
a >> b          /* this is a shift expression */
```

Consider a relational expression such as a < b. If a is less than b, then the expression has the int value 1, which we think of as being *true*. If a is not less than b, then the expression has the int value 0, which we think of as *false*. Observe that the value of a < b is the same as the value of a - b < 0. Because the precedence of the relational operators is less than that of the arithmetic operators, the expression

a - b < 0   is equivalent to   (a - b) < 0

On most machines, an expression such as a < b is implemented as a - b < 0, which is equivalent. The usual arithmetic conversions occur in relational expressions.

Let *e1* and *e2* be arbitrary arithmetic expressions. The following table shows how the value of $e1 - e2$ determines the values of relational expressions.

Values of: e1 − e2	e1 < e2	e1 > e2	e1 <= e2	e1 >= e2
positive	0	1	0	1
zero	0	0	1	1
negative	1	0	1	0

The following table illustrates the use of the rules of precedence and associativity to evaluate relational expressions.

Declarations and initializations		
char c = 'w';		
int i = 1, j = 2, k = -7;		
double x = 7e+33, y = 0.001;		

Expression	Equivalent expression	Value
'a' + 1 < c	('a' + 1) < c	1
- i - 5 * j >= k + 1	((- i) - (5 * j)) >= (k + 1)	0
3 < j < 5	(3 < j) < 5	1
- 3.333 <= x + y	(x - 3.333) <= (x + y)	1
x < x + y	x < (x + y)	0

Two expressions in this table give surprising results in that they do not conform to rules as written mathematically. In mathematics, one writes

$$3 < j < 5$$

to indicate that the variable j has the property of being greater than 3 and less than 5. It can also be considered as a mathematical statement that, depending on the value of j, may or may not be true. For example, if $j = 4$, then the mathematical statement

$$3 < j < 5$$

is true, but if $j = 7$, then the mathematical statement is false. Now consider the C code

```
j = 7;
printf("%d\n", 3 < j < 5);      /* 1 gets printed, not 0 */
```

By analogy with mathematics, one might expect that the expression is *false* and that 0 is printed. However, that is not the case. Because relational operators associate from left to right,

```
3 < j < 5
```
is equivalent to
```
(3 < j) < 5
```

Because the expression `3 < j` is *true*, it has value 1. Thus

```
(3 < j) < 5
```
is equivalent to
```
1 < 5
```

which has value 1. In C, the correct way to write a test for both `3 < j` and `j < 5` is

```
3 < j && j < 5
```

Because the relational operators have higher precedence than the binary logical operators, this is equivalent to

```
(3 < j) && (j < 5)
```

and, as we will see later, this expression is *true* if and only if both operands of the `&&` expression are *true*.

The numbers that are representable in a machine do not have infinite precision. Sometimes, this can cause unexpected results. In mathematics the relation

```
x < x + y
```
is equivalent to
```
0 < y
```

Mathematically, if y is positive, then both of these relations are logically true. Computationally, if x is a floating variable with a large value such as `7e+33` and y is a floating variable with a small value such as `0.001`, then the relational expression

```
x < x + y
```

may be *false*, even though mathematically it is true. An equivalent expression is

$$(x - (x + y)) < 0.0$$

and it is this expression that the machine implements. If, in terms of machine accuracy, the values of x and x + y are equal, the expression will yield the int value 0.

4.3   EQUALITY OPERATORS AND EXPRESSIONS

The equality operators == and != are binary operators acting on expressions. They yield either the int value 0 or the int value 1. The usual arithmetic conversions are applied to expressions that are the operands of the equality operators.

>   *equality_expression* ::= *expr* == *expr* | *expr* != *expr*

Some examples are

```
c == 'A'
k != -2
x + y == 3 * z - 7
```

but not

```
a = b              /* an assignment statement */
a = = b - 1        /* space not allowed */
(x + y) =! 44      /* syntax error: equivalent to (x + y) = (!44) */
```

Intuitively, an equality expression such as a == b is either *true* or *false*. An equivalent expression is a - b == 0, and this is what is implemented at the machine level. If a equals b, then a - b has value 0 and 0 == 0 is *true*. In this case the expression a == b will yield the int value 1, which we think of as *true*. If a is not equal to b, then a == b will yield the int value 0, which we think of as *false*.

The expression a != b uses the not equal operator. It is evaluated in a similar fashion, except that the test here is for inequality rather than for equality. The operator semantics is given by the following table.

Values of:		
expr1 − expr2	expr1 == expr2	expr1 ! = expr2
zero	1	0
nonzero	0	1

The next table shows how the rules of precedence and associativity are used to evaluate some expressions with equality operators.

Declarations and initializations		
int i = 1, j = 2, k = 3;		

Expression	Equivalent expression	Value
i == j	j == i	0
i != j	j != i	1
i + j + k == - 2 * - k	((i + j) + k) == ((- 2) * (- k))	1

Observe that the expression

a != b   is equivalent to   !(a == b)

Also, note carefully that the two expressions

a == b   and   a = b

are *visually* similar. They are close in form but radically different in function. The expression a == b is a test for equality, whereas a = b is an assignment expression. Writing

```
if (a = 1)
    .....          /* do something */
```

instead of

```
if (a == 1)
    .....          /* do something */
```

is a common programming error. The expression in the first if statement is always *true*, and an error such as this can be very difficult to find.

4.4 LOGICAL OPERATORS AND EXPRESSIONS

The logical operator ! is unary, and the logical operators && and || are binary. All of these operators, when applied to expressions, yield either the int value 0 or the int value 1.

Logical negation can be applied to an expression of arithmetic or pointer type. If an expression has value zero, then its negation will yield the int value 1. If the expression has a nonzero value, then its negation will yield the int value 0.

logical_negation_expression ::= ! *expr*

Some examples are

```
!a
!(x + 7.7)
!(a < b || c < d)
```

but not

```
a!         /* out of order */
a != b     /* != is the token for the "not equal" operator */
```

The usual arithmetic conversion rules are applied to expressions that are the operands of !. The following table gives the semantics of the ! operator.

Values of:	
expr	!expr
zero	1
nonzero	0

Although logical negation is a very simple operator, there is one subtlety. The operator ! in C is unlike the *not* operator in ordinary logic. If s is a logical statement, then

$$not\ (not\ s) = s$$

whereas in C the value of !!5, for example, is 1. Because ! associates from right to left, the same as all other unary operators, the expression

```
!!5       is equivalent to        !(!5)
```

and !(!5) is equivalent to !(0), which has value 1. The following table shows how some expressions with logical negation are evaluated.

Declarations and initializations		
`char    c = 'A';`		
`int     i = 7, j = 7;`		
`double  x = 0.0, y = 2.3;`		

Expression	Equivalent expression	Value
`! c`	`! c`	0
`! (i - j)`	`! (i - j)`	1
`! i - j`	`(! i) - j`	−7
`! ! (x + y)`	`! (! (x + y))`	1
`! x * ! ! y`	`(! x) * (!(! y))`	1

The binary logical operators **&&** and **||** also act on expressions and yield either the int value 0 or the int value 1. The syntax for a logical expression is given by

> *logical_expression* ::= *logical_negation_expression*
> | *logical_or_expression*
> | *logical_and_expression*
> *logical_or_expression* ::= *expr* **||** *expr*
> *logical_and_expression* ::= *expr* **&&** *expr*

Some examples are

```
a && b
a || b
!(a < b) && c
3 && (-2 * a + 7)
```

but not

```
a &&        /* one operand missing */
a || b      /* extra space not allowed */
a & b       /* this is a bitwise operation */
&b          /* the address of b */
```

The operator semantics is given by the following table.

Values of:			
expr1	**expr2**	**expr && expr2**	**expr2 || expr2**
zero	*zero*	0	0
zero	*nonzero*	0	1
nonzero	*zero*	0	1
nonzero	*nonzero*	1	1

The precedence of **&&** is higher than **||**, but both operators are of lower precedence than all unary, arithmetic, and relational operators. Their associativity is left to right. The next table shows how the rules of precedence and associativity are used to compute the value of some logical expressions.

Declarations and initializations

```
char     c = 'B';
int      i = 3, j = 3, k = 3;
double   x = 0.0, y = 2.3;
```

Expression	Equivalent expression	Value
i && j && k	(i && j) && k	1
x || i && j - 3	x || (i && (j - 3))	0
i < j && x < y	(i < j) && (x < y)	0
i < j || x < y	(i < j) || (x < y)	1
'A' <= c && c <= 'Z'	('A' <= c) && (c <= 'Z')	1
c - 1 == 'A' || c + 1 == 'Z'	((c - 1) == 'A') || ((c + 1) == 'Z')	1

The usual arithmetic conversions occur in expressions that are the operands of logical operators. Note that many of the expressions in the table are of mixed type. Whenever this occurs, certain values are promoted to match the highest type present in the expression.

Short-Circuit Evaluation

In the evaluation of expressions that are the operands of && and ||, the evaluation process stops as soon as the outcome *true* or *false* is known. This is called *short-circuit* evaluation. It is an important property of these operators. Suppose that *expr1* and *expr2* are expressions and that *expr1* has value zero. In the evaluation of the logical expression

   expr1 && *expr2*

the evaluation of *expr2* will not occur because the value of the logical expression as a whole is already determined to be 0. Similarly, if *expr1* has nonzero value, then in the evaluation of

   expr1 || *expr2*

the evaluation of *expr2* will not occur because the value of the logical expression as a whole is already determined to be 1.

Here is a simple example of how short-circuit evaluation might be used. Suppose that we want to process no more than three characters.

```
int    cnt = 0;

while (++cnt <= 3 && (c = getchar()) != EOF) {
     .....      /* do something */
```

When the expression ++cnt <= 3 is *false*, the next character will not be read.

4.5 THE COMPOUND STATEMENT

A compound statement is a series of declarations and statements surrounded by braces.

compound_statement ::= { { *declaration* }₀₊ { *statement* }₀₊ }

The chief use of the compound statement is to group statements into an executable unit. When declarations come at the beginning of a compound statement, the compound statement is also called a *block*. (Blocks will be discussed in Chapter 5.) In C, wherever it is syntactically correct to place a statement, it is also syntactically correct to place a compound statement. *A compound statement is itself a statement.* An example of a compound statement is

```
{
    a = 1;
    {
        b = 2;
        c = 3;
    }
}
```

Note that in this example there is a compound statement within a compound statement. An important use of the compound statement is to achieve the desired flow of control in if, if-else, while, for, do, and switch statements.

4.6 THE EMPTY STATEMENT

The empty statement is written as a single semicolon. It is useful where a statement is needed syntactically, but no action is required semantically. As we shall see, this is sometimes useful in constructs that affect the flow of control, such as if-else statements and for statements. The empty statement is a special case of the expression statement.

expr_statement ::= { *expr* }*opt* ;

Some examples of expression statements are

```
a = b;                  /* an assignment statement */
a + b + c;              /* legal, but no useful work gets done */
;                       /* an empty statement */
printf("%d\n", a);      /* a function call */
```

4.7   THE if AND THE if-else STATEMENTS

The general form of an if statement is

>   if (*expr*)
>   *statement*

If *expr* is nonzero (*true*), then *statement* is executed; otherwise *statement* is skipped and control passes to the next statement. In the example

```
if (grade >= 90)
    printf("Congratulations!\n");
printf("Your grade is %d.\n", grade);
```

a congratulatory message is printed only when the value of grade is greater than or equal to 90. The second printf() is always executed. The syntax of an if statement is given by

>   *if_statement* ::= if (*expr*) *statement*

Usually the expression in an if statement is a relational, equality, or logical expression, but as the syntax shows, an expression from any domain is permissible. Some other examples of if statements are

```
if (y != 0.0)
    x /= y;

if (c == ' ') {
    ++blank_cnt;
    printf("found another blank\n");
}
```

but not

```
if  b == a                /* parentheses missing */
    area = a * a;
```

Where appropriate, compound statements should be used to group a series of statements under the control of a single if expression. The following code consists of two if statements:

```
if (j < k)
    min = j;
if (j < k)
    printf("j is smaller than k\n");
```

The code can be written to be more efficient and more understandable by using a single if statement with a compound statement for its body.

```
if (j < k) {
    min = j;
    printf("j is smaller than k\n");
}
```

The if-else statement is closely related to the if statement. It has the general form

```
if (expr)
    statement1
else
    statement2
```

If *expr* is nonzero, then *statement1* is executed and *statement2* is skipped; if *expr* is zero, then *statement1* is skipped and *statement2* is executed. In both cases control then passes to the next statement. Consider the code

```
if (x < y)
    min = x;
else
    min = y;
```

If x < y is *true*, then min will be assigned the value of x, and if it is *false*, then min will be assigned the value of y. The syntax is given by

$$if\_else\_statement \quad ::= \quad \text{if } (expr) \ statement$$
$$\text{else } statement$$

An example is

```
if (c >= 'a' && c <= 'z')

else {
    ++other_cnt;
    printf("%c is not a lowercase letter\n", c);
}
```

but not

```
if (i != j) {
   i += 1;
   j += 2;
} ;
else
   i -= j;       /* syntax error */
```

The syntax error occurs because the semicolon following the right brace creates an empty statement, and consequently the else has nowhere to attach.

Because an if statement is itself a statement, it can be used as the statement part of another if statement. Consider the code

```
if (a == 1)
   if (b == 2)
      printf("***\n");
```

This is of the form

```
if (a == 1)
   statement
```

where *statement* is the following if statement

```
if (b == 2)
   printf("***\n");
```

In a similar fashion, an if-else statement can be used as the statement part of another if statement. Consider, for example,

```
if (a == 1)
   if (b == 2)
      printf("***\n");
   else
      printf("###\n");
```

Now we are faced with a semantic difficulty. This code illustrates the *dangling else problem*. It is not clear from the syntax what the else part is associated with. Do not be fooled by the format of the code. As far as the machine is concerned, the following code is equivalent:

```
if (a == 1)
    if (b == 2)
        printf("***\n");
else
    printf("###\n");
```

The rule is that an else attaches to the nearest if. Thus the code is correctly formatted as we first gave it. It has the form

```
if (a == 1)
    statement
```

where *statement* is the if-else statement

```
if (b == 2)
    printf("***\n");
else
    printf("###\n");
```

4.8 THE while STATEMENT

Repetition of action is one reason we rely on computers. When there are large amounts of data, it is very convenient to have control mechanisms that repeatedly execute specific statements. In C, the while, for, and do statements provide for repetitive action.

Although we have already used the while statement, or while loop, in many examples, we now want to explain precisely how this iterative mechanism works. The syntax is given by

while_statement ::= while *(expr) statement*

Some examples are

```
while (i++ < n)
    factorial *= i;

while ((c = getchar()) != EOF) {
    if (c >= 'a' && c <= 'z')
        ++lowercase_letter_cnt;
    ++total_cnt;
}
```

but not

```
while (++i < LIMIT) do {        /* syntax error: do is not allowed */
    j = 2 * i + 3;
    printf("%d\n", j);
}
```

Consider a construction of the form

> while (*expr*)
>   *statement*
> *next statement*

First *expr* is evaluated. If it is nonzero (*true*), then *statement* is executed and control is passed back to the beginning of the while loop. The effect of this is that the body of the while loop, namely *statement*, is executed repeatedly until *expr* is zero (*false*). At that point control passes to *next statement*.

It is possible to inadvertently specify an expression that never becomes zero, and unless other means of escaping the while loop are introduced, the program is stuck in an infinite loop. Care should be taken to avoid this difficulty. As an example, consider the code

```
printf("Input an integer:  ");
scanf("%d", &n);
while (--n)
    .....      /* do something */
```

The intent is for a positive integer to be entered and assigned to the int variable n. Then the body of the while loop is to be executed repeatedly until the expression --n is eventually zero. However, if a negative integer is inadvertently assigned to n, then the loop will be infinite. To guard against this possibility, it would be better to code instead

```
while (--n > 0)
    .....          /* do something */
```

It is sometimes appropriate for a while loop to contain only an empty statement. A typical example would be

```
while ((c = getchar()) == ' ')
    ;     /* empty statement */
```

This code will cause blank characters in the input stream to be skipped. We could have written this as

```
while ((c = getchar()) == ' ');
```

However, it is considered good programming style to place the semicolon on the next line by itself so that it is clearly visible as an empty statement.

Our next program illustrates the ideas that we have presented in this section. The program counts various kinds of characters.

```
/* Count blanks, digits, letters, newlines, and others. */

#include <stdio.h>

int main(void)
{
    int    blank_cnt = 0, c, digit_cnt = 0,
           letter_cnt = 0, nl_cnt = 0, other_cnt = 0;

    while ((c = getchar()) != EOF)        /* braces not necessary */
        if (c == ' ')
            ++blank_cnt;
        else if (c >= '0' && c <= '9')
            ++digit_cnt;
        else if (c >= 'a' && c <= 'z' || c >= 'A' && c <= 'Z')
            ++letter_cnt;
        else if (c == '\n')
            ++nl_cnt;
        else
            ++other_cnt;

    printf("%10s%10s%10s%10s%10s%10s\n\n",
        "blanks", "digits", "letters", "lines", "others", "total");
    printf("%10d%10d%10d%10d%10d%10d\n\n",
        blank_cnt, digit_cnt, letter_cnt, nl_cnt, other_cnt,
        blank_cnt + digit_cnt + letter_cnt + nl_cnt + other_cnt);
    return 0;
}
```

Let us execute this program, using its source file for data. To do this, we give the command

cnt_char < cnt_char.c

Here is the output that appears on the screen:

blanks	digits	letters	lines	others	total
197	31	348	27	180	783

DISSECTION OF THE *cnt_char* PROGRAM

■ `while ((c = getchar()) != EOF)        /* braces not necessary */`
Braces are unnecessary because the long `if-else` construct that follows is a single statement that comprises the body of the `while` loop.

■ ```
if (c == ' ')
    ++blank_cnt;
else if (c >= '0' && c <= '9')
    ++digit_cnt;
else if (c >= 'a' && c <= 'z' || c >= 'A' && c <= 'Z')
    ++letter_cnt;
else if (c == '\n')
    ++nl_cnt;
else
    ++other_cnt;
```
This statement tests a series of conditions. When a given condition evaluates to *true*, its corresponding expression statement is executed and the remaining tests are then skipped. For each character read into the variable c, exactly one of the variables used for counting will be incremented. Note that logically we could have written

■  ```
if (c == ' ')
    ++blank_cnt;
else
    if (c >= '0' && c <= '9')
        ++digit_cnt;
    else
        if (c >= 'a' && c <= 'z' || c >= 'A' && c <= 'Z')
            ++letter_cnt;
        else
            .....
```
When the code is formatted this way, each of the `if-else` pairs lines up to show the logical structure of the code. However, this coding style is not recommended because long chains of `if-else` statements are possible, which can cause the code to march too far to the right.

4.9 THE for STATEMENT

The for statement, like the while statement, is used to execute code iteratively. We can explain its action in terms of the while statement. The construction

```
for (expr1; expr2; expr3)
    statement
next statement
```

is semantically equivalent to

```
expr1;
while (expr2) {
    statement
    expr3
}
next statement
```

provided that *expr2* is present, and provided that a continue statement is not in the body of the for loop. From our understanding of the while statement, we see that the semantics of the for statement are the following. First *expr1* is evaluated. Typically, *expr1* is used to initialize the loop. Then *expr2* is evaluated. If it is nonzero (*true*), then *statement* is executed, *expr3* is evaluated, and control passes back to the beginning of the for loop, except that evaluation of *expr1* is skipped. Typically, *expr2* is a logical expression controlling the iteration. This process continues until *expr2* is zero (*false*), at which point control passes to *next statement*.

The syntax of a for statement is given by

for_statement ::= for (*expr*; *expr*; *expr*) *statement*

Some examples are

```
for (i = 1; i <= n; ++i)
    factorial *= i;

for (j = 2; k % j == 0; ++j) {
    printf("%d is a divisor of %d\n", j, k);
    sum += j;
}
```

but not

```
for (i = 0, i < n, i += 3)      /* semicolons are needed */
    sum += i;
```

Any or all of the expressions in a for statement can be missing, but the two semicolons must remain. If *expr1* is missing, then no initialization step is performed as part of the for loop. The code

```
i = 1;
sum = 0;
for ( ; i <= 10; ++i)
   sum += i;
```

computes the sum of the integers from 1 to 10, and so does the code

```
i = 1;
sum = 0;
for ( ; i <= 10 ; )
   sum += i++;
```

The special rule for when *expr2* is missing is that the test is always *true*. Thus the for loop in the code

```
i = 1;
sum = 0;
for ( ; ; ) {
   sum += i++;
   printf("%d\n", sum);
}
```

is an infinite loop.

A for statement can be used as the statement part of an if, if-else, while, or another for statement. For example, the construction

```
for (...)
   for (...)
      for (...)
         statement
```

is a single for statement.

In many situations, program control can be accomplished by using either a while or a for statement. Which gets used is often a matter of taste. One major advantage of a for loop is that control and indexing can both be kept right at the top. When loops are nested, this can facilitate the reading of the code. The program in the next section illustrates this.

4.10 AN EXAMPLE: BOOLEAN VARIABLES

Boolean algebra plays a major role in the design of computer circuits. In this algebra all variables have only the values zero or one. Transistors and memory technologies implement zero-one value schemes with currents, voltages, and magnetic orientations. Frequently, the circuit designer has a function in mind and needs to check whether, for all possible zero-one inputs, the output has the desired behavior.

We will use int variables b1, b2, ..., b5 to represent five boolean variables. They will be allowed to take on only the values 0 and 1. A boolean function of these variables is one that returns only 0 or 1. A typical example of a boolean function is the majority function; it returns 1 if a majority of the variables have value 1, and 0 otherwise. We want to create a table of values for the functions

```
b1 || b3 || b5        and        b1 && b2 || b4 && b5
```

and the majority function. Recall that logical expressions always have the int value 0 or 1.

```c
/* Print a table of values for some boolean functions. */

#include <stdio.h>

int main(void)
{
   int    b1, b2, b3, b4, b5;                  /* boolean variables */
   int    cnt = 0;

   printf("\n%5s%5s%5s%5s%5s%5s%7s%7s%11s\n\n",    /* headings */
      "Cnt", "b1", "b2", "b3", "b4", "b5",
      "fct1", "fct2", "majority");

   for (b1 = 0; b1 <= 1; ++b1)
      for (b2 = 0; b2 <= 1; ++b2)
         for (b3 = 0; b3 <= 1; ++b3)
            for (b4 = 0; b4 <= 1; ++b4)
               for (b5 = 0; b5 <= 1; ++b5)
                  printf("%5d%5d%5d%5d%5d%5d%6d%7d%9d\n",
                     ++cnt, b1, b2, b3, b4, b5,
                     b1 || b3 || b5, b1 && b2 || b4 && b5,
                     b1 + b2 + b3 + b4 + b5 >= 3);
   putchar('\n');
   return 0;
}
```

The program prints a table of values for all possible inputs and corresponding outputs. It illustrates a typical use of nested for loops. Here is some of the output of the program:

Cnt	b1	b2	b3	b4	b5	fct1	fct2	majority
1	0	0	0	0	0	0	0	0
2	0	0	0	0	1	1	0	0
3	0	0	0	1	0	0	0	0

. . . . .

4.11 THE COMMA OPERATOR

The comma operator has the lowest precedence of all the operators in C. It is a binary operator with expressions as operands.

comma_expression ::= *expr* , *expr*

In a comma expression of the form

expr1 , *expr2*

expr1 is evaluated first, and then *expr2*. The comma expression as a whole has the value and type of its right operand. An example is

```
a = 0, b = 1
```

If b has been declared an int, then this comma expression has value 1 and type int.

The comma operator sometimes gets used in for statements. It allows multiple initializations and multiple processing of indices. For example, the code

```
for (sum = 0, i = 1; i <= n; ++i)
    sum += i;
```

can be used to compute the sum of the integers from 1 to *n*. Carrying this idea further, we can stuff the entire body of the for loop inside the for parentheses. The previous code could be rewritten as

```
for (sum = 0, i = 1; i <= n; sum += i, ++i)
    ;
```

but not as

```
for (sum = 0, i = 1; i <= n; ++i, sum += i)
    ;
```

In the comma expression

```
++i, sum += i
```

the expression ++i is evaluated first, and this will cause sum to have a different value.

The comma operator should be used only in situations where it fits naturally. So far, we have given examples to illustrate its use, but none of the code is natural. In Chapter 10, where we discuss linked lists, we will have occasion to keep track of an index and a pointer at the same time. The comma operator can be used in a natural way to do this by writing

```
for (i = 0, p = head; p != NULL; ++i, p = p -> next)
    . . . . .
```

The comma operator associates from left to right. Examples of comma expressions are given in the following table.

Declarations and initializations

```
int      i, j, k = 3;
double   x = 3.3;
```

Expression	Equivalent expression	Value
i = 1, j = 2, ++ k + 1	((i = 1), (j = 2)), ((++ k) + 1)	5
k != 1, ++ x * 2.0 + 1	(k != 1), (((++ x) * 2.0) + 1)	9.6

Most commas in programs do not represent comma operators. For example, those commas used to separate expressions in argument lists of functions or used within initializer lists are not comma operators. If a comma operator is to be used in these places, the comma expression in which it occurs must be enclosed in parentheses.

4.12 THE do STATEMENT

The do statement can be considered a variant of the while statement. Instead of making its test at the top of the loop, it makes it at the bottom. Its syntax is given by

do_statement ::= do *statement* while (*expr*) ;

An example is

```
do {
    sum += i;
    scanf("%d", &i);
} while (i > 0);
```

Consider a construction of the form

```
do
    statement
while (expr);
next statement
```

First *statement* is executed and *expr* is evaluated. If the value of *expr* is nonzero (*true*), then control passes back to the beginning of the do statement and the process repeats itself. When *expr* is zero (*false*), then control passes to *next statement*.

As an example, suppose that we want to read in a positive integer and that we want to insist that the integer be positive. The following code will do the job:

```
do {
    printf("Input a positive integer: ");
    scanf("%d", &n);
    if (error = (n <= 0))
        printf("\nERROR: Do it again!\n\n");
} while (error);
```

If a nonpositive integer is entered, the user will be notified with a request for a positive integer. Control will exit the loop only after a positive integer has been entered.

Because in C only a small percentage of loops tend to be do loops, it is considered good programming style to use braces even when they are not needed. The braces in the construct

```
do {
    a single statement
} while (...);
```

make it easier for the reader to realize that you have written a do statement rather than a while statement followed by an empty statement.

Now that we have discussed in detail the `if` statement, the `if-else` statement, and the various looping statements, we want to mention the following tip that applies to all of their control expressions. It is considered good programming style to use a relational expression, when appropriate, rather than an equality expression. In many cases this will result in more robust code. For expressions of type `float` or `double`, an equality test can be beyond the accuracy of the machine. Here is an example of this:

```
/* A test that fails. */

#include <stdio.h>

int main(void)
{
    int      cnt = 0;
    double   sum = 0.0, x;

    for (x = 0.0; x != 9.9; x += 0.1) {    /* trouble! */
        sum += x;
        printf("cnt = %5d\n", ++cnt);
    }
    printf("sum = %f\n", sum);
    return 0;
}
```

On most machines this program goes into an infinite loop.

4.13 AN EXAMPLE: FIBONACCI NUMBERS

The sequence of Fibonacci numbers is defined recursively by

$$f_0 = 0, \quad f_1 = 1, \quad f_{i+1} = f_i + f_{i-1} \qquad \text{for } i = 1, 2, \ldots$$

Except for f_0 and f_1, every element in the sequence is the sum of the previous two elements. It is easy to write down the first few elements of the sequence.

0, 1, 1, 2, 3, 5, 8, 13, 21, 34, 55, 89, 144, 233, ...

Fibonacci numbers have lots of uses and many interesting properties. One of the properties has to do with the Fibonacci quotients defined by

$$q_i = f_i / f_{i-1} \qquad \text{for } i = 2, 3, \ldots$$

It can be shown that the sequence of quotients converges to the golden mean, which is the real number $(1 + \sqrt{5})/2$. We want to write a program that prints Fibonacci numbers and quotients. If f1 contains the value of the current Fibonacci number and f0 contains the value of the previous Fibonacci number, then we can do the following:

1   Save the value of f1 (the current Fibonacci number) in a temporary.
2   Add f0 and f1 and store the value in f1, the new Fibonacci number.
3   Store the value of the temporary in f0 so that f0 will contain the previous Fibonacci number.
4   Print, and then repeat this process.

Because the Fibonacci numbers grow large very quickly, we are not able to compute many of them. Here is the program:

```c
/* Print Fibonacci numbers and quotients. */

#include <stdio.h>

#define   LIMIT   46

int main(void)
{
   long    f0 = 0, f1 = 1, n, temp;

   printf("%7s%19s%29s\n%7s%19s%29s\n%7s%19s%29s\n", /* headings */
      "   ", "Fibonacci", "Fibonacci",
      " n", "   number", " quotient",
      "--", "---------", "---------");
   printf("%7d%19d\n%7d%19d\n", 0, 0, 1, 1);   /* first two cases */

   for (n = 2; n <= LIMIT; ++n) {
      temp = f1;
      f1 += f0;
      f0 = temp;
      printf("%7ld%19ld%29.16f\n", n, f1, (double) f1 / f0);
   }
   return 0;
}
```

Here is some of the output of the program:

n	Fibonacci number	Fibonacci quotient
--	---------	---------
0	0	
1	1	
2	1	1.0000000000000000
3	2	2.0000000000000000
4	3	1.5000000000000000
5	5	1.6666666666666667
6	8	1.6000000000000001
7	13	1.6250000000000000
.....		
23	28657	1.6180339901755971
24	46368	1.6180339882053250
25	75025	1.6180339889579021
.....		
44	701408733	1.6180339887498949
45	1134903170	1.6180339887498949
46	1836311903	1.6180339887498949

DISSECTION OF THE *fibonacci* PROGRAM

■ `#define   LIMIT   46`

When for loops are used, they frequently repeat an action up to some limiting value. If a symbolic constant such as LIMIT is used, then it serves as its own comment, and its value can be changed readily.

■ `long   f0 = 0, f1 = 1, n, temp;`

The variables f0, f1, and temp have been declared to be of type long so that the program will work properly on machines having 2-byte words, as well as on machines having 4-byte words. Note that some of the Fibonacci numbers printed are too large to be stored in a 2-byte int. There is no need for n to be of type long; it could just as well be of type int.

■ `for (n = 2; n <= LIMIT; ++n) {`
`    temp = f1;`
`    f1 += f0;`
`    f0 = temp;`
`    .....`

First n is initialized to 2. Then a test is made to see if n is less than or equal to LIMIT. If it is, then the body of the for loop is executed, n is incremented, and control is passed back to the top of the for loop. The test, the execution of the body, and the incrementing of n all get done repeatedly until n has a value greater than LIMIT. Each time through the loop, an appropriate Fibonacci number is computed and printed. The body of the for loop is the compound statement surrounded by braces. The use of the variable temp in the body is essential. Suppose that instead we had written

```
for (n = 2; n <= LIMIT; ++n) {   /* wrong code */
    f1 += f0;
    f0 = f1;
    .....
```

Then each time through the loop f0 would not contain the previous Fibonacci number.

■ `printf("%7ld%19ld%29.16f\n", n, f1, (double) f1 / f0);`
Because variables of type long are being printed, the modifier l is being used with the conversion character d. Note that the field widths specified here match those in the printf() statements used at the beginning of the program. The field widths control the spacing between columns in the output. There is no magic in choosing them—just whatever looks good. Because a cast is a unary operator, it is of higher precedence than division. Thus the expression

```
(double) f1 / f0       is equivalent to       ((double) f1) / f0
```

Because the operands of the division operator are of mixed type, the value of f0 gets promoted to a double before division is performed.

4.14 THE goto STATEMENT

The goto statement is considered a harmful construct in most accounts of modern programming methodology. It causes an unconditional jump to a labeled statement somewhere in the current function. Thus it can undermine all the useful structure provided by other flow of control mechanisms (for, while, do, if, switch).

Because a goto jumps to a labeled statement, we need to discuss this latter construct first. The syntax of a labeled statement is given by

labeled_statement ::= *label* : *statement*
label ::= *identifier*

Some examples of labeled statements are

```
bye: exit(1);
L444: a = b + c;
bug1: bug2: bug3: printf("bug found\n");       /* multiple labels */
```

but not

```
333: a = b + c;      /* 333 is not an identifier */
```

The scope of a label is within the function in which it occurs, except for those blocks where the label identifier has been redefined. Label identifiers have their own name space. This means that the same identifier can be used both for a label and a variable. This practice, however, is considered bad programming style and should be avoided.

Control can be unconditionally transferred to a labeled statement by executing a goto statement of the form

goto *label*;

An example would be

```
goto error;
.....
error: {
   printf("An error has occurred - bye!\n");
   exit(1);
}
```

Both the goto statement and its corresponding labeled statement must be in the body of the same function. Here is a more specific piece of code that uses a goto.

```
while (scanf("%lf", &x) == 1) {
   if (x < 0.0)
      goto negative_alert;
   printf("%f  %f\n", sqrt(x), sqrt(2 * x));
}
negative_alert: printf("Negative value encountered!\n");
```

Note that this example could have been rewritten in a number of ways without using a goto.

In general, the goto should be avoided. It is a primitive method of altering flow of control, which, in a richly structured language, is unnecessary. Labeled statements and goto's are the hallmark of incremental patchwork program design. A programmer who modifies a program by adding goto's to additional code fragments soon makes the program incomprehensible.

When should a goto be used? A simple answer is not at all. Indeed, one cannot go wrong by following this advice. In some rare instances, however, which should be carefully documented, a goto can make the program significantly more efficient. In other cases it can simplify flow of control. This may occur when a special value is tested for in a deeply nested inner loop and, when this value is found, the program control needs to jump to the outermost level of the function.

4.15 THE break AND continue STATEMENTS

Two special statements,

   `break;`   and   `continue;`

interrupt the normal flow of control. The `break` statement causes an exit from the innermost enclosing loop or `switch` statement. In the following example, a test for a negative argument is made, and if the test *is* true, then a `break` statement is used to pass control to the statement immediately following the loop:

```
while (1) {
   scanf("%lf", &x);
   if (x < 0.0)
      break;                      /* exit loop if x is negative */
   printf("%f\n", sqrt(x));
}
/* break jumps to here */
```

This is a typical use of `break`. What would otherwise be an infinite loop is made to terminate upon a given condition tested by the `if` expression.

The `continue` statement causes the current iteration of a loop to stop and causes the next iteration of the loop to begin immediately. The following code processes all characters except digits:

```
for (i = 0; i < TOTAL; ++i) {
   c = getchar();
   if (c >= '0' && c <= '9')
      continue;
   .....               /* process other characters */
/* continue transfers control to here to begin next iteration */
}
```

The `continue` statement may only occur inside `for`, `while`, and `do` loops. As the example shows, `continue` transfers control to the end of the current iteration, whereas `break` would terminate the loop.

In the presence of a `continue` statement, a `for` loop of the form

```
for (expr1; expr2; expr3) {
   .....
   continue;
   .....
}
```

is equivalent to

```
expr1;
while (expr2) {
    .....
    goto next;
    .....
next:
    expr3;
}
```

which is different from

```
expr1;
while (expr2) {
    .....
    continue;
    .....
    expr3;
}
```

(See Exercise 29 for a convenient way to test this.)

4.16 THE switch STATEMENT

The switch is a multiway conditional statement generalizing the if-else statement. Let us first look at the syntax for a switch statement.

$switch\_statement$ ::= switch ($integral\_expression$)
$case\_statement$ | $default\_statement$ | $switch\_block$
$case\_statement$ ::= { case $constant\_integral\_expression$: }$_{1+}$ $statement$
$default\_statement$ ::= default : $statement$
$switch\_block$ ::= { { $declaration\_list$ }$_{opt}$ { $case\_group$ }$_{0+}$ { $default\_group$ }$_{opt}$ }
$case\_group$ ::= {case $constant\_integral\_expression$: }$_{1+}$ {$statement$ }$_{1+}$
$default\_group$ ::= default : {$statement$ }$_{1+}$

The following is a typical example of a switch statement:

```
switch (c) {
case 'a':
   ++a_cnt;
   break;
case 'b':
   ++b_cnt;
   break;
case 'c':
case 'C':
   ++cC_cnt;
   break;
default:
   ++other_cnt;
}
```

Notice that the body of the switch statement in the example is a compound statement. This will be so in all but the most degenerate situations. The controlling expression in the parentheses following the keyword switch must be of integral type. In the example, it is just the int variable c. The usual automatic conversions are performed on the controlling expression. After the expression is evaluated, control jumps to the appropriate case label. The constant integral expressions following the case labels must all be unique. Typically, the last statement before the next case or default label is a break statement. If there is no break statement, then execution "falls through" to the next statement in the succeeding case. Missing break statements are a frequent cause of error in switch statements. There may be at most one default label in a switch. Typically, it occurs last, although it can occur anywhere. The keywords case and default cannot occur outside of a switch.

The effect of a switch

1   Evaluate the switch expression.
2   Go to the case label having a constant value that matches the value of the
     expression found in step 1, or, if a match is not found, go to the
     default label, or, if there is no default label, terminate the switch.
3   Terminate the switch when a break statement is encountered, or terminate
     the switch by "falling off the end."

Let us review the various kinds of jump statements available to us. These include the goto, break, continue, and return statements. The goto is unrestricted in its use and should be avoided as a dangerous construct. The break may be used in loops and is important to the proper structuring of the switch statement. The continue is constrained to use within loops and is often unnecessary. The return statement must be used in functions that return values. It will be discussed in the next chapter.

4.17 THE CONDITIONAL OPERATOR

The conditional operator ?: is unusual in that it is a ternary operator. It takes as operands three expressions.

conditional_expression ::= *expr* ? *expr* : *expr*

In a construct such as

expr1 ? *expr2* : *expr3*

expr1 is evaluated first. If it is nonzero (*true*), then *expr2* is evaluated and that is the value of the conditional expression as a whole. If *expr1* is zero (*false*), then *expr3* is evaluated and that is the value of the conditional expression as a whole. Thus a conditional expression can be used to do the work of an if-else statement. Consider, for example, the code

```
if (y < z)
    x = y;
else
    x = z;
```

The effect of the code is to assign to x the minimum of y and z. This also can be accomplished by writing

```
x = (y < z) ? y : z;
```

Because the precedence of the conditional operator is just above assignment, parentheses are not necessary. However, parentheses often are used to make clear what is being tested for.

The type of the conditional expression

expr1 ? *expr2* : *expr3*

is determined by both *expr2* and *expr3*. If they are of different types, then the usual conversion rules are applied. Note carefully that the type of the conditional expression does not depend on which of the two expressions *expr2* or *expr3* is evaluated. The conditional operator ?: has precedence just above the assignment operators, and it associates from right to left.

Declarations and initializations

```
char      a = 'a', b = 'b';        /* a has decimal value 97 */
int       i = 1, j = 2;
double    x = 7.07;
```

Expression	Equivalent expression	Value	Type
i == j ? a - 1 : b + 1	(i == j) ? (a - 1) : (b + 1)	99	int
j % 3 == 0 ? i + 4 : x	((j % 3) == 0) ? (i + 4) : x	7.07	double
j % 3 ? i + 4 : x	(j % 3) ? (i + 4) : x	5.0	double

4.18 SUMMARY

1 Relational, equality, and logical expressions have the `int` value 0 or 1.

2 The negation operator `!` is unary. A negation expression such as `!a` has the `int` value 0 or 1. Remember: `!!a` and `a` need not have the same value.

3 A chief use of relational, equality, and logical expressions is to test data to affect flow of control.

4 Automatic type conversions can occur when two expressions are compared that are the operands of a relational, equality, or logical operator.

5 The grouping construct `{...}` is a compound statement. It allows enclosed statements to be treated as a single unit.

6 An `if` statement provides a way of choosing whether or not to execute a statement.

7 The `else` part of an `if-else` statement associates with the nearest available `if`. This resolves the "dangling else" problem.

8 The `while`, `for`, and `do` statements provide for the iterative execution of code. The body of a `do` statement executes at least once.

9 The programmer often has to choose between the use of a `while` or a `for` statement. In situations where clarity dictates that both the control and the indexing be kept visible at the top of the loop, the `for` statement is the natural choice.

10 The comma operator is occasionally useful in `for` statements. Of all the operators in C, it has the lowest priority.

11 The four statement types

```
    goto            break           continue            return
```

cause an unconditional transfer of flow of control. Their use should be mini-mized.

12 goto's are considered harmful to good programming. Avoid them.

13 The switch statement provides a multiway conditional branch. It is useful when dealing with a large number of special cases.

4.19 EXERCISES

1 Give equivalent logical expressions of the following without negation:

```
!(a > b)              !(a <= b && c <= d)
!(a + 1 == b + 1)     !(a < 1 || b < 2 && c < 3)
```

2 Complete the following table.

Declarations and initializations
`int       a = 1, b = 2, c = 3;` `double    x = 1.0;`

Expression	Equivalent expression	Value
`a > b && c < d`		
`a < ! b | | ! ! a`		
`a + b < ! c + c`		
`a - x | | b * c && b / a`		

3 Write a program that reads characters from the standard input file until EOF is encountered. Use the variables digit_cnt and other_cnt to count the number of digits and the number of other characters, respectively.

4 Write a program that counts the number of times the first three letters of the alphabet (a, A, b, B, c, C) occur in a file. Do not distinguish between lower- and uppercase letters.

5 Write a program that contains the loop

```
while (scanf("1f", &salary) == 1) {
    .....
}
```

Within the body of the loop compute a 17% federal withholding tax and a 3% state withholding tax and print these values along with the corresponding salary. Accumulate the sums of all salaries and taxes printed. Print these sums after the program exits the `while` loop.

6 What gets printed?

```
char    c = 'A';
int     i = 5, j = 10;

printf("%d %d %d\n", !c, !!c, !!!c);
printf("%d %d %d\n", - ! i, ! - i, ! - i - ! j);
printf("%d %d %d\n", ! (6 * j + i - c), ! i-5, ! j - 10);
```

7 Explain the effect of the following code:

```
int    i;
.....
while (i = 2) {
    printf("Some even numbers: %d %d %d\n", i, i + 2, i + 4);
    i = 0;
}
```

Contrast this code with the following:

```
int    i;
.....
if (i = 2)
    printf("Some even numbers: %d %d %d\n", i, i + 2, i + 4);
```

Both pieces of code are logically wrong. The run-time effect of one of them is so striking that the error is easy to spot, whereas the other piece of wrong code has a subtle effect that is much harder to spot. Explain.

8 What gets printed?

```
char      c = 'A';
double    x = 1e+33, y = 0.001;

printf("%d %d %d\n", c == 'a', c == 'b', c != 'c');
printf("%d\n", c == 'A' && c <= 'B' || 'C');
printf("%d\n", 1 != !!c == !!!c);
printf("%d\n", x + y > x - y);
```

9 What gets printed? Explain.

```
int   i = 7, j = 7;

if (i == 1)
    if (j == 2)
        printf("%d\n", i = i + j);
else
    printf("%d\n", i = i - j);
printf("%d\n", i);
```

10 The syntax error in the following piece of code does not really show up on the line indicated. Run a test program with this piece of code in it to find out which line is flagged with a syntax error. Explain why.

```
while (++i < LIMIT) do {        /* syntax error */
    j = 2 * i + 3;
    printf("j = %d\n", j);
}
    /* Many other languages require "do", but not C. */
```

11 Can the following code ever lead to an infinite loop? Explain. (Assume that the values of i and j are not changed in the body of the loop.)

```
printf("Input two integers: ");
scanf("%d%d", &i, &j);
while (i * j < 0 && ++i != 7 && j++ != 9) {
    .....       /* do something */
}
```

12 In Section 4.8, "The while Statement," we said that if n has a negative value, then

```
while (--n)
    .....               /* do something */
```

is an infinite loop. Actually, that is not true. Can you explain why?

13 Write a program that reads in an integer value for n and then sums the integers from n to 2 * n if n is nonnegative, or from 2 * n to n if n is negative. Write the code in two versions, one using only for loops and the other using only while loops.

14 Answer the following true-false questions:

> In the C language:
>
> Every statement ends in a semicolon.
>
> Every statement contains at least one semicolon.
>
> Every statement contains at most one semicolon.
>
> There exists a statement with precisely 33 semicolons.
>
> There exists a statement made up of 35 characters
>   that contains 33 semicolons.

15 In Section 4.10, "An Example: Boolean Variables," we presented a program that prints a table of values for some boolean functions. Execute the program and examine its output. For the 32 different inputs, exactly half of them (16 in number) have majority value 1. Write a program that prints a table of values for the majority function for, say, 7 boolean variables. Of the 128 different inputs, how many have majority value 1? State the general case as a theorem and try to give a proof. (Your machine can help you find theorems by checking special cases, but in general it cannot give a proof.)

16 Write three versions of a program that computes the sum of the first n even integers and the sum of the first n odd integers. The value for n should be entered interactively. In the first version of your program, use the code

```
for (cnt = 0, i = 1, j = 2; cnt < n; ++cnt, i += 2, j += 2)
    odd_sum += i, even_sum += j;
```

Note the prolific use of the comma operator. The code is not very good, but it will give you confidence that the comma operator works as advertised. In the second version, use one or more `for` statements but no comma operators. In the third version, use only `while` statements.

17 Choose one version of the program that you wrote in Exercise 16 and incorporate into it the following piece of code:

```
do {
    printf("Input a positive integer: ");
    scanf("%d", &n);
    if (error = (n <= 0))
        printf("\nERROR: Do it again!\n\n");
} while (error);
```

Then write another version of the program that uses a `while` statement instead of a `do` statement to accomplish the same effect.

18 Until interrupted, the following code prints TRUE FOREVER on the screen repeatedly. (In UNIX, type a control-c to effect an interrupt; in MS-DOS, type a control-z.)

```
while (1)
    printf(" TRUE FOREVER ");
```

Write a simple program that accomplishes the same thing, but use a `for` statement instead of a `while` statement. The body of the `for` statement should contain just the empty statement ";".

19 The following code is meant to give you practice with short-circuit evaluation:

```
int    a = 0, b = 0, x;

x = 0 && (a = b = 777);
printf("%d %d %d\n", a, b, x);
x = 777 || (a = ++b);
printf("%d %d %d\n", a, b, x);
```

What gets printed? First write down your answers. Then write a test program to check them.

20 The semantics of logical expressions imply that order of evaluation is critical in some computations. Which of the following two alternate expressions is most likely to be the correct one? Explain.

(a) `if ((x != 0.0) && ((z - x) / x * x < 2.0))`
    .....
(b) `if (((z - x) / x * x < 2.0) && (x != 0.0))`
    .....

21 Suppose that we have three statements called *st1, st2,* and *st3.* We wish to write an `if-else` statement that will test the value of an `int` variable i and execute different combinations of the statements accordingly. The combinations are given in the following tables:

(a) i	execute	(b) i	execute	(c) i	execute
1	st1	1	st2	1	st1, st2
2	st2	2	st1, st3	2	st1, st2
3	st3	3	st1	3	st2, st3

Write programs that read in values for i interactively. Use appropriate `printf()` statements to check that the flow of control mimics the action described in the tables. For example, statements such as

```
if (i == 1)
    printf("statement_1 executed\n");
```

can be used to show that your programs run properly.

22 A polynomial in x of at most degree 2 is given by

$$ax^2 + bx + c$$

Its *discriminant* is defined to be

$$b^2 - 4ac$$

We are interested in the square root of the discriminant (see Exercise 23). If the discriminant is nonnegative, then

$$\sqrt{b^2 - 4ac}$$

has its usual interpretation, but if the discriminant is negative, then

$$\sqrt{b^2 - 4ac} \qquad \text{means} \qquad i\sqrt{-(b^2 - 4ac)}$$

where $i = \sqrt{-1}$, or equivalently, $i^2 = -1$. Write a program that reads in values for a, b, and c and prints the value of the square root of the discriminant. For example, if the values 1, 2, and 3 are read in, then i*2.828427 should be printed.

23 Write a program that repeatedly reads in values for a, b, and c and finds the roots of the polynomial

$$ax^2 + bx + c$$

Recall that the roots are real or complex numbers that solve the equation

$$ax^2 + bx + c = 0$$

When both $a = 0$ and $b = 0$, we consider the case "extremely degenerate" and leave it at that. When $a = 0$ and $b \neq 0$, we consider the case "degenerate." In this case the equation reduces to

$$bx + c = 0$$

and has one root given by $x = -c/b$. When $a \neq 0$ (the general case), the roots are given by

$$root_1 = \frac{1}{2a}(-b + \sqrt{b^2 - 4ac}) \qquad root_2 = \frac{1}{2a}(-b - \sqrt{b^2 - 4ac})$$

The expression under the square root sign is the *discriminant* (see Exercise 22). If the discriminant is positive, then two real roots exist. If the discriminant is zero, then the two roots are real and equal. In this case we say that the polynomial (or the associated equation) has *multiple real roots*. If the discriminant is negative, then the roots are complex. For each set of values for a, b, and c, your program should print the computed root(s) along with one of the following messages:

```
degenerate               two real roots
extremely degenerate     two complex roots
multiple real roots
```

For example, if the values 1, 2, and 3 are read in for a, b, and c, respectively, then

```
two complex roots:  root1 = -1.000000 + i*1.414214
                    root2 = -1.000000 - i*1.414214
```

should be printed.

24 A *truth table* for a boolean function is a table consisting of all possible values for its variables and the corresponding values of the boolean function itself. In Section 4.10, "An Example: Boolean Variables," we created a truth table for the majority function and two other functions. In that table we used 1 and 0 to represent *true* and *false*, respectively. Create separate truth tables for the following boolean functions:

```
b1 || b2 || b3 || b4    !(!b1 || b2) && (!b3 || b4)
```

Use the letters T and F in your truth tables to represent *true* and *false*, respectively. *Hint:* Use the #define mechanism to define a BOOLEX, and write your program to operate on an arbitrary BOOLEX.

25 Write a program to check the proper pairing of braces. Your program should have two variables: one to keep track of left braces, say left_cnt, and the other to keep track of right braces, say right_cnt. Both variables should be initialized to zero. Your program should read and print each character in the input file. The appropriate variable should be incremented each time a brace is encountered. If right_cnt ever exceeds the value of left_cnt, your program should insert the character pair ?? at that point in the output. After all the characters in the input file have been processed, the two variables left_cnt and right_cnt should have the same value. If not, and left_cnt is larger than right_cnt, then a message should be printed that includes the number of right braces missing as a series of that many }'s. For example,

```
ERROR: Missing right braces: }}}
```

Use the macros getchar() and putchar() for input/output. Test your program by processing some files containing your own C code.

26   Extend the program that you wrote in Exercise 25 so that it deals with both braces and parentheses simultaneously.

27   In Section 4.8, "The while Statement," we presented a program that counts blanks, digits, and letters. Modify the program so that lower- and uppercase letters are counted separately.

28   Rewrite the following two pieces of code to avoid using break or continue:

```
while (c = getchar()) {
    if (c == 'E')
        break;
    ++cnt;
    if (c >= '0' && c <= '9')
        ++digit_cnt;
}

i = -5;
n = 50;
while (i < n) {
    ++i;
    if (i == 0)
        continue;
    total += i;
    printf("i = %d and total = %d\n", i, total);
}
```

29   Here is a simple way to test the effect of a continue statement in the body of a for loop. What gets printed?

```
for (putchar('1'); putchar('2'); putchar('3')) {
    putchar('4');
    continue;
    putchar('5');
}
```

30   The mathematical operation min(x, y) can be represented by the conditional expression

```
(x < y) ? x : y
```

In a similar fashion, using only conditional expressions, describe the mathematical operations

```
min(x, y, z)        and        max(x, y, z, w)
```

31 In ANSI C, labels have their own name space, whereas in traditional C they do not. This means that in ANSI C the same identifier can be used for a variable and a label, although it is not considered good programming practice to do so. Write a test program containing the following code and execute it on your ANSI C compiler:

```
int   L = -3;                            /* L is a variable */

if (L < 0)
    goto L;
printf("L = %d\n", L);
L: printf("Exiting label test!\n");    /* L is a label */
```

If a traditional C compiler is available to you, check to see that your program will not compile.

32 (Advanced) Let a be a positive real number, and let the sequence of real numbers x_i be given by

$$x_0 = 1, \quad x_{i+1} = \frac{1}{2}\left(x_i + \frac{a}{x_i}\right) \quad \text{for } i = 0, 1, 2, \ldots$$

It can be shown mathematically that

$$x_i \to \sqrt{a} \quad \text{as } i \to \infty$$

This algorithm is derived from the Newton-Raphson method in numerical analysis. Write a program that reads in the value of a interactively and uses this algorithm to compute the square root of a. As you will see, the algorithm is very efficient. (Nonetheless, it is not the algorithm used by the sqrt() function in the standard library.) Declare x0 and x1 to be of type double, and initialize x1 to 1. Inside a loop do the following:

```
x0 = x1;                   /* save the current value of x1 */
x1 = 0.5 * (x1 + a / x1);  /* compute a new value of x1 */
```

The body of the loop should be executed as long as x0 is not equal to x1. Each time through the loop, print out the iteration count and the values of x1 (converging to the square root of a) and a - x1 * x1 (a check on accuracy).

33 (Advanced) The constant e, which is the base of the natural logarithms, is given to 41 significant figures by

$$e = 2.71828\ 18284\ 59045\ 23536\ 02874\ 71352\ 66249\ 77572$$

Define

$$x_n = \left(1 + \frac{1}{n}\right)^n \qquad \text{for } n = 1, 2, \ldots$$

It can be shown mathematically that

$$x_n \to e \qquad \text{as } n \to \infty$$

Investigate how to calculate e to arbitrary precision using this algorithm. You will find that the algorithm is computationally ineffective (see Exercise 34).

34 (Advanced) In addition to the algorithm given in Exercise 33, the value for e is also given by the infinite series

$$e = 1 + 1 + \frac{1}{2!} + \frac{1}{3!} + \frac{1}{4!} + \cdots$$

This algorithm is computationally effective. Use it to compute e to arbitrary precision.

## CHAPTER 5

FUNCTIONS

The heart of effective problem solving is problem decomposition. Taking a problem and breaking it into small, manageable pieces is critical to writing large programs. In C, the function construct is used to implement this "top-down" method of programming.

A program consists of one or more files, with each file containing zero or more functions, one of them being a main() function. Functions are defined as individual objects that cannot be nested. Program execution begins with main(), which can call other functions, including library functions such as printf() and sqrt(). Functions operate with program variables, and which of these variables are available at a particular place in a function is determined by scope rules. In this chapter we discuss function definition, function declaration, scope rules, storage classes, and recursion.

5.1   FUNCTION DEFINITION

The C code that describes what a function does is called the *function definition*. It must not be confused with the function declaration. A function definition has the following general form:

type function_name(parameter list)
{
    declarations
    statements
}

Everything before the first brace comprises the *header* of the function definition, and everything between the braces comprises the *body* of the function definition. The parameter list is a comma-separated list of declarations. An example of a function definition is

```
int factorial(int n)          /* header */
{                             /* body starts here */
    int   i, product = 1;

    for (i = 2; i <= n; ++i)
        product *= i;
    return product;
}
```

The first `int` tells the compiler that the value returned by the function will be converted, if necessary, to an `int`. The parameter list consists of the declaration `int n`. This tells the compiler that the function takes a single argument of type `int`. An expression such as `factorial(7)` causes the function to be invoked, or called. The effect is to execute the code that comprises the function definition, with `n` having the value 7. Thus functions act as useful abbreviating schemes. Here is another example of a function definition:

```
void wrt_address(void)
{
    printf("%s\n%s\n%s\n%s\n%s\n\n",
    "                *********************",
    "                **    SANTA CLAUS    *",
    "                **    NORTH POLE     *",
    "                **    EARTH          *",
    "                *********************");
}
```

The first `void` tells the compiler that this function returns no value; the second `void` tells the compiler that this function takes no arguments. The expression

```
wrt_address()
```

causes the function to be invoked. For example, to call the function three times we can write

```
for (i = 0; i < 3; ++i)
    wrt_address();
```

A function definition starts with the type of the function. If no value is returned, then the type is `void`. If the type is something other than `void`, then the value returned by the function will be converted, if necessary, to this type. The name of the function is followed by a parenthesized list of parameter declarations. The parameters act as placeholders for values that are passed when the function is invoked.

Sometimes, to emphasize their role as placeholders, these parameters are called the *formal parameters* of the function. The function body is a block, or compound statement, and it too may contain declarations. Some examples of function definitions are

```
void nothing(void) { }      /* this function does nothing */

double twice(double x)
{
   return (2.0 * x);
}

int all_add(int a, int b)
{
   int   c;
   .....
   return (a + b + c);
}
```

If a function definition does not specify the function type, then it is `int` by default. For example, the last function definition could be given by

```
all_add(int a, int b)
{
   .....
```

However, it is considered good programming practice to specify the function type explicitly. (See Exercise 5 for further discussion.)

Any variables declared in the body of a function are said to be "local" to that function. Other variables may be declared external to the function. These are called "global" variables. An example is

```
#include <stdio.h>

int   a = 33;      /* a is external and initialized to 33 */

int main(void)
{
   int   b = 77;                /* b is local to main() */

   printf("a = %d\n", a);    /* a is global to main() */
   printf("b = %d\n", b);
   return 0;
}
```

In traditional C, the function definition has a different syntax. The declarations of the variables in the parameter list occur after the parameter list itself and just before the first brace. An example is

```
void f(a, b, c, x, y)
int      a, b, c;
double   x, y;
{
   . . . . .
```

The order in which the parameters are declared is immaterial. If there are no parameters, then a pair of empty parentheses is used. ANSI C compilers will accept this traditional syntax as well as the newer syntax. Thus traditional code can still be compiled by an ANSI C compiler.

There are several important reasons to write programs as collections of many small functions. It is simpler to correctly write a small function to do one job. Both the writing and debugging are made easier. It is also easier to maintain or modify such a program. One can readily change just the set of functions that need to be rewritten, expecting the rest of the code to work correctly. Also, small functions tend to be self-documenting and highly readable. A useful heuristic for writing good programs is to write each function so that its code fits on a single page.

5.2   THE return STATEMENT

The return statement may or may not include an expression.

    return_statement ::= return; | return *expression*;

Some examples are

```
return;
return ++a;
return (a * b);
```

The expression being returned can be enclosed in parentheses, but this is not required.

When a return statement is encountered, execution of the function is terminated and control is passed back to the calling environment. If the return statement contains an expression, then the value of the expression is passed back to the calling environment as well. Moreover, this value will be converted, if necessary, to the type of the function as specified in the function definition.

```
float f(char a, char b, char c)
{
   int   i;
   .....
   return i;   /* the value returned will be converted to a float */
}
```

There can be zero or more `return` statements in a function. If there is no `return` statement, then control is passed back to the calling environment when the closing brace of the body is encountered. This is called "falling off the end." The following function definition illustrates how two `return` statements might be used:

```
double absolute_value(double x)
{
   if (x >= 0.0)
      return x;
   else
      return -x;
}
```

Even though a function returns a value, a program does not need to use it.

```
while (...) {
   getchar();       /* get a char, but do nothing with it */
   c = getchar();   /* c will be processed */
   .....
}
```

5.3 FUNCTION PROTOTYPES

Functions should be declared before they are used. ANSI C provides for a new function declaration syntax called the *function prototype*. A function prototype tells the compiler the number and type of arguments that are to be passed to the function and the type of the value that is to be returned by the function. An example is

```
double   sqrt(double);
```

This tells the compiler that `sqrt()` is a function that takes a single argument of type `double` and returns a `double`. The general form of a function prototype is

   type   function_name (parameter type list);

The parameter type list is typically a comma-separated list of types. Identifiers are optional; they do not affect the prototype. For example, the function prototype

```
void f(char c, int i);          is equivalent to        void f(char, int);
```

The identifiers such as c and i that occur in parameter type lists in function prototypes are not used by the compiler. Their purpose is to provide documentation to the programmer and other readers of the code. The keyword void is used if a function takes no arguments. Also, the keyword void is used if no value is returned by the function. If a function takes a variable number of arguments, then the ellipsis (...) is used. See, for example, the function prototype for printf() in the standard header file *stdio.h*.

Function prototypes allow the compiler to check the code more thoroughly. Also, values passed to functions are properly coerced, if possible. For example, if the function prototype for sqrt() has been specified, then the function call sqrt(4) will yield the correct value. Because the compiler knows that sqrt() takes a double, the int value 4 will be promoted to a double and the correct value will be returned. (See Exercise 5 for further discussion.)

In traditional C, parameter type lists are not allowed in function declarations. For example, the function declaration of sqrt() is given by

```
double   sqrt();      /* traditional C style */
```

Even though ANSI C compilers will accept this style, function prototypes are preferred. With this declaration, the function call sqrt(4) will not yield the correct value (see Exercise 5).

Function Prototypes in C++

In C++, function prototypes are required, and the use of void in the parameter type list in both function prototypes and function definitions is optional. Thus, for example, in C++

```
void f()          is equivalent to        void f(void)
```

Note carefully that this results in a conflict with traditional C. In traditional C, a function declaration such as

```
int f();
```

means that f() takes an unknown number of arguments. In traditional C, void is not a keyword. Thus it cannot be used in a parameter list in a function declaration or function definition.

5.4   AN EXAMPLE: CREATING A TABLE OF POWERS

In this section we give an example of a program that is written using a number of functions. For simplicity, we will write all the functions one after another in one file. The purpose of the program is to print a table of powers.

```c
#include <stdio.h>

#define    N    7

long    power(int, int);
void    prn_heading(void);
void    prn_tbl_of_powers(int);

int main(void)
{
   prn_heading();
   prn_tbl_of_powers(N);
   return 0;
}

void prn_heading(void)
{
   printf("\n:::::  A TABLE OF POWERS  :::::\n\n");
}

void prn_tbl_of_powers(int n)
{
   int    i, j;

   for (i = 1; i <= n; ++i) {
      for (j = 1; j <= n; ++j)
         if (j == 1)
            printf("%ld", power(i, j));
         else
            printf("%9ld", power(i, j));
      putchar('\n');
   }
}

long power(int m, int n)
{
   int    i;
   long    product = 1;

   for (i = 1; i <= n; ++i)
      product *= m;
   return product;
}
```

Here is the output of the program:

```
:::::   A TABLE OF POWERS   :::::

1           1           1           1           1           1           1
2           4           8           16          32          64          128
3           9           27          81          243         729         2187
. . . . .
```

Note that the first column consists of integers raised to the first power, the second column consists of integers raised to the second power, and so forth. In our program we have put the function prototypes near the top of the file. This makes them visible throughout the rest of the file. We used the type `long` so the program will produce the same output whether the machine has 2- or 4-byte words. Note that the function `power()` computes the quantity m^n, which is m raised to the nth power.

Our program illustrates in a very simple way the idea of top-down design. The programmer thinks of the tasks to be performed and codes each task as a function. If a particular task is complicated, then that task, in turn, can be subdivided into other tasks, each coded as a function. An additional benefit of this is that the program as a whole becomes more readable and self-documenting.

5.5   FUNCTION DECLARATIONS FROM THE COMPILER'S VIEWPOINT

To the compiler, function declarations are generated in various ways: by function invocation, by function definition, and by explicit function declarations and function prototypes. If a function call, say `f(x)`, is encountered before any declaration, definition, or prototype for it occurs, then the compiler assumes a default declaration of the form

```
int   f();
```

Nothing is assumed about the parameter list for the function. Now suppose that the following function definition occurs first:

```
int f(x)          /* traditional C style */
double x;
{
    . . . . .
```

This provides both declaration and definition to the compiler. Again, however, nothing is assumed about the parameter list. It is the programmer's responsibility to pass only a single argument of type `double`. A function call such as `f(1)` can be expected to fail because `1` is of type `int`, not `double`. Now suppose that we use, instead, an ANSI C style definition:

```
int f(double x)        /* ANSI C style */
{
    .....
```

The compiler now knows about the parameter list as well. In this case a function call such as `f(1)` can be expected to work properly. When an `int` gets passed as an argument, it will be converted to a `double`.

A function prototype is a special case of a function declaration. A good programming style is to give either the function definition (ANSI C style) or the function prototype or both before a function is used. A major reason for including standard header files is because they contain function prototypes.

Limitations

Function definitions and prototypes have certain limitations. The function storage class specifier (see Section 5.11), if present, can be either `extern` or `static`, but not both; `auto` and `register` cannot be used. The types "array of ..." and "function returning ..." cannot be returned by a function. However, a pointer representing an array or a function can be returned (see Chapter 6). The only storage class specifier that can occur in the parameter type list is `register`. Parameters cannot be initialized.

5.6 AN ALTERNATE STYLE FOR FUNCTION DEFINITION ORDER

Suppose we want to write a program in a single file. If our program contains more than one function definition, we usually put #includes and #defines at the top of the file, other program elements such as templates of enumeration types (Chapter 7) and templates of structures and unions (Chapter 9) next, then a list of function prototypes, and finally the function definitions, starting with `main()`. Because function definitions also serve as function prototypes, an alternate style is to remove the list of function prototypes and to put the function definition of any function that gets called before the function definition of its caller. In particular, `main()` goes last in the file.

Let us illustrate this alternate style by modifying the *tbl_of_powers* program that we wrote in Section 5.4. Here is another way of writing that program:

```
#include <stdio.h>

#define    N    7

void prn_heading(void)
{
    .....
}

long power(int m, int n)
{
    .....
}

void prn_tbl_of_powers(int n)
{
    .....
    printf("%ld", power(i, j));
    .....
}

int main(void)
{
    prn_heading();
    prn_tbl_of_powers(N);
    return 0;
}
```

Because power() is called by prn_tbl_of_powers(), the function definition for power() must come first. Similarly, the function definitions of the two functions called by main() must come before the function definition of main(). (See Exercise 10 for further discussion.)

Although we favor the top-down style that puts main() first, we will occasionally use this alternate style as well.

5.7 FUNCTION INVOCATION AND CALL BY VALUE

A program is made up of one or more function definitions, with one of these being main(). Program execution always begins with main(). When program control encounters a function name, the function is called, or invoked. This means that program control passes to that function. After the function does its work, program control is passed back to the calling environment, which then continues with its work.

Functions are invoked by writing their name and an appropriate list of arguments within parentheses. Typically, these arguments match in number and type (or compatible type) the parameters in the parameter list in the function definition. The compiler enforces type compatibility when function prototypes are used. All arguments are passed "call by value." This means that each argument is evaluated and its value is used locally in place of the corresponding formal parameter. Thus, if a variable is passed to a function, the stored value of that variable in the calling environment will not be changed. Here is an example that clearly illustrates the concept of "call by value":

```
#include <stdio.h>

int main(void)
{
    int   n = 3, sum, compute_sum(int);

    printf("%d\n", n);          /* 3 is printed */
    sum = compute_sum(n);
    printf("%d\n", n);          /* 3 is printed */
    printf("%d\n", sum);        /* 6 is printed */
    return 0;
}

int compute_sum(int n)         /* sum the integers from 1 to n */
{
    int   sum = 0;

    for ( ; n > 0; --n)        /* stored value of n is changed */
        sum += n;
    return sum;
}
```

Even though n is passed to compute_sum() and the value of n in the body of that function is changed, the value of n in the calling environment remains unchanged. It is the *value* of n that is being passed, not n itself.

The "call by value" mechanism is in contrast to that of "call by reference." In Chapter 6, we will explain how to accomplish the effect of "call by reference." This is a way of passing addresses (references) of variables to a function that then allows the body of the function to make changes to the values of variables in the calling environment.

Function invocation means

1   Each expression in the argument list is evaluated.

2   The value of the expression is converted, if necessary, to the type of the formal parameter, and that value is assigned to its corresponding formal parameter at the beginning of the body of the function.

3   The body of the function is executed.

4   If a `return` statement is executed, then control is passed back to the calling environment.

5   If the `return` statement includes an expression, then the value of the expression is converted, if necessary, to the type given by the type specifier of the function, and that value is passed back to the calling environment, too.

6   If the `return` statement does not include an expression, then no useful value is returned to the calling environment.

7   If no `return` statement is present, then control is passed back to the calling environment when the end of the body of the function is reached. No useful value is returned.

8   All arguments are passed "call by value."

5.8   DEVELOPING A LARGE PROGRAM

Typically, a large program is written in a separate directory as a collection of *.h* and *.c* files, with each *.c* file containing one or more function definitions. Each *.c* file can be recompiled as needed, saving time for both the programmer and the machine. We discuss this further in Chapter 11, where we explain about libraries and the use of *make*.

Let us suppose we are developing a large program called *pgm*. At the top of each of our *.c* files we put the line

```
#include "pgm.h"
```

When the preprocessor encounters this directive, it looks first in the current directory for the file *pgm.h*. If there is such a file, then it gets included. If not, then the preprocessor looks in other system-dependent places for the file. If the file *pgm.h* cannot be found, then the preprocessor issues an error message and compilation stops.

Our header file *pgm.h* may contain #includes, #defines, templates of enumeration types, templates of structure and union types, other programming constructs, and finally a list of function prototypes at the bottom. Thus *pgm.h* contains program elements that are appropriate for our program as a whole. Because the header file *pgm.h* occurs at the top of each .c file, it acts as the "glue" that binds our program together.

Create a .h file that gets included in all the .c files

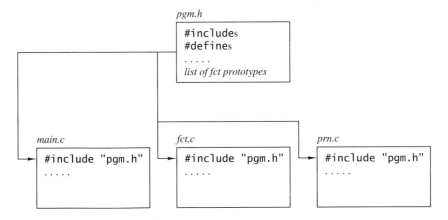

Let us show a very simple example of how this works. We will write our program in a separate directory. It will consist of a *.h* file and three *.c* files. Typically, the name of the directory and the name of the program are the same. Here is our program:

In file pgm.h:

```
#include <stdio.h>
#include <stdlib.h>

#define    N    3

void    fct1(int k);
void    fct2(void);
void    prn_info(char *);
```

In file main.c:

```
#include "pgm.h"

int main(void)
{
    char    ans;
    int     i, n = N;

    printf("%s",
        "This program does not do very much.\n"
        "Do you want more information?   ");
    scanf(" %c", &ans);
    if (ans == 'y' || ans == 'Y')
        prn_info("pgm");
    for (i = 0; i < n; ++i)
        fct1(i);
    printf("Bye!\n");
    return 0;
}
```

In file fct.c:

```
#include "pgm.h"

void fct1(int n)
{
   int   i;

   printf("Hello from fct1()\n");
   for (i = 0; i < n; ++i)
      fct2();
}

void fct2(void)
{
   printf("Hello from fct2()\n");
}
```

In file prn.c:

```
#include "pgm.h"

void prn_info(char *pgm_name)
{
   printf("Usage:  %s\n\n", pgm_name);
   printf("%s\n",
      "This program illustrates how one can write a program\n"
      "in more than one file.  In this example, we have a\n"
      "single .h file that gets included at the top of our\n"
      "three .c files.  Thus the .h file acts as the \"glue\"\n"
      "that binds the program together.\n"
      "\n"
      "Note that the functions fct1() and fct2() when called\n"
      "only say \"hello.\"  When writing a serious program, the\n"
      "programmer sometimes does this in a first working\n"
      "version of the code.\n");
}
```

Note that we used the type char * (pointer to char) in our program. (We will discuss pointers in Chapter 6.) We compile the program with the command

cc −o pgm main.c fct.c prn.c

The compiler makes the executable file *pgm* along with three .o file that correspond to .c files. (In MS-DOS, they are .*obj* files.) The .o files are called *object* files. (For further discussion about these object files and how the compiler can use them, see Section 11.13, "The C Compiler.")

For a more interesting example of a program written in separate files, see Section 7.6, "An Example: The Game of Paper, Rock, Scissors." Other examples are available via *ftp* and the Internet. If you are connected to the Internet, try the following command:

  ftp bc.aw.com

After you have made a connection, you can change directory (*cd*) to *bc*, and then *cd* to *kelley_pohl*, and then look around. A large program is much easier to investigate if you have the source code. Then you can print out whatever is of interest and, with the help of a debugger (see Chapter 11), you can step through the program if you wish to do so.

What Constitutes a Large Program?

For an individual, a large program might consist of just a few hundred lines of code. Which lines get counted? Usually all the lines in any *READ_ME* files (there should be at least one), the *.h* files, the *.c* files, and the *makefile* (discussed in Chapter 11). In UNIX, the word count utility *wc* can be used to do this:

  *wc READ_ME *.h *.c makefile*

In industry, programs are typically written by teams of programmers, and a large program might be considered anything over a hundred thousand lines.

The style of writing a program in its own directory as a collection of *.h* and *.c* files works well for any serious program, whether it is large or small, and all experienced programmers follow this style. To become proficient in the style, the programmer has to learn how to use *make* or some similar tool (see Chapter 11).

5.9   USING ASSERTIONS

The C system supplies the standard header file *assert.h*, which the programmer can include to obtain access to the `assert()` macro. In Chapter 8 we will discuss this macro in detail. Here, we want to show how the programmer can use assertions to facilitate the programming process. Consider the following code:

```
#include <assert.h>
#include <stdio.h>

int    f(int a, int b);
int    g(int c);

int main(void)
{
    int    a, b, c;

    .....
    scanf("%d%d", &a, &b);
    .....
    c = f(a, b);
    assert(c > 0);                /* an assertion */
    .....
}
```

If the expression passed as an argument to assert() is false, the system will print
a message and the program will be aborted. In this example, we are supposing that
f() embodies an algorithm that is supposed to generate a positive integer, which
gets returned. Perhaps someone else wrote the code for the function definition of
f(), and you just want to be sure that the value returned by f() is positive. In the
function definition for f(), it may be important that the arguments a and b satisfy
certain conditions. Let us suppose that we expect a to have either 1 or –1 as its
value and that we expect b to lie in the interval [7, 11]. We can use assertions to
enforce these conditions.

```
int f(int a, int b)
{
    .....
    assert(a == 1 || a == -1);
    assert(b >= 7 && b <= 11);
    .....
}
```

Assertions are easy to write, add robustness to the code, and help other readers of the
code understand its intent. The use of assertions is considered good programming
methodology.

5.10   SCOPE RULES

The basic rule of scoping is that identifiers are accessible only within the block in
which they are declared. They are unknown outside the boundaries of that block.
This would be an easy rule to follow, except that programmers, for a variety of
reasons, choose to use the same identifier in different declarations. We then have
the question of which object the identifier refers to. Let us give a simple example
of this state of affairs.

```
{
    int a = 2;              /* outer block a */
    printf("%d\n", a);      /* 2 is printed */
    {
        int a = 5;          /* inner block a */
        printf("%d\n", a);  /* 5 is printed */
    }                       /* back to the outer block */
    printf("%d\n", ++a);    /* 3 is printed */
}
```

An equivalent piece of code would be

```
{
    int a_outer = 2;
    printf("%d\n", a_outer);
    {
        int a_inner = 5;
        printf("%d\n", a_inner);
    }
    printf("%d\n", ++a_outer);
}
```

Each block introduces its own nomenclature. An outer block name is valid unless an inner block redefines it. If redefined, the outer block name is hidden, or
masked, from the inner block. Inner blocks may be nested to arbitrary depths that
are determined by system limitations. The following piece of code illustrates hidden

variables in three nested blocks:

```
{
    int    a = 1, b = 2, c = 3;

    printf("%3d%3d%3d\n", a, b, c);           /* 1  2  3  */
    {
        int      b = 4;
        float    c = 5.0;

        printf("%3d%3d%5.1f\n", a, b, c);     /* 1  4  5.0  */
        a = b;
        {
            int    c;

            c = b;
            printf("%3d%3d%3d\n", a, b, c);   /* 4  4  4  */
        }
        printf("%3d%3d%5.1f\n", a, b, c);     /* 4  4  5.0  */
    }
    printf("%3d%3d%3d\n", a, b, c);           /* 4  2  3  */
}
```

The int variable a is declared in the outer block and is never redeclared. Therefore, it is available in both nested inner blocks. The variables b and c are redeclared in the first inner block, thus hiding the outer block variables of the same name. Upon exiting this block, both b and c are again available as the outer block variables, with their values intact from the outer block initialization. The innermost block again redeclares c, so that both c (inner) and c (outer) are hidden by c (innermost).

Parallel and Nested Blocks

Two blocks can come one after another, in which case the second block has no knowledge of the variables declared in the first block. Such blocks, residing at the same level, are called *parallel blocks*. Functions are declared in parallel at the outermost level. The following code illustrates two parallel blocks nested in an outer block:

```
{
    int    a, b;
    .....
    {                        /* inner block 1 */
      float    b;
      .....                  /* int a is known, but not int b */
    }
    .....
    {                        /* inner block 2 */
      float    a;
      .....                  /* int b is known, but not int a */
                             /* nothing in inner block 1 in known */
    }
    .....
}
```

Parallel and nested blocks can be combined in arbitrarily complicated schemes. The chief reason for blocks is to allow memory for variables to be allocated where needed. If memory is scarce, block exit will release the storage allocated locally to that block, allowing the memory to be used for some other purpose. Also, blocks associate names in their neighborhood of use, making the code more readable. Functions can be viewed as named blocks with parameters and return statements allowed.

Using a Block for Debugging

One common use for a block is for debugging purposes. Imagine we are in a section of code where a variable, say v, is misbehaving. By inserting a block temporarily into the code, we can use local variables that do not interfere with the rest of the program.

```
{                               /* debugging starts here */
    static int    cnt = 0;

    printf("*** debug: cnt = %d    v = %d\n", ++cnt, v);
}
```

The variable cnt is local to the block. It will not interfere with another variable of the same name in an outer block. Because its storage class is static, it retains its old value when the block is reentered. Here, it is being used to count the number of times the block is executed. (Perhaps we are inside a for loop.) We are assuming that the variable v has been declared in an outer block and is therefore known in this block. We are printing its value for debugging purposes. Later, after we have fixed our code, this block becomes extraneous, and we remove it.

5.11 STORAGE CLASSES

Every variable and function in C has two attributes: *type* and *storage class*. The four storage classes are automatic, external, register, and static, with corresponding keywords

auto   extern   register   static

By far the most common storage class for variables is automatic. However, the programmer needs to know about all the storage classes. They all have important uses.

The Storage Class auto

Variables declared within function bodies are automatic by default. Thus automatic is the most common of the four storage classes. If a compound statement starts with variable declarations, then these variables can be acted on within the scope of the enclosing compound statement. A compound statement with declarations is called a *block* to distinguish it from one that does not begin with declarations.

Declarations of variables within blocks are implicitly of storage class automatic. The keyword auto can be used to explicitly specify the storage class. An example is

```
auto int     a, b, c;
auto float   f;
```

Because the storage class is automatic by default, the keyword auto is seldom used.

When a block is entered, the system allocates memory for the automatic variables. Within that block, these variables are defined and are considered "local" to the block. When the block is exited, the system releases the memory that was set aside for the automatic variables. Thus the values of these variables are lost. If the block is reentered, the system once again allocates memory, but previous values are unknown. The body of a function definition constitutes a block if it contains declarations. If it does, then each invocation of the function sets up a new environment.

The Storage Class extern

One method of transmitting information across blocks and functions is to use external variables. When a variable is declared outside a function, storage is permanently assigned to it, and its storage class is extern. A declaration for an external variable can look just the same as a declaration for a variable that occurs inside a function or block. Such a variable is considered to be global to all functions declared after it, and upon exit from the block or function, the external variable remains in existence.

The following program illustrates these ideas:

```
#include <stdio.h>

int    a = 1, b = 2, c = 3;          /* global variables */
int    f(void);                      /* function prototype */

int main(void)
{
    printf("%3d\n", f());            /* 12 is printed */
    printf("%3d%3d%3d\n", a, b, c);  /* 4  2  3 is printed */
    return 0;
}

int f(void)
{
    int    b, c;                     /* b and c are local */
                                     /* global b, c are masked */
    a = b = c = 4;
    return (a + b + c);
}
```

Note that we could have written

```
extern int    a = 1, b = 2, c = 3;     /* global variables */
```

This use of extern will cause some traditional C compilers to complain. In ANSI C, this use is allowed but not required. Variables defined outside a function have external storage class, even if the keyword extern is not used. Such variables cannot have automatic or register storage class. The keyword static can be used, but its use is special, as explained in Section 5.12, "Static External Variables."

The keyword extern is used to tell the compiler to "look for it elsewhere, either in this file or in some other file." Let us rewrite the last program to illustrate a typical use of the keyword extern.

In file file1.c:

```
#include <stdio.h>

int    a = 1, b = 2, c = 3;       /* external variables */
int    f(void);

int main(void)
{
    printf("%3d\n", f());
    printf("%3d%3d%3d\n", a, b, c);
    return 0;
}
```

In file file2.c:

```
int f(void)
{
    extern int    a;               /* look for it elsewhere */
    int           b, c;

    a = b = c = 4;
    return (a + b + c);
}
```

The two files can be compiled separately. The use of `extern` in the second file tells the compiler that the variable a will be defined elsewhere, either in this file or in some other. The ability to compile files separately is important when writing large programs.

External variables never disappear. Because they exist throughout the execution life of the program, they can be used to transmit values across functions. They may, however, be hidden if the identifier is redefined. Another way of conceiving of external variables is to think of them as being declared in a block that encompasses the whole program.

Information can be passed into a function two ways: by use of external variables and by use of the parameter mechanism. Although there are exceptions, the use of the parameter mechanism is the preferred method. It tends to improve the modularity of the code, and it reduces the possibility of undesirable side effects.

One form of side effect occurs when a function changes a global variable from within its body rather than through its parameter list. Such a construction is error prone. Correct practice is to effect changes to global variables through the parameter and `return` mechanisms. Adhering to this practice improves modularity and readability, and because changes are localized, programs are typically easier to write and maintain.

All functions have external storage class. This means that we can use the keyword `extern` in function definitions and in function prototypes, if we wish to do so. For example,

```
extern double   sin(double);
```

is a valid function prototype for the `sin()` function, and for its function definition we can write

```
extern double sin(double x)
{
    .....
```

The Storage Class `register`

The storage class `register` tells the compiler that the associated variables should be stored in high-speed memory registers, provided it is physically and semantically possible to do so. Because resource limitations and semantic constraints sometimes make this impossible, this storage class defaults to automatic whenever the compiler cannot allocate an appropriate physical register. Typically, the compiler has only a few such registers available. Many of these are required for system use and cannot be allocated otherwise.

Basically, the use of storage class `register` is an attempt to improve execution speed. When speed is a concern, the programmer may choose a few variables that are most frequently accessed and declare them to be of storage class `register`. Common candidates for such treatment include loop variables and function parameters. Here is an example:

```
{
    register int   i;

    for (i = 0; i < LIMIT; ++i) {
        .....
    }
}          /* block exit will free the register */
```

The declaration

```
register i;
```

is equivalent to `register int i;`

If a storage class is specified in a declaration and the type is absent, then the type is `int` by default.

Note that in our example the register variable `i` was declared as close to its place of use as possible. This is to allow maximum availability of the physical registers, using them only when needed. Always remember that a register declaration is taken only as *advice* to the compiler.

The Storage Class `static`

Static declarations have two important and distinct uses. The more elementary use is to allow a local variable to retain its previous value when the block is reentered. This is in contrast to ordinary automatic variables, which lose their value upon block exit and must be reinitialized. The second and more subtle use is in connection with external declarations. We will discuss this in the next section.

As an example of the value-retention use of `static`, we will write the outline of a function that behaves differently depending on how many times it has been called.

```
void f(void)
{
    static int   cnt = 0;

    ++cnt;
    if (cnt % 2 == 0)
        .....                /* do something */
    else
        .....                /* do something different */
}
```

The first time the function is invoked, the variable `cnt` is initialized to zero. On function exit, the value of `cnt` is preserved in memory. Whenever the function is invoked again, `cnt` is not reinitialized. Instead, it retains its previous value from the last time the function was called. The declaration of `cnt` as a `static int` inside of `f()` keeps it private to `f()`. If it were declared outside of the function, then other functions could access it, too.

5.12 STATIC EXTERNAL VARIABLES

The second and more subtle use of `static` is in connection with external declarations. With external constructs it provides a "privacy" mechanism that is very important for program modularity. By privacy, we mean visibility or scope restrictions on otherwise accessible variables or functions.

At first glance, static external variables seem unnecessary. External variables already retain their values across block and function exit. The difference is that static external variables are scope-restricted external variables. The scope is the remainder of the source file in which they are declared. Thus they are unavailable to functions defined earlier in the file or to functions defined in other files, even if these functions attempt to use the `extern` storage class keyword.

```
void f(void)
{
    .....               /* v is not available here */
}

static int  v;    /* static external variable */

void g(void)
{
    .....               /* v can be used here */
}
```

Let us use this facility to provide a variable that is global to a family of functions but, at the same time, is private to the file. We will write two pseudo random number generators, both of which use the same seed. [The algorithm is based on linear congruential methods; see *The Art of Computer Programming*, 2d ed., vol. 2, *Seminumerical Algorithms*, by Donald Ervin Knuth (Reading, Mass.: Addison-Wesley, 1981)].

```
/* A family of pseudo random number generators. */

#define   INITIAL_SEED        17
#define   MULTIPLIER          25173
#define   INCREMENT           13849
#define   MODULUS             65536
#define   FLOATING_MODULUS    65536.0

static unsigned   seed = INITIAL_SEED;   /* external, but
                                             private to this file */
unsigned random(void)
{
    seed = (MULTIPLIER * seed + INCREMENT) % MODULUS;
    return seed;
}

double probability(void)
{
    seed = (MULTIPLIER * seed + INCREMENT) % MODULUS;
    return (seed / FLOATING_MODULUS);
}
```

The function `random()` produces an apparently random sequence of integer values between 0 and `MODULUS`. The function `probability()` produces an apparently random sequence of floating values between 0 and 1.

Notice that a call to random() or probability() produces a new value of the variable seed that depends on its old value. Because seed is a static external variable, it is private to this file and its value is preserved between function calls. We can now create functions in other files that invoke these random number generators without worrying about side effects.

A last use of static is as a storage class specifier for function definitions and prototypes. This use causes the scope of the function to be restricted. Static functions are visible only within the file in which they are defined. Unlike ordinary functions, which can be accessed from other files, a static function is available throughout its own file, but no other. Again, this facility is useful in developing private modules of function definitions.

```
static int   g(void);       /* function prototype */

void f(int a)               /* function definition */
{
    . . . . .               /* g() is available here,
                               but not in other files */
}

static int g(void)          /* function definition */
{
    . . . . .
}
```

5.13   DEFAULT INITIALIZATION

In C, both external variables and static variables that are not explicitly initialized by the programmer are initialized to zero by the system. This includes arrays, strings, pointers, structures, and unions. For arrays and strings, it means that each element is initialized to zero; for structures and unions, it means that each member is initialized to zero. In contrast to this, automatic and register variables usually are not initialized by the system. This means they start with "garbage" values. Although some C systems do initialize automatic variables to zero, this feature should not be relied on; doing so makes the code nonportable.

5.14 RECURSION

A function is said to be recursive if it calls itself, either directly or indirectly. In C, all functions can be used recursively. In its simplest form the idea of recursion is straightforward. Try the following program:

```
#include <stdio.h>

int main(void)
{
    printf("  The universe is never ending!  ");
    main();
    return 0;
}
```

Here is another example of a recursive function. It computes the sum of the first n positive integers.

```
int sum(int n)
{
    if (n <= 1)
        return n;
    else
        return (n + sum(n - 1));
}
```

The recursive function sum( ) is analyzed as illustrated in the following table. First the base case is considered. Then working out from the base case, the other cases are considered.

Function call	Value returned		
sum(1)	1		
sum(2)	2 + sum(1)	or	2 + 1
sum(3)	3 + sum(2)	or	3 + 2 + 1
sum(4)	4 + sum(3)	or	4 + 3 + 2 + 1

Simple recursive routines follow a standard pattern. Typically there is a base case (or cases) that is tested for upon entry to the function. Then there is a general recursive case in which one of the variables, often an integer, is passed as an argument in such a way as to ultimately lead to the base case. In sum( ), the variable n was reduced by 1 each time until the base case with n equal to 1 was reached.

Let us write a few more recursive functions to practice this technique. For a nonnegative integer n, the factorial of n, written $n!$, is defined by

$$0! = 1, \qquad n! = n(n-1)\cdots 3 \cdot 2 \cdot 1 \qquad \text{for } n > 0$$

or equivalently,

$$0! = 1, \qquad n! = n((n-1)!) \qquad \text{for } n > 0$$

Thus, for example, $5! = 5 \cdot 4 \cdot 3 \cdot 2 \cdot 1 = 120$. Using the recursive definition of factorial, it is easy to write a recursive version of the factorial function.

```
int factorial(int n)      /* recursive version */
{
    if (n <= 1)
        return 1;
    else
        return (n * factorial(n - 1));
}
```

This code is correct and will work properly within the limits of integer precision available on a given system. However, because the numbers $n!$ grow large very fast, the function call factorial(n) yields a valid result for only a few values of n. On our system the function call factorial(12) returns a correct value, but if the argument to the function is greater than 12, an incorrect value is returned. This type of programming error is common. Functions that are logically correct can return incorrect values if the logical operations in the body of the function are beyond the integer precision available to the system.

As in sum( ), when an integer n is passed to factorial( ), the recursion activates n nested copies of the function before returning level by level to the original call. This means that n function calls are used for this computation. Most simple recursive functions can be easily rewritten as iterative functions.

```
int factorial(int n)      /* iterative version */
{
    int   product = 1;

    for ( ; n > 1; --n)
        product *= n;
    return product;
}
```

For a given input value, both factorial functions return the same value over the positive integers, but the iterative version requires only one function call regardless of the value passed in.

The next example illustrates a recursive function that manipulates characters. It can easily be rewritten as an equivalent iterative function. We leave this as an exercise. The program first prompts the user to type in a line. Then by means of a recursive function it writes the line backwards.

```
/* Write a line backwards. */

#include <stdio.h>

void  wrt_it(void);

int main(void)
{

    printf("Input a line:   ");
    wrt{_}it();
    printf("\n\n");
    return 0;
}

void wrt_it(void)
{
    int    c;

    if ((c = getchar()) != '\n')
        wrt_it();
    putchar(c);
}
```

If the user types in the line sing a song of sixpence when prompted, then the following appears on the screen:

```
Input a line:   sing a song of sixpence

ecnepxis fo gnos a gnis
```

DISSECTION OF THE *wrt_bkwrds* PROGRAM

■ ```
printf("Input a line: ");
wrt_it();
```
First a prompt to the user is printed. The user writes a line and terminates it by typing a carriage return, which is the character \n. Then the recursive function wrt_it() is invoked.
```

■ `void wrt_it(void)`
   `{`
   `    int    c;`
   We could have declared `c` to be of type `char` because in this function there is
   no test for EOF.

■ `if ((c = getchar()) != '\n')`
   `    wrt_it();`
   If the character read in is not a newline, then `wrt_it()` is invoked again, which
   causes another character to be read in, and so forth. Each call has its own
   local storage for the variable `c`. Each `c` is local to a particular invocation of the
   function `wrt_it()`, and each `c` stores one of the characters in the input stream.
   The function calls are stacked until the newline character is read.

■ `putchar(c);`
   Only after the newline character is read does anything get written. Each invocation of `wrt_it()` now prints the value stored in its local variable `c`. First the
   newline character is printed, then the character just before it, and so on, until
   the first character is printed. Thus the input line is reversed.

Efficiency Considerations

Many algorithms have both iterative and recursive formulations. Typically, recursion
is more elegant and requires fewer variables to make the same calculation. Recursion
takes care of its book-keeping by stacking arguments and variables for each invocation. This stacking of arguments, while invisible to the user, is still costly in time
and space. On some machines a simple recursive call with one integer argument can
require eight 32-bit words on the stack.

Let us discuss efficiency with respect to the calculation of the Fibonacci sequence,
a particularly egregious example. This sequence is defined recursively by

$$f_0 = 0, \qquad f_1 = 1, \qquad f_{i+1} = f_i + f_{i-1} \qquad \text{for } i = 1, 2, \ldots$$

Except for f_0 and f_1, every element in the sequence is the sum of the previous
two elements. The sequence begins 0, 1, 1, 2, 3, 5, ... Here is a function that
computes Fibonacci numbers recursively:

```
int fibonacci(int n)
{
   if (n <= 1)
      return n;
   else
      return (fibonacci(n - 1) + fibonacci(n - 2));
}
```

As the following table shows, a large number of function calls is required to compute the nth Fibonacci number for even moderate values of n.

Value of n	Value of fibonacci(n)	Number of function calls required to recursively compute fibonacci(n)
0	0	1
1	1	1
2	1	3
3	2	5
. . . .		
7	13	41
8	21	67
9	34	109
. . . .		
23	28657	92735
24	46368	150049
25	75025	242785
. . . .		
41	165580141	535828591
42	267914296	866988873
43	433494437	1402817465

Although it is seductive to use recursion, one must be careful about run-time limitations and inefficiencies. It is sometimes necessary to recode a recursion as an equivalent iteration.

Some programmers feel that because the use of recursion is inefficient, it should not be used. The inefficiencies, however, are often of little consequence—as in the example of the quicksort algorithm given in Chapter 8. For many applications, recursive code is easier to write, understand, and maintain. These reasons often prescribe its use.

5.15 SUMMARY

1 Functions are the most general structuring concept in C. They should be used to implement "top-down" problem solving—namely, breaking up a problem into smaller and smaller subproblems until each piece is readily expressed in code.

2 A return statement terminates the execution of a function and passes control back to the calling environment. If the return statement contains an expression, then the value of the expression is passed back to the calling environment as well.

3 A function prototype tells the compiler the number and type of arguments that are to be passed to the function. The general form of a function prototype is

> *type function_name(parameter list)*;

The parameter type list is typically a comma-separated list of types, with optional identifiers. If a function takes no arguments, then the keyword `void` is used. If the function returns no value, then the function type is `void`.

4 Arguments to functions are passed by value. They must be type compatible with the corresponding parameter types given by the function definition or the function prototype.

5 The storage class of a function is always `extern`, and its type specifier is `int` unless otherwise explicitly declared. The `return` statement must return a value compatible with the function type.

6 The principal storage class is automatic. Automatic variables appear and disappear with block entry and exit. They can be hidden when an inner block redeclares an outer block identifier.

7 Scope rules are the visibility constraints associated with identifiers. For example, if in a file we have

```
static void f(void)
{
    . . . . .
}

static int    a, b, c;
    . . . . .
```

then `f()` will be known throughout this file but in no other, and `a`, `b`, and `c` will be known only in this file and only below the place where they are declared.

8 The external storage class is the default class for all functions and all variables declared outside of functions. These identifiers may be used throughout the program. Such identifiers can be hidden by redeclaration but their values cannot be destroyed.

9 The keyword `extern` is used to tell the compiler to "look for it elsewhere, either in this file or in some other file."

10 The storage class `register` can be used to try to improve execution speed. It is semantically equivalent to automatic.

11 The storage class `static` is used to preserve exit values of variables. It is also used to restrict the scope of external identifiers. This latter use enhances modularization and program security by providing a form of privacy to functions and variables.

12 External and static variables that are not explicitly initialized by the programmer are initialized to zero by the system.

13 A function is said to be recursive if it calls itself, either directly or indirectly. In C, all functions can be used recursively.

5.16 EXERCISES

1 Write a function `double power(double x, int n)` that will compute x^n, the nth power of x. Check to see that it computes 3.5^7 correctly. (The answer is 6433.9296875.)

2 Use the library function `sqrt()` to write a function that returns the fourth root of its `int` argument k. The value returned should be a `double`. Use your function to make a table of values.

3 What gets printed? Explain.

```
#include <stdio.h>

int    z;

void f(int x)
{
    x = 2;
    z += x;
}

int main(void)
{
    z = 5;
    f(z);
    printf("z = %d\n", z);
    return 0;
}
```

4 In traditional C, the general form of a function definition is

type function_name (parameter list)
declarations of the parameters
{
    declarations
    statements
}

See Section 5.1, "Function Definition," for an example. Rewrite the function definition for f() in Exercise 3 in this style. Check to see that your compiler will accept it. Does the program produce the same output? (It should.)

5 In this exercise we want to experiment with function declarations. We will use the function pow() from the mathematics library, but instead of including *math.h*, we will supply our own function declaration. Begin by executing the following program:

```
#include <stdio.h>

double   pow(double, double);

int main(void)
{
    printf("pow(2.0, 3.0) = %g\n", pow(2.0, 3.0));
    return 0;
}
```

Next, change the printf() statement to

```
printf("pow(2, 3) = %g\n", pow(2, 3));
```

and run the program again. Even though you have passed int's to pow() instead of double's, do you get the correct answer? You should, because the compiler, knowing that double arguments are required, is able to coerce the values supplied into the right form. Next, replace the function prototype by

```
double   pow();          /* traditional style */
```

What happens now? Finally, remove the function declaration completely. Although your program cannot be expected to run correctly, it should compile. Does it? It is important to remember that even though the C system provides object code for functions in libraries, it is the responsibility of the programmer to provide correct function prototypes.

6 In this exercise we want to experiment with an assertion. Execute the following program so that you understand its effects. *Note:* This is *not* a typical use for an assertion.

```
#include <assert.h>
#include <stdio.h>
#include <stdlib.h>
#include <time.h>

int main(void)
{
    int   a, b, cnt = 0, i;

    srand(time(NULL));
    for (i = 0; i < 1000; ++i) {
        a = rand() % 3 + 1;                /* from 1 to 3 */
        b = rand() % 30 + 1;               /* from 1 to 30 */
        if (b - a <= 1)
            continue;
        assert(b - a > 2);
        printf("%3d\n", ++cnt);
    }
    return 0;
}
```

What values of a and b cause the assertion to fail? On average, how many times do you expect to go through the loop?

7 Use the function probability() that we wrote in Section 5.12 to create two files, one with 100 random numbers and the other with 1000 random numbers. All the numbers will lie in the range from 0 to 1. If the numbers are truly randomly distributed, then we expect the average to approximate 0.5 as we look at larger and larger sets of them. Compute the average of the numbers in each of your files. Typically, the average of the numbers in the larger file will be closer to 0.5 than the average of the numbers in the smaller file. Is it?

8 A polynomial of degree 2 in x is given by

$$ax^2 + bx + c$$

Write the code for the function

```
double f(double a, double b, double c, double x)
{
    .....
```

that will compute the value of an arbitrary polynomial of degree 2. Use the identity

$$(ax + b)x + c = ax^2 + bx + c$$

to minimize multiplications. Use your function to create a file of points that could be used to plot the polynomial $x^2 - 3x + 2$ on the interval [0, 3]. The variable x should go from 0 to 3 in steps of 0.1. By examining your file, can you tell where the roots of the polynomial are?

9 Experiment with the *tbl_of_powers* program presented in Section 5.4. How many rows of the table can you compute before the powers that are printed become incorrect? Where appropriate, try using the type double. Can you get larger numbers this way?

10 In the *tbl_of_powers* program in Section 5.4, we wrote the function definition for main() first. What happens if you remove the function prototypes and put main() last? Your compiler should be happy with this new arrangement. Is it? What happens if you put main() first but do not include any function prototypes? Can you guess what your compiler will complain about? One of our C compilers issues warnings but produces an executable file, whereas our C++ compiler issues errors and refuses to compile the code. What happens on your system?

11 Write a function int is_prime(int n) that returns 1 if n is a prime and 0 otherwise. *Hint:* If k and n are positive integers, then k divides n if and only if n % k has value zero.

12 Write a function, say is_fib_prime(), that checks whether the *n*th Fibonacci number is prime. Your function should call two other functions: the iterative version of fibonacci() that was given in Chapter 4 and the function is_prime() that you wrote in Exercise 11. For *n* between 3 and 10, it is true that the *n*th Fibonacci number is prime if and only if *n* is prime. Use your function is_fib_prime() to investigate what happens when *n* is bigger than 10.

13 A famous conjecture, called the Goldbach conjecture, says that every even integer *n* greater than 2 has the property that it is the sum of two prime numbers. Computers have been used extensively to test this conjecture. No counterexample has ever been found. Write a program that will prove that the conjecture is true for all the even integers between the symbolic constants START and FINISH. For example, if you write

```
#define   START    700
#define   FINISH   1100
```

then the output of your program might look like this:

```
Every even number greater than 2 is the sum of two primes:

     700 = 17 + 683
     702 = 11 + 691
     704 =  3 + 701
     . . . . .
    1098 =  5 + 1093
    1100 =  3 + 1097
```

Hint: Use the function is_prime() that you wrote in Exercise 11.

14 Write a function that finds all factors of any particular number. For example,

$$9 = 3 \times 3, \qquad 17 = 17 \text{ (prime)}, \qquad 52 = 2 \times 2 \times 13$$

Factoring small numbers is easy, and you should have no trouble writing a program to do this. Note, however, that factoring in general is very difficult. If an integer consists of a few hundred digits, then it may be impossible to factor it, even with a very large computer.

15 This exercise gives you practice on understanding the scope of identifiers. What gets printed by the following code? First, hand simulate the code and record your answers. Then write a program to check your answers.

```
int   a = 1, b = 2, c = 3;

a += b += ++c;
printf("%5d%5d%5d\n", a, b, c);
{
    float   b = 4.0;
    int     c;

    a += c = 5 * b;
    printf("%5d%5.1f%5d\n", a, b, c);
}
printf("%5d%5d%5d\n", a, b, c);
```

16 Rewrite "The universe is never ending!" recursion so that it terminates after 17 calls. Your program should consist of a single main() function that calls itself recursively. *Hint:* Use a static variable as a counter.

17 The following function produces incorrect values on some systems:

```
int factorial(int n)             /* wrong */
{
    if (n == 0 || n == 1)
        return 1;
    else
        return (n * factorial(--n));
}
```

Test the function on your system. Explain why the values produced by the function are system-dependent.

18 The greatest common divisor of two positive integers is the largest integer that is a divisor of both of them. For example, 3 is the greatest common divisor of 6 and 15, and 1 is the greatest common divisor of 15 and 22. Here is a recursive function that computes the greatest common divisor of two positive integers:

```
int gcd(int p, int q)
{
    int    r;

    if ((r = p % q) == 0)
        return q;
    else
        return gcd(q, r);
}
```

First, write a program to test the function. Then write and test an equivalent iterative function.

19 In some systems the keyword `extern` is used in function declarations and prototypes in the standard header files. This was a common practice in traditional C systems, but it is usually not done in ANSI C systems. Is this done in your system? *Hint:* Look, for example, in *math.h*.

20 In the program that follows we have purposely declared some external variables
at the bottom of the file. What gets printed?

```
#include <stdio.h>

int main(void)
{
    extern int    a, b, c;        /* look for them elsewhere */

    printf("%3d%3d%3d\n", a, b, c);
    return 0;
}

int    a = 1, b = 2, c = 3;
```

Now change the last line of the program to

```
static int    a = 1, b = 2, c = 3;
```

The variables at the bottom of the file are now static external, so they should not
be available in main(). Because the external variables referred to in main()
are not available, your compiler should complain. Does it? (We find that most
compilers get confused.)

21 When declaring a variable in traditional C, it is permissible to write the storage
class specifier and the type specifier in any order. For example, we can write

```
register int   i;        or        int register   i;
```

In ANSI C, the storage class specifier is supposed to come first. Nonetheless,
most ANSI C compilers will accept either order. (If they did not, then some
traditional code would not compile.) Check to see if the reverse order works on
your compiler.

22 Describe the behavior of the following program:

```
#include <stdio.h>
#include <stdlib.h>

#define    FOREVER    1
#define    STOP       17

int main(void)
{
    void    f(void);

    while (FOREVER)
        f();
    return 0;
}

void f(void)
{
    static int    cnt = 0;

    printf("cnt = %d\n", ++cnt);
    if (cnt == STOP)
        exit(0);
}
```

23 Let n_0 be a given positive integer. For $i = 0, 1, 2, \ldots$ define

$$n_{i+1} = \begin{cases} n_i/2 & \text{if } n_i \text{ is even} \\ 3n_i + 1 & \text{if } n_i \text{ is odd} \end{cases}$$

The sequence stops whenever n_i has the value 1. Numbers that are generated this way are called "hailstones." Write a program that generates some hailstones. The function

```
void hailstones(int n)
{
    .....
```

should be used to compute and print the sequence generated by *n*. The output of your program might look as follows:

```
Hailstones generated by 77:

    77       232       116        58        29        88
    44        22        11        34        17        52
    26        13        40        20        10         5
    16         8         4         2         1

Number of hailstones generated: 23
```

You will find that all the sequences you generate are finite. Whether this is true in general is still an open question.

24 Write a coin-tossing program that uses the random number generator rand() in the standard library to simulate the toss. Use the expression rand() % 2 to generate the int value 0 or 1. Let "heads" be represented by 1 and "tails" by 0. Run the program for 1000, 10000, and 100000 tosses and keep track of the longest sequence of heads and the longest sequence of alternating heads and tails—that is, 101010.... If you know some probability theory, see if this simulation is in line with theory. *Caution:* In some traditional C systems the function rand() is notoriously bad. All you will get is one long sequence of alternating heads and tails. If your ANSI C system has borrowed that particular function, then this exercise, although informative, will not be too interesting.

25 If a random number generator other than rand() is available to you, use it to redo Exercise 24. Are the results of your experiments substantially different?

26 Simulations that involve the repeated use of a random number generator to reproduce a probabilistic event are called Monte Carlo simulations, so-called because Monte Carlo has one of the world's most famous gaming casinos. Let us use this technique to find the break-even point in a variation of the birthday game (see Exercise 34 in Chapter 6). In a roomful of people, at least two of them can be expected to have birthdays on the same day of the year. A common party game is to see if this is true. We wish to find the probability that any two people in a room with *n* people will have been born in the same month. (To do the analysis for the same day rather than the same month requires the use of an array; otherwise the ideas are the same.) It is clear that the probability is 0 if there is only one person in the room. For two people the probability is 1/12. (We are assuming that it is equally likely for a person to be born in any month. In reality this is only an approximation.) Simulate the probability by running, say, 1000 trials with 2, 3, ..., 20 people in the room. (Is 20 too many?) Use

12 variables to count the number of people in the room that were born in each of the 12 months. You can use the expression

```
rand() % 12 + 1
```

to compute the month of birth for each person. (Use a better random number generator, such as lrand48(), if one is available to you.) This expression generates an integer that is randomly distributed in the range from 1 to 12. When any variable gets to 2, that trial is true, meaning that at least two people in the room were born in the same month. The number of true trials divided by 1000 is the computed simulated probability. What value of n yields the break-even point? That is, find the least n for which the probability is 1/2 or more.

ARRAYS, POINTERS, AND STRINGS

Arrays are a data type that uses subscripted variables and makes possible the representation of a large number of homogeneous values. In C, arrays and pointers are closely related concepts. An array name is treated as a constant pointer, and pointers, like arrays, can be subscripted. A distinguishing characteristic of C is its sophisticated use of pointers and pointer arithmetic. Other languages provide "call by reference" so that variables in the calling environment can be changed. In C, pointers are used as parameters in function definitions to obtain the effect of "call by reference." Strings are one-dimensional arrays of characters. They are sufficiently important to be treated as a special topic.

6.1 ONE-DIMENSIONAL ARRAYS

Programs often use homogeneous data. For example, if we want to manipulate some grades, we might declare

```
int    grade0, grade1, grade2;
```

If the number of grades is large, representing and manipulating the data by means of unique identifiers will be cumbersome. Instead, an array, which is a derived type, can be used. An array can be thought of as a simple variable with an index, or subscript, added. The brackets [] are used to contain the array subscripts. To use grade[0], grade[1], and grade[2] in a program, we would declare

```
int    grade[3];
```

The integer 3 in the declaration represents the number of elements in the array. The indexing of array elements always starts at 0.

A one-dimensional array declaration is a type followed by an identifier with a bracketed constant integral expression. The value of the expression, which must be positive, is the size of the array. It specifies the number of elements in the array. The array subscripts can range from 0 to *size* − 1. The lower bound of the array subscripts is 0 and the upper bound is *size* − 1. Thus the following relationships hold:

```
int   a[size];  /* space for a[0],...,a[size- 1] is allocated */
```

lower bound = 0
upper bound = *size* − 1
size = *upper bound* + 1

It is good programming practice to define the size of an array as a symbolic constant.

```
#define   N   100

int   a[N];      /* space for a[0], ..., a[99] is allocated */
```

Given this declaration, the standard programming idiom for processing array elements is with a for loop. For example:

```
for (i = 0; i < N; ++i)
    sum += a[i];    /* process element a[i]
```

This iteration starts with the element a[0] and iteratively processes each element in turn. Because the termination condition is i < N, we avoid the error of falling off the end of the array. The last element processed is, correctly, a[N - 1].

Initialization

Arrays may be of storage class automatic, external, or static, but not register. In traditional C, only external and static arrays can be initialized using an array initializer. In ANSI C, automatic arrays also can be initialized.

one_dimensional_array_initializer ::= { *initializer_list* }
initializer_list ::= *initializer* { , *initializer* }₀₊
initializer ::= *constant_integral_expression*

Consider the example

```
float   f[5] = {0.0, 1.0, 2.0, 3.0, 4.0};
```

This initializes f[0] to 0.0, f[1] to 1.0, and so on. When a list of initializers is shorter than the number of array elements to be initialized, the remaining elements are initialized to zero. For example,

```
int   a[100] = {0};
```

initializes all the elements of a to zero. If an external or static array is not initialized explicitly, then the system initializes all elements to zero by default. In contrast, automatic arrays are not necessarily initialized by the system. Although some compilers do this, others do not. Programmers should assume that uninitialized automatic arrays start with "garbage" values. If an array is declared without a size and is initialized to a series of values, it is implicitly given the size of the number of initializers. Thus

```
int a[] = {2, 3, 5, -7};        and        int a[4] = {2, 3, 5, -7};
```

are equivalent declarations. This feature works with character arrays as well. However, for character arrays an alternate notation is available. A declaration such as

```
char   s[] = "abc";
```

is taken by the compiler to be equivalent to

```
char   s[] = {'a', 'b', 'c', '\0'};
```

Subscripting

If a is an array, we can write a[*expr*], where *expr* is an integral expression, to access an element of the array. We call *expr* a subscript, or index, of a. Let us assume that the declaration

```
int   i, a[N];
```

has been made, where N is a symbolic constant. The expression a[i] can be made to refer to any element of the array by assignment of an appropriate value to the subscript i. A single array element a[i] is accessed when i has a value greater than or equal to 0 and less than or equal to N - 1. If i has a value outside this range, a run-time error will occur when a[i] is accessed. Overrunning the bounds of an array is a common programming error. The effect of the error is system-dependent, and can be quite confusing. One frequent result is that the value of some unrelated variable will be returned or modified. It is the programmer's job to ensure that all subscripts to arrays stay within bounds.

Recall that a parenthesis pair ( ) following an identifier tells the compiler that the identifier is a function name. Examples of this are main() and f(a, b). In C, the parenthesis pair that follows an identifier is treated as an operator. In a similar fashion, the bracket pair [] also is treated as an operator. Both operators ( ) and [] have the highest precedence and have left to right associativity.

6.2 POINTERS

A simple variable in a program is stored in a certain number of bytes at a particular memory location, or address, in the machine. Pointers are used in programs to access memory and manipulate addresses.

If v is a variable, then &v is the location, or address, in memory of its stored value. The address operator & is unary and has the same precedence and right to left associativity as the other unary operators. Addresses are a set of values that can be manipulated. Pointer variables can be declared in programs and then used to take addresses as values. The declaration

```
int    *p;
```

declares p to be of type pointer to int. Its legal range of values always includes the special address 0 and a set of positive integers that are interpreted as machine addresses on the given C system. Some examples of assignment to the pointer p are

```
p = 0;
p = NULL;               /* equivalent to p = 0; */
p = &i;
p = (int *) 1776;       /* an absolute address in memory */
```

In the third example, we think of p as "referring to i" or "pointing to i" or "containing the address of i." In the fourth example, the cast is necessary to avoid a compiler error.

The indirection or dereferencing operator * is unary and has the same precedence and right to left associativity as the other unary operators. If p is a pointer, then *p is the value of the variable of which p is the address. The name "indirection" is taken from machine language programming. The direct value of p is a memory location, whereas *p is the indirect value of p—namely, the value at the memory location stored in p. In a certain sense * is the inverse operator to &. We want to give an explicit, yet elementary, example of how the pointer mechanism works. Let us start with the declaration

```
int    a = 1, b = 2, *p;
```

At this point, we can think of the variables a, b, and p stored in memory as

We think of the pointer p as an arrow, but because it has not yet been assigned a value, we do not know what it points to. Suppose that our next line of code is

```
p = &a;
```

We read this as "p is assigned the address of a," and we have the following picture:

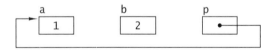

Now let us make the assignment

```
b = *p;
```

We read this as "b is assigned the value pointed to by p." Because p points to a, the statement

```
b = *p;        is equivalent to        b = a;
```

Let us write a simple program that illustrates the distinction between a pointer value and its dereferenced value. We will use the %p format to print the value of a pointer, which on most systems produces a hexadecimal number. On ANSI C systems, the %p format is preferred (see Exercise 6).

```
/* Printing an address, or location. */

#include <stdio.h>

int main(void)
{
   int   i = 7, *p;

   p = &i;
   printf("%s%d\n%s%p\n",
       "    Value of i: ", *p,
       "Location of i: ",  p);
   return 0;
}
```

The output of this program on our system is

```
    Value of i: 7
Location of i: effffb24
```

The actual location of a variable in memory is system-dependent. The operator *
dereferences p. That is, p contains an address, or location, and the expression *p
has the value of what is stored at this location appropriately interpreted according to
the type declaration of p.

A pointer can be initialized in a declaration. However, we must be careful to
interpret the initialization correctly. An example is

```
int    i, *p = &i;
```

Note carefully that this is an initialization of p, not *p. The variable p is of type
int * and its initial value is &i. Also, the declaration of i must occur before we
take its address.

The following table illustrates how some pointer expressions are evaluated:

Declarations and initializations		
int i = 3, j = 5, *p = &i, *q = &j, *r; double x;		

Expression	Equivalent expression	Value
p == & i	p == (& i)	1
* * & p	* (* (& p))	3
r = & x	r = (& x)	/* illegal */
7 * * p / * q + 7	(((7 * (* p))) / (* q)) + 7	11
* (r = & j) *= * p	(* (r = (& j))) *= (* p)	15

In this table we attempted to assign r the value &x. Because r is a pointer to int
and the expression &x is of type pointer to double, this is illegal. Also, note that in
the table we used the expression

```
7 * * p / * q + 7
```

If instead we had written

```
7 * * p /* q + 7                    /* trouble? */
```

we would find that the compiler treats /* as the start of a comment. This can result
in a difficult bug.

In traditional C, conversions during assignment between different pointer types
usually are allowed. In ANSI C, such conversions are not allowed unless one of the
types is pointer to void, or the right side is the constant 0. Thus we can think of

void * as a generic pointer type. This is an important point; see the discussion of
calloc( ) in Section 6.9, "An Example: Merge and Merge Sort."

Declarations

```
int    *p;
float  q;
void   *v;
```

Legal assignments	Illegal assignments
p = 0;	p = 1;
p = (int *) 1;	v = 1;
p = v = q;	p = q;
p = (int *) q;	

Of course, not every value is stored in an accessible memory location. It is useful
to keep in mind the following prohibitions:

Constructs *not* to be pointed at

Do not point at constants.
  &3   /* Illegal */

Do not point at ordinary expressions.
  &(k + 99)   /* Illegal */

Do not point at register variables.
  register v;
  &v   /* Illegal */

The address operator can be applied to variables and array elements. If a is an array,
then expressions such as &a[0] and &a[i+j+3] make sense.

6.3   CALL BY REFERENCE

Whenever variables are passed as arguments to a function, their values are copied to
the corresponding function parameters, and the variables themselves are not changed
in the calling environment. This "call by value" mechanism is strictly adhered to
in C. To change the values of variables in the calling environment, other languages
provide the "call by reference" mechanism. In this section we show how the use of
addresses of variables as arguments to functions can produce the effect of "call by
reference."

For a function to effect "call by reference," pointers must be used in the parameter list in the function definition. Then, when the function is called, addresses of variables must be passed as arguments. As an example of this, let us write a function that swaps the values of two variables in the calling environment.

```
void swap(int *p, int *q)
{
    int    tmp;

    tmp = *p;
    *p = *q;
    *q = tmp;
}
```

To test our function, we can write

```
#include <stdio.h>

void    swap(int *, int *);

int main(void)
{
    int    i = 3, j = 5;

    swap(&i, &j);
    printf("%d  %d\n", i, j);       /* 5  3 is printed */
    return 0;
}
```

Note that in the calling environment we have passed addresses as arguments to the function, and that in the function definition we have used pointers. This is a consistent pattern.

DISSECTION OF THE swap() FUNCTION

■ void swap(int *p, int *q)
  {
      int   tmp;

This function takes two arguments of type pointer to int and returns nothing. The variable tmp is local to this function and is of type int. As the name indicates, we think of this as temporary storage.

■   ```
tmp = *p;
*p = *q;
*q = tmp;
```

The variable tmp is assigned the value pointed to by p. The object pointed to by p is assigned the value pointed to by q. The object pointed to by q is assigned the value tmp. This has the effect of interchanging in the calling environment the stored values of whatever p and q are pointing to.

---

### The effect of "call by reference" is accomplished by

1    Declaring a function parameter to be a pointer
2    Using the dereferenced pointer in the function body
3    Passing an address as an argument when the function is called

## 6.4   THE RELATIONSHIP BETWEEN ARRAYS AND POINTERS

An array name by itself is an address, or pointer value, and pointers, as well as arrays, can be subscripted. Although pointers and arrays are almost synonymous in terms of how they are used to access memory, there are differences, and these differences are subtle and important. A pointer variable can take different addresses as values. In contrast, an array name is an address, or pointer, that is fixed.

Suppose that a is an array and that i is an int. It is a fundamental fact that the expression

    a[i]       is equivalent to       *(a + i)

The expression a[i] has the value of the *i*th element of the array (counting from 0), whereas *(a + i) is the dereferencing of the expression a +, a pointer expression that points i element positions past. If p is a pointer, then in a similar fashion the expression

    p[i]       is equivalent to       *(p + i)

This means that we can (and do) use array notation with pointers. Expressions such as a + i and p + i are examples of pointer arithmetic. The expression a + i has as its value the *i*th offset from the base address of the array a. That is, it points to the *i*th element of the array (counting from 0). In a similar manner, p + i is the *i*th offset from the value of p. The actual address produced by such an offset depends on the type that p points to.

When an array is declared, the compiler must allocate a sufficient amount of contiguous space in memory to contain all the elements of the array. The base address of the array is the initial location in memory where the array is stored; it
```

is the address of the first element (index 0) of the array. Consider the following declarations:

```
#define    N    100

int    a[N], i, *p, sum = 0;
```

Suppose that the system assigns 300 as the base address of the array and that memory bytes numbered 300, 304, 308, ..., 696 are allocated as the addresses of a[0], a[1], a[2], ..., a[99], respectively. We are assuming that each byte is addressable and that 4 bytes are used to store an int. This is system-dependent. The statement

```
p = a;        is equivalent to        p = &a[0];
```

It causes 300 to be assigned to p. Pointer arithmetic provides an alternative to array indexing. The statement

```
p = a + 1;        is equivalent to        p = &a[1];
```

It causes 304 to be assigned to p. Assuming that the elements of a have been assigned values, we can use the following code to sum the array:

```
for (p = a; p < &a[N]; ++p)
    sum += *p;
```

First p is initialized to the base address of the array. In the body of the loop, the variable sum is incremented by the value pointed to by p. Each time through the loop, p is incremented so its successive values are &a[0], &a[1], ..., &a[N-1]. Here is another way of summing the array:

```
for (i = 0; i < N; ++i)
    sum += *(a + i);
```

In the body of the loop the pointer value a is offset by i and then dereferenced. This produces the value a[i]. Finally, here is a third way of summing the array:

```
p = a;
for (i = 0; i < N; ++i)
    sum += p[i];
```

Note that because a is a constant pointer, expressions such as

```
a = p    ++a    a += 2    &a
```

are illegal. We cannot change the value of a.

6.5   POINTER ARITHMETIC AND ELEMENT SIZE

Pointer arithmetic is one of the powerful features of C. If the variable p is a pointer
to a particular type, then the expression p + 1 yields the correct machine address
for storing or accessing the next variable of that type. In a similar fashion, pointer
expressions such as p + i and ++p and p += i all make sense. If p and q are both
pointing to elements of an array, then p - q yields the int value representing the
number of array elements between p and q. Even though pointer expressions and
arithmetic expressions have a similar appearance, there is a critical difference in interpretation between the two types of expressions. The following code illustrates this:

```
double    a[2], *p, *q;

p = a;                          /* points to base of array */
q = p + 1;                      /* equivalent to q = &a[1]; */
printf("%d\n", q - p);                  /* 1 is printed */
printf("%d\n", (int) q - (int) p);    /* 8 is printed */
```

On most machines a double is stored in 8 bytes. Because p points to a double and
q points to the next double, the difference in terms of array elements is 1, but the
difference in memory locations is 8.

6.6   ARRAYS AS FUNCTION ARGUMENTS

In a function definition, a formal parameter that is declared as an array is actually
a pointer. Corresponding to this, when an array is passed as an argument to a
function, the base address of the array is passed "call by value." The array elements
themselves are not copied. As a notational convenience, the compiler allows array
bracket notation to be used in declaring pointers as parameters. To illustrate these
ideas, we write a function that sums the elements of an array of type double.

```
double sum(double a[], int n)      /* n is the size a[] */
{
   int       i;
   double    sum = 0.0;

   for (i = 0; i < n; ++i)
      sum += a[i];
   return sum;
}
```

Note carefully that in the header to the function definition the declaration of the parameter a as an array is equivalent to its declaration as a pointer. This means that an equivalent function definition is given by

```
double sum(double *a, int n)       /* n is the size a[] */
{
    .....
```

Although an array declaration is equivalent to a pointer declaration in a parameter list, this equivalence does *not* hold for external declarations or for declarations within the body of a function.

Suppose that in main() we have an array, or vector, v declared with 100 elements. After the elements of the vector have been assigned values, we can use the above function sum() to add various of the elements of v. The following table illustrates some of the possibilities:

Various ways that sum() might be called

Invocation	What gets computed and returned
sum(v, 100)	v[0] + v[1] + ... + v[99]
sum(v, 88)	v[0] + v[1] + ... + v[87]
sum(&v[7], k - 7)	v[7] + v[8] + ... + v[k - 1]
sum(v + 7, 2 * k)	v[7] + v[8] + ... + v[2 * k + 6]

The last call illustrates again the use of pointer arithmetic. The base address of v is offset by 7, causing the local pointer variable a in sum() to be initialized to this value. This causes all address calculations inside the function call to be similarly offset.

6.7 AN EXAMPLE: BUBBLE SORT

Although we presented a bubble sort in Chapter 1, we will do so again here and illustrate in some detail how the function works on a particular array of integers. We will use the function swap() from the previous section.

```
void bubble(int a[], int n)       /* n is the size of a[] */
{
    int     i, j;
    void    swap(int *, int *);

    for (i = 0; i < n - 1; ++i)
        for (j = n - 1; j > i; --j)
            if (a[j-1] > a[j])
                swap(&a[j-1], &a[j]);
}
```

Because of pointer arithmetic, the expressions a + i and &a[i] are equivalent. Thus the function call to swap() could have been written

```
swap(a + i, a + j);
```

Now we describe how the bubble sort works. Suppose that in main() we have

```
int    a[] = {7, 3, 66, 3, -5, 22, 77, 2};

bubble(a, 8);
```

The following table shows the elements of a[] after each pass of the outer loop in the function bubble():

Unordered data:	7	3	66	3	-5	22	-77	2
First pass:	-77	7	3	66	3	-5	22	2
Second pass:	-77	-5	7	3	66	3	2	22
Third pass:	-77	-5	2	7	3	66	3	22
Fourth pass:	-77	-5	2	3	7	3	66	22
Fifth pass:	-77	-5	2	3	3	7	22	66
Sixth pass:	-77	-5	2	3	3	7	22	66
Seventh pass:	-77	-5	2	3	3	7	22	66

At the start of the first pass a[6] is compared with a[7]. Because the values are in order, they are not exchanged. Then a[5] is compared with a[6], and because these values are out of order, they are exchanged. Then a[4] is compared with a[5], and so on. Adjacent out-of-order values are exchanged. The effect of the first pass is to "bubble" the smallest value in the array into the element a[0]. In the second pass, a[0] is left unchanged and a[6] is compared first with a[7], and so on. After the second pass the next to the smallest value is in a[1]. Because each pass bubbles the next smallest element to its appropriate array position, the algorithm will, after $n - 1$ passes, have all the elements ordered. Notice that in this example all the elements have been ordered after the fifth pass. It is possible to modify the algorithm so it terminates earlier by adding a variable that detects if no exchanges are made in a given pass. We leave this as an exercise.

A bubble sort is very inefficient. If the size of the array is n, then the number of comparisons performed is proportional to n^2. The merge sort discussed in Section 6.9 is much more efficient; it is an $n \log n$ algorithm.

6.8 DYNAMIC MEMORY ALLOCATION WITH calloc() AND malloc()

C provides the functions calloc() and malloc() in the standard library, and their function prototypes are in *stdlib.h*. The name calloc stands for "contiguous allocation," and the name malloc stands for "memory allocation."

The programmer uses calloc() and malloc() to dynamically create space for arrays, structures, and unions (see Chapters 9 and 10 for structures and unions). Here is a typical example that shows how calloc() can be used to allocate space dynamically for an array:

```
#include <stdio.h>
#include <stdlib.h>

int main(void)
{
    int    *a;                  /* to be used as an array */
    int    n;                   /* the size of the array */

    .....                       /* get n from somewhere, perhaps
                                   interactively from the user */

    a = calloc(n, sizeof(int)); /* get space for a */
    .....                       /* use a as an array */
```

The function calloc() takes two arguments, both of type size_t. In ANSI C, size_t must be an unsigned integral type. Typically, a typedef is used in *stdlib.h* to make size_t equivalent to the type unsigned int. A function call of the form

```
calloc(n,  el_size)
```

allocates contiguous space in memory for an array of n elements, with each element having *el_size* bytes. The space is initialized with all bits set to zero. If the call is successful, a pointer of type void * that points to the base of the array in memory is returned; otherwise, NULL is returned. Note that the use of the sizeof operator makes the code appropriate for machines having either 2- or 4-byte words.

The programmer uses malloc() in a similar fashion. This function takes a single argument of type size_t. If the call is successful, it returns a pointer of type void * that points to the requested space in memory; otherwise, NULL gets returned. Instead of writing

```
a = calloc(n, sizeof(int));
```

we could have written

```
a = malloc(n * sizeof(int));
```

Unlike `calloc()`, the function `malloc()` does not initialize the space in memory that it makes available. If there is no reason to initialize the array to zero, then the use of either `calloc()` or `malloc()` is acceptable. In a large program, `malloc()` may take less time.

Space that has been dynamically allocated with either `calloc()` or `malloc()` does not get returned to the system upon function exit. The programmer must use `free()` explicitly to return the space. A call of the form

```
free(ptr)
```

causes the space in memory pointed to by `ptr` to be deallocated. If `ptr` is NULL, the function has no effect. If `ptr` is not NULL, it must be the base address of space previously allocated by a call to `calloc()`, `malloc()`, or `realloc()` that has not yet been deallocated by a call to `free()` or `realloc()`. Otherwise the call is in error. The effect of the error is system-dependent.

Let us write a small program that illustrates the ideas we have presented in this section. The first `printf()` statement in the program tells the user exactly what the program does.

```c
#include <stdio.h>
#include <stdlib.h>
#include <time.h>

void    fill_array(int *a, int n);
void    prn_array(int *a, int n);
int     sum_array(int *a, int n);

int main(void)
{
   int    *a, n;

   srand(time(NULL));      /* seed the random number generator */
   printf("\n%s\n",
      "This program does the following repeatedly:\n"
      "\n"
      "   1   creates space for an array of size n\n"
      "   2   fills the array with randomly distributed digits\n"
      "   3   prints the array and the sum of its element\n"
      "   4   deallocates the space\n");
   for ( ; ; ) {
      printf("Input n:   ");
      scanf("%d", &n);
      if (n < 1) {
         printf("\nBye!\n\n");
         exit(1);
      }
      putchar('\n');
      a = calloc(n, sizeof(int));      /* get space for a */
      fill_array(a, n);
      prn_array(a, n);
      printf("Sum of the elements = %d\n\n", sum_array(a, n));
      free(a);
   }
   return 0;
}

void fill_array(int *a, int n)
{
   int    i;

   for (i = 0; i < n; ++i)
      a[i] = rand() % 19 - 9;
}
```

```
void prn_array(int *a, int n)
{
   int   i;

   printf("a = [");
   for (i = 0; i < n - 1; ++i)
      printf("%d, ", a[i]);
   printf("%d]\n", a[n - 1]);
}

int sum_array(int *a, int n)
{
   int   i, sum = 0;

   for (i = 0; i < n; ++i)
      sum += a[i];
   return sum;
}
```

Offsetting the Pointer

For arrays (vectors) intended for mathematical use, we often want to index the arrays from 1 instead 0. In a small program we can do something like the following:

```
int       n;
double    *a;

.....
a = calloc(n + 1, sizeof(double));
```

Because the size of a is one more than n, we can disregard a[0] and use a[1], ..., a[n] as needed. This is certainly an acceptable scheme. However, an alternative scheme is to do the following. First we write

```
a = calloc(n, sizeof(double));
```

At this point, here is what we have in memory:

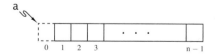

Next, we write

```
--a;          /* offset the pointer */
```

The picture of what is in memory changes to the following:

Notice that the dotted lines indicate memory the programmer does not own. Thus a[0] should not be accessed: neither written to nor read. The elements a[1], . . . , a[n], however, are now accessible for use by the programmer. To deallocate the space, we can write free(a + 1).

In Chapter 12, we will expand on the ideas presented in this section when we deal with mathematical matrices.

6.9 AN EXAMPLE: MERGE AND MERGE SORT

Suppose we have two ordered arrays of integers, say a[] and b[]. If we want to merge them into another ordered array, say c[], then the algorithm to do so is simple. First, compare a[0] and b[0]. Whichever is smaller, say b[0], put into c[0]. Next compare a[0] and b[1]. Whichever is smaller, say b[1], put into c[1]. Next compare a[0] and b[2]. Whichever is smaller, say a[0], put into c[2]. Next compare a[1] and b[2], and so on. Eventually one of the arrays a[] or b[] will be exhausted. At that point, the remainder of the elements in the other array must be copied into c[]. The function that does this is the following:

```
/* Merge a[] of size m and b[] of size n into c[]. */

void merge(int a[], int b[], int c[], int m, int n)
{
    int   i = 0, j = 0, k = 0;

    while (i < m && j < n)
        if (a[i] < b[j])
            c[k++] = a[i++];
        else
            c[k++] = b[j++];
    while (i < m)                    /* pick up any remainder */
        c[k++] = a[i++];
    while (j < n)
        c[k++] = b[j++];
}
```

The array c[] is assumed to contain enough space to hold both a[] and b[]. The programmer must make certain that the bounds on c[] are not overrun.

In contrast to a bubble sort, a merge sort is very efficient. We will write a function called mergesort() to act on an array key[], which has a size that is a power of 2. The "power of 2" requirement will help to make the explanation simpler. In Exercise 16, we indicate how this restriction can be removed. To understand how merge sort works, let us suppose that key[] contains the following 16 integers:

   4   3   1   67   55   8   0   4   −5   37   7   2   9   1   −1

The algorithm will work on the data in a number of passes. The following table shows how we want the data to look after each pass:

Unordered data:	4	3	1	67	55	8	0	4	−5	37	7	4	2	9	1	−1
First pass:	3	4	1	67	8	55	0	4	−5	37	4	7	2	9	−1	1
Second pass:	1	3	4	67	0	4	8	55	−5	4	7	37	−1	1	2	9
Third pass:	0	1	3	4	4	8	55	67	−5	−1	1	2	4	7	9	37
Fourth pass:	−5	−1	0	1	1	2	3	4	4	4	7	8	9	37	55	67

After the first pass we want each successive pair of integers to be in order. After the second pass we want each successive quartet of integers to be in order. After the third pass we want each successive octet of integers to be in order. Finally, after the fourth pass we want all 16 of the integers to be in order. At each stage merge() is used to accomplish the desired ordering. For example, after the third pass we have the two subarrays

   0   1   3   4   8   55   67   and   −5   −1   1   2   4   7   9   37

which are both in order. By merging these two subarrays, we obtain the completely ordered array given in the last line of the table above. Surprisingly, the code that accomplishes this is quite short. Moreover, it illustrates the power of pointer arithmetic.

```
/* Mergesort: Use merge() to sort an array of size n. */

#include <stdio.h>
#include <stdlib.h>
#include <assert.h>

void    merge(int *, int *, int *, int, int);

void mergesort(int key[], int n)
{
    int     j, k, m, *w;

    for (m = 1; m < n; m *= 2)
        ;
    if (m != n) {
        printf("ERROR: Array size is not a power of 2 - bye!\n");
        exit(1);
    }
    w = calloc(n, sizeof(int));          /* allocate workspace */
    assert(w != NULL);                   /* calloc() worked */
    for (k = 1; k < n; k *= 2) {
        for (j = 0; j < n - k; j += 2 * k)
            merge(key + j, key + j + k, w + j, k, k);/* merge into w */
        for (j = 0; j < n; ++j)
            key[j] = w[j];               /* write w back into key */
    }
    free(w);                             /* free the workspace */
}
```

DISSECTION OF THE mergesort() FUNCTION

■ `for (m = 1; m < n; m *= 2)`
     `;`

After this loop the value of m is the smallest power of 2 that is greater than or equal to n.

■ ```
   if (m != n) {
       printf("ERROR: Array size is not a power of 2 - bye!\n");
       exit(1);
   }
   ```

First we test to see if n is a power of 2. If it is not a power of 2, we exit the program with an appropriate message.
   ```

■   w = calloc(n, sizeof(int));   /* allocate workspace */
       assert(w != NULL);   /* calloc() worked */

The function calloc() is in the standard library, and its function prototype is in the header file *stdlib.h*. The function is used to allocate space in memory for an array dynamically. The first argument to the function specifies the number of elements in the array, and the second argument specifies the size in bytes needed to store each element. The function returns a pointer of type void * to the allocated space. Because its type is void *, the pointer can be assigned to w without a cast. In traditional C, we would have written

```
w = (int *) calloc(n, sizeof(int));
```

Although w is a pointer to int, we can use it just as we would an array.

■   assert(w != NULL);   /* calloc() worked */

If calloc() fails to allocate space—for example, the system free store (heap) is exhausted—then NULL is returned. We used the assert() macro in *assert.h* to make sure this did not happen. If the expression w != NULL is false, then the program will be aborted at this point.

■   for (k = 1; k < n; k *= 2) {
      for (j = 0; j < n - k; j += 2 * k)
         merge(key + j, key + j + k, w + j, k, k);/* merge into w */
      for (j = 0; j < n; ++j)
         key[j] = w[j];   /* write w back into key */
    }

This is the heart of the algorithm. Suppose we start with key[] having the data given as unordered in the table above. In the first pass of the outer loop, k is 1. Consider the first inner loop

```
for (j = 0; j < n - k; j += 2 * k)
    merge(key + j, key + j + k, w + j, k, k); /* merge into w */
```

The first call to merge() is equivalent to

```
merge(key + 0, key + 0 + 1, w + 0, 1, 1);
```

The arrays based at key and key + 1, both of size 1, are being merged and put into the array based at w. This will result in w[0] and w[1] being in order. The next call to merge() is equivalent to

```
merge(key + 2, key + 2 + 1, w + 2, 1, 1);
```

The arrays based at key + 2 and key + 3, both of size 1, are being merged and put into the array based at w + 2. This will result in w[2] and w[3] being in order. The next call ..., and so on. After the first pass of the outer loop, each successive pair of elements in w[] is in order; see the table above. At this point the array w[] is copied into key[]. In the second pass of the outer loop, k is 2, and the next call to merge() is equivalent to

```
merge(key + 0, key + 0 + 2, w + 0, 2, 2);
```

The arrays based at key and key + 2, both of size 2, are being merged and put into the array based at w. This will result in w[0], w[1], w[2], w[3] being in order. The next call to merge() is equivalent to

```
merge(key + 4, key + 4 + 2, w + 4, 2, 2);
```

The arrays based at key + 4 and key + 6, both of size 2, are being merged and put into the array based at w + 4. This will result in w[4], w[5], w[6], w[7] being in order. The next call ..., and so on. After the second pass of the outer loop, each successive quartet of elements in w[] is in order; see the table above. At this point the array w[] is copied into key[]. In the third pass of the outer loop, k is 4, and the next call to merge()..., and so on.

■ free(w);   /* free the workspace */
This function is in the standard library, and its function prototype is in *stdlib.h*. It causes the space pointed to by w to be deallocated. The system is then able to use this space for some other purpose. Unlike automatic storage, space allocated by calloc() is not relinquished automatically upon exit from a function. The programmer must explicitly free this space.

Here is a function that can be used to test `mergesort()`. The interested reader should modify the program to print out the array after each pass of the outer loop in order to check that the above table is reproduced.

```
/* Mergesort test program. */

#include <stdio.h>

#define   KEYSIZE   16

void   mergesort(int *, int);

int main(void)
{
   int   i, key[] = { 4, 3, 1, 67, 55, 8, 0, 4,
                      -5, 37, 7, 4, 2, 9, 1, -1 };

   mergesort(key, KEYSIZE);
   printf("After mergesort:\n");
   for (i = 0; i < KEYSIZE; ++i)
      printf("%4d", key[i]);
   putchar('\n');
   return 0;
}
```

The amount of work that a merge sort does when sorting *n* elements is proportional to *n* log *n*. Compared to a bubble sort, this is a very significant improvement. Sorting is critical to the efficient handling of large amounts of stored information. However, it is beyond the scope of this text to discuss the topic in detail; see *The Art of Computer Programming*, vol. 3, *Sorting and Searching*, by Donald Ervin Knuth (Reading, Mass.: Addison-Wesley, 1973).

6.10 STRINGS

Strings are one-dimensional arrays of type `char`. By convention, a string in C is terminated by the end-of-string sentinel \0, or null character. Because of this, dealing with strings has its own flavor, and we treat the topic separately. It is useful to think of strings as having a variable length, delimited by \0, but with a maximum length determined by the size of the string. The size of a string must include the storage needed for the end-of-string sentinel. As with all arrays, it is the job of the programmer to make sure that string bounds are not overrun.

String constants are written between double quotes. For example, `"abc"` is a character array of size 4, with the last element being the null character \0. Note that

string constants are different from character constants. For example, "a" and 'a'
are not the same. The array "a" has two elements, the first with value 'a' and the
second with value '\0'.

A string constant, like an array name, is treated by the compiler as a pointer. Its
value is the base address of the string. Consider the following code:

```
char    *p = "abc";

printf("%s %s\n", p, p + 1);    /* abc bc is printed */
```

The variable p is assigned the base address of the character array "abc". When a
pointer to char is printed in the format of a string, each successive character in the
array is printed until the end-of-string sentinel is reached. Thus, in the printf()
statement, the expression p causes abc to be printed, and the expression p + 1,
which points to the letter b in the string "abc", causes bc to be printed. Because a
string constant such as "abc" is treated as a pointer, expressions such as

   "abc"[1]   and   *("abc" + 2)

make sense (see Exercise 20). Such expressions are not used in serious code, but
they help to emphasize that string constants are treated as pointers.

As we have already seen, arrays and pointers have similar uses. They also have
differences. Let us consider the two declarations

   char   *p = "abcde";   and   char   s[] = "abcde";

In the first declaration the compiler allocates space in memory for p, puts the string
constant "abcde" in memory, and initializes p with the base address of the string
constant. We now think of p as pointing to the string. The second declaration is
equivalent to

```
char    s[] = {'a', 'b', 'c', 'd', 'e', '\0'};
```

Because the brackets are empty, the compiler allocates 6 bytes of memory for the
array s. The first byte is initialized with 'a', the second byte is initialized with 'b',
and so on. Here is how we think of these objects stored in memory:

A char is always stored in 1 byte, and on most machines a pointer is stored in a
word. Thus, on our machine, p is stored in 4 bytes and s is stored in 6 bytes. Of
course, p contains the address of a string that requires another 6 bytes of storage.
(See Exercise 22 for further discussion.)

For technical reasons, it is better not to print null characters. [If null characters are put into a file and then another utility is used to process the file, the result can be confusing (see Exercise 23).] However, the printing of null strings is perfectly acceptable. One natural instance of this occurs when dealing with plurals:

```
char    *s;
int     nfrogs;


.....
s = (nfrogs == 1) ? "" : "s";
printf("We found %d frog%s in the pond!\n", nfrogs, s);
```

To illustrate string processing, we will write a function that counts the number of words in a string. We assume that words in the string are separated by white space. Our function will use the macro isspace(), which is defined in the standard header file *ctype.h*. This macro is used to test whether a character is a blank, tab, or newline. If it is one of these, then a nonzero (*true*) value is returned; otherwise, zero (*false*) is returned.

```
/* Count the number of words in a string. */

#include <ctype.h>

int word_cnt(char *s)
{
    int     cnt = 0;

    while (*s != '\0') {
        while (isspace(*s))         /* skip white space */
            ++s;
        if (*s != '\0') {           /* found a word */
            ++cnt;
            while (!isspace(*s) && *s != '\0')
                ++s;                /* skip the word */
        }
    }
    return cnt;
}
```

This is a typical string processing function. Pointer arithmetic and dereferencing are used to search for various characters or patterns.

6.11 STRING HANDLING FUNCTIONS IN THE STANDARD LIBRARY

Traditional C provides a number of useful string handling functions, and ANSI C has added new ones. See the Appendix "The Standard Library" for details. The function prototypes for string handling functions are given in the standard header file *string.h*.

In this section we want to illustrate the use of a few string handling functions. We will see that some of the parameters in the functions are declared to have the type const char *. The type qualifier const in this context is telling the compiler that the character pointed to in memory should not be changed (see Exercise 26). The pointer itself, however, can be changed.

Some string handling functions in the standard library

- char *strcat(char *s1, const char *s2);
  This function takes two strings as arguments, concatenates them, and puts the result in s1. The programmer must ensure that s1 points to enough space to hold the result. The string s1 is returned.

- int strcmp(const char *s1, const char *s2);
  Two strings are passed as arguments. An integer is returned that is less than, equal to, or greater than zero, depending on whether s1 is lexicographically less than, equal to, or greater than s2.

- char *strcpy(char *s1, const char *s2);
  The string s2 is copied into s1 until \0 is moved. Whatever exists in s1 is overwritten. It is assumed that s1 has enough space to hold the result. The value s1 is returned.

- unsigned strlen(const char *s);
  A count of the number of characters before \0 is returned.

There is nothing special about these functions. They are written in C and are all quite short. Variables in them are often declared to have storage class register to make them execute more quickly. Here is one way the function strlen() could be written:

```
unsigned strlen(const char *s)
{
    register int   n;

    for (n = 0; *s != '\0'; ++s)
        ++n;
    return n;
}
```

The loop continues counting until the end-of-string character `'\0'` is detected. For example, `strlen("abc")` returns the value 3 and `strlen("")` returns the value 0. The function `strcpy()` is even simpler.

```
char *strcpy(char *s1, const char *s2)
{
    while (*s1++ = *s2++)
        ;
    return s1;
}
```

When first seen, this C idiom seems obscure. A character-by-character assignment is made from the source string starting at `s2` to the destination string starting at `s1`. The postincrement advances each pointer address through its respective string. Termination occurs when the zero value is assigned.

The function `strcat()` is more interesting. It can be written in a number of ways. Here is one of them:

```
char *strcat(char *s1, const char *s2)
{
    register char   *p = s1;

    while (*p)
        ++p;
    while (*p++ = *s2++)
        ;
    return s1;
}
```

DISSECTION OF THE strcat() FUNCTION

■   `register char   *p = s1;`

The pointer p is initialized to the pointer value `s1`. Thus p and `s1` point to the same memory location.

■ while (*p)
     ++p;
As long as the value pointed to by p is nonzero, p is incremented, causing it
to point at the next character in the string. When p points to the end-of-string
sentinel \0, the expression *p has the value zero. This causes control to pass
beyond the while statement. Notice that we could have written

while (*p != '\0')   instead of   while (*p)

to achieve the same effect. Functions in the C library often are written in a
sparse manner. Although one might think that sparse C code produces faster
running object code, most C compilers produce the same object code for both
forms of these while statements.

■ *p++
Because unary operators associate from right to left, this expression is equivalent
to *(p++). Thus p itself is being incremented. In contrast, the expression
(*p)++ would increment what p is pointing to, leaving the value of p itself
unchanged. The value of the expression p++ is the current value of p. This
value is dereferenced; then the value of p in memory in incremented, causing it
to point to the next character in the string.

■ while (*p++ = *s2++)
     ;
At the beginning of this while loop, p points to the null character at the end
of the string pointed to by s1. The value pointed to by s2 is assigned to the
object pointed to by p, and this is the value of the assignment expression as a
whole. Then both p and s2 are incremented, causing them to point to the next
character in their respective strings. When s2 points to the null character, the
expression *s2++ has the value 0. This value is assigned to the object pointed
to by p, producing the null character \0, which serves as the end-of-string for
s1. The effect of this while statement is to append a copy of the string s2,
including the null character, to the end of s1.

String handling functions are illustrated in the next table. Note carefully that it is the programmer's responsibility to allocate sufficient space for strings that are passed as arguments to functions.

Declarations and initializations

```
char  s1[] = "beautiful big sky country",
      s2[] = "how now brown cow";
```

Expression	Value
strlen(s1)	25
strlen(s2 + 8)	9
strcmp(s1, s2)	*negative integer*

Statements	What gets printed
printf("%s", s1 + 10);	big sky country
strcpy(s1 + 10, s2 + 8);	
strcat(s1, "s!");	
printf("%s", s1);	beautiful brown cows!

6.12 MULTIDIMENSIONAL ARRAYS

The C language allows arrays of any type, including arrays of arrays. With two bracket pairs, we obtain a two-dimensional array. This idea can be iterated to obtain arrays of higher dimension. With each bracket pair we add another array dimension.

Examples of declarations of arrays	Remarks
int a[100];	a one-dimensional array
int b[2][7];	a two-dimensional array
int c[5][3][2];	a three-dimensional array

A k-dimensional array has a size for each of its k dimensions. If we let s_i represent the size of its ith dimension, then the declaration of the array will allocate space for $s_1 \times s_2 \times \ldots \times s_k$ elements. In the preceding table, b has 2×7 elements, and c has $5 \times 3 \times 2$ elements. Starting at the base address of the array, all the array elements are stored contiguously in memory. *Caution:* The multidimensional array mechanism described here is often unsuitable for dealing with mathematical matrices. See Section 12.6, "Dynamic Allocation of Matrices," for further discussion.

Two-Dimensional Arrays

Even though array elements are stored contiguously one after the other, it is often convenient to think of a two-dimensional array as a rectangular collection of elements with rows and columns. For example, if we declare

```
int   a[3][5];
```

then we can think of the array elements arranged as follows:

	col 1	col 2	col 3	col 4	col 5
row 1	a[0][0]	a[0][1]	a[0][2]	a[0][3]	a[0][4]
row 2	a[1][0]	a[1][1]	a[1][2]	a[1][3]	a[1][4]
row 3	a[2][0]	a[2][1]	a[2][2]	a[2][3]	a[2][4]

Because of the relationship between arrays and pointers, there are numerous ways to access elements of a two-dimensional array.

Expressions equivalent to a[i][j]

```
*(a[i] + j)
(*(a + i))[j]
*((*(a + i)) + j)
*(&a[0][0] + 5*i + j)
```

The parentheses are necessary because the brackets [] have higher precedence than the indirection operator *. We can think of a[i] as the *i*th row of a (counting from 0), and we can think of a[i][j] as the element in the *i*th row, *j*th column of the array (counting from 0). The array name a by itself is equivalent to &a[0]; it is a pointer to an array of 5 ints. The base address of the array is &a[0][0], not a. Starting at the base address of the array, the compiler allocates contiguous space for 15 ints. For any array, the mapping between pointer values and array indices is called the *storage mapping function*. For the array a, the storage mapping function is specified by noting that

a[i][j]   is equivalent to   *(&a[0][0] + 5*i + j)

When a multidimensional array is a formal parameter in a function definition, all sizes except the first must be specified so that the compiler can determine the correct storage mapping function. (Because of this, multidimensional arrays are often inappropriate for use in mathematical programming; see Section 12.6, "Dynamic Allocation of Matrices.") After the elements of the array a given above have been assigned values, the following function can be used to sum the elements of the array.

Note carefully that the column size must be specified.

```
int sum(int a[][5])
{
    int   i, j, sum = 0;

    for (i = 0; i < 3; ++i)
        for (j = 0; j < 5; ++j)
            sum += a[i][j];
    return sum;
}
```

In the header of the function definition, the following parameter declarations are equivalent:

```
int a[][5]            int (*a)[5]            int a[3][5]
```

Because of operator precedence, the parentheses are necessary. The constant 3 acts as a reminder to human readers of the code, but the compiler disregards it.

Three-Dimensional Arrays

Arrays of dimension higher than two work in a similar fashion. Let us describe how three-dimensional arrays work. If we declare

```
int   a[7][9][2];
```

then the compiler will allocate space for $7 \times 9 \times 2$ contiguous ints. The base address of the array is &a[0][0][0], and the storage mapping function is specified by noting that

```
a[i][j][k]        is equivalent to        *(&a[0][0][0] + 9*2*i + 2*j + k)
```

If an expression such as a[i][j][k] is used in a program, the compiler uses the storage mapping function to generate object code to access the correct array element in memory. Although normally it is not necessary to do so, the programmer can make direct use of the storage mapping function. Here is a function that will sum the elements of the array a:

```
int sum(int a[][9][2])
{
    int   i, j, k, sum = 0;

    for (i = 0; i < 7; ++i)
        for (j = 0; j < 9; ++j)
            for (k = 0; k < 2; ++k)
                sum += a[i][j][k];
    return sum;
}
```

In the header of the function definition the following parameter declarations are equivalent:

```
int a[][9][2]          int a[7][9][2]          int (*a)[9][2]
```

The constant 7 acts as a reminder to human readers of the code, but the compiler disregards it. The other two constants are needed by the compiler to generate the correct storage mapping function.

Initialization

There are a number of ways to initialize a multidimensional array. Let us begin our discussion by considering the following three initializations, which are equivalent:

```
int   a[2][3] = {1, 2, 3, 4, 5, 6};
int   a[2][3] = {{1, 2, 3}, {4, 5, 6}};
int   a[ ][3] = {{1, 2, 3}, {4, 5, 6}};
```

If there are no inner braces, then each of the array elements a[0][0], a[0][1], ..., a[1][2] is initialized in turn. Note that the indexing is by rows. If there are fewer initializers than elements in the array, then the remaining elements are initialized to zero. If the first bracket pair is empty, then the compiler takes the size from the number of inner brace pairs. All sizes except the first must be given explicitly.

If we are willing to put in a lot of braces, then we do not have to specify all the zeros. Consider the initialization

```
int   a[2][2][3] = {
          {{1, 1, 0}, {2, 0, 0}},
          {{3, 0, 0}, {4, 4, 0}}
      };
```

An equivalent initialization is given by

```
int   a[][2][3] = {{{1, 1}, {2}}, {{3}, {4, 4}}};
```

If the initializers are fully and consistently braced, then wherever there are not enough initializers listed, the remaining elements are initialized to zero.

In general, if an array of storage class automatic is not explicitly initialized, then array elements start with "garbage" values. Here is a simple way to initialize all array elements to zero:

```
int   a[2][2][3] = {0};        /* all element initialized to zero */
```

Unlike automatic arrays, all static and external arrays are initialized to zero by default.

The Use of `typedef`

Let us illustrate the use of `typedef` by defining a small number of functions that operate on vectors and matrices.

```
#define    N    3        /* the size of all vectors and matrices */

typedef    double    scalar;
typedef    scalar     vector[N];
typedef    scalar     matrix[N][N];
```

We have used the `typedef` mechanism to create the types `scalar`, `vector`, and `matrix`, which is both self-documenting and conceptually appropriate. Our programming language has been extended in a natural way to incorporate these new types as a domain. Notice how `typedef` can be used to build hierarchies of types. For example, we could have written

```
typedef    vector    matrix[N];
```

in place of

```
typedef    scalar    matrix[N][N];
```

The use of `typedef` to create type names such as `scalar`, `vector`, and `matrix` allows the programmer to think in terms of the application. Now we are ready to create functions that provide operations over our domain.

```
void add(vector x, vector y, vector z)      /* x = y + z */
{
    int i;

    for (i = 0; i < N; ++i)
        x[i] = y[i] + z[i];
}

scalar dot_product(vector x, vector y)
{
    int       i;
    scalar    sum = 0.0;

    for (i = 0; i < N; ++i)
        sum += x[i] * y[i];
    return sum;
}

void multiply(matrix a, matrix b, matrix c)      /* a = b * c */
{
    int    i, j, k;

    for (i = 0; i < N; ++i)
        for (j = 0; j < N; ++j) {
            a[i][j] = 0.0;
            for (k = 0; k < N; ++k)
                a[i][j] += b[i][k] * c[k][j];
        }
}
```

These routines are not generic because they work only with matrices of fixed size. We show how this limitation is removed in Section 12.6, "Dynamic Allocation of Matrices."

6.13   ARRAYS OF POINTERS

Arrays of pointers have many uses. In this section we write a program that uses an array of pointers to sort words in a file lexicographically. As we will see, an array of type char * can be thought of as an array of strings.

To explain how our program works, we need to imagine first how we are going to test it. Let us create the file *input* with the following two lines in it:

A is for apple or alphabet pie
which all get a slice of, come taste it and try.

To sort the words in this file, we give the command

  sort_words < input

This causes the following to be printed on the screen:

```
A
a
all
alphabet
.....
which
```

Now we are ready to discuss our program. It will consist of three functions written in a single file. Here is the top of the file and the first function:

```
/* Sort words lexicographically. */

#include <stdio.h>
#include <stdlib.h>
#include <string.h>

#define   MAXWORD   50          /* max word size */
*/ #define   N         1000       /* array size */

void    sort_words(char *[], int);
void    swap(char **, char **);

int main(void)
{
    char    *w[N];                  /* an array of pointers */
    char    word[MAXWORD];          /* work space */
    int     n;                      /* number of words to be sorted */
    int     i;

    for (i = 0; scanf("%s", word) == 1; ++i) {
        if (i >= N) {
            printf("Sorry, at most %d words can be sorted.", N);
            exit(1);
        }
        w[i] = calloc(strlen(word) + 1, sizeof(char));
        strcpy(w[i], word);
    }
    n = i;
    sort_words(w, n);
    for (i = 0; i < n; ++i)          /* print the sorted words */
        printf("%s\n", w[i]);
    return 0;
}
```

DISSECTION OF main() IN THE *sort_words* PROGRAM

■
```
#define   MAXWORD   50        /* max word size */
#define   N         1000      /* array size */
```
We are assuming that no word in the file has more than 50 characters and that there are at most 1000 words in the file.

■
```
char    *w[N];                /* an array of pointers */
char    word[MAXWORD];        /* work space */
```
Because of operator precedence,

`char    *w[N];`   is equivalent to   `char    *(w[N]);`

Thus w is an array of pointers to char. We will use word to temporarily store each word that is read from the file.

■
```
for (i = 0; scanf("%s", word) == 1; ++i) {
    .....
```
As long as scanf() is able to read characters from the standard input file and store them in word, the body of the for loop is executed. Recall that scanf() takes as arguments a control string followed by addresses that are matched with the formats in the control string. Note that because word is the name of an array, it is itself an address. Technically, it is an error to use &word instead of word as the second argument to scanf(). However, many compilers simply ignore the & operator used in this context, and some compilers ignore it and do not even tell you they are doing so!

■
```
w[i] = calloc(strlen(word) + 1, sizeof(char));
```
The function calloc() is in the standard library and its function prototype is in *stdlib.h*. A function call such as

`calloc(n, sizeof(...))`

dynamically allocates space for an array of n elements, with each element requiring sizeof(...) bytes in memory, and returns a pointer to the allocated space. The minimum number of bytes needed to store the string word, including the end-of-string sentinel \0, is strlen(word) + 1. The function calloc() dynamically allocates this space and returns a pointer to it. The pointer is assigned to w[i].

■   `strcpy(w[i], word);`

After space has been allocated, the function `strcpy()` is used to copy `word` into memory starting at the address `w[i]`. At the end of the `for` loop we can think of `w` as an array of words.

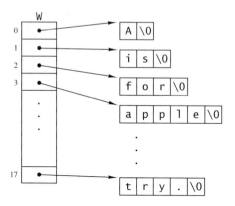

■   `sort_words(w, n);`
```
for (i = 0; i < n; ++i)          /* print the sorted words */
    printf("%s\n", w[i]);
```
The function `sort_words()` is used to sort the words in the array lexicograph-ically. Then the words are printed.

Now we want to look at the function `sort_words()`. It uses a transposition sort that is similar in flavor to a bubble sort.

```
void sort_words(char *w[], int n)    /* n elements will be sorted */
{
    int    i, j;

    for (i = 0; i < n; ++i)
        for (j = i + 1; j < n; ++j)
            if (strcmp(w[i], w[j]) > 0)
                swap(&w[i], &w[j]);
}
```

Notice that `strcmp()` is used to compare the two strings pointed to by `w[i]` and `w[j]`. If they are out of order, we use the function `swap()` to interchange the two pointer values. The addresses of the pointers are passed so that the pointer values themselves can be changed in the calling environment by the function call. The underlying character strings in memory do not get swapped; only the pointers to them are interchanged.

Finally, we look at the function swap(). Each of the two arguments passed to the function is an address of a pointer to char, or equivalently, a pointer to pointer to char.

```
void swap(char **p, char **q)
{
    char    *tmp;

    tmp = *p;
    *p = *q;
    *q = tmp;
}
```

Because p is a pointer to pointer to char, the expression *p that dereferences p is of type pointer to char, or char *. Thus the variable tmp is declared to be of type char *. This swap() function is similar to the one we wrote previously, except that the types are different.

Before swapping:

After swapping:

Of course, if the *sort_words* program were intended for serious work on a large amount of data, we would use a more efficient sorting algorithm. We could, for example, modify our merge() and merge_sort() functions to work on arrays of pointers to char rather than on arrays of ints (see Exercise 36).

6.14   ARGUMENTS TO main()

Two arguments, conventionally called argc and argv, can be used with main() to communicate with the operating system. Here is a program that prints its command line arguments. It is a variant of the *echo* command in MS-DOS and UNIX.

```
/* Echoing the command line arguments. */

#include <stdio.h>

int main(int argc, char *argv[])
{
    int    i;

    printf("argc = %d\n", argc);
    for (i = 0; i < argc; ++i)
        printf("argv[%d] = %s\n", i, argv[i]);
    return 0;
}
```

The variable argc provides a count of the number of command line arguments. The array argv is an array of pointers to char that can be thought of as an array of strings. The strings are the words that make up the command line. Because the element argv[0] contains the name of the command itself, the value of argc is always 1 or more.

   Suppose we compile the above program and put the executable code in the file *my_echo*. If we give the command

   my_echo a is for apple

the following is printed on the screen:

```
argc = 5
argv[0] = my_echo
argv[1] = a
argv[2] = is
argv[3] = for
argv[4] = apple
```

On an MS-DOS system, the string in argv[0] consists of the full pathname of the command, and it is capitalized. As we will see in Chapter 11, file names are often passed as arguments to main().

6.15   RAGGED ARRAYS

We want to contrast a two-dimensional array of type char with a one-dimensional array of pointers to char. Both similarities and differences exist between these two constructs.

```
#include <stdio.h>

int main(void)
{
   char   a[2][15] = {"abc:", "a is for apple"};
   char   *p[2]    = {"abc:", "a is for apple"};

   printf("%c%c%c %s %s\n%c%c%c %s %s\n",
      a[0][0], a[0][1], a[0][2], a[0], a[1],
      p[0][0], p[0][1], p[0][2], p[0], p[1]);
   return 0;
}
```

The output of this program is the following:

```
abc abc: a is for apple
abc abc: a is for apple
```

The program and its output illustrate similarities in how the two constructs are used. Let us consider the program in some detail.

The identifier a is a two-dimensional array, and its declaration causes space for 30 chars to be allocated. The two-dimensional initializer is equivalent to

```
{{'a', 'b', 'c', ':', '\0'}, {'a', ' ', 'i', 's', ... }}
```

The identifier a is an array, each of whose elements is an array of 15 chars. Thus a[0] and a[1] are arrays of 15 chars. Because arrays of characters are strings, a[0] and a[1] are strings. The array a[0] is initialized to

```
{'a', 'b', 'c', ':', '\0'}
```

and because only five elements are specified, the rest are initialized to zero (the null character). Even though not all elements are used in this program, space has been allocated for them. The compiler uses a storage mapping function to access a[i][j]. Each access requires one multiplication and one addition.

The identifier p is a one-dimensional array of pointers to char. Its declaration causes space for two pointers to be allocated (4 bytes for each pointer on our machine). The element p[0] is initialized to point at "abc:", a string that requires space for 5 chars. The element p[1] is initialized to point at "a is ...", a string that requires space for 15 chars, including the null character \0 at the end of the string. Thus p does its work in less space than a. Moreover, the compiler does not generate code for a storage mapping function to access p[i][j], which means that p does its work faster than a. Note that a[0][14] is a valid expression, but that p[0][14] is not. The expression p[0][14] overruns the bounds of the string pointed to by p[0]. Of course, a[0][14] overruns the string a[0], but it does not overrun the array a[0]. Hence the expression a[0][14] is acceptable.

An array of pointers whose elements are used to point to arrays of varying sizes is called a *ragged array*. Because, in the above program, the rows of p have different lengths, it is an example of a ragged array. If we think of the elements p[i][j] arranged as a "rectangular" collection of elements in rows and columns, the disparate row lengths give the "rectangle" a ragged look. Hence the name "ragged array."

A ragged array

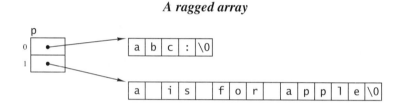

6.16   FUNCTIONS AS ARGUMENTS

In C, pointers to functions can be passed as arguments, used in arrays, returned from functions, and so forth. In this section we describe how this facility works.

Suppose we want to carry out a computation with a variety of functions. For example, consider the computation

$$\sum_{k=m}^{n} f^2(k)$$

where in one instance $f(k) = \sin(k)$ and in another instance f is given by

$$f(k) = \frac{1}{k}$$

The following routine accomplishes the task:

```
double sum_square(double f(double), int m, int n)
{
    int      k;
    double   sum = 0.0;

    for (k = m; k <= n; ++k)
        sum += f(k) * f(k);
    return sum;
}
```

Notice that in the header to the function definition the first parameter declaration tells the compiler that f is a function that takes an argument of type double and returns a double. When a function occurs in a parameter declaration, the compiler interprets it as a pointer. Here is an equivalent header to the function definition:

```
double sum_square(double (*f)(double), int m, int n)
{
    .....
```

The first parameter declaration is read as "f is a pointer to function that takes a single argument of type double and returns a double." The parentheses are necessary because () binds tighter than *. In contrast, consider the declaration

```
double   *g(double);
```

This declares g to be a function that takes an argument of type double and returns a pointer to double.

In the body of the function definition for sum_square() we can either treat the pointer f as if it were a function, or we can explicitly dereference the pointer. For example, we could have written

```
sum += (*f)(k) * (*f)(k);        instead of        sum += f(k) * f(k);
```

It is helpful to think of the construct (*f)(k) as follows:

f	the pointer to a function
*f	the function itself
(*f)(k)	the call to the function

To illustrate how the function `sum_square()` might be used, let's write a complete program. In `main()`, we will use `sin()` from the standard library and the function `f()`, which we will write ourselves.

```c
#include <stdio.h>

double    f(double);
double    sin(double);
double    sum_square(double (*)(double), int, int);

int main(void)
{
    printf("%s%.7f\n%s%.7f\n",
        " First computation: ", sum_square(sin, 2, 13),
        "Second computation: ", sum_square(f, 1, 10000));
    return 0;
}

double sum_square(double (*f)(double), int m, int n)
{
    int       k;
    double    sum = 0.0;

    for (k = m; k <= n; ++k)
        sum += f(k) * f(k);
    return sum;
}

double f(double x)
{
    return 1.0 / x;
}
```

The output of this program is

```
 First computation: 5.7577885
Second computation: 1.6448341
```

In mathematics it is known that the sum of $1/k^2$ from 1 to infinity is $\pi^2/6$. Notice that the second number in the output of the program approximates this. The function prototype of `sum_square()` that we gave in `main()` can be written in a number of equivalent ways. We will illustrate this in the next section. *Caution:* ANSI C expects function prototypes and headers to function definitions to agree, or to be of equivalent form. If your compiler complains about the function prototype for `sum_square()`, take instead a copy of the header of the function definition as the prototype. (Your compiler is not supposed to complain.)

6.17 AN EXAMPLE: USING BISECTION TO FIND THE ROOT OF A FUNCTION

An important problem that arises in engineering, mathematics, and physics is to find the root of a given real-valued function. A real number x that satisfies the equation $f(x) = 0$ is called a root of f. In simple cases—for example, if f is a quadratic polynomial—a formula for the roots is known. In general, however, there is no formula, and a root must be found by numerical methods.

Suppose that f is a continuous real-valued function defined on the interval $[a, b]$. If $f(a)$ and $f(b)$ are of opposite sign, then the continuity of the function guarantees that it has a root in the interval $[a, b]$.

Finding a root by bisection

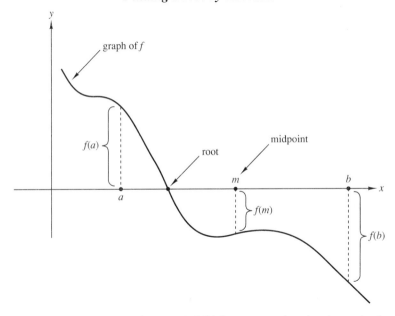

Notice that the condition that $f(a)$ and $f(b)$ have opposite sign is equivalent to the product $f(a) f(b)$ being negative. The method of bisection proceeds as follows. Let m be the midpoint of the interval. If $f(m)$ is zero, we have found a root. If not, then either $f(a)$ and $f(m)$ are of opposite sign or $f(m)$ and $f(b)$ are of opposite sign. Suppose that the first case holds. We then know that f has a root in the interval $[a, m]$, and we now start the process over again. After each iteration we obtain an interval that is half the length of the previous interval. When the interval is sufficiently small, we take its midpoint as an approximation to a root of f. In general, we cannot hope to find the exact root. For most functions the precise mathematical root will not have an exact machine representation.

```
/* Find a root of f() by the bisection method. */

#define   EPS   1e-12                    /* epsilon */

double root(double f(double), double a, double b)
{
   double   m = (a + b) / 2.0;      /* midpoint */

   if (f(m) == 0.0 || b - a < EPS)
      return m;
   else if (f(a) * f(m) < 0.0)
      return root(f, a, m);
   else
      return root(f, m, b);
}
```

Now we want to test our function. We first write main(), which invokes root()
with a polynomial p() as an argument. Then we write the code for a particular
fifth-degree polynomial p().

```
#include <stdio.h>

double    p(double);
double    root(double (*)(double), double, double);

int main(void)
{
   double   x;

   x = root(p, 0.0, 3.0);
   printf("%s%.16f\n%s%.16f\n",
      "Approximate root: ", x,
      " Function value: ", p(x));
   return 0;
}

double p(double x)
{
   return (x * x * x * x * x  -  7.0 * x  -  3.0);
}
```

The output of the program is

```
Approximate root: 1.7196280914844584
  Function value: 0.0000000000000317
```

Here is a list of equivalent function prototypes for root():

```
double    root(double (*)(double), double, double);
double    root(double (*f)(double), double, double);
double    root(double f(double), double, double);
double    root(double f(double), double a, double b);
double    root(double f(double x), double a, double b);
```

In the last three declarations the identifier f is being interpreted by the compiler as a pointer to a function. Other than this, f is not used. Nonetheless, we may not discard it. The following prototype is incorrect:

```
double    root(double (double), double, double);    /* wrong */
```

The Kepler Equation

In the early 1600s Johannes Kepler wanted to solve the equation

$$m = x - e \sin(x)$$

for various values of the parameters m and e. One way to view the problem is to graph

$$y = x \qquad \text{and} \qquad y = m + e \sin(x)$$

together. A solution to the Kepler equation then corresponds to the point where the two graphs intersect.

A solution to the Kepler equation

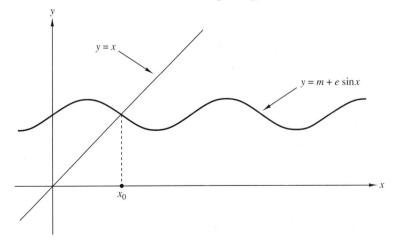

We want to write a program that solves the Kepler equation when the parameters have the values $m = 2.2$ and $e = 0.5$. Here is the complete program:

```
#include <stdio.h>
#include <math.h>

#define    E      0.5
#define    M      2.2
#define    EPS    1e-15

double    kepler(double x);
double    root(double f(double x), double a, double b);

int main(void)
{
    double    x;
    x = root(kepler, -100.0, +100.0);
    printf("%s%.16f\n%s%.16f\n",
        "Approximate root: ", x,
        " Function value: ", kepler(x));
    return 0;
}

double kepler(double x)
{
    return (x - E * sin(x) - M);
}

/* Find a root of f() by the bisection method. */

double root(double f(double), double a, double b)
{
    double    m = (a + b) / 2.0;      /* midpoint */

    if (f(m) == 0.0 || b - a < EPS)
        return m;
    else if (f(a) * f(m) < 0.0)
        return root(f, a, m);
    else
        return root(f, m, b);
}
```

Here is the output of this program.

```
Approximate root: 2.4994545281635010
 Function value: 0.0000000000000004
```

6.18 ARRAYS OF POINTERS TO FUNCTION

The function root() that we discussed in Section 6.17 takes as its first argument
a function, or more precisely, a pointer to function. In C, a function name by itself
is treated by the compiler as a pointer to the function. This is similar to how C
treats array names. Technically speaking, when we pass kepler as an argument to
root(), it is the address of kepler() that gets passed. To illustrate how a pointer
could be used, here is another way to write main():

```
int main(void)
{
    double   x;
    double   (*pfdd)(double);    /* ptr to fct taking double
                                    and returning double    */

    pfdd = &kepler;
    x = root(pfdd, -100.0, +100.0);
    . . . . .
```

Observe that pfdd is a pointer of type "pointer to function taking a single argument
of type double and returning a double." Like other C pointers, pfdd is strongly
typed and can only be assigned pointer values of the same type. Because kepler()
is a function taking a double and returning a double, we can assign &kepler to
pfdd. However, because a function name by itself is treated as a pointer, we could
just as well have written

```
pfdd = kepler;
```

Because the type for pfdd matches the type of the first parameter in the function
prototype for root(), we can pass pfdd as an argument to root().

In our next program we create an array of pointers, each of type "pointer to function taking a `double` and returning a `double`." We then deal with each array element (function pointer) in a `for` loop.

```
/* Find the roots of several functions. */

#include <stdio.h>
#include <math.h>

#define    EPS    1e-12
#define    N      3

typedef double (*PFDD)(double);    /* ptr to fct taking double
                                      and returning double */
double    f1(double x);
double    f2(double x);
double    f3(double x);
double    root(double f(double x), double a, double b);

int    cnt = 0;           /* global variable */

int main(void)
{
    PFDD       g[N] = {&f1, &f2, &f3};
    int        i;
    int        begin_cnt;
    double     x0;

    for (i = 0; i < N; ++i) {
        begin_cnt = cnt;
        x0 = root(g[i], -100.0, +100.0);
        printf("For g[%d] (x) an approximate root"
                " is x0 = %.16f\n", i, x0);
        printf(" Fct evaluation at the root:"
                " g[%] (x0) = %.16f\n", i, g[i] (x0));
        printf(" Number of function calls"
                " to root() =%3d\n\n", cnt - begin_cnt);
    }
    return 0;
}

double f1(double x)
{
    return (x*x*x - x*x + 2.0*x - 2.0);
}
```

```
double f2(double x)
{
    return (sin(x) - 0.7*x*x*x + 3.0);
}

double f3(double x)
{
    return (exp(0.13*x) - x*x*x);
}

double root(double f(double), double a, double b)
{
    double   m = (a + b) / 2.0;       /* midpoint */

    ++cnt;                            /* global */
    if (f(m) == 0.0 || b - a < EPS)
        return m;
    else if (f(a) * f(m) < 0.0)
        return root(f, a, m);
    else
        return root(f, m, b);
}
```

When we execute this program, here is what gets printed on the screen:

```
For g[0](x) an approximate root is x0 = 1.0000000000001563
 Fct evaluation at the root: g[0](x0) = 0.0000000000004690
    Number of function calls to root() = 49

For g[1](x) an approximate root is x0 = 1.7844142783818739
 Fct evaluation at the root: g[1](x0) = 0.0000000000023137
    Number of function calls to root() = 49

For g[2](x) an approximate root is x0 = 1.0463871738071617
 Fct evaluation at the root: g[2](x0) = -0.0000000000002731
    Number of function calls to root() = 49
```

DISSECTION OF THE *find_roots* PROGRAM

■ `typedef double (*PFDD)(double);`   /* ptr to fct taking double
                                            and returning double */
  This `typedef` makes PFDD a new name for the type "pointer to function taking a single argument of type `double` and returning a `double`." We will see that the use of PFDD makes the code easier to write and easier to read.

- ```
  double    root(double f(double x), double a, double b);
  ```
  This is the function prototype for `root()`. We could just as well have written

  ```
  double    root(PFDD f, double a, double b);
  ```

  Although this is shorter, the longer form is just as clear.

- ```
  int    cnt = 0;        /* global variable */
  ```
  Because this variable is declared at the top of the file outside of any function definition, it is a global variable. Every time the function `root()` gets called, `cnt` gets incremented.

- ```
  PFDD      g[N] = {&f1, &f2, &f3};
  ```
  We declare g to be an array of N elements, with each element having type PFDD. The array is initialized with three pointer values. The following declarations are equivalent:

  ```
  PFDD      g[N] = {f1, f2, f3};
  PFDD      g[N] = {&f1, &f2, &f3};
  double    (*g[N])(double) = {f1, f2, f3};
  double    (*g[N])(double) = {&f1, &f2, &f3};
  ```

  We can choose any one from this list to use as our declaration of g.

- ```
  x0 = root(g[i], -100.0, +100.0);
  ```
  Here, the pointer `g[i]` is being passed as an argument to `root()`. Equivalently, we could have written

  ```
  x0 = root(*g[i], -100.0, +100.0);
  ```

  When we dereference the pointer, we get the function that it points to. But the compiler treats a function by itself as a pointer to the function, so the two ways of writing this are equivalent. The words "function by itself" mean that the function is not followed by parentheses. If a function name or a function pointer or a dereferenced function pointer is followed by parentheses, then we have a call to the function.

- ```
  g[i](x)
  ```
  This is a call to the function pointed to by `g[i]`. If we wish, we can write

  ```
  (*g[i])(x)
  ```

  instead. Because x0 is the computed root, the value of `g[i](x0)` should be close to zero. When we print this value, we see that it is indeed close to zero.
  ```

Note that each of our functions f1(), f2(), and f3() takes on values with opposite signs at the end points of the interval [−100, 100]. Our calls to root() will not work if this condition does not hold.

6.19 THE TYPE QUALIFIERS const AND volatile

The keywords const and volatile have been added to the C language by the ANSI C committee. These keywords are not available in traditional C. They are called *type qualifiers* because they restrict, or qualify, the way an identifier of a given type can be used.

Let us first discuss how const is used. Typically, in a declaration const comes after the storage class, if any, but before the type. Consider the declaration

```
static const int   k = 3;
```

We read this as "k is a constant int with static storage class." Because the type for k has been qualified by const, we can initialize k, but thereafter k cannot be assigned to, incremented, or decremented.

In C, even though a variable has been qualified with const, it still cannot be used to specify an array size in another declaration. In C++, however, it can be used for this purpose. This is one of the few places where C and C++ differ.

```
const int   n = 3;
int         v[n];        /* any C compiler will complain */
```

In some situations we can use a const-qualified variable instead of a symbolic constant; in other situations, we cannot.

An unqualified pointer should not be assigned the address of a const-qualified variable. The following code illustrates the problem:

```
const int   a = 7;
int         *p = &a;     /* the compiler will complain */
```

Here is the reason why the compiler complains. Because p is an ordinary pointer to int, we could use it later in an expression such as ++*p to change the stored value of a, violating the concept that a is constant. If, however, we write

```
const int   a = 7;
const int   *p = &a;
```

then the compiler will be happy. The last declaration is read "p is a pointer to a constant int and its initial value is the address of a." Note that p itself is not constant. We can assign to it some other address. We may not, however, assign a value to *p. The object pointed to by p should not be modified.

Suppose we want p itself to be constant, but not a. This is achieved with the declarations

```
int             a;
int * const     p = &a;
```

We read the last declaration as "p is a constant pointer to int, and its initial value is the address of a." Thereafter, we may not assign a value to p, but we may assign a value to *p. Now consider

```
const int             a = 7;
const int * const     p = &a;
```

The last declaration tells the compiler that p is a constant pointer to a constant int. Neither p nor *p can be assigned to, incremented, or decremented.

In contrast to const, the type qualifier volatile is seldom used. A volatile object is one that can be modified in some unspecified way by the hardware. Consider the declaration

```
extern const volatile int   real_time_clock;
```

The extern means "look for it elsewhere, either in this file or in some other file." The qualifier volatile indicates that the object may be acted on by the hardware. Because const is also a qualifier, the object may not be assigned to, incremented, or decremented within the program. The hardware can change the clock, but the code cannot.

6.20 SUMMARY

1 The brackets [] are used in a declaration to tell the compiler that an identifier is an array. The integral constant expression in the brackets specifies the size of the array. For example, the declaration

```
int   a[100];
```

causes the compiler to allocate contiguous space in memory for 100 ints. The elements of the array are numbered from 0 to 99. The array name a by itself is a constant pointer; its value is the base address of the array.

2 A pointer variable takes addresses as values. Some typical values are NULL, addresses of variables, string constants, and pointer values, or addresses, returned from functions such as calloc(). If allocation fails—for example, the system free store (heap) is exhausted—then NULL is returned.

3   The address operator & and the indirection or dereferencing operator ∗ are unary operators with the same precedence and right to left associativity as other unary operators. If v is a variable, then the expression

     ∗&v   is equivalent to   v

4   Pointers are used as formal parameters in headers to function definitions to effect "call by reference." When addresses of variables are passed as arguments, they can be dereferenced in the body of the function to change the values of variables in the calling environment.

5   In C, arrays and pointers are closely related topics. If a is an array and i is an int, then the expression

     a[i]   is equivalent to   ∗(a + i)

These expressions can be used to access elements of the array. The expression a + i is an example of pointer arithmetic. Its value is the address of the element of the array that is i elements beyond a itself. That is, a + i is equivalent to &a[i].

6   In the header to a function definition, the declaration of a parameter as an array is equivalent to its declaration as a pointer. For example,

     int a[]   is equivalent to   int ∗a

This equivalence does *not* hold elsewhere.

7   When an array is passed as an argument to a function, a pointer is actually passed. The array elements themselves are not copied.

8   Strings are one-dimensional arrays of characters. By convention, they are terminated with the null character \0, which acts as the end-of-string sentinel.

9   The standard library contains many useful string handling functions. For example, strlen() returns the length of a string and strcat() concatenates two strings.

10   Arrays of any type can be created, including arrays of arrays. For example,

     double   a[3][7];

declares a to be an array of "array of 7 doubles." The elements of a are accessed by expressions such as a[i][j]. The base address of the array is &a[0][0], not a. The array name a by itself is equivalent to &a[0].

11   In the header to a function definition, the declaration of a multidimensional array must have all sizes specified except the first. This allows the compiler to generate the correct storage mapping function.

12 Arguments to main() are typically called argc and argv. The value of argc is the number of command line arguments. The elements of the array argv are addresses of the command line arguments. We can think of argv as an array of strings.

13 Ragged arrays are constructed from arrays of pointers. The elements of the array can point to arrays with different sizes.

14 Like an array name, a function name that is passed as an argument is treated as a pointer. In the body of the function the pointer can be used to call the function in the normal way, or it can be explicitly dereferenced.

15 The type qualifiers const and volatile have been added to ANSI C. They are not available in traditional C.

6.21   EXERCISES

1 Four values get printed when the following code is executed. How many of those values are the same? Explain.

```
char    *format = "%p %d %d %d\n";
int     i = 3;
int     *p = &i;

printf(format, p, *p + 7, 3 * **&p + 1, 5 * (p - (p - 2)));
```

2 One of our compilers warned us about integer overflow for the expression p - (p - 2) in Exercise 1. Modify the program that you wrote in Exercise 1 so that it prints the integer values of both p and p - 2. Does it seem possible that integer overflow can occur? (See Exercise 3 for further discussion.)

3 Consider the following program:

```
#include <stdio.h>
#include <stddef.h>

int main(void)
{
    int         a, b, *p = &a, *q = &b;
    ptrdiff_t   diff = p - q;

    printf("diff = %d\n", diff);
    return 0;
}
```

In ANSI C, the difference of two pointer expressions must be a signed integral type. On most UNIX systems, the type is int and on most MS-DOS systems the type is long. On all ANSI C systems, the type is given in the standard header file *stddef.h* by a type definition of the following form:

```
typedef    type    ptrdiff_t;
```

Find this `typedef` in *stddef.h* on your system so you will know the type for
`diff`. Note that `%d` is appropriate in the `printf()` statement if `diff` has type
`int` and that `%ld` is appropriate if `diff` has type `long`. Run the program so you
understand its effects. Then modify the program by adding the following two
lines:

```
diff = p - (int *) 0;
printf("diff = %d\n", diff);
```

Are you surprised by what gets printed now? Do you understand the reason for
the compiler warning that was discussed in Exercise 2? Explain. If `int *` is
replaced by `ptrdiff_t *`, does the program act any differently?

4 If `i` and `j` are `int`s and `p` and `q` are pointers to `int`, which of the following
assignment expressions are not legal?

```
p = &i        p = &*&i      i = (int) p      q = &p
*q = &j        i = (*&)j     i = *&*&j        i = *p++ + *q
```

5 When variables are declared, are they located in memory contiguously? Write
a program with the declaration

```
char    a, b, c, *p, *q, *r;
```

and print out the locations that are assigned to all these variables by your compiler. Are the locations in order? If the locations are in order, are they increasing
or decreasing? Is the address of each pointer variable divisible by 4? If so, this
probably means that each pointer value gets stored in a machine word.

6 The following program uses `%p` formats to print out some addresses:

```
#include <stdio.h>

int main(void)
{
    int    a = 1, b = 2, c = 3;

    printf("%s%p\n%s%p\n%s%p\n",
        "&a = ", &a,
        "&b = ", &b,
        "&c = ", &c);
    return 0;
}
```

If the variables a, b, and c are not initialized, does the program produce the same output? What happens on your system if you change %p to %d? Does your compiler complain? (It should.) If possible, run your program on an MS-DOS system. Because a pointer is 4 bytes and an int is 2 bytes, the %d format is inappropriate and can cause a negative number to be printed.

7 If you want to see addresses printed as decimal numbers rather than hexadecimals, it is usually safe to cast an address as an unsigned long and use the %lu format. Try this on your system by replacing the printf() statement in Exercise 6 by

```
printf("%s%lu\n%s%lu\n%s%lu\n",
    "&a = ", (unsigned long) &a,
    "&b = ", (unsigned long) &b,
    "&c = ", (unsigned long) &c);
```

8 What gets printed? Explain.

```
#include <stdio.h>

typedef    unsigned long    ulong;

int main(void)
{
    char            *pc = NULL;
    int             *pi = NULL;
    double          *pd = NULL;
    long double     *pld = NULL;

    printf("%5lu%5lu\n%5lu%5lu\n%5lu%5lu\n",
        (ulong)(pc + 1), (ulong)(pi + 1),
        (ulong)(pd + 1), (ulong)(pld + 1),
        (ulong)(pc + 3), (ulong)(pld + 3));
    return 0;
}
```

9 The following array declarations have several errors. Identify each of them.

```
#define    N    4

int    a[N] = {0, 2, 2, 3, 4};
int    b[N - 5];
int    c[3.0];
```

10 In the following program the invocation of change_it() seems to have no
    effect. Explain.

```
#include <stdio.h>

void    change_it(int []);

int main(void)
{
   int    a[5], *p;

   p = a;
   printf("p has the value %p\n", p);
   change_it(a);
   p = a;
   printf("p has the value %p\n", p);
   return 0;
}

void change_it(int a[])
{
   int    i = 777, *q = &i;

   a = q;      /* a is assigned a different value */
}
```

11 What is wrong with the following program? Correct the program and explain
    the meaning of its output.

```
#include <stdio.h>

int main(void)
{
   int    a[] = {0, 2, 4, 6, 8},
          *p = a + 3;

   printf("%s%d%s\n%s%d%s\n",
      "a[?]    = ", *p,       "?",
      "a[?+1] = ", *p + 1, "?");
   return 0;
}
```

12 A real polynomial $p(x)$ of degree n or less is given by

$$p(x) = a_0 + a_1 x + a_2 x^2 + \ldots + a_n x^n$$

with the coefficients $a_0, a_1, \ldots, a_n$ representing real numbers. If $a_n \neq 0$, then the degree of $p(x)$ is n. Polynomials can be represented in a machine by an array such as

```
#define   N   5          /* N is the max degree */

double    p[N + 1];
```

Write a function

```
double eval(double p[], double x, int n) /* n is max degree */
{
    . . . . .
```

that returns the value of the polynomial p evaluated at x. Write two versions of the function. The first version should be written with a straightforward naive approach. The second version should incorporate Horner's Rule. For fifth-degree polynomials, Horner's Rule is expressed by writing

$$p(x) = a_0 + x\,(a_1 + x\,(a_2 + x\,(a_3 + x\,(a_4 + x\,(a_5)))))$$

How many additions and multiplications are used in each of your two versions of the eval() function?

13 Write a function that adds two polynomials of at most degree n.

```
/* f = g + h;   n is the max degree of f, g, and h */

void add(double f[], double g[], double h[], n)
{
    . . . . .
```

14 Write an algorithm to multiply two polynomials of at most degree n. Use your function add() to sum intermediate results. This is not very efficient. Can you write a better routine?

15 Modify the function bubble() so that it terminates after the first pass in which no two elements are interchanged.

16 Modify `mergesort()` so that it can be used with an array of any size, not just with a size that is a power of 2. Recall that any positive integer can be expressed as a sum of powers of 2—for example,

   $$27 = 16 + 8 + 2 + 1$$

   Consider the array as a collection of subarrays of sizes that are powers of 2. Sort the subarrays and then use `merge()` to produce the final sorted array.

17 Write a program that will test the relative efficiency of the function `bubble()` given in Section 6.7 versus the function `mergesort()` that you wrote in Exercise 16. Generate test data by using `rand()` to fill arrays. Run your program on arrays of various sizes, say with 10, 100, 500, and 1000 elements. Plot the running time for each sort versus the size of the array. For large array sizes you should see the growth indicated by the formulas given in the text. For small array sizes there is too much overhead to detect this growth pattern. If you are unfamiliar with how to time program execution, see Section 11.16, "How To Time C Code." (If you are on a UNIX system, you can give the command

   time pgm

   to time a program.)

18 A palindrome is a string that reads the same both forward and backward. Some examples are

   `"ABCBA"`   `"123343321"`   `"otto"`   `"i am ma i"`   `"C"`

   Write a function that takes a string as an argument and returns the `int` value 1 if the string is a palindrome and returns 0 otherwise. If UNIX is available to you, how many palindromes can you find in the file */usr/dict/words*?

19 Modify your palindrome function from Exercise 18 so that blanks and capitals are ignored in the matching process. Under these rules, the following are examples of palindromes:

   `"Anna"`   `"A man a plan a canal Panama"`   `"ott o"`

   If UNIX is available to you, how many more palindromes can you find in the file */usr/dict/words*?

20 What gets printed? Explain.

```
printf("%c%c%c%c%c!\n",
    "ghi"[1], *("def" + 1),
    *"abc" + 11, "klm"[1], *"ghi" + 8);
```

21 In Chapter 3 we saw that the largest value that can be stored in an `int` is
approximately 2 billion. In many applications, such numbers are not big enough.
For example, the federal government has to deal with figures in the trillions of
dollars. (Or is it quadrillions?) In this exercise we want to explore, in a primitive
fashion, how two large integers can be added. Here is a program that will do
this:

```
#include <stdio.h>

#define   N    20

static void    add(int sum[], int a[], int b[]);
static void    prn_num(int a[]);

int main(void)
{
    int    a[N] = {7, 5, 9, 8, 9, 7, 5, 0, 0, 9, 9, 0, 8, 8};
    int    b[N] = {7, 7, 5, 3, 1, 2, 8, 8, 9, 6, 7, 7};
    int    sum[N];

    printf("Integer a: ");
    prn_num(a);
    printf("Integer b: ");
    prn_num(b);
    add(sum, a, b);
    printf("     Sum: ");
    prn_num(sum);
    return 0;
}
```

```
static void add(int sum[], int a[], int b[])
{
   int   carry, i;

   carry = 0;
   for (i = 0; i < N; ++i) {
      sum[i] = a[i] + b[i] + carry;
      if (sum[i] < 10)
         carry = 0;
      else {
         carry = sum[i] / 10;
         sum[i] %= 10;
      }
   }
}

static void prn_num(int a[])
{
   int   i;

   for (i = N - 1; i >= 0; --i) {
      if (a[i] == 0)
         putchar(' ');
      else
         break;
   }
   for ( ; i >= 0; --i)
      printf("%d", a[i]);
   putchar('\n');
}
```

When we execute this program, here is what appears on the screen:

```
Integer a:      88099005798957
Integer b:        776988213577
     Sum:      88875994012534
```

Note that the digits are stored in array elements going from element 0 to element $N - 1$, but that the digits are printed in the opposite order. To understand this program, review how you learned to do addition in grade school. Write a similar program that computes the product of two integers.

22 The `sizeof` operator can be used to find the number of bytes needed to store a
    type or an expression. When applied to arrays, it does *not* yield the size of the
    array. What gets printed? Explain.

```
#include <stdio.h>

void    f(int a[]);

int main(void)
{
    char     s[]  = "deep in the heart of texas";
    char     *p   = "deep in the heart of texas";
    int      a[3];
    double   d[5];

    printf("%s%d\n%s%d\n%s%d\n%s%d\n",
        "sizeof(s) = ", sizeof(s),
        "sizeof(p) = ", sizeof(p),
        "sizeof(a) = ", sizeof(a),
        "sizeof(d) = ", sizeof(d));
    f(a);
    return 0;
}

void f(int a[])
{
    printf("In f(): sizeof(a) = %d\n", sizeof(a));
}
```

23 If UNIX is available to you and you are familiar with the *diff* utility, try the
    following experiment. Use the two statements

```
printf("abc\n");        and        printf("a%cb%cc\n", '\0', '\0');
```

to write two versions of an elementary program that writes on the screen. Use
redirection to put the printout of the respective programs into two files, say *tmp1*
and *tmp2*. If you use the UNIX utility *cat* to print first one file on the screen
and then the other, you will not see any difference. Now try the command

   diff tmp1 tmp2

Do you see what the confusion is? Explain. *Hint:* Use the *od* command with
the *−c* option to get a more complete view of what is in the files. By the way,
why did we use the %c format? Why not just print the string "a\0b\0c\n"?

24 In traditional C, changing the contents of a string constant was allowed, although it was considered poor programming practice to do so. In ANSI C, the programmer is not supposed to be able to change a string constant. However, compilers vary in their ability to enforce this. Consider the following code:

```
char    *p = "abc";

*p = 'X';                   /* illegal? */
printf("%s\n", p);          /* Xbc gets printed? */
```

On our system, one of our compilers does not complain and the program executes, whereas another compiler exhibits a run-time error. What happens on your system?

25 Consider the following code:

```
char    *p = "abc", *q = "abc";

if (p == q)
    printf("The two strings have the same address!\n");
else
    printf("As I expected, the addresses are different.\n");
```

Both p and q have been initialized to the base address in memory of a string constant—namely, "abc". Note that p == q tests whether two pointer values are the same; it is *not* a test for equality of the contents of the strings pointed to by p and q. Are there two string constants in memory or only one? This is compiler-dependent. Moreover, many compilers provide an option that determines whether all string constants with the same content get stored separately or as just one string. In traditional C, because string constants could be overwritten (see Exercise 24), string constants with the same content were usually stored separately. In contrast to this, many ANSI C compilers store them in the same place. What happens on your system?

26 The ANSI C committee has introduced the type qualifier `const` as a new key-
    word in the C language. Here is an example of its use:

```
const char   *p;
```

Here, the type qualifier `const` tells the compiler that the character in memory
pointed to by p should not be changed. (Read "p is a pointer to a constant
`char`.") Compilers vary on their ability to enforce this. Try the following code:

```
char        s[] = "abc";
const char  *p = s;

*p = 'A';                    /* illegal? */
printf("%s\n", s);
```

Does your compiler complain? (It should.)

27 A lot of effort has been expended on the problem of machine translation. How
    successful is a naive approach? Go to a library to find out what the most
    common, say 100, English words are. Consult, for example, *The American
    Heritage Word Frequency Book* by John Carroll et al. (Boston, Mass.: Houghton
    Mifflin, 1971). Write down the 100 words and, with the help of a foreign
    language dictionary, write down their translation. Write a program that uses two
    arrays such as

```
char   *foreign[100], *english[100];
```

to translate foreign text to English. Test your program. (You may be surprised
at the results.) Instead of 100 words, try 200. Does your program produce a
significantly better translation?

28 A simple encryption scheme is to interchange letters of the alphabet on a one-
    to-one basis. This can be accomplished with a translation table for the 52 lower-
    and uppercase letters. Write a program that uses such a scheme to encode text.
    Write another program that will decode text that has been encoded. This is not
    a serious encryption scheme. Do you know why? If you are interested, learn
    about a more secure encryption system and then program it. If UNIX is available
    to you, read the online manual concerning *crypt* to get the flavor of some of the
    concerns in the area of encryption.

29 What gets printed? Explain.

```
#include <stdio.h>

void    try_me(int [][3]);

int main(void)
{
    int    a[3][3] = {{2, 5, 7}, {0, -1, -2}, {7, 9, 3}};

    try_me(a);
    return 0;
}

void try_me(int (*a)[3])
{
    printf("%d %d %d %d  . . .  infinity\n",
        a[1][0], -a[1][1], a[0][0], a[2][2]);
}
```

Now, change the declaration of the parameter in the header of the function definition of try_me( ) to

```
int *a[3]
```

and leave the rest of the code alone. Does your compiler complain? (It should.) Explain.

30 Choose a character and use a two-dimensional array that matches the size of your screen to graph on the screen the functions sin( ) and cos( ) from 0 to 2π. Because, on most screens, the space in which a character is printed is not square, there is horizontal/vertical distortion. Experiment with your graphs to see if you can remove this distortion.

31 Write out a dissection for the following program. An understanding of the storage mapping function is needed to explain it. A complete explanation of the last `printf()` statement is rather technical and should only be attempted by advanced computer science students.

```
#include <stdio.h>

int main(void)
{
    int    a[3][5], i, j,
           *p = *a;     /* a nice initialization! */

    for (i = 0; i < 3; ++i)
       for (j = 0; j < 5; ++j)
          a[i][j] = i * 5 + j;
    for (i = 0; i < 3; ++i)
       for (j = 0; j < 5; ++j)
          printf("%s%12d", (j == 0) ? "\n" : "", a[i][j]);
    printf("\n");
    for (i = 0; i < 15; ++i)
          printf("%s%12d", (i % 5 == 0) ? "\n" : "", *(p + i));
    printf("\n\n%12d%12d\n%12d%12d\n%12d%12d\n%12d%12d\n\n",
       **a, **(a + 1),
       *(a[0] + 1), *(*a + 1),
       *(a[1] + 2), *(*(a + 1) + 2),
       *(a[2] + 3), *(*(a + 2) + 3));
    printf("%-11s%s%12d\n%-11s%s%12d\n%-11s%s%12d\n\n",
       "(int) a", "=", (int) a,
       "(int) *a", "=", (int) *a,
       "(int) **a", "=", (int) **a);
    return 0;
}
```

32 Modify the *my_echo* program so that it will print out its arguments in capital letters if the option −*c* is present. Do not print out the argument that contains the option.

33 Complete the following table.

Declarations and initializations

```
char    *p[2][3] = {"abc", "defg", "hi",
                    "jklmno", "pqrstuvw", "xyz" };
```

Expression	Equivalent expression	Value
***p	p[0][0][0]	'a'
**p[1]		
**(p[1] + 2)		
((p + 1) + 1)[7]		/* error */
(*(*(p + 1) + 1))[7]		
*(p[1][2] + 2)		

34 Simulations that involve the repeated use of a random number generator to reproduce a probabilistic event are called Monte Carlo simulations, so-called because Monte Carlo has one of the world's most famous gaming casinos. In this exercise we want to find the probability that at least two people in a room with n people have birthdays that fall on the same day of the year. Assume that there are 365 days in a year, and assume that the chance of a person being born on each day of the year is the same. A single trial experiment consists of filling an array of size n with integers that are randomly distributed from 1 to 365. If any two elements in the array have the same value, then we say that the trial is "true." Thus a true trial corresponds to the case when at least two people in the room were born on the same day of the year. Simulate the probability by running, say, 10,000 trials with n people in the room. Do this for $n = 2, 3, \ldots,$ 100. You can use the expression

```
rand() % 365 + 1
```

to compute the day of birth for each person. (Use a better random number generator, such as lrand48(), if one is available to you.) The number of true trials divided by 10000 is the computed simulated probability. What value of n yields the break-even point? That is, find the least n for which the probability is 1/2 or more.

35 The computational methodology that we suggested in Exercise 34 will certainly work, but so will other techniques. For this exercise, write another version of the program that you wrote in Exercise 34, this time using the computational methodology suggested in Exercise 27 in Chapter 5. Which methodology is better? There are at least three ways to consider this question:

>   Which program runs faster?
>
>   Which program is easier to code?
>
>   Which program uses the least amount of memory?

Address each one of these questions.

36 Modify the function `merge()` given in the text and the function `mergesort()` that you wrote in Exercise 16 to work on arrays of pointers to `char` rather than on arrays of `int`s. Modify the *sort_words* program to use these functions. Time both versions of the program on a large file. The program that uses `mergesort()` should run much faster. Does it?

37 The following code can be used to reverse the characters in a string:

```
char *reverse(char *s)
{
    char    *p, *q, tmp;
    int     n;

    n = strlen(s);
    q = (n > 0) ? s + n - 1 : s;
    for (p = s; p < q; ++p, --q) {
        tmp = *p;
        *p = *q;
        *q = tmp;
    }
    return s;
}
```

Test this function by writing a program that contains the following lines:

```
char    str[] = "abcdefghijklmnopqrstuvwxyz";

printf("%s\n", reverse(str));
```

Execute your program so that you understand its effects. The following shows
what is in memory at the beginning of the for loop:

Explain why this picture is correct. Draw a series of similar pictures that describe
the state of the memory after each iteration of the for loop.

38 Recall that argc and argv are typically used as arguments to main(). Because
argc is the number of command line arguments, one might think that the size
of the array argv is argc, but that is not so. The array argv has size argc +
1, and the last element in the array is the null pointer. Here is another version
of the *echo* command:

```
#include <stdio.h>

int main(int argc, char **argv)
{
    while (*argv != NULL)
        printf("%s  ", *argv++);
    putchar('\n');
    return 0;
}
```

Run the program so you understand its effects. Give a detailed explanation of
how it works. *Hint:* If a pointer to pointer to char is dereferenced, then the
result is a pointer to char. Also, reread the dissection of the strcat() function
in Section 6.11.

39 In C, a function prototype can occur more than once. Moreover, equivalent
    function prototypes do not conflict. Modify the *find_roots* program that we
    wrote in Section 6.18 by replacing the function prototype

```
double   root(double f(double x), double a, double b);
```

with the following list of function prototypes:

```
double   root(PFDD, double, double);
double   root(PFDD fp, double a, double b);
double   root(double (*)(double), double, double);
double   root(double (*f)(double), double, double);
double   root(double f(double), double a, double b);
double   root(double f(double x), double a, double b);
```

Does your compiler complain? (It shouldn't.)

40 In Section 6.18, "Arrays of Pointers to Function," we saw that the *find_roots*
    program made 49 calls to root( ) each time a root of a function was computed.
    Use a hand calculator to explain why precisely 49 calls were made. *Hint:* Most
    of the calls to root( ) cut the interval in half.

41 Compile and execute the following program so that you understand its effects:

```
#include <stdio.h>
#include <string.h>

void   tell_me(int f(const char *, const char *));

int main(void)
{
    tell_me(strcmp);
    tell_me(main);
    return 0;
}

void tell_me(int f(const char *, const char *))
{
    if (f == strcmp)
        printf("Address of strcmp(): %p\n", f);
    else
        printf("Function address: %p\n", f);
}
```

Because the pointer being passed in the second call to tell_me() has the wrong type, your compiler should complain. Does it? Modify the program to get rid of the warning by using the generic void * pointer type.

42 (Advanced) The following program has an error in it.

```
#include <stdio.h>
#include <string.h>

int main(void)
{
    char   *p1 = "abc", *p2 = "pacific sea";

    printf("%s   %s   %s\n", p1, p2, strcat(p1, p2));
    return 0;
}
```

On our system, what happens is compiler-dependent. With one of our compilers, the program exhibits a run-time error. With another compiler, we get the following written to the screen:

abcpacific sea   acific sea   abcpacific sea

This output makes sense and tells us something about the compiler. What programming error did we make? What does the output tell us about our compiler? Which is the preferred behavior: a compiler that produces executable code that exhibits a run-time error, or a compiler that produces (sometimes) logically incorrect output?

43 A function name by itself is treated by the compiler as a pointer. This is a general rule in C. Is the following code legal?

```
#include <stdio.h>

void    f(void);
void    g(void);
void    h(void);

int main(void)
{
    (*f)();
    return 0;
}

void f(void)
{
    printf("Hello from f().\n");
    (((*g)))();
}

void g(void)
{
    printf("Hello from g().\n");
    (*(*(*h)))();
}

void h(void)
{
    printf("Hello from h().\n");
}
```

Write your answer before you try to compile the program. Your answer should be based on your general knowledge about how well a C compiler can be expected to follow a rule, even if the rule is applied in some strange way.

44 A precondition for the root() solver to work is that f(a) and f(b) must have opposite signs. Use an assertion at the beginning of root() to check this condition.

45 The ancient Egyptians wrote in hieroglyphics. In this system of writing, vowel sounds are not represented, only consonants. Is written English generally understandable without vowels? To experiment, write a function is_vowel() that returns 1 if a letter is a vowel and 0 otherwise. Use your function in a program that reads the standard input file and writes to the standard output file, deleting all vowels. Use redirection on a file containing some English text to test your program.

CHAPTER **7**

BITWISE OPERATORS AND ENUMERATION TYPES

There are two additional ways to represent discrete values: as bits and as elements in a finite set. In this chapter we first discuss the bitwise operators. Even though expressions involving bitwise operators are explicitly system-dependent, they are very useful. We illustrate their usefulness in packing and unpacking data.

In the second half of the chapter, we discuss the enumeration types. These are user-defined types that allow the programmer to name a finite set together with its elements, which are called *enumerators*. These types are defined and used by the programmer as the need arises. We illustrate much of this material by implementing a completely worked out interactive game program.

7.1 BITWISE OPERATORS AND EXPRESSIONS

The bitwise operators act on integral expressions represented as strings of binary digits. These operators are explicitly system-dependent. We will restrict our discussion to machines having 8-bit bytes, 4-byte words, the two's complement representation of integers, and ASCII character codes.

Bitwise operators		
Logical operators:	(unary) bitwise complement:	~
	bitwise and:	&
	bitwise exclusive or:	^
	bitwise inclusive or:	|
Shift operators:	left shift:	<<
	right shift:	>>

Like other operators, the bitwise operators have rules of precedence and associativity that determine precisely how expressions involving them are evaluated.

Operators	Associativity
() ++ *(postfix)* -- *(postfix)*	left to right
++ *(prefix)* -- *(prefix)* ! ~ sizeof (*type*) + *(unary)* - *(unary)* & *(address)*	right to left
* / %	left to right
+ -	left to right
<< >>	left to right
< <= > >=	left to right
== !=	left to right
&	left to right
^	left to right
|	left to right
&&	left to right
||	left to right
?:	right to left
= += *= <<= >>= *etc*	right to left
, *(comma operator)*	left to right

The operator ~ is unary; all the other bitwise operators are binary. They operate on integral expressions. We will discuss each of the bitwise operators in detail.

Bitwise Complement

The operator ~ is called the *complement operator*, or the *bitwise complement operator*. It inverts the bit string representation of its argument; the 0s become 1s, and the 1s become 0s. Consider, for example, the declaration

```
int   a = 70707;
```

The binary representation of a is

```
00000000 00000001 00010100 00110011
```

The expression ~a is the bitwise complement of a, and this expression has the binary representation

    11111111 11111110 11101011 11001100

The int value of the expression ~a is -70708.

Two's Complement

The *two's complement representation* of a nonnegative integer n is the bit string obtained by writing n in base 2. If we take the bitwise complement of the bit string and add 1 to it, we obtain the two's complement representation of $-n$. The next table gives some examples. To save space, we show only the two low-order bytes.

Value of n	Binary representation	Bitwise complement	Two's complement representation of $-n$	Value of $-n$
7	00000000 00000111	11111111 11111000	11111111 11111001	-7
8	00000000 00001000	11111111 11110111	11111111 11111000	-8
9	00000000 00001001	11111111 11110110	11111111 11110111	-9
-7	11111111 11111001	00000000 00000110	00000000 00000111	7

The preceding table is read from left to right. If we start with a positive integer n, consider its binary representation, and take its bitwise complement and add 1, then we obtain the two's complement representation of $-n$. A machine that uses the two's complement representation as its binary representation in memory for integral values is called a *two's complement machine*.

On a two's complement machine, if we start with the binary representation of a negative number $-n$ and take its bitwise complement and add 1, we obtain the two's complement representation, or binary representation, of n. This is illustrated in the last line in the above table.

The two's complement representations of both 0 and -1 are special. The value 0 has all bits off; the value -1 has all bits on. Note that if a binary string is added to its bitwise complement, then the result has all bits on, which is the two's complement representation of -1. Negative numbers are characterized by having the high bit on.

On a two's complement machine, the hardware that does addition and bitwise complementation can be used to implement subtraction. The operation a - b is the same as a + (-b), and -b is obtained by taking the bitwise complement of b and adding 1.

Bitwise Binary Logical Operators

The three operators & (and), ∧ (exclusive or), and | (inclusive or) are binary operators. They take integral expressions as operands. The two operands, properly widened, are operated on bit position by bit position. The following table shows the bitwise operators acting on 1-bit fields. The table defines the semantics of the operators.

Values of:				
a	b	a & b	a ∧ b	a | b
0	0	0	0	0
1	0	0	1	1
0	1	0	1	1
1	1	1	0	1

The next table contains examples of the bitwise operators acting on int variables.

Declarations and initializations		
int a = 33333, b = -77777;		
Expression	Representation	Value
a	00000000 00000000 10000010 00110101	33333
b	11111111 11111110 11010000 00101111	−77777
a & b	00000000 00000000 10000000 00100101	32805
a ∧ b	11111111 11111110 01010010 00011010	−110054
a | b	11111111 11111110 11010010 00111111	−77249
~(a | b)	00000000 00000001 00101101 11000000	77248
(~a & ~b)	00000000 00000001 00101101 11000000	77248

Left and Right Shift Operators

The two operands of a shift operator must be integral expressions. The integral promotions are performed on each of the operands. The type of the expression as a whole is that of its promoted left operand. An expression of the form

   expr1 << *expr2*

causes the bit representation of *expr1* to be shifted to the left by the number of places specified by *expr2*. On the low-order end, 0s are shifted in.

Declaration and initialization		

`char    c = 'Z';`

Expression	Representation	Action
c	00000000 00000000 00000000 01011010	unshifted
c << 1	00000000 00000000 00000000 10110100	left-shifted 1
c << 4	00000000 00000000 00000101 10100000	left-shifted 4
c << 31	00000000 00000000 00000000 00000000	left-shifted 31

Even though c is stored in 1 byte, in an expression it gets promoted to an int. When shift expressions are evaluated, integral promotions are performed on the two operands separately, and the type of the result is that of the promoted left operand. Thus the value of an expression such as c << 1 gets stored in 4 bytes.

The right shift operator >> is not quite symmetric to the left shift operator. For unsigned integral expressions, 0s are shifted in at the high end. For the signed types, some machines shift in 0s, while others shift in sign bits (see Exercise 4). The sign bit is the high-order bit; it is 0 for nonnegative integers and 1 for negative integers.

Declarations and initializations		

```
int        a = 1 << 31;  /* shift 1 to the high bit */
unsigned   b = 1 << 31;
```

Expression	Representation	Action
a	10000000 00000000 00000000 00000000	unshifted
a >> 3	11110000 00000000 00000000 00000000	right-shifted 3
b	10000000 00000000 00000000 00000000	unshifted
b >> 3	00010000 00000000 00000000 00000000	right-shifted 3

Note that on our machine, sign bits are shifted in with an int. On another machine, 0s might be shifted in. To avoid this difficulty, programmers often use unsigned types when using bitwise operators.

If the right operand of a shift operator is negative or has a value that equals or exceeds the number of bits used to represent the left operand, then the behavior is undefined. It is the programmer's responsibility to keep the value of the right operand within proper bounds.

Our next table illustrates the rules of precedence and associativity with respect to the shift operators. To save space, we show only the two low-order bytes.

Declaration and assignments			
unsigned a = 1, b = 2;			
Expression	**Equivalent expression**	**Representation**	**Value**
a << b >> 1	(a << b) >> 1	00000000 00000010	128
a << 1 + 2 << 3	(a << (1 + 2)) << 3	00000000 01000000	64
a + b << 12 * a >> b	((a + b) << (12 * a)) >> b	00001100 00000000	3072

In C++, the two shift operators are *overloaded* and used for input/output. Overloading in C++ is a method of giving existing operators and functions additional meanings. See Chapter 13 for examples and explanation.

7.2   MASKS

A mask is a constant or variable that is used to extract desired bits from another variable or expression. Because the `int` constant 1 has the bit representation

```
00000000 00000000 00000000 00000001
```

it can be used to determine the low-order bit of an `int` expression. The following code uses this mask and prints an alternating sequence of 0s and 1s:

```
int    i, mask = 1;

for (i = 0; i < 10; ++i)
    printf("%d", i & mask);
```

If we wish to find the value of a particular bit in an expression, we can use a mask that is 1 in that position and 0 elsewhere. For example, we can use the expression 1 << 2, as a mask for the third bit, counting from the right. The expression

```
(v & (1 << 2)) ? 1 : 0
```

has the value 1 or 0 depending on the third bit in v.

Another example of a mask is the constant value 255, which is $2^8 - 1$. It has the following bit representation:

```
00000000 00000000 00000000 11111111
```

Because only the low-order byte is turned on, the expression

    v & 255

will yield a value having a bit representation with all its high-order bytes zero and its low-order byte the same as the low-order byte in v. We express this by saying, "255 is a mask for the low-order byte."

7.3 SOFTWARE TOOLS: PRINTING AN int BITWISE

Software tools are utilities that the programmer can use to write software. Most systems provide a variety of software tools. Examples are compilers, debuggers, and the *make* utility. We will discuss these in Chapter 11. Programmers often write other software tools for their own use as the need arises. The bit_print() function that we discuss in this section is a typical example. For anyone writing software that deals with the machine at the bit level, the bit_print() utility is essential; it allows the programmer to see what is happening. For the beginning programmer, exploration with bit_print() helps to provide a conceptual framework that is very useful.

Our bit_print() function uses a mask to print out the bit representation of an int. The function can be used to explore how values of expressions are represented in memory. We used it, in fact, to help create the tables in this chapter.

```
/* Bit print an int expression. */

#include <limits.h>

void bit_print(int a)
{
    int    i;
    int    n = sizeof(int) * CHAR_BIT;          /* in limits.h */
    int    mask = 1 << (n - 1);                 /* mask = 100...0 */

    for (i = 1; i <= n; ++i) {
        putchar(((a & mask) == 0) ? '0' : '1');
        a <<= 1;
        if (i % CHAR_BIT == 0 && i < n)
            putchar(' ');
    }
}
```

DISSECTION OF THE `bit_print()` FUNCTION

■ `#include <limits.h>`

In ANSI C, the symbolic constant CHAR_BIT is defined in *limits.h*. In traditional C, this header file is not usually available. The value of CHAR_BIT on most systems is 8. It represents the number of bits in a char, or equivalently, the number of bits in a byte. ANSI C requires at least 8 bits in a byte.

■ `int   n = sizeof(int) * CHAR_BIT;        /* in limits.h */`

Because we want this function to work on machines having either 2- or 4-byte words, we use the variable n to represent the number of bits in a machine word. We expect the value of the expression sizeof(int) to be either 2 or 4, and we expect that the symbolic constant CHAR_BIT, which is defined in the standard header file *limits.h*, will be 8. Thus we expect n to be initialized to either 16 or 32, depending on the machine.

■ `int   mask = 1 << (n - 1);                /* mask = 100...0 */`

Because of operator precedence, the parentheses are not needed in the initialization. We put them there to make the code more readable. Because << has higher precedence than =, the expression 1 << (n - 1)) gets evaluated first. Suppose that n has value 32. The constant 1 has only its low-order bit turned on. The expression 1 << 31 shifts that bit to the high-order end. Thus mask has all its bits off except for its high-order bit (sign bit), which is on.

■
```
for (i = 1; i <= n; ++i) {
   putchar(((a & mask) == 0) ? '0' : '1');
   a <<= 1;
   .....
```

First consider the expression

```
(a & mask) == 0
```

If the high-order bit in a is off, then the expression a & mask has all its bits off, and the expression (a & mask) == 0 is *true*. Conversely, if the high-order bit in a is on, then the expression a & mask has its high-order bit on, and the expression (a & mask) == 0 is *false*. Now consider the expression

```
((a & mask) == 0) ? '0' : '1'
```

If the high-order bit in a is off, then the conditional expression has the value '0'; otherwise, it has the value '1'. Thus putchar() prints a 0 if the high-order bit is off and prints a 1 if it is on.

■ `putchar(((a & mask) == 0) ? '0' : '1');`
   `a <<= 1;`
   After the high-order bit in a has been printed, we left-shift the bits in a by 1
   and place the result back in a. Recall that

   `a <<= 1;`   is equivalent to   `a = a << 1;`

   The value of the expression a << 1 has the same bit pattern as a, except that it
   has been left-shifted by 1. The expression by itself does not change the value of
   a in memory. In contrast to this, the expression a <<= 1 does change the value
   of a in memory. Its effect is to bring the next bit into the high-order position,
   ready to be printed the next time through the loop.

■ `if (i % CHAR_BIT == 0 && i < n)`
   `    putchar(' ');`
   If we assume that the value of the symbolic constant CHAR_BIT is 8, then this
   code causes a blank to be printed after each group of 8 bits has been printed. It
   is not necessary to do this, but it certainly makes the output easier to read.

7.4 PACKING AND UNPACKING

The use of bitwise expressions allows for data compression across byte boundaries.
This is useful in saving space, but it can be even more useful in saving time. On
a machine with 4-byte words, each instruction cycle processes 32 bits in parallel.
The following function can be used to pack four characters into an int. It uses shift
operations to do the packing byte by byte.

```
/* Pack 4 characters into an int. */

#include <limits.h>

int pack(char a, char b, char c, char d)
{
    int   p = a;                     /* p will be packed with a, b, c, d */

    p = (p << CHAR_BIT) | b;
    p = (p << CHAR_BIT) | c;
    p = (p << CHAR_BIT) | d;
    return p;
}
```

To test our function, we write a program with the lines

```
printf("abcd = ");
bit_print(pack('a', 'b', 'c', 'd'));
putchar('\n');
```

in main(). Here is the output of our test program:

```
abcd = 01100001 01100010 01100011 01100100
```

Observe that the high-order byte has value 97, or 'a', and that the values of the remaining bytes are 98, 99, and 100. Thus pack() did its work properly.

Having written pack(), we now want to be able to retrieve the characters from within the 32-bit int. Again, we can use a mask to do this.

```
/* Unpack a byte from an int. */

#include <limits.h>

char unpack(int p, int k)                /* k = 0, 1, 2, or 3 */
{
    int        n = k * CHAR_BIT;         /* n = 0, 8, 16, or 24 */
    unsigned   mask = 255;               /* low-order byte */

    mask <<= n;
    return ((p & mask) >> n);
}
```

DISSECTION OF THE unpack() FUNCTION

■ `#include <limits.h>`
We have included this header file because it contains the definition of the symbolic constant CHAR_BIT. It represents the number of bits in a byte. On most machines its value is 8.

■ `char unpack(int p, int k)`   /* k = 0, 1, 2, or 3 */
`{`
`. . . . .`
We think of the parameter p as a packed int with its bytes numbered 0 through 3. The parameter k will indicate which byte we want: If k has value 0, then we want the low-order byte; if k has value 1, then we want the next byte; and so forth.

- `int        n = k * CHAR_BIT;`   `/* n = 0, 8, 16, or 24 */`
  If we assume that CHAR_BIT is 8 and that k has value 0, 1, 2, or 3, then n will be initialized with the value 0, 8, 16, or 24.

- `unsigned   mask = 255;`   `/* low-order byte */`
  The constant 255 is special; to understand it, first consider 256. Because $256 = 2^8$, the bit representation of 256 has all bits 0 except for a 1 in the 9th bit, counting from the low-order bit. Because 255 is one less than 256, the bit representation of 255 has all bits 0, except for the first 8 bits, which are all 1 (see Exercise 8). Thus the binary representation of mask is

      00000000 00000000 00000000 11111111

- `mask <<= n;`
  Let us assume that CHAR_BIT is 8. If n has value 0, then the bits in mask are not changed. If n has value 8, then the bits in mask are left-shifted by 8. In this case we think of mask stored in memory as

      00000000 00000000 11111111 00000000

  If n has value 16, then the bits in mask are left-shifted by 16. In this case we think of mask stored in memory as

      00000000 11111111 00000000 00000000

  In a similar fashion, if n has value 24, then mask will have only the bits in its high-order byte turned on.

- `(p & mask) >> n`
  Parentheses are needed because & has lower precedence than >>. Suppose that p has value −3579753 (which we chose because it has a suitable bit pattern), and suppose that n has value 16. The following table illustrates what happens:

Expression	Binary representation	Value
p	11111111 11001001 01100000 10010111	−3579753
mask	00000000 11111111 00000000 00000000	16711680
p & mask	00000000 11001001 00000000 00000000	13172736
(p & mask) >> n	00000000 00000000 00000000 11001001	201

- `return ((p & mask) >> n);`
  Because the function type for unpack() is char, the int expression (p & mask) >> n gets converted to a char before it gets passed back to the calling environment. When an int is converted to a char, only the low-order byte is retained; the other bytes are discarded.

Imagine wanting to keep an abbreviated employee record in one integer. We will suppose that an "employee identification number" can be stored in 9 bits and that a "job type" can be stored in 6 bits, which provides for a total of up to 64 different job types. The employee's "gender" can be stored in 1 bit. These three fields will require 16 bits, which, on a machine with 4-byte words, is a short integer. We can think of the three bit fields as follows:

Identification	Job type	Gender
bbbbbbbbb	bbbbbb	b

The following function can be used in a program designed to enter employee data into a short. The inverse problem of reading data out of the short would be accomplished with the use of masks.

```
/* Create employee data in a short int. */

short create_employee_data(int id_no, int job_type, char gender)
{
   short   employee = 0;      /* start with all bits off */

   employee |= (gender == 'm' || gender == 'M') ? 0 : 1;
   employee |= job_type << 1;
   employee |= id_no << 7;
   return employee;
}
```

Multicharacter Character Constants

Multibyte characters are allowed in ANSI C. An example is 'abc'. On a machine with 4-byte words, this causes the characters 'a', 'b', and 'c' to be packed into a single word. However, the order in which they are packed is machine-dependent. Some machines put 'a' in the low-order byte; others put it in the high-order byte (see Exercise 12).

7.5   ENUMERATION TYPES

The keyword enum is used to declare enumeration types. It provides a means of naming a finite set, and of declaring identifiers as elements of the set. Consider, for example, the declaration

```
enum day {sun, mon, tue, wed, thu, fri, sat};
```

This creates the user-defined type enum day. The keyword enum is followed by the tag name day. The enumerators are the identifiers sun, mon, ..., sat. They are constants of type int. By default, the first one is 0, and each succeeding one has the next integer value. This declaration is an example of a type specifier, which we also think of as a *template*. No variables of type enum day have been declared yet. To do so, we can now write

```
enum day    d1, d2;
```

This declares d1 and d2 to be of type enum day. They can take on as values only the elements (enumerators) in the set. Thus

```
d1 = fri;
```

assigns the value fri to d1, and

```
if (d1 == d2)
    .....          /* do something */
```

tests whether d1 is equal to d2. Note carefully that the type is enum day. The keyword enum by itself is not a type.

The enumerators can be initialized. Also, we can declare variables along with the template, if we wish to do so. The following is an example:

```
enum suit {clubs = 1, diamonds, hearts, spades}    a, b, c;
```

Because clubs has been initialized to 1, diamonds, hearts, and spades have the values 2, 3, and 4, respectively. In this example

```
enum suit {clubs = 1, diamonds, hearts, spades}
```

is the type specifier, and a, b, and c are variables of this type. Here is another example of initialization:

```
enum fruit {apple = 7, pear, orange = 3, lemon}    frt;
```

Because the enumerator apple has been initialized to 7, pear has value 8. Similarly, because orange has value 3, lemon has value 4. Multiple values are allowed, but the identifiers themselves must be unique.

```
enum veg {beet = 17, carrot = 17, corn = 17}    vege1, vege2;
```

The tag name need not be present. Consider, for example,

```
enum {fir, pine}   tree;
```

Because there is no tag name, no other variables of type enum {fir, tree} can be declared.

The following is the syntax for the enumeration declaration:

> *enum_declaration* ::= *enum_type_specifier identifier* { , *identifier* }$_{0+}$;
> *enum_type_specifier* ::=   enum *e_tag* { *e_list* }
> | enum *e_tag*
> | enum { *e_list* }
> *e_tag* ::= *identifier*
> *e_list* ::= *enumerator* { , *enumerator* }$_{0+}$
> *enumerator* ::= *identifier* { = *constant_integral_expression* }$_{opt}$

In general, one should treat enumerators as programmer-specified constants and use them to aid program clarity. If necessary, the underlying value of an enumerator can be obtained by using a cast. The variables and enumerators in a function must all have distinct identifiers. The tag names, however, have their own name space. This means that we can reuse a tag name as a variable or as an enumerator. The following is an example:

```
enum veg {beet, carrot, corn}   veg;
```

Although this is legal, it is not considered good programming practice.

We illustrate the use of the enumeration type by writing a function that computes the next day. The typedef facility is used to replace the enum keyword in the type declaration.

```
/* Compute the next day. */

enum day {sun, mon, tue, wed, thu, fri, sat};

typedef   enum day   day;   /*the usual typedef trick */

day find_next_day(day d)
{
    day   next_day;

    switch (d) {
    case sun:
        next_day = mon;
        break;
    case mon:
        next_day = tue;
        break;
    case tue:
        next_day = wed;
        break;
    case wed:
        next_day = thu;
        break;
    case thu:
        next_day = fri;
        break;
    case fri:
        next_day = sat;
        break;
    case sat:
        next_day = sun;
        break;
    }
    return next_day;
}
```

Recall that only a constant integral expression can be used in a `case` label. Because enumerators are constants, they can be used in this context. The following is another version of this function; this version uses a cast to accomplish the same ends:

```
/* Compute the next day with a cast. */

enum day {sun, mon, tue, wed, thu, fri, sat};

typedef   enum day   day;

day find_next_day(day d)
{
    day   next_day;

    return ((day)(((int) d + 1) % 7));
}
```

Enumeration types can be used in ordinary expressions provided type compatibility is maintained. However, if one uses them as a form of integer type and constantly accesses their implicit representation, it is better just to use integer variables instead. The importance of enumeration types is their self-documenting character, where the enumerators are themselves mnemonic. Furthermore, enumerators force the compiler to provide programmer-defined type checking so that one does not inadvertently mix apples and diamonds.

7.6   AN EXAMPLE: THE GAME OF PAPER, ROCK, SCISSORS

We will illustrate some of the concepts introduced in this chapter by writing a program to play the traditional children's game called "paper, rock, scissors." In this game each child uses her or his hand to represent one of the three objects. A flat hand held in a horizontal position represents "paper," a fist represents "rock," and two extended fingers represent "scissors." The children face each other and at the count of three display their choices. If the choices are the same, then the game is a tie. Otherwise, a win is determined by the rules:

Paper covers the rock.
Rock breaks the scissors.
Scissors cut the paper.

We will write this program in its own directory. The program will consist of a *.h* file and a number of *.c* files. Each of the *.c* files will include the header file at the top of the file. In the header file we put #include directives, templates for our enumeration types, type definitions, and function prototypes:

In file p_r_s.h:

```
/* The game of paper, rock, scissors. */

#include <ctype.h>          /* for isspace() */
#include <stdio.h>          /* for printf(), etc */
#include <stdlib.h>         /* for rand() and srand() */
#include <time.h>           /* for time() */

enum p_r_s {paper, rock, scissors,
            game, help, instructions, quit};

enum outcome {win, lose, tie, error};

typedef    enum p_r_s       p_r_s;
typedef    enum outcome     outcome;

outcome    compare(p_r_s player_choice, p_r_s machine_choice);
void       prn_final_status(int win_cnt, int lose_cnt);
void       prn_game_status(int win_cnt, int lose_cnt, int tie_cnt);
void       prn_help(void);
void       prn_instructions(void);
void       report_tabulate(outcome result,
               int *win_cnt_ptr, int *lose_cnt_ptr, int *tie_cnt_ptr);
p_r_s      selection_by_machine(void);
p_r_s      selection_by_player(void);
```

We do not normally comment our #include lines, but here we are trying to make the code more readable for the novice programmer. Here is our main() function:

In file main.c:

```c
#include "p_r_s.h"

int main(void)
{
    int         win_cnt = 0, lose_cnt = 0, tie_cnt = 0;
    outcome     result;
    p_r_s       player_choice, machine_choice;

    srand(time(NULL));        /* seed the random number generator */
    prn_instructions();
    while ((player_choice = selection_by_player()) != quit)
        switch (player_choice) {
        case paper:
        case rock:
        case scissors:
            machine_choice = selection_by_machine();
            result = compare(player_choice, machine_choice);
            report_tabulate(result, &win_cnt, &lose_cnt, &tie_cnt);
            break;
        case game:
            prn_game_status(win_cnt, lose_cnt, tie_cnt);
            break;
        case instructions:
            prn_instructions();
            break;
        case help:
            prn_help();
            break;
        default:
            printf("\nPROGRAMMER ERROR: Cannot get to here!\n\n");
            exit(1);
        }
    prn_game_status(win_cnt, lose_cnt, tie_cnt);
    prn_final_status(win_cnt, lose_cnt);
    return 0;
}
```

The first executable statement in main( ) is

```
srand(time(NULL));
```

This seeds the random number generator rand( ), causing it to produce a different sequence of integers each time the program is executed. More explicitly, passing srand( ) an integer value determines where rand( ) will start. The function call time(NULL) returns a count of the number of seconds that have elapsed since 1 January 1970 (the approximate birthday of UNIX). Both srand( ) and time( ) are provided in the standard library. The function prototype for srand( ) is in *stdlib.h*, and the function prototype for time( ) is in *time.h*. Both of these header files are provided by the system. Note that we included them in *p_r_s.h*.

The next executable statement in main( ) calls prn_instructions( ). This provides instructions to the user. Embedded in the instructions are some of the design considerations for programming this game. We wrote this function, along with other printing functions, in *prn.c*:

In file prn.c:

```
#include "p_r_s.h"

void prn_final_status(int win_cnt, int lose_cnt)
{
    if (win_cnt > lose_cnt)
        printf("CONGRATULATIONS - You won!\n\n");
    else if (win_cnt == lose_cnt)
        printf("A DRAW - You tied!\n\n");
    else
        printf("SORRY - You lost!\n\n");
}

void prn_game_status(int win_cnt, int lose_cnt, int tie_cnt)
{
    printf("\n%s\n%s%4d\n%s%4d\n%s%4d\n%s%4d\n\n",
        "GAME STATUS:",
        "   Win:    ", win_cnt,
        "   Lose:   ", lose_cnt,
        "   Tie:    ", tie_cnt,
        "   Total: ", win_cnt + lose_cnt + tie_cnt);
}
```

```
void prn_help(void)
{
   printf("\n%s\n",
      "The following characters can be used for input:\n"
      "     p   for paper\n"
      "     r   for rock\n"
      "     s   for scissors\n"
      "     g   print the game status\n"
      "     h   help, print this list\n"
      "     i   reprint the instructions\n"
      "     q   quit this game\n");
}

void prn_instructions(void)
{
   printf("\n%s\n",
      "PAPER, ROCK, SCISSORS:\n"
      "\n"
      "   In this game\n"
      "\n"
      "       p is for \"paper\"\n"
      "       r is for \"rock\"\n"
      "       s is for \"scissors\"\n"
      "\n"
      "   Both the player and the machine will choose one\n"
      "   of p, r, or, s. If the two choices are the same,\n"
      "   then the game is a tie. Otherwise:\n"
      "\n"
      "       \"paper covers the rock\"     (a win for paper),\n"
      "       \"rock breaks the scissors\"  (a win for rock),\n"
      "       \"scissors cut the paper\"    (a win for scissors).\n"
      "\n"
      "   There are other allowable inputs:\n"
      "\n"
      "       g   for game status     (the number of wins so far),\n"
      "       h   for help,\n"
      "       i   for instructions  (reprint these instructions),\n"
      "       q   for quit           (to quit the game).\n"
      "\n"
      "   This game is played repeatedly until q is entered.\n"
      "\n"
      "   Good luck!\n");
}
```

To play the game, both the machine and the player (user) need to make a selection from "paper, rock, scissors." We write these routines in *selection.c*:

In file selection.c:

```c
#include "p_r_s.h"

p_r_s selection_by_machine(void)
{
    return ((p_r_s) (rand() % 3));
}

p_r_s selection_by_player(void)
{
    char    c;
    p_r_s   player_choice;

    printf("Input p, r, or s:  ");
    while (isspace(c = getchar()))      /* skip white space */
        ;
    switch (c) {
    case 'p':
        player_choice = paper;
        break;
    case 'r':
        player_choice = rock;
        break;
    case 's':
        player_choice = scissors;
        break;
    case 'g':
        player_choice = game;
        break;
    case 'i':
        player_choice = instructions;
        break;
    case 'q':
        player_choice = quit;
        break;
    default:
        player_choice = help;
        break;
    }
    return player_choice;
}
```

The machine's selection is computed by the uses of the expression rand( ) % 3 to produce a randomly distributed integer between 0 and 2. Because the type of the function is p_s_r, the value returned will be converted to this type, if necessary. We provided an explicit cast to make the code more self-documenting.

Note that in selection_by_player( ) we use the macro isspace( ) from *ctype.h* to skip white space. (The macros in *ctype.h* are discussed in Chapter 8.) After white space is skipped, all other characters input at the terminal are processed, most of them through the default case of the switch statement.

The value returned by selection_by_player( ) determines which case gets executed in the switch statement in main( ). The value returned depends on what the player types. If the character g is input, then prn_game_status( ) is invoked; if any character other than white space or p, r, s, g, i, or q is input, then prn_help( ) is invoked.

Once the player and the machine have made a selection, we need to compare the two selections in order to determine the outcome of the game. The following function does this:

In file compare.c:

```
#include "p_r_s.h"

outcome compare(p_r_s player_choice, p_r_s machine_choice)
{
   outcome    result;

   if (player_choice == machine_choice)
      return tie;
   switch (player_choice) {
   case paper:
      result = (machine_choice == rock) ? win : lose;
      break;
   case rock:
      result = (machine_choice == scissors) ? win : lose;
      break;
   case scissors:
      result = (machine_choice == paper) ? win : lose;
      break;
   default:
      printf("\nPROGRAMMER ERROR: Unexpected choice!\n\n");
      exit(1);
   }
   return result;
}
```

The value returned by compare() in main() gets passed to the function report_and_tabulate(). This function reports to the user the result of a round of play and increments as appropriate the number of wins, losses, and ties.

In file report.c:

```
#include "p_r_s.h"

void report_tabulate(outcome result,
    int *win_cnt_ptr, int *lose_cnt_ptr, int *tie_cnt_ptr)
{
    switch (result) {
    case win:
        ++*win_cnt_ptr;
        printf("%27sYou win.\n", "");
        break;
    case lose:
        ++*lose_cnt_ptr;
        printf("%27sYou lose.\n", "");
        break;
    case tie:
        ++*tie_cnt_ptr;
        printf("%27sA tie.\n", "");
        break;
    default:
        printf("\nPROGRAMMER ERROR: Unexpected result!\n\n");
        exit(1);
    }
}
```

We are now ready to compile our program. We can do this with the command

cc −o p_r_s main.c compare.c prn.c report.c selection.c

Later, after we have learned about the *make* utility (see Chapter 11), we can facilitate program development by using an appropriate makefile.

7.7 SUMMARY

1 The bitwise operators provide the programmer with a means of accessing the bits in an integral expression. Typically, we think of the operands of these operators as bit strings.

2 The use of bitwise expressions allows for data compression across byte boundaries. This capability is useful in saving space, but it is even more useful in saving time. On a machine with 4-byte words, each instruction cycle processes 32 bits in parallel.

3 Most machines use the two's complement representation for integers. In this representation the high-order bit is the sign bit. It is 1 for negative integers and 0 for nonnegative integers.

4 Bitwise operations are explicitly machine-dependent. A left shift causes 0s to be shifted in. The situation for a right shift is more complicated. If the integral expression is `unsigned`, then 0s are shifted in. If the expression is one of the signed types, then what gets shifted in is machine-dependent. Some machines shift in sign bits. This means that if the sign bit is 0, then 0s are shifted in, and if the sign bit is 1, then 1s are shifted in. Some machines shift in 0s in all cases.

5 Masks are particular values used typically with the & operator to extract a given series of bits. Packing is the act of placing a number of distinct values into various subfields of a given variable. Unpacking extracts these values.

6 The keyword `enum` allows the programmer to define enumeration types. A variable of such a type can take values from the set of enumerators associated with the type.

7 Enumerators are distinct identifiers chosen for their mnemonic significance. Their use provides a type-checking constraint for the programmer, as well as self-documentation for the program.

8 Enumerators are constants of type `int`. Thus they can be used in `case` labels in a `switch`. A cast can be used to resolve type conflicts.

7.8 EXERCISES

1 Suppose that integers have a 16-bit two's complement representation. Write the binary representation for $-1, -5, -101, -1023$. Recall that the two's complement representation of negative integers is obtained by taking the bit representation of the corresponding positive integer, complementing it, and adding 1.

2 Alice, Betty, and Carole all vote on 16 separate referendums. Assume that each individual's vote is stored bitwise in a 16-bit integer. Write a function definition that begins

```
short majority(short a, short b, short c)
{
    .....
```

This function should take as input the votes of Alice, Betty, and Carole stored in a, b, and c, respectively. It should return the bitwise majority of a, b, and c.

3 Write a function definition that begins

```
int circular_shift(int a, int n)
{
    .....
```

This function should left-shift a by n positions, where the high-order bits are reintroduced as the low-order bits. Here are two examples of a circular shift operation defined for a char instead of an int:

10000001	circular shift 1 yields	00000011
01101011	circular shift 3 yields	01011011

4 Does your machine shift in sign bits? Here is some code that will help you determine this:

```
int       i = -1;        /* turn all bits on */
unsigned  u = -1;

if (i >> 1 == u >> 1)
    printf("Zeros are shifted in.\n");
else
    printf("Sign bits are shifted in.\n");
```

Explain why this code works.

5 Write a function that will reverse the bit representation of an int. Here are two examples of a reversing operation defined for a char instead of an int:

01110101	reversed yields	10101110
10101111	reversed yields	11110101

6 Write a function that will extract every other bit position from a 32-bit expression. The result should be returned as a 16-bit expression. Your function should work on machines having either 2- or 4-byte words.

7 Write a function that takes as its input a string of decimal integers. Each character in the string can be thought of as a decimal digit. The digits should be converted to 4-bit binary strings and packed into an int. If an int has 32 bits, then eight digits can be packed into it. When you test your function, here is what you might see on the screen:

```
Input a string of decimal digits:  12345678

12345678 = 0001 0010 0011 0100 0101 0110 0111 1000
```

Also, write an inverse function. It should unpack an `int` and return the original string. *Hint:* Here is one way to begin a conversion function:

```
int convert(char *s)
{
    char   *p;
    int     a = 0;    /* turn all bits off */

    for (p = s; *p != '\0'; ++p) {
        a <<= 4;
        switch (*p) {
        case '1':
            a |= 1;
            break;
        case '2':
        .....
```

8 Use the `bit_print()` function to create a table containing n, the binary representation for 2^n, and the binary representation for $2^n - 1$, for $n = 0, 1, 2, \ldots, 32$. If your machine has 2-byte words, then the output of your program should look like this:

```
 0:   00000000 00000001     00000000 00000000
 1:   00000000 00000010     00000000 00000001
 2:   00000000 00000100     00000000 00000011
.....
15:   10000000 00000000     01111111 11111111
.....
```

After you have done this, write down a similar table by hand that contains n, 10^n, and $10^n - 1$ for $n = 0, 1, 2, \ldots, 7$. Write the numbers in base 10 in your table. Do you see the similarity between the two tables? *Hint:* Use the following code:

```
int    i, power = 1;

for (i = 0; i < 32; ++i) {
    printf("%2d:   ", i);
    bit_print(power);
    printf("   ");
    bit_print(power - 1);
    putchar('\n');
    power *= 2;
}
```

9 Some of the binary representations in the tables in this chapter are easy to check for correctness, and some are not. Use bit_print() to check some of the more difficult representations.

10 Write a version of the bit_print() function that will work on machines with either 2- or 4-byte words. *Hint:* Use the sizeof operator to find the number of bytes in an int.

11 If you are not familiar with the use of the constants 0xff, 0xff00, 0xff0000, and 0xff000000 as masks, write a test program that uses bit_print() to print these values as bit strings.

12 If your machine has 4-byte words, use the function bit_print() to find out how the multibyte character 'abc' is stored on your machine. If your machine has 2-byte words, then you can put only two characters into a multibyte character. In that case, try 'ab'.

13 Write a roulette program. The roulette (machine) will select a number between 0 and 35 at random. The player can place an odd/even bet, or can place a bet on a particular number. A winning odd/even bet is paid off at 2 to 1, except that all odd/even bets lose if the roulette selects 0. If the player places a bet on a particular number and the roulette selects it, then the player is paid off at 35 to 1. If you play this game and make one-dollar bets, how long can you play before you lose ten dollars?

14 Write a function called previous_month() that returns the previous month. Start with the code

```
enum month {jan, feb, ..., dec};
typedef   enum month   month;
```

If dec is passed as an argument to the function, then jan should be returned. Write another function that prints the name of a month. More explicitly, if the enumerator jan is passed as an argument, then January should be printed. Write main() so that it calls your functions and produces a table of all twelve months, each one listed next to its predecessor month. *Caution:* When printf() is used, a variable of an enumeration type is printed as its implicit integer value. That is,

```
printf("%d\n", jan);
```

prints 0, not jan.

15 Write a next-day program for a particular year. The program should take as input two integers, say 17 and 5, which represents 17 May, and it should print as output 18 May, which is the next day. Use enumeration types in the program. Pay particular attention to the problem of crossing from one month to the next.

16 A twentieth-century date can be written with integers in the form *day/month/year*. An example is 1/7/33, which represents 1 July 1933. Write a function that stores the day, month, and year compactly. Because we need 31 different values for the day, 12 different values for the month, and 100 different values for the year, we can use 5 bits to represent the day, 4 bits to represent the month, and 7 bits to represent the year. Your function should take as input the day, month, and year as integers, and it should return the date packed into a 16-bit integer. Write another function that does the unpacking. Write a program to test your functions.

17 Write a function that acts directly on a packed date (see Exercise 16) and produces the next calendar day in packed form. Contrast this to the program you wrote in Exercise 15.

18 Rewrite the program given in Section 4.10, "An Example: Boolean Variables." Use the five low-order bits in the char variable b to represent the five boolean variables b1, ..., b5.

19 Rewrite the program from Exercise 18 to take advantage of machine arithmetic. Show by hand simulation that the effect of adding 1 to the bit representation for b is equivalent to the effect of the nested for statements. In this exercise, your program should generate the table using a single unnested for statement.

20 (Balanced Meal Program) Use enumeration types to define five basic food groups: fish, fruits, grains, meats, and vegetables. Use a random number generator to select an item from each food group. Write a function meal() that picks an item from each of the five groups and prints out this menu. Print 20 menus. How many different menus are available?

21 Write a function that picks out five cards at random from a deck of cards. Your function should check that all the cards in the hand are distinct. Recall that the spots on a playing card that represent its numeric value are called "pips." A playing card such as the seven of hearts has a pip value 7 and a suit value hearts. The pip value for an ace is 1, a deuce is 2, ..., and a king is 13. Use enumeration types to represent the pips and suit values in your function. Write another function that prints out the hand in a visually pleasing way.

22 Write a set of routines that test whether the hand generated by the function in Exercise 21 is a straight, a flush, or a full house. A straight consists of five cards that can be placed in consecutive sequence by pip value. A flush consists of five cards of the same suit. A full house is three of a kind plus a pair. Run your random hand generator and print out any hand that is one of these three kinds, along with the hand number. Continue to print out hands until one of each of the three kinds has been generated, or until you have generated 5000 hands. If the latter happens, there is probably something wrong with your program. Do you know why?

23 In the game "paper, rock, scissors," an outcome that is not a tie is conveyed to the player by printing

```
You win.        or        You lose.
```

Rewrite the program so that messages like the following are printed:

```
You chose paper and I chose rock.  You win.
```

24 Consider the function pack() given in Section 7.4, "Packing and Unpacking." The body of the function consists of four statements. Rewrite the function so these four statements are collapsed into a single return statement.

25 Rewrite the function pack() so that only arithmetic operations are used.

26 On any machine, a mask of type long is acceptable. However, when we tried the following initialization on a 2-byte machine, our code did not work as expected:

```
long    mask = 1 << 31;    /* turn the high bit on: error! */
```

We made an egregious error. Can you explain what it is?

27 How multicharacter character constants such as 'abc' get stored is system-dependent. Because programmers sometimes write 'abc' instead of "abc", some compilers provide a warning when multicharacter character constants get used, even if the use is proper. What happens on your system? Try the following code:

```
int    c = 'abc';

printf("'abc' = ");
bit_print(c);
printf("\n");
```

Here is the output on a Sun workstation:

```
'abc' = 00000000 01100011 01100010 01100001
```

28 A useful implementation of the mathematical concept of set is an `unsigned long` treated as a set of up to 32 elements.

```
typedef    unsigned long    set;

const set    empty = 0X0;        /* use hexadecimal constants */
```

Write a routine that does set union using bit operators. *Caution:* Because `union` is a keyword, use another name.

```
/* This function returns the union of a and b. */

set    Union(set a, set b);
```

By using masks you can examine whether a bit position is 1. Use this idea to write a function

```
void    display(set a);
```

that informatively prints out the members of a set. To test your functions, you could write

```
set    a = 0X7;           /* a has elements 1, 2, 3 */
set    b = 0X55;          /* b has elements 1, 3, 5, 7 */

display(Union(a, b));     /* 1, 2, 3, 5, 7 is in the union */
```

29 (Project) Use the ideas presented in Exercise 28 to develop a complete set manipulation package for sets whose size is 32 members or less. Thus you need to write

```
set    Union(set a, set b);
set    intersection(set a, set b);
set    complement(set a);
```

After you have written these functions and tested them, use arrays of `int`s to represent larger sets. The size of the arrays should allow for sets with 1000 members or less. Modify your functions to work with these sets.

CHAPTER **8**

THE PREPROCESSOR

The C language uses the preprocessor to extend its power and notation. In this chapter we present a detailed discussion of the preprocessor, including new features added by the ANSI C committee. We begin by explaining the use of #include. Then we thoroughly discuss the use of the #define macro facility. Macros can be used to generate in-line code that takes the place of a function call. Their use can reduce program execution time.

Lines that begin with a # are called *preprocessing directives*. These lines communicate with the preprocessor. In ANSI C, the # can be preceded on the line by white space, whereas in traditional C, it must occur in column 1. The syntax for preprocessing directives is independent of the rest of the C language. The effect of a preprocessing directive starts at its place in a file and continues until the end of that file, or until its effect is negated by another directive. It is always helpful to keep in mind that the preprocessor does not "know C."

8.1 THE USE OF #include

We have already used preprocessing directives such as

```
#include <stdio.h>
#include <stdlib.h>
```

Another form of the #include facility is given by

```
#include "filename"
```

This causes the preprocessor to replace the line with a copy of the contents of the named file. A search for the file is made first in the current directory and then in other system-dependent places. With a preprocessing directive of the form

```
#include <filename>
```

the preprocessor looks for the file only in the other places and not in the current directory. In UNIX systems, the standard header files such as *stdio.h* and *stdlib.h* are typically found in */usr/include*. In general, where the standard header files are stored is system-dependent.

There is no restriction on what a #include file can contain. In particular, it can contain other preprocessing directives that will be expanded by the preprocessor in turn.

8.2   THE USE OF #define

Preprocessing directives with #define occur in two forms:

> #define   *identifier*   *token_string$_{opt}$*
> #define   *identifier(identifier, . . . , identifier)*   *token_string$_{opt}$*

The *token_string* is optional. A long definition of either form can be continued to the next line by placing a backslash \ at the end of the current line. If a simple #define of the first form occurs in a file, the preprocessor replaces every occurrence of *identifier* by *token_string* in the remainder of the file, except in quoted strings. Consider the example

> #define   SECONDS_PER_DAY   (60 * 60 * 24)

In this example the token string is (60 * 60 * 24), and the preprocessor will replace every occurrence of the symbolic constant SECONDS_PER_DAY by that string in the remainder of the file.

The use of simple #defines can improve program clarity and portability. For example, if special constants such as π or the speed of light c are used in a program, they should be defined.

> #define   PI   3.14159
> #define   C   299792.458   /* speed of light in km/sec */

Other special constants that are used in programs are also best coded as symbolic constants.

> #define   EOF   (-1)   /* typical end-of-file value */
> #define   MAXINT   2147483647   /* largest 4-byte integer */

Program limits that are programmer decisions can also be specified symbolically.

> #define   ITERS   50   /* number of iterations */
> #define   SIZE   250   /* array size */
> #define   EPS   1.0e-9   /* a numerical limit */

In general, symbolic constants aid documentation by replacing what might otherwise be a mysterious constant with a mnemonic identifier. They aid portability by allowing constants that may be system-dependent to be altered once. They aid reliability by restricting to one place the check on the actual representation of the constant.

Syntactic Sugar

It is possible to alter the syntax of C toward some user preference. A frequent programming error is to use the token = in place of the token == in logical expressions. A programmer could use

```
#define    EQ    ==
```

to defend against such a mistake. This superficial alteration of the programming syntax is called *syntactic sugar*. Another example of this is to change the form of the while statement by introducing "do," which is an ALGOL style construction.

```
#define    do    /* blank */
```

With these two #define lines at the top of the file, the code

```
while (i EQ 1) do {
   . . . . .
```

will become, after the preprocessor pass,

```
while (i == 1) {
   . . . . .
```

One must keep in mind that because do will disappear from anywhere in the file, the do-while statement cannot be used.

8.3 MACROS WITH ARGUMENTS

So far, we have considered only simple #define preprocessing directives. We now want to discuss how we can use the #define facility to write macro definitions with parameters. The general form is given by

```
#define    identifier( identifier, ... ,identifier )    token_string_opt
```

There can be no space between the first identifier and the left parenthesis. Zero or more identifiers can occur in the parameter list. An example of a macro definition with a parameter is

```
#define    SQ(x)    ((x) * (x))
```

The identifier x in the #define is a parameter that is substituted for in later text. The substitution is one of string replacement without consideration of syntactic correctness. For example, with the argument 7 + w the macro call

SQ(7 + w)   expands to   ((7 + w) * (7 + w))

In a similar fashion

SQ(SQ(*p))   expands to   ((((*p) * (*p))) * (((*p) * (*p))))

This seemingly extravagant use of parentheses is to protect against the macro expanding an expression so that it led to an unanticipated order of evaluation. It is important to understand why all the parentheses are necessary. First, suppose we had defined the macro as

#define   SQ(x)   x * x

With this definition

SQ(a + b)   expands to   a + b * a + b

which, because of operator precedence, is not the same as

((a + b) * (a + b))

Now suppose we had defined the macro as

#define   SQ(x)   (x) * (x)

With this definition

4 / SQ(2)   expands to   4 / (2) * (2)

which, because of operator precedence, is not the same as

4 / ((2) * (2))

Finally, let us suppose that we had defined the macro as

#define   SQ (x)   ((x) * (x))

With this definition

SQ(7)   expands to   (x) ((x) * (x)) (7)

which is not even close to what was intended. If, in the macro definition, there is a space between the macro name and the left parenthesis that follows, then the rest of the line is taken as replacement text.

A common programming error is to end a #define line with a semicolon, making it part of the replacement string when it is not wanted. As an example of this, consider

```
#define   SQ(x)   ((x) * (x));      /* error */
```

The semicolon here was typed by mistake, one that is easily made because programmers often end a line of code with a semicolon. When used in the body of a function, the line

```
x = SQ(y);      gets expanded to      x = ((y) * (y));;
```

The last semicolon creates an unwanted null statement. If we were to write

```
if (x == 2)
    x = SQ(y);
else
    ++x;
```

we would get a syntax error caused by the unwanted null statement. The extra semicolon does not allow the else to be attached to the if statement.

Macros are frequently used to replace function calls by in-line code, which is more efficient. For example, instead of writing a function to find the minimum of two values, a programmer could write

```
#define   min(x, y)   (((x) < (y)) ? (x) : (y))
```

After this definition, an expression such as

```
m = min(u, v)
```

gets expanded by the preprocessor to

```
m = (((u) < (v)) ? (u) : (v))
```

The arguments of min() can be arbitrary expressions of compatible type. Also, we can use min() to build another macro. For example, if we need to find the minimum of four values, we can write

```
#define   min4(a, b, c, d)   min(min(a, b), min(c, d))
```

A macro definition can use both functions and macros in its body. Here are some examples:

```
#define    SQ(x)       ((x) * (x))
#define    CUBE(x)     (SQ(x) * (x))
#define    F_POW(x)    sqrt(sqrt(CUBE(x)))/* fractional power: 3/4 */
```

A preprocessing directive of the form

   #undef *identifier*

will undefine a macro. It causes the previous definition of a macro to be forgotten.

   Caution: Debugging code that contains macros with arguments can be difficult. To see the output from the preprocessor, you can give the command

   cc –E file.c

After the preprocessor has done its work, no further compilation takes place (see Exercise 1).

8.4   THE TYPE DEFINITIONS AND MACROS IN *stddef.h*

C provides the `typedef` facility so that an identifier can be associated with a specific type. A simple example is

```
typedef    char    uppercase;
```

This makes `uppercase` a type that is synonymous with `char`, and it can be used in declarations, just as other types are used. An example is

```
uppercase    c, u[100];
```

The `typedef` facility allows the programmer to use type names that are appropriate for a specific application (see Chapters 9 and 10).

   In this section we are concerned with the implementation-specific type definitions and macros that are given in the header file *stddef.h*. They can occur in other standard header files as well. Here is how the type definitions might appear:

```
typedef    int        ptrdiff_t;    /* pointer difference type */
typedef    short      wchar_t;      /* wide character type */
typedef    unsigned   size_t;       /* the sizeof type */
```

The type `ptrdiff_t` tells what type is obtained with an expression involving the difference of two pointers (see Exercise 7). The type `wchar_t` is provided to support languages with character sets that will not fit into a `char`. Some C compilers are not interested in providing such support. If that is the case, the type definition would probably be

```
typedef   char   wchar_t;      /* same as a plain char */
```

Recall that the `sizeof` operator is used to find the size of a type or an expression. For example, `sizeof(double)` on most systems is 8. The type `size_t` is the type of the result of the `sizeof` operator. This is system-dependent, but it must be an unsigned integral type. We will see the use of `size_t` in our discussion of `qsort( )` in the next section.

The macro `NULL` is also given in `stddef.h`. It is an implementation-defined null pointer constant. Typically, `NULL` is defined to be 0, but on some systems it is given by

```
#define   NULL   ((void *) 0)
```

8.5 AN EXAMPLE: SORTING WITH qsort( )

Programmers, for a variety of reasons, need to be able to sort data. If the amount of data is small, or the program does not have to run fast, we can use a bubble sort or a transposition sort to accomplish the task. If, however, there is a lot of data, and speed of execution is a concern, then we can use the function `qsort( )` provided by the standard library. (The name *qsort* stands for "quick sort.")

The function `qsort( )` is useful because it is a lot faster than a bubble sort or a simple transposition sort and it is quite easy to implement. Another quicksort implementation, (`quicksort( )`), however, is even faster (see Exercises 33 and 34), but it requires more coding effort. We will discuss quicksort in Section 8.15.

The function prototype for `qsort( )` is in *stdlib.h*. It is equivalent to

```
void qsort(void *array, size_t n_els, size_t el_size,
           int compare(const void *, const void *));
```

Notice that the type `size_t` is used. Many other functions in the standard library also use this type. When `qsort( )` is called, its first argument is the array to be sorted, its second argument is the number of elements in the array, its third argument is the number of bytes in an element, and its fourth argument is a function, called the *comparison function*, which is used to compare elements in the array. In this function prototype for qsort(), the declaration of the fourth parameter is

```
int compare(const void *, const void *)
```

This is itself a function prototype, the prototype for the comparison function. The comparison function takes as arguments two pointers to void. When qsort() gets invoked, these two pointers will point to elements of the array. The comparison function returns an int that is less than, equal to, or greater than zero, depending on whether its first argument is considered to be less than, equal to, or greater than its second argument. The two pointers are of type void * because they are meant to be generic. As we will see, qsort() can be used to sort arrays of any type. The type qualifier const tells the compiler that the objects pointed to by the two pointers should not be modified (see Section 6.19).

Let us write a test program that illustrates the use of qsort(). In our program we fill an array, print it, sort it with qsort(), and then print it again.

```
#include <stdio.h>
#include <stdlib.h>
#include <time.h>

#define    N    11                         /* size of the array */

enum when {before, after};

typedef    enum when    when;

int     cmp(const void *vp, const void *vq);   /* comparison fct */
void    fill_array(double *a, int n);
void    prn_array(when val, double *a, int n);

int main(void)
{
    double    a[N];

    fill_array(a, N);
    prn_array(before, a, N);
    qsort(a, N, sizeof(double), cmp);
    prn_array(after, a, N);
    return 0;
}
```

```
int cmp(const void *vp, const void *vq)
{
   const double   *p = vp;
   const double   *q = vq;
   double          diff = *p - *q;

   return ((diff >= 0.0) ? ((diff > 0.0) ? -1 : 0) : +1);
}

void fill_array(double *a, int n)
{
   int   i;

   srand(time(NULL));                    /* seed rand() */
   for (i = 0; i < n; ++i)
      a[i] = (rand() % 1001) / 10.0;
}

void prn_array(when val, double *a, int n)
{
   int   i;

   printf("%s\n%s%s\n",
      "---",
      ((val == before) ? "Before " : "After "), "sorting:");
   for (i = 0; i < n; ++i) {
      if (i % 6 == 0)
         putchar('\n');
      printf("%11.1f", a[i]);
   }
   putchar('\n');
}
```

We want to discuss a number of points about this test program, but before we do, let us look at some typical output:

```
---
Before sorting:

        1.5        17.0        99.5        45.3        52.6        66.3
        3.4        70.2        23.4        57.4         6.4
---
After sorting:

       99.5        70.2        66.3        57.4        52.6        45.3
       23.4        17.0         6.4         3.4         1.5
```

DISSECTION OF THE *try_qsort* PROGRAM

■ `#define   N   11`   `/* size of the array */`

To test the function `qsort()`, we will create an array of size N. After we get
the code to work for a small array, we can test it on a larger array.

■ `int     cmp(const void *vp, const void *vq);  /* comparison fct */`
`void    fill_array(double *a, int n);`
`void    prn_array(when val, double *a, int n);`

These are function prototypes. We can name our comparison function whatever
we want, but the type of the function and the number and type of its arguments
must agree with the last parameter in the function prototype for `qsort()`.

■ ```
int main(void)
{
    double   a[N];

    fill_array(a, N);
    prn_array(before, a, N);
    qsort(a, N, sizeof(double), cmp);
    prn_array(after, a, N);
    return 0;
}
```

In `main()`, we declare a to be an array of `doubles`. Because the purpose of
our program is to test `qsort()`, we do not do anything exciting. All we do is
fill the array, print it, use `qsort()` to sort it, and then print the array again.

■ `qsort(a, N, sizeof(double), cmp);`

When `qsort()` is invoked, we must pass it the base address of the array to
be sorted, the number of elements in the array, the number of bytes required to
store an element, and the name of our comparison function.

■ ```
int cmp(const void *vp, const void *vq)
{
    .....
```

This is the start of the function definition for our comparison function. The letter
v in vp and vq is mnemonic for "void." In the body of `main()`, we pass the
name of our comparison function as the last argument to `qsort()`. This occurs
in the statement

`qsort(a, N, sizeof(double), cmp);`

In the body of `qsort()`, which the programmer does not have access to, pointers
to elements of the array a will be passed to `cmp()`. The programmer is not
concerned with the internal details of `qsort()`. The programmer only has to
write the comparison function with the understanding that the parameters vp and
vq are pointers to elements of the array.

■
```
int cmp(const void *vp, const void *vq)
{
    const double   *p = vp;
    const double   *q = vq;
    double         diff = *p - *q;
    . . . . .
```
In the body of our comparison function, we initialize vp to p and vq to q. If we do not qualify p and q with const, the compiler will complain (see Section 6.19). The variables p and q are of type pointer to double because the elements of the array a are of type double. We initialize diff to the difference of the objects pointed to by p and q.

■ `return ((diff >= 0.0) ? ((diff > 0.0) ? -1 : 0) : +1);`
If diff is positive, we return –1; if diff is zero, we return 0; and if diff is negative, we return 1. This causes the array to be sorted in descending order. Suppose we replace this line with

```
if (diff < 0.0)
    return -1;
if (diff == 0.0)
    return 0;
return 1;
```

This will cause the array to be sorted in ascending order.

■
```
void fill_array(double *a, int n)
{
    int    i;

    srand(time(NULL));                        /* seed rand() */
    . . . . .
```
Typically, the function call time(NULL) returns the number of seconds that have elapsed since 1 January 1970. ANSI C does not guarantee this, but this convention is widely followed. Passing time(NULL) to srand( ) causes the array a to be filled with different values every time the program is invoked.

■
```
for (i = 0; i < n; ++i)
    a[i] = (rand() % 1001) / 10.0;
```
The expression rand( ) % 1001 has an int value in the interval 0 to 1000. Because we are dividing this by the double value 10.0, the value of what is assigned to a[i] is in the interval 0 to 100.

8.6   AN EXAMPLE: MACROS WITH ARGUMENTS

In this section we again fill arrays and sort them with qsort( ), but this time we use macros with arguments. We will call our program *sort*.

Let us write our program in three files: a header file *sort.h* and two *.c* files. In the header file we put our #includes, our #defines, and a list of function prototypes.

In file sort.h:

```
#include <stdio.h>
#include <stdlib.h>
#include <string.h>
#include <time.h>

#define    M    32                                     /* size of a[] */
#define    N    11                                     /* size of b[] */

#define    fractional_part(x)    (x - (int) x)
#define    random_char()         (rand() % 26 + 'a')
#define    random_float()        (rand() % 100 / 10.0)

#define    FILL(array, sz, type)         \
    if (strcmp(type, "char") == 0)        \
       for (i = 0; i < sz; ++i)           \
          array[i] = random_char();      \
    else                                  \
       for (i = 0; i < sz; ++i)           \
          array[i] = random_float()

#define    PRINT(array, sz, cntrl_string)  \
    for (i = 0; i < sz; ++i)               \
       printf(cntrl_string, array[i]);     \
    putchar('\n')

int    compare_fractional_part(const void *, const void *);
int    lexico(const void *, const void *);
```

DISSECTION OF THE *sort.h* HEADER FILE

■ ```
#include <stdio.h>
#include <stdlib.h>
#include <string.h>
#include <time.h>
```
The header file *stdio.h* contains the macro definition for NULL and the function prototype for printf(). The header file *stdlib.h* contains the function prototypes for rand(), srand(), and qsort(). The header file *time.h* contains the function prototype for time(). The function call time(NULL) will be used to seed the random number generator.

■ ```
#define    fractional_part(x)    (x - (int) x)
```
If x is a positive float, then the expression x - (int) x yields the fractional part of x.

■ ```
#define   random_char()   (rand() % 26 + 'a')
```
When rand() is invoked, it returns an integer value randomly distributed between 0 and MAX_RAND, a symbolic constant defined in *stdlib.h*. Because MAX_RAND is typically more than 32 thousand, the expression rand() % 26 yields an integer value randomly distributed between 0 and 25. Because 0 + 'a' has the value 'a' and 25 + 'a' has the value 'z', the expression

```
    rand() % 26 + 'a'
```

produces a character value randomly distributed between 'a' and 'z'.

■ ```
#define   random_float()   (rand() % 100 / 10.0)
```
The value of the expression rand() % 100 is an integer randomly distributed between 0 and 99. Because the expression 10.0 is of type double, the value produced by rand() % 100 is promoted to a double, and the expression

```
    rand() % 100 / 10.0
```

as a whole is also of type double. Its value is between 0 and 9.9.

■
```
#define   FILL(array, sz, type)        \
    if (strcmp(type, "char") == 0)      \
        for (i = 0; i < sz; ++i)        \
            array[i] = random_char();   \
    else                                \
        for (i = 0; i < sz; ++i)        \
            array[i] = random_float()
```
In this macro definition, array, sz, and type are parameters. Unlike function definitions, no type checking gets done. It is the programmer's responsibility to call the macro with arguments of the appropriate type. Note that the variable i is used in the body of the macro. Because it is not declared here, it has to be declared in main(), where the macro gets called. Consider the macro call

```
FILL(a, n, "char");
```

When the macro gets expanded, we obtain

```
if (strcmp("char", "char") == 0)
    for (i = 0; i < n; ++i)
        a[i] = random_char();
else
    for (i = 0; i < n; ++i)
        a[i] = random_float();
```

The identifiers array, sz, and type have been replaced by a, n, and "char", respectively. Note carefully that all but the last semicolon came from the preprocessor expansion mechanism.

■
```
#define   PRINT(array, sz, cntrl_string)  \
    for (i = 0; i < sz; ++i)               \
        printf(cntrl_string, array[i]);    \
    putchar('\n')
```
This macro can be used to print the values of elements of an array. Note that the control string for printf() is a parameter in the macro definition.

■
```
int   compare_fractional_part(const void *, const void *);
int   lexico(const void *, const void *);
```
These are prototypes of comparison functions that will be passed to qsort(). Notice that with respect to type, they match the function prototype of the comparison function in the function prototype for qsort().

Now let us consider the rest of the code for our program. In `main()`, we fill an array, print it, sort it, and print it again. Then we repeat the process, but this time with an array of a different type.

In file main.c:

```
#include "sort.h"

int main(void)
{
    char    a[M];
    float   b[N];
    int     i;

    srand(time(NULL));
    FILL(a, M , "char");
    PRINT(a, M, "%-2c");
    qsort(a, M, sizeof(char), lexico);
    PRINT(a, M, "%-2c");
    printf("---\n");
    FILL(b, N, "float");
    PRINT(b, N, "%-6.1f");
    qsort(b, N, sizeof(float), compare_fractional_part);
    PRINT(b, N, "%-6.1f");
    return 0;
}
```

Notice that each time we invoke `qsort()`, we use a different comparison function. Here is the output of our program:

```
q m z r h l a j o e t b k w l t z t v i e m h p f y b p s w a j
a a b b e e f h h i j j k l l m m o p p q r s t t t v w w y z z
---
9.4   0.2   5.1   6.7   5.4   5.3   6.1   9.6   2.8   8.8   8.5
6.1   5.1   0.2   5.3   5.4   9.4   8.5   9.6   6.7   8.8   2.8
```

Finally, we want to look at the two comparison functions. Pointers to `void` are used because this is required by the function prototype of `qsort()` in *stdlib.h*. We will carefully explain how these pointers get used in the comparison functions.

In file compare.c:

```
#include "sort.h"

int compare_fractional_part(const void *vp, const void *vq)
{
   const float   *p = vp, *q = vq;
   float          x;

   x = fractional_part(*p) - fractional_part(*q);
   return ((x < 0.0) ? -1 : (x == 0.0) ? 0 : +1);
}

int lexico(const void *vp, const void *vq)
{
   const char   *p = vp, *q = vq;

   return (*p - *q);
}
```

DISSECTION OF THE `compare_fractional_part()` FUNCTION

■   `int compare_fractional_part(const void *vp, const void *vq)`
    `{`
        `. . . . .`
    This function takes two `const` qualified pointers to `void` as arguments and
    returns an `int`. Because of this, the function can be passed as an argument to
    `qsort()`.

■   `int compare_fractional_part(const void *vp, const void *vq)`
    `{`
        `const float   *p = vp, *q = vq;`
        `float          x;`
        `. . . . .`
    The letter v in vp and vq is mnemonic for "void." Because pointers to `void`
    cannot be dereferenced, we declare p and q to be pointers to `float` and initialize
    them with vp and vq, respectively. Because an ANSI C compiler will complain
    if a `const`-qualified pointer is assigned to one that is not `const` qualified, we
    declare p and q to be `const` qualified. Notice that we did not declare x to be
    `const` qualified. If we had done so, we would be able to give x a value only
    by initializing it.

■ x = fractional_part(*p) - fractional_part(*q);
   return ((x < 0.0) ? -1 : (x == 0.0) ? 0 : +1);
   The difference of the fractional parts of the objects pointed to by p and q is
   assigned to x. Then −1, 0, or +1 is returned, depending on whether x is negative,
   zero, or positive. Thus, when we call qsort() with compare_decimal_part()
   passed as an argument, the elements in the array get sorted according to their
   fractional parts.

Observe that in the function lexico() we defined p and q to be pointers to
const char and initialized them with vp and vq, respectively. Then we returned
the difference of what is pointed to by p and q. Thus, when we call qsort() with
lexico passed as an argument, the elements in the array get sorted lexicographically.

8.7   THE MACROS IN `stdio.h` AND `ctype.h`

The C system provides the macros getc() and putc() in *stdio.h*. The first is used
to read a character from a file, the second to write a character to a file. We will
see their use in Chapter 11, where we discuss files. Because the header file *stdio.h*
contains the lines

```
#define    getchar()    getc(stdin)
#define    putchar(c)   putc((c), stdout)
```

we see that getchar() and putchar() are also macros. They read characters from
the keyboard and write characters to the screen, respectively.

The C system also provides the standard header file *ctype.h*, which contains a
set of macros that test characters and a set of prototypes of functions that convert
characters. The preprocessing directive

```
#include <ctype.h>
```

includes these macros and function prototypes. In the table that follows we list the
macros that test characters. These macros all take an argument of type int and
return an int.

Macro	Nonzero (true) is returned if:
isalpha(c)	c is a letter
isupper(c)	c is an uppercase letter
islower(c)	c is a lowercase letter
isdigit(c)	c is a digit
isalnum(c)	c is a letter or digit
isxdigit(c)	c is a hexadecimal digit
isspace(c)	c is a white space character
ispunct(c)	c is a punctuation character
isprint(c)	c is a printable character
isgraph(c)	c is printable, but not a space
iscntrl(c)	c is a control character
isascii(c)	c is an ASCII code

In the next table we list the functions `toupper()` and `tolower()`, which are in the standard library, and the macro `toascii()`. The macro and the prototypes for the two functions are in *ctype.h*. The functions and the macro each take an `int` and return an `int`. In the table we assume that `c` is a variable of integral type, such as `char` or `int`. Note carefully that the value of `c` stored in memory does not get changed.

Call to the function or macro	Value returned
toupper(c)	corresponding uppercase value or c
tolower(c)	corresponding lowercase value or c
toascii(c)	corresponding ASCII value

If `c` is not a lowercase letter, then the value returned by `toupper(c)` is c. Similarly, if `c` is not an uppercase letter, then the value returned by `tolower(c)` is c.

8.8   CONDITIONAL COMPILATION

The preprocessor has directives for conditional compilation. They can be used for program development and for writing code that is more easily portable from one machine to another. Each preprocessing directive of the form

```
#if        constant_integral_expression
#ifdef     identifier
#ifndef    identifier
```

provides for conditional compilation of the code that follows until the preprocessing directive

```
#endif
```

is reached. For the intervening code to be compiled, after #if, the constant expression must be nonzero (*true*), and after #ifdef or after #if defined, the named identifier must have been defined previously in a #define line, without an intervening

```
#undef   identifier
```

having been used to undefine the macro. After #ifndef, the named identifier must be currently undefined.

The integral constant expression used in a preprocessing directive cannot contain the sizeof operator or a cast. It may, however, use the defined preprocessing operator. This operator is available in ANSI C, but not necessarily in traditional C. The expression

```
defined   identifier        is equivalent to        defined(identifier)
```

It evaluates to 1 if the identifier is currently defined, and evaluates to 0 otherwise. Here is an example of how it can be used:

```
#if defined(HP9000) || defined(SUN4) && !defined(VAX)
   .....        /* machine-dependent code */
#endif
```

Sometimes printf() statements are useful for debugging purposes. Suppose that at the top of a file we write

```
#define   DEBUG   1
```

and then throughout the rest of the file we write lines such as

```
#if DEBUG
   printf("debug: a = %d\n", a);
#endif
```

Because the symbolic constant DEBUG has nonzero value, the printf() statements will be compiled. Later, these lines can be omitted from compilation by changing the value of the symbolic constant DEBUG to 0.

An alternate scheme is to define a symbolic constant having no value. Suppose that at the top of a file we write

```
#define   DEBUG
```

Then we can use the #ifdef or #if defined forms of conditional compilation. For example, if we write

```
#ifdef DEBUG
   . . . . .
#endif
```

then the intervening lines of code will be compiled. When we remove the #define line that defines DEBUG from the top of the file, the intervening lines of code will not be compiled.

Suppose we are writing code in a large software project. We may be expected to include at the top of all our code certain header files supplied by others. Our code may depend on some of the function prototypes and on some of the macros in these header files, but because the header files are for the project as a whole, our code might not use everything. Moreover, we may not even know all the things that eventually will be in the header files. To prevent the clash of macro names, we can use the #undef facility:

```
#include "everything.h"

#undef    PIE
#define   PIE    "I like apple."
. . . . .
```

If PIE happens to be defined in *everything.h*, then we have undefined it. If it is not defined in *everything.h*, then the #undef directive has no effect.

Here is a common use of conditional compilation. Imagine that you are in the testing phase of program development and that your code has the form

statements
more statements
and still more statements

For debugging or testing purposes, you may wish to temporarily disregard, or block out, some of your code. To do this, you can try to put the code into a comment.

statements
/*
more statements
*/
and still more statements

However, if the code to be blocked out contains comments, this method will result in a syntax error. The use of conditional compilation solves this problem.

```
statements
#if 0
more statements
#endif
and still more statements
```

The preprocessor has control structures that are similar to the if-else statement in C. Each of the #if forms can be followed by any number of lines, possibly containing preprocessing directives of the form

```
#elif   constant_integral_expression
```

possibly followed by the preprocessing directive

```
#else
```

and, finally, followed by the preprocessing directive

```
#endif
```

Note that #elif is a contraction for "else-if." The flow of control for conditional compilation is analogous to that provided by if-else statements.

8.9   THE PREDEFINED MACROS

In ANSI C there are five predefined macros. They are always available, and they cannot be undefined by the programmer. Each of these macro names includes two leading and two trailing underscore characters.

Predefined macro	Value
__DATE__	A string containing the current date
__FILE__	A string containing the file name
__LINE__	An integer representing the current line number
__STDC__	If the implementation follows ANSI Standard C, then the value is a nonzero integer.
__TIME__	A string containing the current time

In Exercise 6 we show how to test what the effects of these macros are on your system.

8.10   THE OPERATORS # AND

The preprocessing operators # and ## are available in ANSI C but not in traditional
C. The unary operator # causes "stringization" of a formal parameter in a macro
definition. Here is an example of its use:

```
#define    message_for(a, b)  \
           printf(#a " and " #b ": We love you!\n")

int main(void)
{
   message_for(Carole, Debra);
   return 0;
}
```

When the macro is invoked, each parameter in the macro definition is replaced by
its corresponding argument, with the # causing the argument to be surrounded by
double quotes. Thus, after the preprocessor pass, we obtain

```
int main(void)
{
   printf("Carole" " and " "Debra" ": We love you!\n");
   return 0;
}
```

Because string constants separated by white space are concatenated, this `printf()`
statement is equivalent to

```
printf("Carole and Debra: We love you!\n");
```

In the next section we will see how the "stringization" operator # is used in assertions.
   The binary operator ## is used to merge tokens. Here is an example of how the
operator is used:

```
#define    X(i)    x ## i

X(1) = X(2) = X(3);
```

After the preprocessor pass, we are left with the line

```
x1 = x2 = x3;
```

8.11   THE assert( ) MACRO

ANSI C provides the assert( ) macro in the standard header file *assert.h*. This
macro can be used to ensure that the value of an expression is what you expect it to
be. Suppose that you are writing a critical function and that you want to be sure the
arguments satisfy certain conditions. Here is an example of how assert( ) can be
used to do this:

```
#include <assert.h>

void f(char *p, int n)
{
    .....
    assert(p != NULL);
    assert(n > 0 && n < 7);
    .....
```

If an assertion fails, then the system will print out a message and abort the program.
Although the assert( ) macro is implemented differently on each system, its general
behavior is always the same. Here is one way the macro might be written:

```
#include <stdio.h>
#include <stdlib.h>                             /* for abort() */

#if defined(NDEBUG)
    #define   assert(ignore)   ((void) 0)       /* ignore it */
#else
    #define   assert(expr)                                \
        if (!(expr)) {                                    \
            printf("\n%s%s\n%s%s\n%s%d\n\n",              \
                "Assertion failed: ", #expr,              \
                "in file ", __FILE__,                     \
                "at line ", __LINE__);                    \
            abort();                                      \
        }
#endif
```

Note that if the macro NDEBUG is defined, then all assertions are ignored. This allows
the programmer to use assertions freely during program development, and then to
effectively discard them later by defining the macro NDEBUG. The function abort( )
is in the standard library (see Appendix A).

8.12   THE USE OF #error AND #pragma

ANSI C has added the #error and #pragma preprocessing directives. The following code demonstrates how #error can be used:

```
#if A_SIZE < B_SIZE
    #error "Incompatible sizes"
#endif
```

If during compilation the preprocessor reaches the #error directive, then a compile-time error will occur, and the string following the directive will be printed on the screen. In our example, we used the #error macro to enforce the consistency of two symbolic constants. In an analogous fashion, the directive can be used to enforce other conditions.

The #pragma directive is provided for implementation-specific uses. Its general form is

   #pragma *tokens*

It causes a behavior that depends on the particular C compiler. Any #pragma that is not recognized by the compiler is ignored.

8.13   LINE NUMBERS

A preprocessing directive of the form

   #line *integral_constant "filename"*

causes the compiler to renumber the source text so the next line has the specified constant and causes it to believe that the current source file name is *filename*. If no file name is present, then only the renumbering of lines takes place. Normally, line numbers are hidden from the programmer and occur only in reference to warnings and syntax errors.

8.14   CORRESPONDING FUNCTIONS

In ANSI C, many of the macros with parameters that are given in the standard header files also have corresponding functions in the standard library. As an example, suppose we want to access the function isalpha() instead of the macro. One way to do this is to write

   #undef isalpha

somewhere in the file before isalpha() is invoked. This has the effect of discarding the macro definition, forcing the compiler to use the function instead. We would still include the header file *ctype.h* at the top of the file, however, because in addition to macros, the file contains function prototypes.

Another way to obtain the function instead of the macro is to write

```
(isalpha)(c)
```

The preprocessor does not recognize this construct as a macro, but the compiler recognizes it as a function call (see Exercise 8).

8.15 AN EXAMPLE: QUICKSORT

Quicksort was created by C. Anthony R. Hoare and described in his 1962 paper "Quicksort" (*Computer Journal*, vol. 5, no. 1). Of all the various sorting techniques, quicksort is perhaps the most widely used internal sort. An internal sort is one in which all the data to be sorted fit entirely within main memory.

Our quicksort code makes serious use of macros. When sorting lots of data, speed is essential, and the use of macros instead of functions helps to make our code run faster. As we will see, all the macros that we use are quite simple. We could replace them by in-line code, but their use makes the code more readable. Because quicksort is important, we will explain it in some detail.

Let us suppose that we want to sort an array of integers of size n. If the values of the elements are randomly distributed, then, on average, the number of comparisons done by quicksort is proportional to $n \log n$. But in the worst case, the number of comparisons is proportional to n^2. This is a disadvantage of quicksort. Other sorts—mergesort, for example—even in the worst case, do work proportional to $n \log n$. However, of all the $n \log n$ sorting methods known, quicksort is, on average, the fastest by a constant factor. Another advantage of quicksort is that it does its work in place. No additional work space is needed.

Our quicksort code is written in a single file. We will describe the elements of
the code as we present it. At the top of the file we have

```
/* Quicksort!  Pointer version with macros. */

#define    swap(x, y)     { int t; t = x; x = y; y = t; }
#define    order(x, y)    if (x > y) swap(x, y)
#define    o2(x, y)       order(x, y)
#define    o3(x, y, z)    o2(x, y); o2(x, z); o2(y, z)

typedef    enum {yes, no}    yes_no;

static yes_no    find_pivot(int *left, int *right, int *pivot_ptr);
static int       *partition(int *left, int *right, int pivot);
```

We have not written our macros to be robust. They are intended for use only in
this file. A typedef has been used to make the type yes_no synonymous with the
enumeration type enum yes, no. Because the two functions find_pivot() and
partition() have static storage class, they are known only in this file.

```
void quicksort(int *left, int *right)
{
    int    *p, pivot;

    if (find_pivot(left, right, &pivot) == yes) {
        p = partition(left, right, pivot);
        quicksort(left, p - 1);
        quicksort(p, right);
    }
}
```

Quicksort is usually implemented recursively. The underlying idea is to "divide and
conquer." Suppose that in main() we have declared a to be an array of size N.
After the array has been filled, we can sort it with the call

```
quicksort(a, a + N - 1);
```

The first argument is a pointer to the first element of the array; the second argument is
a pointer to the last element of the array. In the function definition for quicksort(),
it is convenient to think of these pointers as being on the left and right side of the
array, respectively. The function find_pivot() chooses, if possible, one of the
elements of the array to be a "pivot element." The function partition() is used to

rearrange the array so that the first part consists of elements all of whose values are less than the pivot and the remaining part consists of elements all of whose values are greater than or equal to the pivot. In addition, partition() returns a pointer to an element in the array. Elements to the left of the pointer all have value less than the pivot, and elements to the right of the pointer, as well as the element pointed to, all have value greater than or equal to the pivot. Once the array has been rearranged with respect to the pivot, quicksort() is invoked on each subarray.

```
static yes_no find_pivot(int *left, int *right, int *pivot_ptr)
{
    int    a, b, c, *p;

    a = *left;                              /* left value */
    b = *(left + (right - left) / 2);       /* middle value */
    c = *right;                             /* right value */
    o3(a, b, c);                      /* order these 3 values */
    if (a < b) {            /* pivot will be higher of 2 values */
        *pivot_ptr = b;
        return yes;
    }
    if (b < c) {
        *pivot_ptr = c;
        return yes;
    }
    for (p = left + 1; p <= right; ++p)
        if (*p != *left) {
            *pivot_ptr = (*p < *left) ? *left : *p;
            return yes;
        }
    return no;               /* all elements have the same value */
}
```

Ideally, the pivot should be chosen so that at each step the array is partitioned into two parts, each with an equal (or nearly equal) number of elements. This would minimize the total amount of work performed by quicksort(). Because we do not know a priori what this value should be, we try to select for the pivot the middle value from among the first, middle, and last elements of the array. In order for there to be a partition, there has to be at least one element that is less than the pivot. If all the elements have the same value, a pivot does not exist and no is returned by the function (see Exercises 26 and 27 for further discussion).

```
   static int *partition(int *left, int *right, int pivot)
   {
       while (left <= right) {
           while (*left < pivot)
               ++left;
           while (*right >= pivot)
               --right;
           if (left < right) {
               swap(*left, *right);
               ++left;
               --right;
           }
       }
       return left;
   }
```

The major work is done by partition(). We want to explain in detail how this function works. Suppose we have an array a[] of 12 elements:

7   4   3   5   2   5   8   2   1   9   −6   −3

When find_pivot() is invoked, the first, middle, and last elements of the array are compared. The middle value is 5, and because this is larger than the smallest of the three values, this value is chosen for the pivot value. The following table shows the values of the elements of the array after each pass of the outer while loop in the partition() function. The elements that were swapped in that pass are boxed.

Unordered data:	7	4	3	5	2	5	8	2	1	9	−6	−3
First pass:	−3	4	3	5	2	5	8	2	1	9	−6	7
Second pass:	−3	4	3	−6	2	5	8	2	1	9	5	7
Third pass:	−3	4	3	−6	2	1	8	2	5	9	5	7
Fourth pass:	−3	4	3	−6	2	1	2	8	5	9	5	7

Notice that after the last pass the elements with index 0 to 6 have value less than the pivot and that the remaining elements have value greater than or equal to the pivot. The address of a[7] is returned when the function exits.

8.16 SUMMARY

1   The preprocessor provides facilities for file inclusion and for defining macros. Files may be included by using preprocessing directives of the form

```
#include  <filename>
#include  "filename"
```

2 A #define preprocessing directive can be used to give a symbolic name to a token string. The preprocessor substitutes the string for the symbolic name in the source text before compilation.

3 The use of the #define facility to define symbolic constants enhances readability and portability of programs.

4 The preprocessor provides a general macro facility with argument substitution. A macro with parameters is defined by a preprocessing directive of the form

   #define   *identifier*(*identifier*, ... , *identifier*)   *token_string*$_{opt}$

An example is given by

   #define   swap(x, y)   {int t; t = x; x = y; y = t;}

This macro provides in-line code to perform the swap of two values. It is not a function call.

5 The preprocessor provides for conditional compilation to aid in program testing, to facilitate porting, and so on. Lines beginning with #if, #ifdef, #ifndef, #elif, #else, and #endif are used for this.

6 The defined operator can be used with preprocessing directives. An example is

   #if (defined(HP3000) || defined(SUN3)) && !defined(SUN4)
       .....   /* machine-dependent code */
   #endif

7 An effective way to block out sections of code for debugging purposes is to use

   #if 0
       .....
   #endif

8 ANSI C has introduced the preprocessing operators # and ##. The # operator is unary. It can be applied to a formal parameter in the body of a macro, causing replacement text to be surrounded by double quotes. This effect is called "stringization." The ## operator is binary. It causes the pasting together of two tokens.

9 ANSI C provides the assert() macro in the header file *assert.h*. Assertions can be used to ensure that an expression has an appropriate value.

10 The function qsort() is provided by the C system. Its function prototype is in *stdlib.h*. Although qsort() is faster than a bubble sort or a simple transposition sort, it is not as fast as quicksort. An advantage of qsort() is that it is easy to implement.

11 Quicksort is one of the most widely used sorting algorithms. It is faster by a constant factor than all other known $n \log n$ sorting methods.

8.17 EXERCISES

1 A program that contains macros with arguments can be difficult to debug. Most
   C compilers provide an option that causes the preprocessor to write its output
   on the screen with no further compilation taking place. Put the following code
   in a file, say *try_me.c*:

```
#include <stdio.h>

#define   PRN(x)    printf("x\n");

int main(void)
{
   PRN(Hello from main());
   return 0;
}
```

   Next, compile the program and run it. You will see that it does not print what
   was expected. To see how the preprocessor treats this code, give the command

   cc –E try_me.c

   (Use redirection if you want to take a careful look at what gets produced.) If
   the *–E* option is not the right one for your compiler, find out what the correct
   option is. Note that the identifier PRN does not get generated by the preprocessor.
   Explain why. Fix the code. *Hint:* Use stringization.

2 Consider the following macro definition:

```
#define   forever(x)    forever(forever(x))

forever(more)
```

   This looks like it will produce infinite recursion, but in ANSI C the preprocessor
   is supposed to be smart enough to know that infinite recursion is not what is
   intended. How does your preprocessor expand this macro?

3 Suppose that x, y, and z are variables of type float in a program. If these
   variables have the values 1.1, 2.2, and 3.3, respectively, then the statement

```
PRN3(x, y, z);
```

   should cause the line

```
x has value 1.1 and y has value 2.2 and z has value 3.3
```

   to be printed. Write the macro definition for PRN3().

4 Suppose we have

In file a_b_c.h:

```
#define   TRUE   1
#define   A_B_C  int main(void)                               \
                 {                                            \
                     printf("A Big Cheery \"hello\"!\n");  \
                     return 0;                                \
                 }
```

In file a_b_c.c:

```
#if TRUE
   #include <stdio.h>
   #include "a_b_c.h"
   A_B_C
#endif
```

When we try to compile the program, the compiler complains. Why? Can you permute two lines in one of the files so that the program compiles and runs? Explain.

5 Macros are not always as safe as functions, even when all the parameters in the body of the macro definition are enclosed in parentheses. Define a macro

```
MAX(x, y, z)
```

that produces a value corresponding to the largest of its three arguments. Construct some expressions to use in MAX() that produce unanticipated results.

6 Are all of the predefined macros available on your system? Try the following code:

```
printf("%s%s\n%s%s\n%s%d\n%s%d\n%s%s\n",
    "__DATE__ = ", __DATE__,
    "__FILE__ = ", __FILE__,
    "__LINE__ = ", __LINE__,
    "__STDC__ = ", __STDC__,
    "__TIME__ = ", __TIME__);
```

7 Do you have access to an ANSI C compiler on a small system? On small systems, compilers such as Borland C and Microsoft C provide for different memory models, and each memory model usually requires a specific type definition for ptrdiff_t. Look in *stddef.h* and see if this is the case on your small system. Can you explain why the different memory models require their own ptrdiff_t type?

8   In ANSI C, many of the macros with arguments defined in the standard header
    files are required to be available also as functions. Does your system provide
    these functions? See, for example, if your system will accept the code

```
#include <ctype.h>        /* function prototype here? */

if ((isalpha)('a'))
    printf("Found the isalpha() function!\n");
```

Do not be too surprised if your system does not provide the corresponding
functions. After all, they do not get used very much.

9   C has the reputation for being an excellent language for character processing.
    This reputation is due, in part, to the fact that macros rather than functions
    are used extensively in character processing. Programmers believe that the use
    of macros can reduce execution time significantly. Is this really true? In this
    exercise we want to test this belief. Begin by writing a program that uses the
    macros in *stdio.h* and *ctype.h* extensively.

```
#include <ctype.h>
#include <stdio.h>
#include <time.h>

int main(void)
{
    int   c;

    printf("Clock ticks: %ld\n", clock()); /* start the clock */
    while ((c = getchar()) != EOF)
        if (islower(c))
            putchar(toupper(c));
        else if (isupper(c))
            putchar(tolower(c));
        else if (isdigit(c))
            . . . . .
```

Complete this program. (Read about clock() in Appendix A.) If c is a digit,
write the character x; if c is a punctuation character, do not write anything; if c
is a white space character, write it twice. Just before the return from main(),
write the line

```
printf("Clock ticks: %ld\n", clock()); /* ticks up to now */
```

Now, write another version of your program in which each macro is replaced
by its corresponding function. For example, instead of islower(c) write

```
(islower)(c)
```

Use redirection to process character files with each version of your program. On a small file, due to system overhead, there should not be much difference in running time, but as the file gets larger, the difference should be more pronounced. Is it? *Hint:* Give the command

    pgm < *input* > *output*

so that you will not have to waste time printing the file on the screen.

10 In ANSI C, the standard header files can be included repeatedly and in any order. Change the first version of the program that you wrote in Exercise 9 by duplicating the #include lines at the top of the file a number of times:

```
#include <ctype.h>
#include <stdio.h>
#include <time.h>
#include <ctype.h>
#include <stdio.h>
#include <time.h>
.....                       /* repeat a number of times */

int main(void)
{
    .....
```

Does your compiler complain? Although the program might compile a little more slowly, it should execute just as fast. Does it?

11 We listed isascii() as a macro in *ctype.h*. However, this macro is not really specified in the ANSI C documents. (Perhaps the ANSI C committee did not want to show any favoritism for ASCII codes over any other.) Check to see if isascii() is provided by your system.

12 In this exercise we want to warn you about a subtle difference between traditional C and ANSI C. In traditional C, tolower() and toupper() are provided as macros in *ctype.h*. In ANSI C, the corresponding macros are available in *ctype.h*, but they have been renamed as _tolower() and _toupper(). (Check to see that they are available on your system.) In traditional C, it makes sense to use an expression such as toupper(c) only if you already know that c is a lowercase letter. In ANSI C, toupper() is implemented as a function, and the expression toupper(c) makes sense no matter what integral value c might have. If c is not a lowercase letter, then toupper(c) has no effect; that is, it returns c. Similar remarks hold with respect to tolower(). Experiment with your system. See what is produced by the expressions

    tolower('a')   _tolower('a')   toupper('A')   _toupper('A')

13 The stringization operator # causes an argument that is passed to a macro to be surrounded by double quotes. What happens if the argument is already surrounded by double quote characters? Write a test program that contains the following code:

```
#define    YANK(x)    s = #x

char    *s;

YANK("Go home, Yankee!");
printf("%s\n", s);
```

Write another version of your program that does not contain the # operator. Execute both versions. How does the output of one version differ from the other? Use the –E option (or whatever is required by your system) to get the preprocessor to expand your code. What does the preprocessor do differently when the # operator is present?

14 What gets printed? Explain.

```
#define    GREETINGS(a, b, c) \
           printf(#a ", " #b ", and " #c ": Hello!\n")

int main(void)
{
   GREETINGS(Alice, Bob, Carole);
   return 0;
}
```

Look what is produced by the preprocessor before compilation. Can you find GREETINGS?

15 Consider the directive

```
#undef    TRY_ME
```

If TRY_ME was previously defined with a #define macro, this line causes the macro to be discarded. If TRY_ME was not previously defined, then the line should have no effect. Write some code to test what happens on your system. If TRY_ME was not previously defined, does your system complain?

16 The assert() macro is supposed to be discarded if the macro NDEBUG is defined. Does it work as expected on your system? Try the following program:

```
#define    NDEBUG
#include <assert.h>

int main(void)
{
    int    a = 1, b = 2;

    assert(a > b);
    return 0;
}
```

What happens if you interchange the first two lines of the program?

17 In the program in Exercise 16, replace the two lines at the top with the following three lines:

```
#include <assert.h>
#define    NDEBUG
#include <assert.h>
```

Does your C compiler complain? Should your C compiler complain? *Hint:* Check to see if the line

```
#undef    assert
```

is in the *assert.h* header file.

18 Suppose you are moving a large C program from a machine that has 4-byte words to one that has 2-byte words. On a machine with 2-byte words, an int is restricted to values that lie (approximately) between −32000 and +32000. Suppose that this range of values is too restrictive for some parts of the program that you are moving. If you put the line

```
#define    int    long
```

into a header file that gets included with each of the files making up your program, will this work? Explain.

19 Find the `typedef` for `size_t` in the header file *stddef.h* on your system. Search for this `typedef` in *stdlib.h* also. Suppose you are writing some code that starts with

```
#include <stddef.h>
#include <stdlib.h>
```

Because duplicate type definitions do not work, your system must be able to prevent the `typedef` for `size_t` from being included twice. Explain how this mechanism works.

20 If you want to use `qsort()`, you have to know what its function prototype is. On some ANSI C systems it is given in *stdlib.h* as

```
void qsort(void *base, size_t nelem,
           size_t width, int (*compare)());
```

What is provided by your system? Is it equivalent to this? Remember, in a function prototype the parameter identifiers are discarded by the compiler. Thus an equivalent function prototype is given by

```
void qsort(void *, size_t, size_t, int (*)());
```

21 In the *qsort* program we used two comparison functions. What happens if you rewrite the comparison functions in such a way that they do not match the last parameter in the function prototype for `qsort()`? Rewrite them as

```
int lexico(char *p, char *q)
{
    return (*p - *q);
}

int compare_decimal_part(float *p, float *q)
{
    float   x;

    x = decimal_part(*p) - decimal_part(*q);
    return ((x == 0.0) ? 0 : (x < 0.0) ? -1 : +1);
}
```

Also, change the corresponding function prototypes in `main()`. Will the program compile now? If it does, take a careful look at the function prototype for `qsort()` as given in *stdlib.h* on your system. Is it the case that the last parameter is something like `(compare *)()`? If the program does not compile, can you cast the last argument in the two calls to `qsort()` so that it does?

22 Write a program to test the quicksort code. Begin with the following code:

```
#include <stdio.h>
#include <stdlib.h>
#include <time.h>

void   quicksort(int *, int *);

#define   N   10000

int main(void)
{
   int   a[N], i;

   srand(time(NULL));     /* seed the random number generator */
   for (i = 0; i < N; ++i)
      a[i] = rand() % 1000;
   quicksort(a, a + N - 1);
   .....
```

Complete this program by writing code that prints the sorted array elements. If you get tired of looking at all those elements, you can print just enough of the beginning, middle, and end of the array so that you believe it has been sorted.

23 In Exercise 22 you sorted an array of size 10000 with integer entries that were randomly distributed in the interval [0, 999]. Run the program again, this time keeping track of its running time. Now change the program so that the entries in the array are randomly distributed in the interval [0, 9]. Give a heuristic argument to explain why the times are so different.

24 The quicksort algorithm can be used to sort all kinds of arrays, not just arrays of integers. Rewrite the quicksort code so that it can be used to sort an array of strings. Write a program to test your code.

25 If an array has just a few elements, say 7 or less, then a bubble sort or a
    transposition sort should be faster than quicksort. The following version of
    `quicksort()` takes this into account:

```
int quicksort(int *left, int *right)
{
    int          *p, *q, pivot;
    static int    cnt = 0;

    if (right - left < 7) {
        for (p = left; p < right; ++p)
            for (q = p + 1; q <= right; ++q)
                if (*p > *q)
                    swap(*p, *q);
    }
    else if (find_pivot(left, right, &pivot) == yes) {
        p = partition(left, right, pivot);
        quicksort(left, p - 1);
        quicksort(p, right);
    }
    return ++cnt;
}
```

Note the use of the variable `cnt`. The value returned to the calling environment
is the number of times the function gets called. Experiment to see if this new
version of `quicksort()` executes faster. Is there a correlation between running
time and the number of times the function gets called?

26 Having a good algorithm for finding the pivot element in quicksort can be crucial.
    A simple algorithm is to find two distinct elements of the array and to choose the
    larger value as the pivot. With this algorithm, quicksort takes time proportional
    to n^2 instead of $n \log n$ if the array happens to be already in order, or nearly so.
    This is an important point because, in practice, arrays are often partially in order
    to begin with. Rewrite the quicksort code to implement this algorithm and write
    a test program that illustrates the poor behavior of quicksort when the array is
    in order to begin with. What happens if the array starts in reverse order?

27 To find the pivot element, we choose from among three elements of the array.
    Choosing from among five elements should reduce the running time somewhat.
    Implement this strategy by rewriting the quicksort code, using macros where
    appropriate. Write a program to test whether the running time is less. The
    optimal strategy for finding the pivot depends on the data in the array. Choosing
    from among five elements is a common strategy. What about choosing from
    among seven elements? If you are ambitious, try that strategy as well.

28 Suppose that a[] is an array of integers of size 100, and that for each i the element a[i] has value i. If quicksort(a, a + 99) is invoked, how many function calls to quicksort() are made? Compute this number for each version of find_pivot().

29 The pointer that is returned by partition() is used to break the original array into two subarrays. The size of the first subarray is called the *partition break size*. Use a random number generator to fill an array of size 100. Invoke find_pivot() and partition() to find the partition break size for the array. Do this repeatedly, say 100 times, and keep track of the running average of the break size. One expects the average break size to correspond to the middle of the array. Does this seem to be true from your experimentation?

30 The optimal break size for an array of size n is n/2. This identifies two subarrays of equal, or nearly equal, size for further processing. For example, given an array of size 100, a break size of 50 is optimal. Notice that a break size of 49 identifies subarrays of sizes 49 and 51, and that a break size of 51 identifies subarrays of sizes 51 and 49. Thus the break sizes 49 and 51 are both of equal merit. Modify the program you wrote in Exercise 27 so that you keep track of the running average of the absolute value of the difference k - 50, where k is the break size obtained from partition(). This number corresponds inversely to how good the break size is. More generally, define

$$m = \frac{|k - (n/2)|}{n}$$

where k is the partition break size obtained from partition() acting on an array of size n. Fill arrays randomly and run some machine experiments to see what, if anything, can be said about m.

31 In the discussion that follows the code for the partition() function, we presented a table that shows the elements of the array a[] after each pass of the outer while loop. Find an array of 12 distinct elements that will produce the maximum number of passes. Write a table that shows the elements of the array after each pass. Box the elements that were swapped. After you have done this by hand, write a program to create this table. To indicate the elements that were swapped in each pass, you can surround them with double quotes.

32 Compare quicksort() with mergesort() (see Chapter 6). Time both functions with arrays having 100, 1000, and 10,000 elements. For a small amount of data, run-time overhead dominates. That is, setting up the functions, initializing values, and other miscellaneous steps dominate the actual work required to perform the sorting. For large arrays, quicksort() should be faster than mergesort(). Is this true?

33 If you have a small amount of data to be sorted, a bubble sort or transposition
    sort works fine. If you have more data, then qsort() can be used. Although
    qsort() certainly is a lot faster than a bubble sort, it is not as fast as qsort().
    The advantage of qsort() over quicksort() is that it can be implemented
    with just a few lines of code. The advantage of quicksort() over qsort()
    is that it is faster. By how much? The answer is that it is a *lot* faster. Write a
    program to demonstrate this. In your program declare two large arrays. Fill the
    first array with randomly distributed integers and copy it into the second array.
    Time how long it takes qsort() to sort the first array and how long it takes
    quicksort() to sort the second array. Print these two values and their quotient.
    Because of system overhead, the size of the quotient will depend on the size of
    the arrays being sorted. It will also depend on how much effort you put into
    fine-tuning your quicksort algorithm. In any case, remember what quotients you
    get (or jot them down in the margin). Anyone who does serious work with
    machines should have a general sense of how much faster quicksort() is than
    qsort().

34 In Exercise 33, you computed the quotient of running times required to sort a
    large array, first with qsort() and then with quicksort(). In this exercise,
    you are to compute those quotients again, first with your array elements randomly
    distributed in the interval [0, 100000] and then with array elements randomly
    distributed in the interval [0, 1]. The results of this exercise are quite surprising.
    Try it.

## CHAPTER 9

STRUCTURES AND UNIONS

C is an easily extensible language. It can be extended by providing macros that are stored in header files and by providing functions that are stored in libraries. It can also be extended by defining data types that are constructed from the fundamental types. An array type is an example of this; it is a derived type that is used to represent homogeneous data. In contrast, the structure type is used to represent heterogeneous data. A structure has components, called *members*, that are individually named. Because the members of a structure can be of various types, the programmer can create aggregates of data that are suitable for a particular application.

9.1 STRUCTURES

The structure mechanism provides a means to aggregate variables of different types. As a simple example, let us define a structure that describes a playing card. The spots on a card that represent its numeric value are called "pips." A playing card such as the three of spades has a pip value, 3, and a suit value, spades. We can declare the structure type

```
struct card {
    int     pips;
    char    suit;
};
```

to capture the information needed to represent a playing card. In this declaration struct is a keyword, card is the structure tag name, and the variables pips and suit are members of the structure. The variable pips will take values from 1 to 13, representing ace to king; the variable suit will take values from 'c', 'd', 'h', and 's', representing the suits clubs, diamonds, hearts, and spades, respectively.

This declaration creates the derived data type struct card. It is an example of a user-defined type. The declaration can be thought of as a template; it creates the type struct card, but no storage is allocated. The tag name, along with the keyword struct, can now be used to declare variables of this type.

```
struct card    c1, c2;
```

This declaration allocates storage for the identifiers c1 and c2, which are of type struct card. An alternative scheme is to write

```
struct card {
    int     pips;
    char    suit;
} c1, c2;
```

which defines the type struct card and declares c1 and c2 to be of this type, all at the same time.

To access the members of a structure, we use the member access operator ".". Let us assign to c1 the values representing the three of spades.

```
c1.pips = 3;
c1.suit = 's';
```

A construct of the form

   structure_variable . member_name

is used as a variable in the same way that a simple variable or an element of an array is used. If we want c2 to represent the same playing card as c1, then we can write

```
c2 = c1;
```

This causes each member of c2 to be assigned the value of the corresponding member of c1.

Programmers commonly use the typedef mechanism when using structure types. An example of this is

```
typedef   struct card   card;
```

Now, if we want more variables to represent playing cards, we can write

```
card    c3, c4, c5;
```

Note that in the type definition the identifier card is used twice. In C, the name space for tags is separate from that of other identifiers. Thus the type definition for card is appropriate.

Within a given structure the member names must be unique. However, members in different structures are allowed to have the same name. This does not create confusion because a member is always accessed through a structure identifier or expression. Consider the following code:

```
struct fruit {
    char    *name;
    int     calories;
};

struct vegetable {
    char    *name;
    int     calories;
};

struct fruit        a;
struct vegetable    b;
```

Having made these declarations, it is clear that we can access a.calories and b.calories without ambiguity.

Structures can be complicated. They can contain members that are themselves arrays or structures. Also, we can have arrays of structures. Before presenting some examples, let us give the syntax of a structure declaration:

structure_declaration ::= *struct_specifier declarator_list* ;
struct_specifier ::= struct *tag_name* | struct *tag_name$_{opt}$* { { *mem_decl* }$_{1+}$ }
tag_name ::= *identifier*
mem_decl ::= *member_declaration*
member_declaration ::= *type_specifier declarator_list* ;
declarator_list ::= *declarator* { , *declarator* }$_{0+}$

An example is

```
struct card {
    int     pips;
    char    suit;
} deck[52];
```

Here, the identifier deck is declared to be an array of struct card.

If a tag name is not supplied, then the structure type cannot be used in later declarations. An example is

```
struct {
    int     day, month, year;
    char    day_name[4];        /* Mon, Tue, Wed, etc. */
    char    month_name[4];      /* Jan, Feb, Mar, etc. */
} yesterday, today, tomorrow;
```

This declares `yesterday`, `today`, and `tomorrow` to represent three dates. Because a tag name is not present, more variables of this type cannot be declared later. In contrast, the declaration

```
struct date {
    int     day, month, year;
    char    day_name[4];            /* Mon, Tue, Wed, etc. */
    char    month_name[4];          /* Jan, Feb, Mar, etc. */
};
```

has `date` as a structure tag name, but no variables are declared of this type. We think of this as a template. We can write

```
struct date   yesterday, today, tomorrow;
```

to declare variables of this type.

It is usually good programming practice to associate a tag name with a structure type. It is both convenient for further declarations and for documentation. However, when using `typedef` to name a structure type, the tag name may be unimportant. An example is

```
typedef struct {
    float   re;
    float   im;
} complex;

complex   a, b, c[100];
```

The type `complex` now serves in place of the structure type. The programmer achieves a high degree of modularity and portability by using `typedef` to name such derived types and by storing them in header files.

9.2   ACCESSING MEMBERS OF A STRUCTURE

In this section we discuss methods for accessing members of a structure. We have already seen the use of the member access operator ".". We will give further examples of its use and introduce the member access operator ->.

Suppose we are writing a program called *class_info*, which generates information about a class of 100 students. We begin by creating a header file.

In file class_info.h:

```
#define    CLASS_SIZE    100

struct student {
    char    *last_name;
    int     student_id;
    char    grade;
};
```

This header file can now be used to share information with the modules making up the program. Suppose in another file we write

```
#include "class_info.h"

int main(void)
{
    struct student    tmp, class[CLASS_SIZE];
    .....
```

We can assign values to the members of the structure variable tmp by using statements such as

```
tmp.grade = 'A';
tmp.last_name = "Casanova";
tmp.student_id = 910017;
```

Now suppose we want to count the number of failing students in a given class. To do this, we write a function named fail() that counts the number of F grades in the array class[]. The grade member of each element in the array of structures must be accessed.

```
/* Count the failing grades. */

#include "class_info.h"

int fail(struct student class[])
{
    int    i, cnt = 0;

    for (i = 0; i < CLASS_SIZE; ++i)
        cnt += class[i].grade == 'F';
    return cnt;
}
```

DISSECTION OF THE fail() FUNCTION

■ int fail(struct student class[])
   {
        int   i, cnt = 0;

The parameter class is of type pointer to struct student. An equivalent declaration for this parameter would be

        struct student *class

We can think of class as a one-dimensional array of structures. Parameters of any type, including structure types, can be used in headers to function definitions.

■ for (i = 0; i < CLASS_SIZE; ++i)

We are assuming that when this function is called, an array of type struct student of size CLASS_SIZE will be passed as an argument.

■ cnt += class[i].grade == 'F';

An expression such as this demonstrates how concise C can be. C is operator rich. To be fluent in its use, the programmer must be careful about precedence and associativity. This statement is equivalent to

        cnt += (((class[i]).grade) == 'F');

The member grade of the *i*th element (counting from zero) of the array of structures class is selected. A test is made to see if it is equal to 'F'. If equality holds, then the value of the expression

        class[i].grade == 'F'

is 1 and the value of cnt is incremented. If equality does not hold, then the value of the expression is 0 and the value of cnt remains unchanged.

■ return cnt;

The number of failing grades is returned to the calling environment.

C provides the member access operator -> to access the members of a structure via a pointer. (This operator is typed on the keyboard as a minus sign followed by a greater than sign.) If a pointer variable is assigned the address of a structure, then a member of the structure can be accessed by a construct of the form

   pointer_to_structure -> *member_name*

A construct that is equivalent to this is

   (**pointer_to_structure*).*member_name*

The parentheses are necessary. Along with ( ) and [], the operators "." and ->
have the highest precedence and associate from left to right. Thus the preceding
construct without parentheses would be equivalent to

*(*pointer_to_structure*.*member_name*)

This is in error because only a structure can be used with the "." operator, not a
pointer to a structure.

Let us illustrate the use of -> by writing a function that adds complex numbers.
First, suppose we have the following typedef in a header file:

In file complex.h:

```
struct complex {
    double   re;        /* real part */
    double   im;        /* imag part */
};

typedef   struct complex   complex;
```

Then in another file we write

```
#include "complex.h"

void add(complex *a, complex *b, complex *c)      /* a = b + c */
{
    a -> re = b -> re + c -> re;
    a -> im = b -> im + c -> im;
}
```

Note that a, b, and c are pointers to structures. If we think of the pointers as
representing complex numbers, then we are adding b and c and putting the result
into a. That is the sense of the comment that follows the header to the function
definition.

In the following table we have illustrated some of the ways that the two member
access operators can be used. In the table we assume that the user-defined type
struct student, which we presented earlier, has already been declared.

Declarations and assignments

```
struct student    tmp, *p = &tmp;

tmp.grade = 'A';
tmp.last_name = "Casanova";
tmp.student_id = 910017;
```

Expression	Equivalent expression	Conceptual value
tmp.grade	p -> grade	A
tmp.last_name	p -> last_name	Casanova
(*p).student_id	p -> student_id	910017
* p -> last_name + 1	(*(p -> last_name)) + 1	D
*(p -> last_name + 2)	(p -> last_name)[2]	s

9.3   OPERATOR PRECEDENCE AND ASSOCIATIVITY: A FINAL LOOK

We now want to display the entire precedence and associativity table for all the C operators. The operators "." and -> have been introduced in this chapter. These operators, together with ( ) and [], have the highest precedence.

Operators	Associativity
( ) [] . -> ++ (*postfix*) -- (*postfix*)	left to right
++ (*prefix*) -- (*prefix*) ! ~ sizeof (*type*) + (*unary*) - (*unary*) & (*address*)	right to left
* / %	left to right
+ -	left to right
<< >>	left to right
< <= > >=	left to right
== !=	left to right
&	left to right
^	left to right
|	left to right
&&	left to right
||	left to right
?:	right to left
= += *= <<= >>= *etc*	right to left
, (*comma operator*)	left to right

Although the complete table of operators is extensive, some simple rules apply. The primary operators are function parentheses, subscripting, and the two member access operators. These four operators are of highest precedence. Unary operators come next, followed by the arithmetic operators. Arithmetic operators follow the usual convention; namely, multiplicative operators have higher precedence than additive operators. Assignments of all kinds are of lowest precedence, with the exception of the still more lowly comma operator. If a programmer does not know the rules of precedence and associativity in a particular situation, he or she should either look up the rules or use parentheses. If you work at a particular location on a regular basis, you should consider copying this table and pasting it on the wall right next to where you work.

9.4 USING STRUCTURES WITH FUNCTIONS

In C, structures can be passed as arguments to functions and can be returned from them. When a structure is passed as an argument to a function, it is passed by value, meaning that a local copy is made for use in the body of the function. If a member of the structure is an array, then the array gets copied as well. If the structure has many members, or members that are large arrays, then passing the structure as an argument can be relatively inefficient. For most applications an alternate scheme is to write functions that take an address of the structure as an argument instead. Business applications often use structures that have lots of members. Let us imagine that we have such a structure:

```
typedef struct {
    char                name[25];
    int                 employee_id;
    struct dept         department;
    struct home_address *a_ptr;
    double              salary;

    .....
} employee_data;
```

Notice that the department member is itself a structure. Because the compiler has to know the size of each member, the declaration for struct dept has to come first. Let us suppose that it was given by

```
struct dept {
    char    dept_name[25];
    int     dept_no;
};
```

Notice that the `a_ptr` member in the type definition of `employee_data` is a pointer to a structure. Because the compiler already knows the size of a pointer, this structure need not be defined first.

Now, suppose we want to write a function to update employee information. There are two ways we can proceed. The first way is as follows:

```
employee_data update(employee_data e)
{
    .....
    printf("Input the department number:   ");
    scanf("%d", &n);
    e.department.dept_no = n;
    .....
    return e;
}
```

Notice that we are accessing a member of a structure within a structure, because

    `e.department.dept_no`   is equivalent to   `(e.department).dept_no`

To use the function `update()`, we could write in `main()` or in some other function

    `employee_data   e;`

    `e = update(e);`

Here, `e` is being passed by value, causing a local copy of `e` to be used in the body of the function, and when a structure is returned from `update()`, it is assigned to `e`, causing a member-by-member copy to be performed. Because the structure is large, the compiler must do a lot of copy work. An alternate way to proceed is to write

```
void update(employee_data *p)
{
    .....
    printf("Input the department number:   ");
    scanf("%d", &n);
    p -> department.dept_no = n;
    .....
```

In this example, the construct

    `p -> department.dept_no`   is equivalent to   `(p -> department).dept_no`

This illustrates how a member of a structure within a structure can be accessed via a pointer. To use this version of the update() function, we could write in main() or in some other function

```
employee_data    e;

update(&e);
```

Here, the address of e is being passed, so no local copy of the structure is needed within the update() function. For most applications this is the more efficient of the two methods (see Exercise 5 for further discussion).

9.5 INITIALIZATION OF STRUCTURES

All external and static variables, including structures, that are not explicitly initialized by the programmer are automatically initialized by the system to zero. In traditional C, only external and static variables can be initialized. ANSI C allows automatic variables, including structures, to be initialized as well.

The syntax for initializing structures is similar to that for initializing arrays. A structure variable in a declaration can be initialized by following it with an equals sign and a list of constants contained within braces. If not enough values are used to assign all the members of the structure, the remaining members are assigned the value zero by default. Some examples are

```
card   c = {13, 'h'};    /* the king of hearts */

complex   a[3][3] = {
    {{1.0, -0.1}, {2.0, 0.2}, {3.0, 0.3}},
    {{4.0, -0.4}, {5.0, 0.5}, {6.0, 0.6}},
};   /* a[2][] is assigned zeroes */

struct fruit    frt = {"plum", 150};

struct home_address {
    char    *street;
    char    *city_and_state;
    long    zip_code;
} address = {"87 West Street", "Aspen, Colorado", 80526};

struct home_address    previous_address = {0};
```

The last example illustrates a convenient way to initialize all members of a structure to have value zero. It causes pointer members to be initialized with the pointer value NULL and array members to have their elements initialized to zero.

9.6   AN EXAMPLE: PLAYING POKER

Let us use the concepts that we have presented thus far in this chapter to write a
program to play poker. The program will compute the probability that a flush is
dealt, meaning that all five cards in a hand are of the same suit. In the exercises we
will discuss ways of extending the program. *Caution:* We are going to redesign our
card structure.

Our program consists of many small functions. The simplest scheme is to put
them all in one file. We will present the functions one after another as they occur in
the file. Where appropriate, we will discuss key ideas. Here is what occurs at the
top of the file:

```
#include <stdio.h>
#include <stdlib.h>
#include <time.h>

#define    NDEALS     3000    /* number of deals */
#define    NPLAYERS   6       /* number of players */

typedef    enum {clubs, diamonds, hearts, spades}    cdhs;

struct card {
   int     pips;
   cdhs    suit;
};

typedef    struct card    card;
```

We are envisioning a game with six players. Because we are interested in the
probability of a flush occurring, we want to deal many hands. Notice that the
member suit is an enumeration type. As we will see, the use of the enumeration
type makes the code very readable. Next in the file comes the function prototypes:

```
card    assign_values(int pips, cdhs suit);
void    prn_card_values(card *c_ptr);
void    play_poker(card deck[52]);
void    shuffle(card deck[52]);
void    swap(card *p, card *q);
void    deal_the_cards(card deck[52], card hand[NPLAYERS][5]);
int     is_flush(card h[5]);
```

We begin our program development with main(). Every time we need a new function, we write it at the bottom of the file and put its function prototype in the list just above main().

```
int main(void)
{
    cdhs    suit;
    int     i, pips;
    card    deck[52];

    for (i = 0; i < 52; ++i) {
        pips = i % 13 + 1;
        if (i < 13)
            suit = clubs;
        else if (i < 26)
            suit = diamonds;
        else if (i < 39)
            suit = hearts;
        else
            suit = spades;
        deck[i] = assign_values(pips, suit);
    }
    for (i = 26; i < 39; ++i)                    /* print out the hearts */
        prn_card_values(&deck[i]);
    play_poker(deck);
    return 0;
}
```

In main(), we first assign values to each element in the array deck. We think of these elements as playing cards in a deck. To check that the code works as expected, we print out the hearts.

```
card assign_values(int pips, cdhs suit)
{
    card    c;

    c.pips = pips;
    c.suit = suit;
    return c;
}
```

Notice that the identifiers pips and suit are parameters in the function definition as well as members of the structure c. This sort of dual use of names is common.

```
void prn_card_values(card *c_ptr)
{
   int     pips = c_ptr -> pips;
   cdhs    suit = c_ptr -> suit;
   char    *suit_name;

   if (suit == clubs)
      suit_name = "clubs";
   else if (suit == diamonds)
      suit_name = "diamonds";
   else if (suit == hearts)
      suit_name = "hearts";
   else if (suit == spades)
      suit_name = "spades";
   printf("card: %2d of %s\n", pips, suit_name);
}
```

In the function `prn_card_values()` we use `pips` and `suit` as local variables.
The compiler cannot confuse these identifiers with the members of `card` because
members of a structure can be accessed only via the "." and -> operators.

Our next function is `play_poker()`. Because it is central to this program and
contains some crucial ideas, we will look at it in detail.

```
void play_poker(card deck[52])
{
   int     flush_cnt = 0, hand_cnt = 0;
   int     i, j;
   card    hand[NPLAYERS][5];   /* each player is dealt 5 cards */

   srand(time(NULL));        /* seed the random number generator */
   for (i = 0; i < NDEALS; ++i) {
      shuffle(deck);
      deal_the_cards(deck, hand);
      for (j = 0; j < NPLAYERS; ++j) {
         ++hand_cnt;
         if (is_flush(hand[j])) {
            ++flush_cnt;
            printf("%s%d\n%s%d\n%s%f\n\n",
               "       Hand number:  ", hand_cnt,
               "      Flush number:  ", flush_cnt,
               "Flush probability:  ",
                  (double) flush_cnt / hand_cnt);
         }
      }
   }
}
```

DISSECTION OF THE `play_poker()` FUNCTION

- `card   hand[NPLAYERS][5];   /* each player is dealt 5 cards */`
  The identifier `hand` is a two-dimensional array. It can be viewed also as an array of arrays. Because the symbolic constant `NPLAYERS` has value 6, we can think of `hand` as 6 hands, each with 5 cards.

- `srand(time(NULL));     /* seed the random number generator */`
  The function `srand()` is used to seed the random number generator invoked by `rand()`. The value supplied as an argument to `srand()` is called the seed. Here, we have used for the seed the value returned by the function call `time(NULL)`. This function is in the standard library, and its function prototype is in the header file *time.h*. Because `time()` produces an integer value that is obtained from the internal clock, each time we run the program a different seed is produced, causing different numbers to be generated by `rand()`. Hence, every time we run the program different hands are dealt.

- ```
  for (i = 0; i < NDEALS; ++i) {
      shuffle(deck);
      deal_the_cards(deck, hand);
  ```
  Before dealing the cards, we shuffle the deck. As we will see, this is where we use `rand()` to simulate the shuffling.

- ```
  for (j = 0; j < NPLAYERS; ++j) {
      ++hand_cnt;
      if (is_flush(hand[j])) {
          ++flush_cnt;
          .....
  ```
  After the cards are dealt, we check each player's hand to see if it is a flush. If it is, then we increment `flush_cnt` and print.

The function that shuffles the cards comes next. It is quite simple. We go through the deck swapping each card with another card that is chosen randomly. Note that the 52 in the header to the function definition is only for the benefit of the human reader. The compiler disregards it.

```
void shuffle(card deck[52])
{
    int   i, j;

    for (i = 0; i < 52; ++i) {
        j = rand() % 52;
        swap(&deck[i], &deck[j]);
    }
}

void swap(card *p, card *q)
{
    card   tmp;

    tmp = *p;
    *p = *q;
    *q = tmp;
}
```

Even though the swap() function is used to swap structures, its general form is the same.

```
void deal_the_cards(card deck[52], card hand[NPLAYERS][5])
{
    int   card_cnt = 0, i, j;

    for (j = 0; j < 5; ++j)
        for (i = 0; i < NPLAYERS; ++i)
            hand[i][j] = deck[card_cnt++];
}
```

Because the compiler disregards the first size in an array in a parameter declaration, an equivalent header for this function definition is

```
void deal_the_cards(card deck[], card hand[][5])
```

Also, because arrays in parameter declarations are really pointers, another equivalent header is given by

```
void deal_the_cards(card *deck, card (*hand)[5])
```

In each of these headers, the 5 is needed by the compiler to generate the correct storage mapping function. Notice that in the function the cards are dealt one at a time to each of the hands in turn. In contrast, the code

```
for (i = 0; i < NPLAYERS; ++i)
    for (j = 0; j < 5; ++j)
        hand[i][j] = deck[cnt++];
```

would have the effect of dealing 5 cards all at once to each of the hands. Because we are trying to simulate a poker game as it is actually played, the code that we used in deal_the_cards() is preferable.

```
int is_flush(card h[5])
{
    int   i;

    for (i = 1; i < 5; ++i)
        if (h[i].suit != h[0].suit)
            return 0;
    return 1;
}
```

The function is_flush() checks to see if the cards in a hand are all of the same suit. It is invoked in the function play_poker() with the expression is_flush(hand[j]). Recall that hand is an array of arrays, making hand[j] itself an array of type card. When is_flush() is called, the elements of this array are accessed.

9.7 UNIONS

A union, like a structure, is a derived type. Unions follow the same syntax as structures but have members that share storage. A union type defines a set of alternative values that may be stored in a shared portion of memory. The programmer is responsible for interpreting the stored values correctly. Consider the declaration

```
union int_or_float {
    int     i;
    float   f;
};
```

In this declaration, union is a keyword, int_or_float is the union tag name, and the variables i and f are members of the union. This declaration creates the derived data type union int_or_float. The declaration can be thought of as a template; it creates the type, but no storage is allocated. The tag name, along with the keyword union, can now be used to declare variables of this type.

```
union int_or_float    a, b, c;
```

This declaration allocates storage for the identifiers a, b, and c. For each variable the compiler allocates a piece of storage that can accommodate the largest of the specified members. The notation used to access a member of a union is identical to that used to access a member of a structure.

The following example shows how what is stored in a union can be interpreted in different ways:

```
typedef union int_or_float {
    int     i;
    float   f;
} number;

int main(void)
{
    number    n;

    n.i = 4444;
    printf("i: %10d     f: %16.10e\n", n.i, n.f);
    n.f = 4444.0;
    printf("i: %10d     f: %16.10e\n", n.i, n.f);
    return 0;
}
```

This little experiment demonstrates how your system overlays an int and a float. The output of this program is system-dependent. Here is what is printed on our system:

```
i:        4444      f: 0.6227370375e-41
i: 1166729216      f: 4.4440000000e+03
```

DISSECTION OF THE *int_or_float* PROGRAM

■   typedef union int_or_float {
       int   i;
       float   f;
   } number;
   As with structures, the typedef mechanism can be used to abbreviate long type names.

■ number   n;

The type number is equivalent to union int_or_float. This declaration causes the system to allocate space for the union variable n. That space must accommodate the larger of the two members of n. If we assume that an int is stored in 2 or 4 bytes and that a float is stored in 4 bytes, then the system will allocate 4 bytes for n.

■ n.i = 4444;
   printf("i: %10d   f: %16.10e\n", n.i, n.f);

The int member n.i is assigned the int value 4444. When we print the value of n.i in the format of a decimal integer, 4444, of course, is printed. However, the same piece of memory is interpreted as a float when we print the member n.f in the %e format. In this case, something radically different from 4444 is printed.

■ n.f = 4444.0;
   printf("i: %10d   f: %16.10e\n", n.i, n.f);

Now we are playing the game the other way. The float member n.f is assigned the float value 4444.0. When n.f is printed in the %e format, we get the correct value, but when we print the underlying storage in the %d format, we get something quite different.

The point is that the system will interpret the same stored values according to which member component is selected. It is the programmer's responsibility to choose the right one.

Unions are used in applications that require multiple interpretations for a given piece of memory. But more commonly, they are used to conserve storage by allowing the same space in memory to be used for a variety of types. The members of a union can be structures or other unions. The following is an example:

```
struct flower {
   char                    *name;
   enum {red, white, blue}  color;
};

struct fruit {
   char   *name;
   int    calories;
};

struct vegetable {
   char   *name;
   int    calories;
   int    cooking_time;      /* in minutes */
};

union flower_fruit_or_vegetable {
   struct flower       flw;
   struct fruit        frt;
   struct vegetable    veg;
};

union flower_fruit_or_vegetable   ffv;
```

Having made these declarations, we can use a statement such as

```
ffv.veg.cooking_time = 7;
```

to assign a value to the member cooking_time of the member veg in the union ffv.

9.8   BIT FIELDS

An int or unsigned member of a structure or union can be declared to consist of a specified number of bits. Such a member is called a *bit field*, and the number of associated bits is called its *width*. The width is specified by a nonnegative constant integral expression following a colon. The width is at most the number of bits in a machine word. Typically, bit fields are declared as consecutive members of a structure, and the compiler packs them into a minimal number of machine words.

An example is

```
struct pcard {                    /* a packed representation */
    unsigned   pips : 4;
    unsigned   suit : 2;
};
```

A variable of type `struct pcard` has a 4-bit field called `pips` that is capable of
storing the 16 values 0 to 15, and a 2-bit field called `suit` that is capable of storing
the values 0, 1, 2, and 3, which can be used to represent clubs, diamonds, hearts,
and spades, respectively. Thus the 13 `pips` values and the 4 `suit` values needed to
represent playing cards can be represented compactly with 6 bits. Suppose that we
make the declaration

```
struct pcard   c;
```

To assign to c the nine of diamonds, we can write

```
c.pips = 9;
c.suit = 1;
```

The syntax for a bit field within a structure or union is given by

bit_field_member ::= { `int` | `unsigned` }₁ { *identifier* }*opt* : *expr*
expr ::= *constant_integral_expression*

Whether the compiler assigns the bits in left-to-right or right-to-left order is machine-
dependent. Although some machines assign bit fields across word boundaries, most
of them do not. Thus on a machine with 4-byte words, the declaration

```
struct abc {
    int   a : 1, b : 16, c : 16;
} x;
```

typically would cause x to be stored in two words, with a and b stored in the first
word and c stored in the second. Only nonnegative values can be stored in `unsigned`
bit fields. For `int` bit fields, what happens is system-dependent. On some systems
the high-order bit in the field is treated as the sign bit (see Exercise 25). In most
applications `unsigned` bit fields are used.

The chief reason for using bit fields is to conserve memory. On machines with 4-byte words, we can store 32 1-bit variables in a single word. Alternatively, we could use 32 char variables. Clearly, the amount of memory saved by using bit fields can be substantial.

There are some restrictions, however. Arrays of bit fields are not allowed. Also, the address operator & cannot be applied to bit fields. This means that a pointer cannot be used to address a bit field directly, although use of the member access operator -> is acceptable.

One last point: Unnamed bit fields can be used for padding and alignment purposes. Suppose our machine has 4-byte words, and suppose we want to have a structure that contains six 7-bit fields with three of the bit fields in the first word and three in second. The following declaration accomplishes this:

```
struct small_integers {
    unsigned   i1 : 7, i2 : 7, i3 : 7,
               : 11,                      /* align to next word */
             i4 : 7, i5 : 7, i6 : 7;
};
```

Another way to cause alignment to a next word is to use an unnamed bit field with zero width. Consider the code

```
struct abc {
    unsigned   a : 1, : 0, b : 1, : 0, c : 1;
};
```

This creates three 1-bit fields in three separate words.

9.9   AN EXAMPLE: ACCESSING BITS AND BYTES

In this section we give an example of how the bits and bytes of a word in memory can be accessed. One way we can do this is through the use of bitwise operators and masks, as explained in Chapter 7. Here, we illustrate how it can be done using bit fields. Our program will be for machines having 4-byte words.

```c
#include <stdio.h>

typedef struct {
    unsigned   b0 : 8, b1 : 8, b2 : 8, b3 : 8;
} word_bytes;

typedef struct {
    unsigned
        b0  : 1, b1  : 1, b2  : 1, b3  : 1, b4  : 1, b5  : 1,
        b6  : 1, b7  : 1, b8  : 1, b9  : 1, b10 : 1, b11 : 1,
        b12 : 1, b13 : 1, b14 : 1, b15 : 1, b16 : 1, b17 : 1,
        b18 : 1, b19 : 1, b20 : 1, b21 : 1, b22 : 1, b23 : 1,
        b24 : 1, b25 : 1, b26 : 1, b27 : 1, b28 : 1, b29 : 1,
        b30 : 1, b31;
} word_bits;

typedef union {
    int          i;
    word_bits    bit;
    word_bytes   byte;
} word;

int main(void)
{
    word   w = {0};
    void   bit_print(int);

    w.bit.b8 = 1;
    w.byte.b0 = 'a';
    printf("w.i = %d\n", w.i);
    bit_print(w.i);
    return 0;
}
```

The code in main() shows how a particular bit or byte in a word can be accessed. We use the function bit_print(), which we presented in Chapter 7, to see precisely what is happening to the word in memory. Because machines vary on whether bits and bytes are counted from the high-order or low-order end of a word, the use of a utility such as bit_print() is essential. On one machine our program caused the following to be printed:

```
w.i = 353
00000000 00000000 00000001 01100001
```

whereas on another machine we obtained

```
w.i = 1635778560
01100001 10000000 00000000 00000000
```

Because machines vary with respect to word size and with respect to how bits and bytes are counted, code that uses bit fields may not be portable.

9.10 THE ADT STACK

The term *abstract data type* (ADT) is used in computer science to mean a data structure together with its operations, without specifying an implementation. Suppose we wanted a new integer type, one that could hold arbitrarily large values. The new integer type together with its arithmetic operations is an ADT. It is up to each individual system to determine how the values of integer data are represented and manipulated computationally. Native types such as char, int, and double are implemented by the C compiler.

Programmer-defined types are frequently implemented with structures. In this section we develop and implement the ADT *stack*, one of the most useful standard data structures. A stack is a data structure that allows insertion and deletion of data to occur only at a single restricted element, the top of the stack. This is the *last-in-first-out* (LIFO) discipline. Conceptually, a stack behaves like a pile of trays that pops up or is pushed down when trays are removed or added. The typical operations that can be used with a stack are *push*, *pop*, *top*, *empty*, *full*, and *reset*. The push operator places a value on the stack. The pop operator retrieves and deletes a value off the stack. The top operator returns the top value from the stack. The empty operator tests if the stack is empty. The full operator tests if the stack is full. The reset operator clears the stack, or initializes it. The stack, along with these operations, is a typical ADT.

We will use a fixed-length char array to store the contents of the stack. (Other implementation choices are possible; in Chapter 10, we will implement a stack as a linked list.) The top of the stack will be an integer-valued member named top. The various stack operations will be implemented as functions, each of whose parameter lists includes a parameter of type pointer to stack. By using a pointer, we avoid copying a potentially large stack to perform a simple operation.

```c
/* An implementation of type stack. */

#define    MAX_LEN      1000
#define    EMPTY        -1
#define    FULL         (MAX_LEN - 1)

typedef    enum boolean {false, true}    boolean;

typedef struct stack {
    char    s[MAX_LEN];
    int     top;
} stack;

void reset(stack *stk)
{
    stk -> top = EMPTY;
}

void push(char c, stack *stk)
{
    stk -> top++;
    stk -> s[stk -> top] = c;
}

char pop(stack *stk)
{
    return (stk -> s[stk -> top--]);
}

char top(const stack *stk)
{
    return (stk -> s[stk -> top]);
}

boolean empty(const stack *stk)
{
    return ((boolean) (stk -> top == EMPTY));
}

boolean full(const stack *stk)
{
    return ((boolean) (stk -> top == FULL));
}
```

DISSECTION OF THE *stack* IMPLEMENTATION

■ `typedef    enum boolean {false, true}    boolean;`
We use this `typdef` to give a new name, `boolean`, to the enumeration type, `enum boolean`. Note that the new name coincides with the tag name. Programmers often do this.

■ `typedef struct stack {`
    `char    s[MAX_LEN];`
    `int     top;`
`} stack;`
This code declares the structure type `struct stack`, and at the same time uses a `typedef` to give `struct stack` the new name `stack`. Here is an equivalent way to write this:

```
struct stack {
    char    s[MAX_LEN];
    int     top;
};

typedef    struct stack    stack;
```

The structure has two members, the array member `s` and the `int` member `top`.

■ `void reset(stack *stk)`
`{`
    `stk -> top = EMPTY;`
`}`
The member `top` in the stack pointed to by `stk` is assigned the value `EMPTY`. This conceptually resets the stack, making it empty. In the calling environment, if `st` is a stack, we can write

    `reset(&st);`

to reset `st` or initialize it. At the beginning of a program, we usually start with an empty stack.

■ `void push(char c, stack *stk)`
`{`
    `stk -> top++;`
    `stk -> s[stk -> top] = c;`
`}`

```
char pop(stack* stk)
{
    return (stk -> s[stk -> top--]);
}
```

The operation *push* is implemented as a function of two arguments. First the member top is incremented. Note that

```
stk -> top++          is equivalent to          (stk -> top)++
```

Then the value of c is shoved onto the top of the stack. This function assumes that the stack is not full. The operation *pop* is implemented in like fashion. It assumes the stack is not empty. The value of the expression

```
stk -> top--
```

is the value that is currently stored in the member top. Suppose this value is 7. Then

```
stk -> s[7]
```

gets returned, and the stored value of top in memory gets decremented, making its value 6.

■
```
boolean empty(const stack *stk)
{
    return ((boolean) (stk -> top == EMPTY));
}

boolean full(const stack *stk)
{
    return ((boolean) (stk -> top == FULL));
}
```
Each of these functions tests the stack member top for an appropriate condition and returns a value of type boolean, either true or false. Suppose the expression

```
stk -> top == EMPTY
```

in the body of empty() is true. Then the expression has the int value 1. This value gets cast to the type boolean, making it true, and that is what gets returned.

To test our stack implementation, we can put the above code in a *.c* file and add the following code at the bottom. Our function `main()` enters the characters of a string onto a stack and then pops them, printing each character out in turn. The effect is to print in reverse order the characters that were pushed onto the stack.

```
/* Test the stack implementation by reversing a string. */

#include <stdio.h>

int main(void)
{
    char    str[] = "My name is Laura Pohl!";
    int     i;
    stack   s;

    reset(&s);                                /* initialize the stack */
    printf(" In the string: %s\n", str);
    for (i = 0; str[i] != '\0'; ++i)
        if (!full(&s))
            push(str[i], &s);                 /* push a char on the stack */
    printf("From the stack: ");
    while (!empty(&s))
        putchar(pop(&s));                     /* pop a char off the stack */
    putchar('\n');
    return 0;
}
```

The output from this test program is

```
 In the string: My name is Laura Pohl!
From the stack: !lhoP aruaL si eman yM
```

Note that the expression `&s`, the address of the `stack` variable `s`, is used as an argument whenever we call a stack function. Because each of these functions expects a pointer of type `stack *`, the expression `&s` is appropriate.

9.11 SUMMARY

1 Structures and unions are principal methods by which the programmer can define new types.

2 The `typedef` facility can be used to give new names to types. Programmers routinely use `typedef` to give a new name to a structure or union type.

3 A structure is an aggregation of components that can be treated as a single variable. The components of the structure are called members.

4 Members of structures can be accessed by using the member access operator "`.`". If s is a structure variable with a member named m, then the expression `s.m` refers to the value of the member m within the structure s.

5 Members of structures can also be accessed by the member access operator `->`. If p is a pointer that has been assigned the value &s, then the expression `p -> m` also refers to `s.m`. Both "`.`" and `->` have highest precedence among C operators.

6 In ANSI C, if a and b are two variables of the same structure type, then the assignment expression `a = b` is valid. It causes each member of a to be assigned the value of the corresponding member of b. Also, a structure expression can be passed as an argument to a function and returned from a function. (Many traditional C compilers also have these capabilities, but not all of them.)

7 When a structure variable is passed as an argument to a function, it is passed "call by value." If the structure has many members, or members that are large arrays, this may be an inefficient way of getting the job done. If we redesign the function definition so that a pointer to the structure instead of the structure itself is used, then a local copy of the structure will not be created.

8 A union is like a structure, except that the members of a union share the same space in memory. Unions are used principally to conserve memory. The space allocated for a union variable can be used to hold a variety of types, specified by the members of the union. It is the programmer's responsibility to know which representation is currently stored in a union variable.

9 The members of structures and unions can be arrays or other structures and unions. Considerable complexity is possible when nesting arrays, structures, and unions within each other. Care must be taken that the proper variables are being accessed.

10 A bit field is an `int` or `unsigned` member of a structure or union that has a specified number of bits. The number of bits is given as an integral constant expression following a colon. This number is called the width of the bit field. The width is limited to the number of bits in a machine word. Consecutive bit fields in a structure are stored typically as contiguous bits in a machine word, provided that they fit.

11 Bit fields can be unnamed, in which case they are used for padding or word alignment purposes. The unnamed bit field of width 0 is special. It causes immediate alignment on the next word.

12 How bit fields are implemented is system-dependent. Hence their use need not be portable. Nonetheless, bit fields have important uses.

13 The stack is an abstract data type (ADT) that has many uses, especially in computer science. An ADT can be implemented many different ways.

9.12 EXERCISES

1   In some situations a `typedef` can be replaced by a `#define`. Here is a simple example:

```
typedef   float   DOLLARS;

int main(void)
{
   DOLLARS   amount = 100.0, interest = 0.07 * amount;

   printf("DOLLARS = %.2f\n", amount + interest);
   return 0;
}
```

First execute this program so you understand its effects. Then replace the type-def by

```
#define   DOLLARS   float
```

When you recompile the program and execute it, does it behave as it did before?

2   In some situations a `typedef` cannot be replaced by a `#define`. Consider the following program:

```
typedef   float   DOLLARS;

int main(void)
{
   DOLLARS   amount = 100.00,
             interest = 0.07 * amount;

   {                            /*  new block  */
      float   DOLLARS;

      DOLLARS = amount + interest;
      printf("DOLLARS = %.2f\n", DOLLARS);
   }
   return 0;
}
```

Execute this program so you understand its effects. If the `typedef` is replaced by the line

```
#define    DOLLARS    float
```

then the program will not compile. Explain why the `typedef` works but the `#define` does not.

3 The program in Exercise 2 used a new block to illustrate a certain point. Because of this, the code was not very natural. In this exercise we use a `typedef` again, and this time the code is quite straightforward.

```
typedef   char *   string;

int main(void)
{
    string   a[] = {"I", "like", "to", "fight,"},
             b[] = {"pinch,", "and", "bight."};

    printf("%s %s %s %s %s %s %s\n",
        a[0], a[1], a[2], a[3], b[0], b[1], b[2]);
    return 0;
}
```

Execute the program so you understand its effects. If the `typedef` is replaced by the line

```
#define    string    char *
```

then the program will not compile. Explain why the `typedef` works, but the `#define` does not. To make the program work with the `#define`, a single character needs to be added. What is the character?

4 Write a function `add(a, b, c)`, where the variables a, b, and c are of type `matrix`. Write a program to test your function.

5 Speed is not everything, but it counts for a lot in the computing world. If a structure is large, it is more efficient to pass an address of the structure than it is to pass the structure itself. Does this hold true if the structure is small? After all, there is a cost for dealing with pointers, too. Suppose you have many complex numbers to multiply. How should you design your multiplication function? You could pass structures as arguments:

```
complex mult(complex b, complex c)
{
    complex a;

    a.re = b.re * c.re - b.im * c.im;
    a.im = b.im * c.re + b.re * c.im;
    return a;
}
```

But it may be faster to pass addresses:

```
void mult(complex *a, complex *b, complex *c)
{
    .....
```

Complete this version of the mult() function, and write a test program to see which version is faster.

6 The program in this exercise uses a typedef to name the type "pointer to a function that takes a double and returns a double." First run the program so you understand its effects.

```
#include <stdio.h>
#include <math.h>

#define    PI    3.14159

typedef    double    dbl;              /* an abbreviation */
typedef    dbl       (*PFDD)(dbl);     /* ptr to fct taking
                                          dbl and returning dbl */

int main(void)
{
    PFDD    f = sin, g = cos;

    printf("f(%f) = %f\n", PI, f(PI));
    printf("g(%f) = %f\n", PI, g(PI));
    return 0;
}
```

Now modify the code so the second `typedef` is replaced by

```
typedef   dbl    FDD(dbl);    /* fct of dbl returning a dbl */
typedef   FDD    *PFDD;       /* ptr to FDD */
```

Does the program still run? (It should.) Carefully explain how the `typedef` for PFDD works.

7 Write a function to do complex subtraction. Write two versions: one that returns a pointer to `complex` and one that returns a value of type `complex`.

8 Write a small collection of functions that perform operations on complex vectors and matrices. Include in your collection functions that print complex vectors and matrices on the screen. Write a program to test your functions.

9 Write a program that is able to produce a balanced meal. Start by defining a structure that contains the name of a food, its calories per serving, its food type such as meat or fruit, and its costs. The foods should be stored as an array of structures. The program should construct a meal that comes from four different food types and that meets calorie and cost constraints. The program should be capable of producing a large number of different menus.

10 Create a structure that can describe a restaurant. It should have members that include the name, address, average cost, and type of food. Write a routine that prints out all restaurants of a given food type in order of cost, with the least costly first.

11 Put a list of student names, identification numbers, and grades into a file called *data*. For example, the beginning of the file might look like

```
Casanova    910017    A
Smith       934422    C
Jones       878766    B
.....
```

Write a program called *reorder* that can be used to read the data in the file and put it into the array `class` of type `struct student`. This can be done with redirection

   reorder < *data*

The program should print out an ordered list of students and grades. Students with A grades should be listed first, students with B grades next, and so forth. Among all students having the same grade, the students should be listed alphabetically by name.

12 Modify the program that you wrote in Exercise 11 by adding the function `class_average()` to compute the class average and print it. Assume that an A grade has value 4, a B grade has value 3, and so forth.

13 Experiment with the *poker* program. After dealing many hands, the last computed probability of getting a flush should approximate the mathematical probability. What is the mathematical probability of getting a flush? If you are dealt one card, then it will be of a certain suit, say hearts. What is the chance that the second card you are dealt will be a heart? Well, there are 51 cards left in the deck and 12 of them are hearts, so the probability is 12/51. What is the chance that the third card you are dealt will also be a heart? Because there are now 50 cards left in the deck and 11 of them are hearts, the probability that the second and third cards are hearts is $(12/51) \times (11/50)$. Continuing in this fashion, we see that the mathematical probability of getting a flush is

$$\frac{12}{51} \times \frac{11}{50} \times \frac{10}{49} \times \frac{9}{48}$$

This product is approximately 0.00198. (Use your hand calculator to check that this is so.) When your machine plays poker, some of the computed probabilities should be larger than this number and some smaller. Is that the case?

14 Modify the *poker* program by adding the function `is_straight()`, which tests whether a poker hand is a straight. Whenever a straight is dealt, print the computed probability. Because a flush beats a straight, one expects that the probability of a flush is lower than the probability of a straight. Does your *poker* program confirm this?

15 Modify the *poker* program by adding the function `is_fullhouse()`, which tests whether a poker hand is a full house. Whenever a full house is dealt, print the computed probability. Because a full house beats a flush, one expects that the probability of a full house is lower than the probability of a flush. Does your *poker* program confirm this?

16 The experienced poker player arranges the hand to reflect its values. Write a program that arranges and prints out a hand of five cards in sorted order by pips value. Assume that an ace is highest in value, a king is next highest in value, and so forth.

17 (Advanced) Write a function `hand_value()`, which returns the poker value of the hand. The best possible hand is a straight flush, and the worst possible hand is no pair. Write another function that compares two hands to see which is best.

18 Consider the following version of the function `assign_values()`:

```
void assign_values(card c, int pips, cdhs suit)
{
    c.pips = pips;
    c.suit = suit;
}
```

When we test this function with the code

```
card    c;

assign_values(c, 13, diamonds);    /* the king of diamonds */
prn_card_values(&c);
```

we find that it does not work as expected. Explain.

19 Consider the following `union` declaration:

```
union a {
    int     a;
    char    b;
    float   a;
} a, b, c;
```

There is only one thing wrong. What is it?

20 Write a `typedef` for a structure that has two members. One member should be a union of `double` and `complex`, and the other member should be a "flag" that tells which domain is being used. Write functions that can add and multiply over both domains. Your functions should decide on appropriate conversions when mixing arguments from both domains.

21 In commercial applications, it is sometimes useful to use binary coded decimal codes (BCD), where 4 bits are used to represent a decimal digit. A 32-bit word can be used to represent an 8-digit decimal number. Use bit fields to implement this code. Write two conversion routines, one from binary to BCD and the second from BCD to binary.

22 In Chapter 4 we wrote a program that printed a table of values for some boolean functions. Rewrite that program using bit fields. Represent each boolean variable as a 1-bit field.

23 (Sieve of Eratosthenes) Use an array of structures, where each structure contains a word that is divided into bit fields, to implement the sieve algorithm for primes. On a machine with 4-byte words, we can use an array of a 1000 elements to find all primes less than 32,000. Let each bit represent an integer, and initialize all bits to zero. The idea is to cross out all the multiples of a given prime. A bit that is 1 will represent a composite number. Start with the prime 2. Every second bit is made 1 starting with bit 4. Then bit 3 is still 0. Every third bit is made 1, starting with bit 6. Bit 4 is 1, so it is skipped. Bit 5 is the next bit with value 0. Every fifth bit is made 1, starting with bit 10. At the end of this process, only those bits that are still zero represent primes.

24 What gets printed by the following program? Explain.

```
#include <stdio.h>

struct test {
   unsigned   a : 1, b : 2, c : 3;
};

int main(void)
{
   int           i;
   struct test   x;

   for (i = 0; i < 23; ++i) {
      x.a = x.b = x.c = i;
      printf("%s%d%s%d%s%d\n",
         "   x.a = ", x.a,
         "   x.b = ", x.b,
         "   x.c = ", x.c);
   }
   return 0;
}
```

What happens if you replace

```
x.a = x.b = x.c = i;        by        x.c = x.b = x.a = i;
```

25 Does your system implement signed arithmetic for int bit fields? Try the
    following code:

```
struct test {
   int   a : 3, b : 4;
} x = {0};

for ( ; ; )
   printf("x.a = %2d   x.b = %2d\n", x.a++, x.b++);
```

26 What gets printed? Explain.

```
typedef struct a { unsigned a : 1, : 0, b : 1; } a;
typedef struct b { unsigned a : 1, b : 1; } b;

printf("%.1f\n", (float) sizeof(a) / sizeof(b));
```

27 In this exercise we want to consider = and == with respect to their use with structures. Suppose a and b are two structure variables of the same type. Then the expression a = b is valid, but the expression a == b is not. The operands of the == operator cannot be structures. (Beginning programmers often overlook this subtle point.) Write a small test program to see what your compiler does if you try to use the expression a == b, where a and b are structures of the same type.

28 (Project) The double ended queue is a very useful ADT. To implement this ADT, start with the following constructs:

```
struct deque {          /* double ended queue */
   .....
};

typedef    struct deque          deque;
typedef    enum {false, true}    boolean;
typedef    data                  char;
```

The programmer-defined type deque implements a double ended queue with an array. If you want the data stored in the queue to be ints, use

```
typedef    data                  int;
```

Function prototypes of useful operations include

```
void       add_to_front(deque *, data);
void       add_to_rear(deque *, data);
data       take_from_front(deque *);
data       take_from_rear(deque *);
boolean    empty(deque *);
boolean    full(deque *);
```

Write and test an implementation of the double ended queue ADT. (In Chapter 10 we will see how to do this with a linked list.)

29 Although the program in this exercise is system-dependent, it will run correctly
on many different systems. See if it runs correctly on your machine.

```c
/* The mystery program. */

#if (VAX || PC)
    #define   HEX0    0x6c6c6548
    #define   HEX1    0x77202c6f
    #define   HEX2    0x646c726f
    #define   HEX3    0x00000a21
#else
    #define   HEX0    0x48656c6c
    #define   HEX1    0x6f2c2077
    #define   HEX2    0x6f726c64
    #define   HEX3    0x210a0000
#endif

typedef union {
    char   what[16];
    long   cipher[4];
} mystery;

int main(void)
{
    mystery   x;

    x.cipher[0] = HEX0;        /* put a hex on the mystery */
    x.cipher[1] = HEX1;
    x.cipher[2] = HEX2;
    x.cipher[3] = HEX3;
    printf("%s", x.what);
    return 0;
}
```

Explain how the mystery program works. If the phrase that is printed is unfamiliar to you, ask a programmer who has worked in C for a number of years
what its significance is.

## CHAPTER 10

STRUCTURES AND LIST PROCESSING

In this chapter we explain self-referential structures. We define structures with pointer members that refer to the structure containing them. Such data structures are called *dynamic data structures*. Unlike arrays or simple variables that are normally allocated at block entry, dynamic data structures often require storage management routines to explicitly obtain and release memory.

10.1 SELF-REFERENTIAL STRUCTURES

Let us define a structure with a member field that points at the same structure type. We wish to do this in order to have an unspecified number of such structures nested together.

```
struct list {
    int         data;
    struct list *next;
} a;
```

This declaration of `list` can be stored in two words of memory. One word stores the member `data` and the second word stores the member `next`. The pointer variable `next` is called a *link*. Each structure is linked to a succeeding structure by way of the member `next`. These structures are conveniently displayed pictorially with links shown as arrows.

*A **structure of type** struct list*

data   next

   The pointer variable `next` contains an address of either the location in memory of the successor `list` element or the special value NULL defined as 0. NULL is used to denote the end of the list. Let us see how all this works by manipulating

```
struct list  a, b, c;
```

We will perform some assignments on these structures:

```
a.data = 1;
b.data = 2;
c.data = 3;
a.next = b.next = c.next = NULL;
```

Pictorially, the result of this code is the following:

After assignment

1	NULL		2	NULL		3	NULL
data	next		data	next		data	next

Let us chain these together.

```
a.next = &b;
b.next = &c;
```

These pointer assignments result in linking a to b to c.

After chaining

Now the links allow us to retrieve data from successive elements. Thus

```
a.next -> data
```

has a value 2 and

```
a.next -> next -> data
```

has value 3.

10.2   LINEAR LINKED LISTS

A *linear linked list* is like a clothes line on which the data structures hang sequentially. A head pointer addresses the first element of the list, and each element points at a successor element, with the last element having a link value NULL. This discussion will use the following header file:

In file list.h:

```
#include <stdio.h>
#include <stdlib.h>

typedef   char   DATA;           /* will use char in examples */

struct linked_list {
    DATA                    d;
    struct linked_list    *next;
};

typedef   struct linked_list   ELEMENT;
typedef   ELEMENT              *LINK;
```

Storage Allocation

The specifications in *list.h* do not allocate storage. The system can allocate storage if we declare variables and arrays of type ELEMENT. But what makes these structures especially useful is that utility functions exist to allocate storage dynamically. The system provides malloc() in the standard library, and its prototype is in *stdlib.h*. A function call of the form

```
malloc(size)
```

returns a pointer to enough storage for an object of *size* bytes. The storage is not initialized. The argument to malloc() is of type size_t, and the value returned is of type pointer to void. Recall that size_t is the unsigned integer type that is defined in both *stddef.h* and *stdlib.h*. It is the type that results when the sizeof operator is used. If head is a variable of type LINK, then

Link head;
```
head = malloc(sizeof(ELEMENT));
```

obtains a piece of memory from the system adequate to store an ELEMENT and assigns its address to the pointer head. As in the example, malloc() is used with the sizeof operator. A cast is unnecessary because malloc() returns a pointer to void, which can be assigned to a variable of any pointer type. The sizeof operator calculates the required number of bytes for the particular data structure.

In the code that follows, we will dynamically create a linear linked list storing the three characters *n*, *e*, and *w*. The code

```
head = malloc(sizeof(ELEMENT));
head -> d = 'n';
head -> next = NULL;
```

creates a single-element list.

*The start of a dynamically
created linked list*

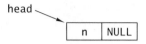

A second element is added by the assignments

```
head -> next = malloc(sizeof(ELEMENT));
head -> next -> d = 'e';
head -> next -> next = NULL;
```

It is now a two-element list.

A two-element linked list

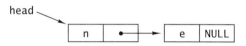

Finally, we add a last element:

```
head -> next -> next = malloc(sizeof(ELEMENT));
head -> next -> next -> d = 'w';
head -> next -> next -> next = NULL;
```

We have a three-element list pointed to by head, and the list ends when *next* has the sentinel value NULL.

A three-element linked list

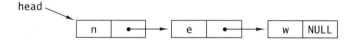

10.3 LIST OPERATIONS

Some of the basic operations on linear lists include:

1   Creating a list
2   Counting the elements
3   Looking up an element
4   Concatenating two lists
5   Inserting an element
6   Deleting an element

We will demonstrate the techniques for programming such operations on lists using both recursion and iteration. The use of recursive functions is natural because lists are a recursively defined construct. Each routine will require the specifications in file *list.h*. Observe that d in these examples could be redefined as an arbitrarily complicated data structure.

As a first example, we will write a function that will produce a list from a string. The function will return a pointer to the head of the resulting list. The heart of the function creates a list element by allocating storage and assigning member values.

```
/* List creation using recursion. */

#include <stdlib.h>
#include "list.h"

LINK string_to_list(char s[])
{
    LINK    head;

    if (s[0] == '\0')        /* base case */
        return NULL;
    else {
        head = malloc(sizeof(ELEMENT));
        head -> d = s[0];
        head -> next = string_to_list(s + 1);
        return head;
    }
}
```

pointer arithmetic

Notice once more how recursion has a base case, the creation of the empty list, and a general case, the creation of the remainder of the list. The general recursive call returns as its value a LINK pointer to the remaining sublist.

DISSECTION OF THE string_to_list() FUNCTION

■ LINK string_to_list(char s[])
```
    {
        LINK    head;
```
When a string is passed as an argument, a linked list of the characters in the string is created. Because a pointer to the head of the list will be returned, the type specifier in the header to this function definition is LINK.

■ `if (s[0] == '\0')        /* base case */`
    `return (NULL);`

When the end-of-string sentinel is detected, NULL is returned, and, as we will see, the recursion terminates. The value NULL is used to mark the end of the linked list.

■ `else {`
    `head = malloc(sizeof(ELEMENT));`

If the string s[] is not the null string, then malloc() is used to retrieve enough bytes to store an object of type ELEMENT. Because malloc() returns a pointer to void, it can be assigned to the variable head, which is a different pointer type. A cast is unnecessary. The pointer variable head now points at the block of storage provided by malloc().

■ `head -> d = s[0];`

The member d of the allocated ELEMENT is assigned the first character in the string s[].

■ `head -> next = string_to_list(s + 1);`

The pointer expression s + 1 points to the remainder of the string. The function is called recursively with s + 1 as an argument. The pointer member next is assigned the pointer value that is returned by string_to_list(s + 1). This recursive call returns as its value a LINK or, equivalently, a pointer to ELEMENT that points to the remaining sublist.

■ `return head;`

The function exits with the address of the head of the list.

This function can also be written as an iterative routine with the help of the additional auxiliary pointer tail. We will name the iterative version s_to_l() to distinguish it from the recursive version string_to_list().

```
/* List creation using iteration. */

#include <stdlib.h>
#include "list.h"

LINK s_to_l(char s[])
{
    LINK    head = NULL, tail;
    int     i;

    if (s[0] != '\0') {                          /* first element */
        head = malloc(sizeof(ELEMENT));
        head -> d = s[0];
        tail = head;
        for (i = 1; s[i] != '\0'; ++i) {    /* add to tail */
            tail -> next = malloc(sizeof(ELEMENT));
            tail = tail -> next;
            tail -> d = s[i];
        }
        tail -> next = NULL;                     /* end of list */
    }
    return head;
}
```

Functions operating on lists often require local pointer variables such as head and tail. One should use such auxiliary pointers freely to simplify code. It is also important to hand-simulate these routines. It is useful to try your program on the empty list, the unit or single-element list, and the two-element list. Frequently, the empty list and the unit list are special cases.

Passing a null string to s_to_l() creates the empty list by having the routine return with value NULL. Creating the first element is done by the first part of the code. The one-element list created from the string "A" is shown in the following diagram. This is the state of the computation before the member next is assigned the value NULL.

A one-element list

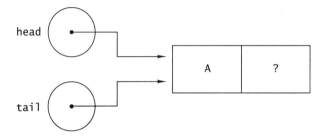

For the two-element case, say "AB", list creation is as pictured. First, the one-element list containing 'A' is created. The for statement is then executed, with i having value 1 and s[1] having value 'B'. A new element is then allocated and attached to the list.

A second element is attached

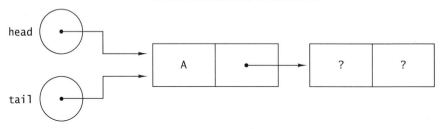

The statement tail = tail -> next; advances tail to the new element. Then its d member is assigned 'B'.

Updating the tail

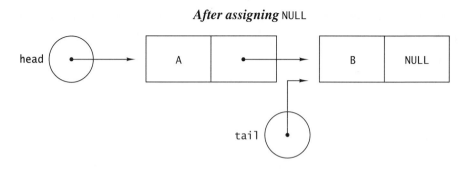

Now s[2] has value \0 and the for statement is exited with a two-element list. Finally, the end of the list is marked with a NULL.

After assigning NULL

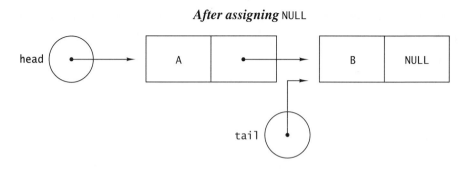

The undefined member values occur because malloc() is not required to initialize memory to zero.

10.4 SOME LIST PROCESSING FUNCTIONS

We will write two additional recursive functions. The first counts the elements in a list and the second prints the elements of a list. Both involve recurring down the list and terminating when the NULL pointer is found. All these functions use the header file *list.h*.

The function count( ) returns 0 if the list is empty; otherwise it returns the number of elements in the list.

```
/* Count a list recursively. */

int count(LINK head)
{
    if (head == NULL)
        return 0;
    else
        return (1 + count(head -> next));
}
```

An iterative version of this function replaces the recursion with a for loop.

```
/* Count a list iteratively. */

int count_it(LINK head)
{
    int    cnt = 0;

    for ( ; head != NULL; head = head -> next)
        ++cnt;
    return cnt;
}
```

Keep in mind that head is passed "call-by-value," so that invoking count_it( ) does not destroy access to the list in the calling environment.

The routine `print_list()` recursively marches down a list printing the value of member variable **d**.

```
/* Print a list recursively. */

void print_list(LINK head)
{
    if (head == NULL)
        printf("NULL");
    else {
        printf("%c --> ", head -> d);
        print_list(head -> next);
    }
}
```

To illustrate the use of these functions, we will write a program that will convert the string "ABC" to a list and print it:

```
#include <stdio.h>
#include <stdlib.h>
#include "list.h"

LINK    string_to_list(char []);
void    print_list(LINK);
int     count(LINK);

int main(void)
{
    LINK    h;

    h = string_to_list("ABC");
    printf("The resulting list is\n");
    print_list(h);
    printf("\nThis list has %d elements.\n", count(h));
    return 0;
}
```

The program produces the following output:

```
The resulting list is
A --> B --> C --> NULL
This list has 3 elements.
```

Often one wishes to take two lists and return a single combined list. The concatenation of lists a and b, where a is assumed to be nonempty, will be the list b added to the end of list a. A function to concatenate will march down list a looking for its end, as marked by the null pointer. It will keep track of its last non-null pointer and will attach the b list to the **next** link in this last element of list a.

```
/* Concatenate list a and b with a as head. */

void concatenate(LINK a, LINK b)
{
   if (a -> next == NULL)    /* a is assumed to not be NULL */
      a -> next = b;
   else
      concatenate(a -> next, b);
}
```

Recursion allows us to avoid using any auxiliary pointers to march down the a list. In general, the self-referential character of list processing makes recursion natural to use. The form of these recursive functions is as follows:

```
void generic_recursion(LINK head)
{
   if (head == NULL)
      do the base case
   else
      do the general case and recur with
      generic_recursion(head -> next)
}
```

Insertion

One of the most useful properties of lists is that insertion takes a fixed amount of time once the position in the list is found. In contrast, if one wished to place a value in a large array, retaining all other array values in the same sequential order, the insertion would take, on average, time proportional to the length of the array. The values of all elements of the array that come after the newly inserted value would have to be moved over one element.

Let us illustrate insertion into a list by having two adjacent elements pointed at by p1 and p2, and inserting between them an element pointed at by q.

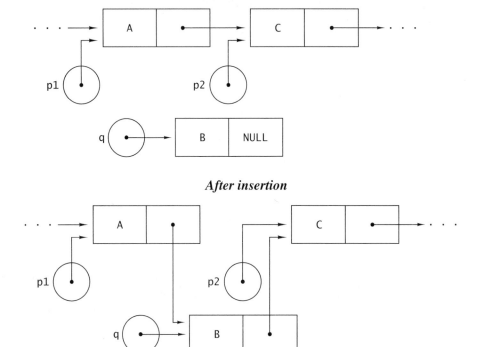

The following function `insert()` places the element pointed at by q between the elements pointed at by p1 and p2:

```
/* Inserting an element in a linked list. */

void insert(LINK p1, LINK p2, LINK q)
{
    p1 -> next = q;          /* insert */
    q -> next = p2;
}
```

Deletion

Deleting an element is very simple in a linked linear list. The predecessor of the element to be deleted has its link member assigned the address of the successor to the deleted element. Again, let us first illustrate the delete operation graphically. Here is the picture that we start with:

Before deletion

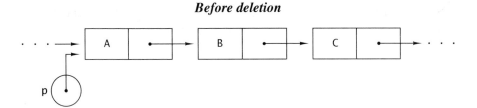

Now we execute the following code:

```
p -> next = p -> next -> next;
```

After deletion

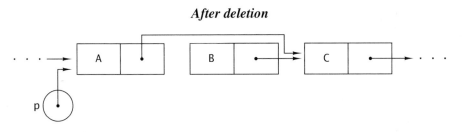

As the diagram shows, the element containing 'B' is no longer accessible and is of no use. Such an inaccessible element is called *garbage*. Because memory is frequently a critical resource, it is desirable that this storage be returned to the system for later use. This may be done with the *stdlib.h* function free(). When called as follows,

```
free(p);
```

makes previously allocated storage for the object pointed to by p available to the system. The formal argument to free() is pointer to void.

Using free(), we can write a deletion routine that returns allocated list storage to the system.

```
/* Recursive deletion of a list. */

void delete_list(LINK head)
{
    if (head != NULL) {
        delete_list(head -> next);
        free(head);                        /* release storage */
    }
}
```

Because `free()` takes a single argument of type `void *`, we can pass a pointer of any type to `free()`. We do not have to use a cast because `void *` is the generic pointer type.

10.5 STACKS

We presented the abstract data type stack as an array in Section 9.10, "The ADT Stack." Here, we will reimplement the ADT stack with a linear linked list. A stack has access restricted to the head of the list, which will be called its *top*. Furthermore, insertion and deletion occur only at the top, and under these restrictions the operations are known as *push* and *pop*, respectively.

A stack can be visualized as a pile of trays. A tray is always picked up from the top and a tray is always returned to the top. Graphically, stacks are drawn vertically.

A stack implementation

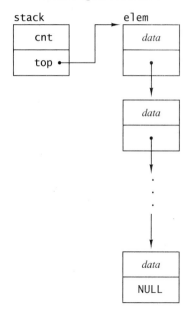

We will write a stack program that consists of a *.h* file and two *.c* files. Here is the header file:

In file stack.h:

```
/* A linked list implementation of a stack. */

#include <stdio.h>
#include <stdlib.h>

#define    EMPTY       0
#define    FULL        10000

typedef    char                data;
typedef    enum {false, true}  boolean;

struct elem {                         /* an element on the stack */
    data        d;
    struct elem *next;
};

typedef    struct elem   elem;

struct stack {
    int     cnt;                 /* a count of the elements */
    elem    *top;               /* ptr to the top element */
};

typedef    struct stack    stack;

void       initialize(stack *stk);
void       push(data d, stack *stk);
data       pop(stack *stk);
data       top(stack *stk);
boolean    empty(const stack *stk);
boolean    full(const stack *stk);
```

The function prototypes of the six standard stack operations that we are going to implement are listed at the bottom of our header file. Conceptually, these functions behave like those we presented in Section 9.10. Here, our use of the type data makes our code reusable (see Section 10.6, where we use the code again).

In file stack.c:

```
/* The basic stack routines. */

#include "stack.h"

void initialize(stack *stk)
{
    stk -> cnt = 0;
    stk -> top = NULL;
}

void push(data d, stack *stk)
{
    elem    *p;

    p = malloc(sizeof(elem));
    p -> d = d;
    p -> next = stk -> top;
    stk -> top = p;
    stk -> cnt++;
}

data pop(stack *stk)
{
    data    d;
    elem    *p;

    d = stk -> top -> d;
    p = stk -> top;
    stk -> top = stk -> top -> next;
    stk -> cnt--;
    free(p);
    return d;
}

data top(stack *stk)
{
    return (stk -> top -> d);
}
```

```
boolean empty(const stack *stk)
{
    return ((boolean) (stk -> cnt == EMPTY));
}

boolean full(const stack *stk)
{
    return ((boolean) (stk -> cnt == FULL));
}
```

The push() routine uses the storage allocator malloc() to create a new stack element, and the pop() routine returns the freed-up storage back to the system.

A stack is a *last-in-first-out* (LIFO) data structure. The last item to be pushed onto the stack is the first to be popped off. So if we were to push first 'a' and second 'b' onto a stack, then pop() would first pop 'b'. In main(), we use this property to print a string in reverse order. This serves as a test of our implementation of the ADT stack.

In file main.c:

```
/* Test the stack implementation by reversing a string. */

#include "stack.h"

int main(void)
{
    char    str[] = "My name is Joanna Kelley!";
    int     i;
    stack   s;

    initialize(&s);                          /* initialize the stack */
    printf(" In the string: %s\n", str);
    for (i = 0; str[i] != '\0'; ++i)
        if (!full(&s))
            push(str[i], &s);                /* push a char on the stack */
    printf("From the stack: ");
    while (!empty(&s))
        putchar(pop(&s));                    /* pop a char off the stack */
    putchar('\n');
    return 0;
}
```

Observe that our function main() is very similar to what we wrote in Chapter 9. Although here we have implemented the ADT as a linked list and in Chapter 9 we implemented the ADT as a string, the use of the operations is similar. Here is the output of our program:

```
In the string: My name is Joanna Kelley!
From the stack: !yelleK annaoJ si eman yM
```

10.6   AN EXAMPLE: POLISH NOTATION AND STACK EVALUATION

Ordinary notation for writing expressions is called *infix*, where operators separate arguments. Another notation for expressions, one that is very useful for stack-oriented evaluation, is called *Polish*, or parenthesis-free, *notation*. In Polish notation the operator comes after the arguments. Thus, for example,

3, 7, +   is equivalent to the infix notation   3 + 7

In Polish notation, going from left to right, the operator is executed as soon as it is encountered. Thus

17, 5, 2, *, +   is equivalent to   17 + (5 * 2)

A Polish expression can be evaluated by an algorithm using two stacks. The Polish stack contains the Polish expression, and the evaluation stack stores the inter-mediate values during execution. Here is a two-stack algorithm that evaluates Polish expressions where all operators are binary:

A two-stack algorithm to evaluate Polish expressions

1. If the Polish stack is empty, halt with the top of the evaluation stack as the answer.
2. If the Polish stack is not empty, pop the Polish stack into d. (We will use d, d1, and d2 to hold data.)
3. If d is a value, push d onto the evaluation stack.
4. If d is an operator, pop the evaluation stack twice, first into d2 and then into d1. Compute d1 and d2 operated on by d and push the result onto the evaluation stack. Go to step 1.

We illustrate this algorithm in the following diagram, where the expression

    13, 4, -, 2, 3, *, +

is evaluated.

A two-stack algorithm to evaluate Polish expressions

	E											
	v											
	a											
	l	13										
P	u	4	4									
o	a	—	—		—							
l	t	2	2		2		2					
i	i	3	3		3		3		3		3	
s	o	*	*		*	4	*		*	2	2	6
h	n	+	+	13	+	13| +	9	+	9	+	9	+	9	15

Let us write a program that implements this two-stack algorithm. A key idea will be to redefine data so that it can store either a value in the form of an integer or an operator in the form of a character. Our program will consist of a *.h* file and five *.c* files. Here is our header file:

In file polish.h:

```
/* A linked list implementation of a Polish stack. */

#include <assert.h>
#include <ctype.h>
#include <stdio.h>
#include <stdlib.h>

#define    EMPTY       0
#define    FULL       10000

struct data {
    enum {operator, value}   kind;
    union {
        char    op;
        int     val;
    }                            u;
};

typedef    struct data          data;
typedef    enum {false, true}   boolean;

struct elem {                           /* an element on the stack */
    data           d;
    struct elem    *next;
};

typedef    struct elem    elem;

struct stack {
    int     cnt;                        /* a count of the elements */
    elem    *top;                       /* ptr to the top element */
};

typedef    struct stack    stack;

boolean    empty(const stack *stk);
int        evaluate(stack *polish);
void       fill(stack *stk, const char *str);
boolean    full(const stack *stk);
void       initialize(stack *stk);
data       pop(stack *stk);
void       prn_data(data *dp);
void       prn_stack(stack *stk);
void       push(data d, stack *stk);
data       top(stack *stk);
```

Observe that this header file is similar to the one we used in our stack program in Section 10.5. The main difference is that we have defined data to be a structure type. The structure contains a union that can hold either an int value or an operator in the form of a char. It also contains a "flag" in the form of an enumeration type. The flag will tell us which kind of data is being stored.

In file main.c:

```
/* Test the two-stack Polish evaluation algorithm. */

#include "polish.h"

int main(void)
{
    char    str[] = "13, 4, -, 2, 3, *, +";
    stack   polish;

    printf("\n%s%s\n\n",
        "Polish expression: ", str);
    fill(&polish, str);               /* fill stack from string */
    prn_stack(&polish);               /* print the stack */
    printf("\n%s%d\n\n",
        "Polish evaluation: ", evaluate(&polish));
    return 0;
}
```

In main( ), we fill the Polish stack from a string and print the stack to check that everything is working properly. The function that is of most interest is the one that evaluates the Polish stack. Let us present that function next.

In file eval.c:

```
/* Evaluation of the Polish stack. */

#include "polish.h"

int evaluate(stack *polish)
{
   data    d, d1, d2;
   stack   eval;

   initialize(&eval);
   while (!empty(polish)) {
      d = pop(polish);
      switch (d.kind) {
      case value:
         push(d, &eval);
         break;
      case operator:
         d2 = pop(&eval);
         d1 = pop(&eval);
         d.kind = value;                /* begin overwriting d */
         switch (d.u.op) {
         case '+':
            d.u.val = d1.u.val + d2.u.val;
            break;
         case '-':
            d.u.val = d1.u.val - d2.u.val;
            break;
         case '*':
            d.u.val = d1.u.val * d2.u.val;
         }
         push(d, &eval);
      }
   }
   d = pop(&eval);
   return d.u.val;
}
```

The evaluate() function embodies the two-stack algorithm that we presented earlier. We first pop d from the polish stack. If it is a value, we push it onto the eval stack. If it is an operator, we pop d2 and d1 off the eval stack, perform the indicated operation, and push the results onto the eval stack. When the polish stack is empty, we pop d from the eval stack and return the int value d.u.val.

We write the stack operations in the file *stack.c*. Except for the inclusion of a different header file, there is no difference at all from the file *stack.c*, which we wrote in Section 10.5.

In file stack.c:

```
/* The basic stack routines. */

#include "polish.h"

void initialize(stack *stk)
{
    stk -> cnt = 0;
    stk -> top = NULL;
}

void push(data d, stack *stk)
{
    elem    *p;

    p = malloc(sizeof(elem));
    p -> d = d;
    p -> next = stk -> top;
    stk -> top = p;
    stk -> cnt++;
}

. . . . .
```

In the stack implementation in Section 10.5, the type data was equivalent to char; here data is a structure type. By using a typedef to embody the idea of "data," we have made the ADT stack implementation reusable. This is an important point. By using code that has already been written and tested, the programmer has less work to do in the current project. We need to be able to fill a stack from a string that contains a Polish expression. Here is our function that does this:

In file fill.c:

```
#include "polish.h"

void fill(stack *stk, const char *str)
{
    const char    *p = str;
    char          c1, c2;
    boolean       b1, b2;
    data          d;
    stack         tmp;

    initialize(stk);
    initialize(&tmp);
    /*
    // First process the string and push data on tmp.
    */
    while (*p != '\0') {
        while (isspace(*p) || *p == ',')
            ++p;
        b1 = (boolean) ((c1 = *p) == '+' || c1 == '-' || c1 == '*');
        b2 = (boolean) ((c2 = *(p + 1)) == ',' || c2 == '\0');
        if (b1 && b2) {
            d.kind = operator;
            d.u.op = c1;
        }
        else {
            d.kind = value;
            assert(sscanf(p, "%d", &d.u.val) == 1);
        }
        if (!full(&tmp))
            push(d, &tmp);                  /* push data on tmp */
        while (*p != ',' && *p != '\0')
            ++p;
    }
    /*
    // Now pop data from tmp and push on stk.
    */
    while (!empty(&tmp)) {
        d = pop(&tmp);                      /* pop data from tmp */
        if (!full(stk))
            push(d, stk);                   /* push data on stk */
    }
}
```

First we process the string to extract the data. As we find the data, we push it onto the stack tmp. After we finish processing the string, we pop the data off of tmp and push it onto the stack pointed to by stk. We do this so the element in the stack pointed to by stk will be in the right order.

We write two printing functions so we are able to check that our code is working properly. Here are the functions:

In file print.c:

```
#include "polish.h"

void prn_data(data *dp)
{
    switch (dp -> kind) {
    case operator:
        printf("%s%3c\n",
            "kind: operator      op:", dp -> u.op);
        break;
    case value:
        printf("%s%3d\n",
            "kind: value         val:", dp -> u.val);
    }
}

void prn_stack(stack *stk)
{
    data    d;

    printf("stack count:%3d%s",
        stk -> cnt, (stk -> cnt == 0) ? "\n" : "      ");
    if (!empty(stk)) {
        d = pop(stk);          /* pop the data */
        prn_data(&d);          /* print the data */
        prn_stack(stk);        /* recursive call */
        push(d, stk);          /* push the data */
    }
}
```

The algorithm to print the stack is quite simple. First pop d off the stack and print it. Then make a recursive call to `prn_stack()`. Finally, push d back onto the stack. The effect of this is to print all the data in the stack, and to leave the stack in its original state. Here is the output from our program:

```
Polish expression: 13, 4, -, 2, 3, *, +

stack count:  7      kind: value      val: 13
stack count:  6      kind: value      val:  4
stack count:  5      kind: operator     op:  -
stack count:  4      kind: value      val:  2
stack count:  3      kind: value      val:  3
stack count:  2      kind: operator     op:  *
stack count:  1      kind: operator     op:  +
stack count:  0

Polish evaluation: 15
```

10.7   QUEUES

A queue is another abstract data type (ADT) that we can implement as a linear linked list. A queue has a *front* and a *rear*. Insertion occurs at the rear of the list and deletion occurs at the front of the list.

A queue implementation

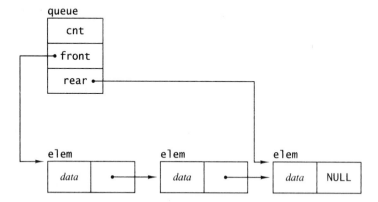

Our implementation of the ADT queue will include a number of the standard
queue functions. Here is our header file:

In file queue.h:

```
/* A linked list implementation of a queue. */

#include <assert.h>
#include <stdio.h>
#include <stdlib.h>

#define    EMPTY       0
#define    FULL        10000

typedef    unsigned int        data;
typedef    enum {false, true}   boolean;

struct elem {                          /* an element in the queue */
    data         d;
    struct elem  *next;
};

typedef    struct elem    elem;

struct queue {
    int    cnt;                 /* a count of the elements */
    elem   *front;              /* ptr to the front element */
    elem   *rear;              /* ptr to the rear element */
};

typedef    struct queue    queue;

void       initialize(queue *q);
void       enqueue(data d, queue *q);
data       dequeue(queue *q);
data       front(const queue *q);
boolean    empty(const queue *q);
boolean    full(const queue *q);
```

At the bottom of the header file we put the list of function prototypes. We write the function definitions in the file *queue.c*. These functions, together with this header file, implement the ADT queue.

In file queue.c:

```
/* The basic queue routines. */

#include "queue.h"

void initialize(queue *q)
{
    q -> cnt = 0;
    q -> front = NULL;
    q -> rear = NULL;
}

data dequeue(queue *q)
{
    data    d;
    elem    *p;

    d = q -> front -> d;
    p = q -> front;
    q -> front = q -> front -> next;
    q -> cnt--;
    free(p);
    return d;
}

void enqueue(data d, queue *q)
{
    elem    *p;

    p = malloc(sizeof(elem));
    p -> d = d;
    p -> next = NULL;
    if (!empty(q)) {
        q -> rear -> next = p;
        q -> rear = p;
    }
    else
        q -> front = q -> rear = p;
    q -> cnt++;
}
```

```
data front(const queue *q)
{
    return (q -> front -> d);
}

boolean empty(const queue *q)
{
    return ((boolean) (q -> cnt == EMPTY));
}

boolean full(const queue *q)
{
    return ((boolean) (q -> cnt == FULL));
}
```

The enqueue() routine uses the storage allocator malloc() to create a new queue element, and the dequeue() routine returns the freed-up storage back to the system.

A queue is a *first-in-first-out* (FIFO) data structure. The first item to be placed onto the queue is the first to be removed. Queues are very useful for a variety of system programming applications. For example, they are often used to schedule resources in an operating system. They are also useful in writing event simulators.

As an example, let us write an elementary resource scheduler for a two-processor system. We will assume that a process can request to be serviced by either processor A or processor B. The process will have a unique process identification (pid) number. After reading all the requests, the scheduler will print the schedule of processes served by each processor.

In file main.c:

```
/* Using queues to schedule two resources. */

#include "queue.h"

int main(void)
{
    int     c;
    int     cnt_a = 0;
    int     cnt_b = 0;
    data    pid;                    /* process id number */
    queue   a, b;

    initialize(&a);
    initialize(&b);
    /*
    // Enqueue the requests.
    */
    while ((c = getchar()) != EOF) {
        switch (c) {
        case 'A':
            assert(scanf("%u", &pid) == 1);
            if (!full(&a))
                enqueue(pid, &a);
            break;
        case 'B':
            assert(scanf("%u", &pid) == 1);
            if (!full(&a))
                enqueue(pid, &b);
        }
    }
    /*
    // Dequeue the requests and print them.
    */
    printf("\nA's schedule:\n");
    while (!empty(&a)) {
        pid = dequeue(&a);
        printf("   JOB %u is %d\n", ++cnt_a, pid);
    }
    printf("\nB's schedule:\n");
    while (!empty(&b)) {
        pid = dequeue(&b);
        printf("   JOB %u is %d\n", ++cnt_b, pid);
    }
    return 0;
}
```

To test our program, we create the following input file:

In file input:

```
B   7702
A   1023
B   3373
A   5757
A   1007
```

When we give the command

scheduler < input

the following gets printed on the screen:

```
A's schedule:
    JOB 1 is 1023
    JOB 2 is 5757
    JOB 3 is 1007

B's schedule:
    JOB 1 is 7702
    JOB 2 is 3373
```

10.8   BINARY TREES

A *tree* is a finite set of elements called *nodes*. A tree has a unique node, called the *root* node, where the remaining nodes are a disjoint collection of subtrees. If node r has $T_1, T_2, \ldots, T_n$ as subtrees, then $r_1, r_2, \ldots, r_n$, the roots of these subtrees, are the children of r. A node with no children is called a *leaf* node.

A general tree

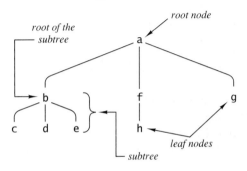

A *binary tree* is a tree whose elements have two children. A binary tree considered as a data structure is an object made up of elements that are characterized by two link fields, called left child and right child. Each link must point at a new object not already pointed at or be NULL. In this representation, a leaf node has both left and right child as the value NULL. The following structures and type specifications will be used to define binary trees.

In file tree.h:

```
#include <assert.h>
#include <stdio.h>
#include <stdlib.h>

typedef    char    DATA;

struct node {
    DATA          d;
    struct node   *left;
    struct node   *right;
};

typedef    struct node    NODE;
typedef    NODE           *BTREE;

#include "fct_proto.h"              /* function prototypes */
```

The file *tree.h* must be included with all binary tree functions defined in this section.

A key advantage of a binary tree over a linear list is that elements are normally reached, on average, in a logarithmic number of link traversals. This gain in time efficiency for retrieving information is at the expense of the space needed to store the extra link field per element. We illustrate this advantage in the exercises.

Binary Tree Traversal

There is one way to march down a linear list, namely from head to tail. However, there are several natural ways to visit the elements of a binary tree. The three commonest are

Inorder:	left subtree	*Preorder:*	root	*Postorder:*	left subtree
	root		left subtree		right subtree
	right subtree		right subtree		root

These standard methods of visitation are the basis for recursive algorithms that manipulate binary trees.

```
/* Inorder binary tree traversal. */

void inorder(BTREE root)
{
    if (root != NULL) {
        inorder(root -> left);       /* recur left */
        printf("%c ", root -> d);
        inorder(root -> right);      /* recur right */
    }
}
```

The function `inorder()` will print the values of each node in the binary tree pointed at by root. The pictured binary tree would be traversed by `inorder()`, printing

A B C D E F G H I J

A binary tree

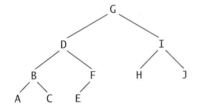

The corresponding preorder and postorder functions are:

```
/* Preorder and postorder binary tree traversal. */

void preorder(BTREE root)
{
   if (root != NULL) {
      printf("%c ", root -> d);
      preorder(root -> left);
      preorder(root -> right);
   }
}

void postorder(BTREE root)
{
   if (root != NULL) {
      postorder(root -> left);
      postorder(root -> right);
      printf("%c ", root -> d);
   }
}
```

Preorder visitation of the binary tree shown above would print

```
G  D  B  A  C  F  E  I  H  J
```

Postorder visitation would print

```
A  C  B  E  F  D  H  J  I  G
```

The reader unfamiliar with these methods should carefully verify these results by hand. Visitation is at the heart of most tree algorithms.

Creating Trees

We will create a binary tree from data values stored as an array. As with lists, we will use the dynamic storage allocator malloc().

```
/* Creating a binary tree. */

BTREE new_node()
{
   return (malloc(sizeof(NODE)));
}
```

```
BTREE init_node(DATA d1, BTREE p1, BTREE p2)
{
    BTREE    t;

    t = new_node();
    t -> d = d1;
    t -> left = p1;
    t -> right = p2;
    return t;
}
```

We will use these routines as primitives to create a binary tree from data values stored in an array. There is a very nice mapping from the indices of a linear array into nodes of a binary tree. We do this by taking the value a[i] and letting it have as child values a[2*i+1] and a[2*i+2]. Then we map a[0] into the unique root node of the resulting binary tree. Its left child will be a[1] and its right child will be a[2]. The function create_tree() embodies this mapping. The formal parameter size is the number of nodes in the binary tree.

```
/* Create a linked binary tree from an array. */

BTREE create_tree(DATA a[], int i, int size)
{
    if (i >= size)
        return NULL;
    else
        return (init_node(a[i],
                create_tree(a, 2 * i + 1, size),
                create_tree(a, 2 * i + 2, size)));
}
```

10.9   GENERAL LINKED LISTS

For some data structures, we wish to combine the use of arrays with the use of lists. The arrays provide random accessing and the lists provide sequential accessing. We will show one such example in this section, an implementation of a general tree. In a general tree, a node can have an arbitrary number of children. It would be very wasteful to specify a structure using the maximum number of links for each node.

We will represent a general tree as a number of linear linked lists, one for each node in the tree. Each list will be the children of a single node. The lists will have an array that will point at the first child of the corresponding node. The base element of the array will point at the root node. The following diagram shows such a representation, in this case for the general tree at the beginning of Section 10.8.

A general tree and associated list structure

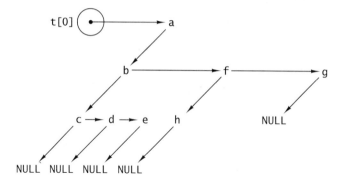

Such trees can be represented using the following header file:

In file gtree.h:

```
#include <assert.h>
#include <stdio.h>
#include <stdlib.h>

typedef    char    DATA;

struct node {
    int           child_no;
    DATA          d;
    struct node   *sib;
};

typedef    struct node    NODE;
typedef    NODE           *GTREE;

#include "fct_proto.h"                /* function prototypes */
```

We will use an array of type GTREE, say t, where t[0] points to the root element represented as type NODE. Siblings will be reached by linear list chaining, and children by array indexing. Let us examine the creation of a particular such tree. We first write routines to create a single node.

```
/* Create a new node. */

GTREE new_gnode()
{
    return (malloc(sizeof(NODE)));
}

GTREE init_gnode(DATA d1, int num, GTREE sibs)
{
    GTREE    tmp;

    tmp = new_gnode();
    tmp -> d = d1;
    tmp -> child_no = num;
    tmp -> sib = sibs;
    return tmp;
}
```

Let us use these routines to create the tree of the previous diagram. Because it contains eight nodes, we need an array t[] of size 9 and type NODE, where t[0] is the pointer to the root node.

```
t[0] = init_gnode('a', 1, NULL);
t[1] = init_gnode('b', 2, NULL);
t[1] -> sib = init_gnode('f', 6, NULL);
t[1] -> sib -> sib = init_gnode('g', 7, NULL);
t[2] = init_gnode('c', 3, NULL);
t[2] -> sib = init_gnode('d', 4, NULL);
t[2] -> sib -> sib = init_gnode('e', 5, NULL);
t[3] = t[4] = t[5] = NULL;
t[6] = init_gnode('h', 8, NULL);
t[7] = t[8] = NULL;
```

It is easy to detect certain properties in this representation, such as whether a node is a leaf node or how many children a node has. For node n, if t[n] points at NULL, then the node is a leaf.

Traversal

Traversal becomes a combination of (1) moving along lists and (2) indexing into array elements that point at the lists. Generalizing the traversal ordering of preorder, postorder, and inorder to these structures is quite straightforward. Once again, these algorithms are prototypes for more complicated functions that can be done on a tree, because they guarantee that each element will be reached in linear time.

```
/* Preorder traversal of general trees. */

void preorder_g(GTREE t, int ind)
{
   GTREE   tmp;      /* tmp traverses the sibling list */

   tmp = t[ind];                 /* t[ind] is the root node */
   while (tmp != NULL) {
      printf("%c  %d\n", tmp -> d, tmp -> child_no);
      preorder_g(t, tmp -> child_no);
      tmp = tmp -> sib;
   }
}
```

The function `preorder_g()` differs from the corresponding binary tree function in that a `while` loop is necessary to move along the linear list of siblings. Notice that recursion allows each subtree to be handled cleanly.

The Use of `calloc()` and Building Trees

The library function `calloc()` provides contiguous allocation of storage that can be used for arrays. Its function prototype is given in *stdlib.h* as

```
void *calloc(size_t n, size_t size);
```

Thus the arguments to `calloc()` are converted to type `size_t`, and the value returned is of type pointer to `void`. Typically, `size_t` is equivalent to `unsigned`. A function call of the form

```
calloc(n, size)
```

returns a pointer to enough contiguous storage for *n* objects, each of *size* bytes. This storage is initialized to zero by the system. Thus `calloc()` can be used to dynamically allocate storage for a run-time defined array. This allows the user to allocate space as needed rather than specifying during compilation an array size that is very large so as to accommodate all cases that might be of interest.

For example, we will want a routine that can build a general tree from a list of edges and an array of type DATA. If we wish to have an array of size 10 to store the tree headers, we can write

```
t = calloc(10, sizeof(GTREE));
```

Now we can pass the dynamically allocated array t of type pointer to GTREE to a function `buildtree()` in order to construct a general tree. This function will take an edge list representation of a tree and compute its general list structure representation.

```
/* Function buildtree creates a tree from an array of edges. */

typedef struct {      /* PAIR represents an edge in a tree */
   int   out;
   int   in;
} PAIR;

void buildtree(PAIR edges[], DATA d[], int n, GTREE t[])
{
   int   i;
   int   x, y;      /* points of edge */

   t[0] = init_gnode(d[1], 1, NULL);/* t[0] takes node 1 as root */
   for (i = 1; i <= n; ++i)
      t[i] = NULL;
   for (i = 0; i < n - 1; ++i) {
      x = edges[i].out;
      y = edges[i].in;
      t[x] = init_gnode(d[y], y, t[x]);
   }
}
```

Similar data structures and functions can be used to develop representations of general graphs, sparse matrices, and complicated networks.

10.10 SUMMARY

1 Self-referential structures use pointers to address identically specified elements.

2 The simplest self-referential structure is the linear linked list. Each element points to its next element, with the last element pointing at NULL, defined as 0.

3 The function malloc() is used to dynamically allocate storage. It takes an argument of type size_t and returns a pointer to void that is the address of the allocated storage.

4 The function free() is a storage management routine that returns to available storage the block of memory pointed at by its argument.

5 Standard algorithms for list processing are naturally implemented recursively. Frequently, the base case is the detection of the NULL link. The general case recurs by moving one link over in the list structure.

6 When algorithms are implemented iteratively, one uses an iterative loop, terminating when NULL is detected. Iterative algorithms trade the use of auxiliary pointers for recursion.

7 The abstract data type (ADT) stack is implementable as a linked list, with access restricted to its first element, which is called the top. The stack has a LIFO (last-in-first-out) discipline implemented by the routines push() and pop().

8 The ADT queue is also implementable as a linked list, with access restricted to its front and rear ends. The queue has a FIFO (first-in-first-out) discipline implemented by the routines enqueue() and dequeue().

9 Binary trees are represented as structures with two link members. They combine the dynamic qualities of linear lists with, on average, significantly shorter access paths to each element. These distances to elements of binary trees are usually logarithmic.

10 Binary trees are traversed most often in one of three major patterns: preorder, inorder, or postorder. Each ordering is determined by when the root is visited. Preorder visits the root first; inorder, after the left subtree; and postorder, last. These traversal patterns are readily implemented as recursions, chaining down both left and right subtrees.

11 Data structures of formidable complexity, involving both lists and arrays, can be specified. One example of their use is in the implementation of a general tree, where a node has an arbitrary number of children. The children of a node are represented as a list pointed to by an array of header elements.

10.11 EXERCISES

1 Try the following code. Why does your compiler complain? Fix the code so it compiles correctly:

```
struct husband {
    int           age;
    char          name[10];
    struct wife   spouse;
} a;

struct wife {
    int              age;
    char             name[10];
    struct husband   spouse;
} b;
```

2 Change the type definition of DATA in the file *list.h* to

```
typedef struct {
    char    name[10];
    int     age;
    int     weight;
}   DATA;
```

and write a function create_1() that transforms an array of such data into a
linear list. Write another routine, one that will count the number of people above
a given weight and age.

3 Given a linear list of the type found in Exercise 2, write a routine sort_age()
that will sort the list according to its age values. Write a function sort_name()
that will sort in lexicographic order based on the name values.

4 Combine the sorting functions in Exercise 3 so they share the most code. This
is best done by defining a routine called compare() that returns either 0 or 1,
depending on which element is larger. Use this function as a parameter to a
linear list sorting function.

5 Draw the list that would result from concatenate(a, a), where a points at a
list of two elements. What happens if the resulting list pointed at by a is passed
to print_list(a)?

6 Exercise 5 was used to construct a cycle. A cycle is a pointer chain that points
back to itself. Cycles are particularly nasty run-time bugs that can be hard to
recognize. Write a function iscycle(head) that returns 1 if a cycle is detected
and 0 otherwise. *Hint:* Save the address of the initial element of the list and
move around until either NULL is reached or the initial address is encountered.

7 Write an iterative version of the function print_list().

8 Modify concatenate() so it returns the address of the head of the resulting
list. Also, if the first list is NULL, it should return the second list. Have it test
to see if both lists are the same. If they are, a cycle will result (see Exercises 5
and 6) and the program should return a warning to that effect.

9 Write a routine copy_cat(a, b) that returns a concatenated copy of the lists a
and b. The original lists a and b should remain undisturbed.

10 Write an iterative version of the function concatenate() that you wrote in
Exercise 8.

11 Write an insertion function that inserts an element at the head of the list.

12 Write an insertion function that inserts an element at the tail of the list.

13 Write an insertion function that inserts an element at the first position in the list
following an element storing a particular DATA item.

14 Generalize the previous three exercises. Write an insertion function that inserts an element in the *n*th position in a list, where 0 means the element is placed at the head of the list. If *n* is larger than the length of the list, insert the element at the tail of the list.

15 An element of a doubly linked linear list can be defined as

```
typedef struct dllist {
    DATA              d;
    struct dllist    *prev;
    struct dllist    *next;
} ELEMENT;
```

This adds an extra member but allows easier traversal along the list.

A doubly linked list

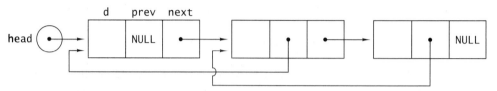

Write iterative routines to perform insertion and deletion.

16 Write a routine `del_dupl()` that deletes duplicate valued elements in a doubly linked list.

17 Evaluate the following Polish expressions by hand:

    (a) 7, 6, -, 3, *
    (b) 9, 2, 3, *, 4, -, +
    (c) 1, 2, +, 3, 4, +, *

18 Write corresponding Polish expressions for the following:

    (a) (7 + 8 + 9) * 4
    (b) (6 - 2) * (5 + 15 * 2)
    (c) 6 - 2 * 5 + 15 * 2

19 Use the *polish* program that we wrote in Section 10.6 to evaluate the six Polish expressions given or derived in Exercises 17 and 18.

20 The following lines occur in the `evaluate()` function in the *polish* program:

```
case operator:
    d2 = pop(&eval);
    d1 = pop(&eval);
```

What happens if we write

```
case operator:
    d1 = pop(&eval);
    d2 = pop(&eval);
```

instead? The program should work properly on some Polish expressions but not
on others. Explain.

21 Create another version of the *polish* program. First, write a routine that reverses
the order of the elements in a stack. Next, append this routine to the file *stack.c*,
and add the function prototype to the header file. Then rewrite the function
fill() so that it makes use of your routine. Finally, test your program.

22 Write a routine that allows you to interactively initialize the contents of a Polish
stack. Write a program to test your routine.

23 When we tested our *polish* program, the Polish expression we used did not have
any unary operators in it. Try the program with the following expression:

```
2, -3, -, -4, 7, +, -1, -1, +, *, *
```

Is the *polish* program able to handle this correctly? (It should be able to.) Write
another version of the *polish* program that can handle both unary plus and unary
minus operators in the list. For example, your program should be able to handle
the following Polish expression:

```
2, -, 3, -, -, 4, +, 7, +, -1, -, +, +, 1, +, *, *
```

In this expression, some of the plus and minus signs are unary and some are
binary.

24 Write a function whose prototype is

```
queue data_to_queue(data d[], int n);
```

where n is the size of the array d. When passed an array of type data, this
function should use the elements in the array to build a queue that gets returned.

25 Write a function whose prototype is

```
data *queue_to_data(queue q);
```

that builds a data array out of the values found in the queue. The size of the
array should be q.cnt.

26 When we tested the scheduler program that we wrote in Section 10.7, our input file was rather simple. Try the following input:

```
x x x A 2323  B 1188  yyy zzz C 3397 3398 A 4545  X  surprise?
```

Are you surprised that it works? Explain.

27 Write a four-resource version of the scheduler program.

28 Modify the program that you wrote for Exercise 27 to allow for priorities. Change the type data to a structure that has both a processor ID number and a priority. The priority should be an unsigned number between 0 and 9. Create schedules where the highest priority processes are serviced first. *Caution:* Do not confuse the concepts of "process" and "processor."

29 Write routines for binary trees that

   (a) count the number of nodes
   (b) count the number of nodes having a particular value, say 'b'
   (c) print out the value of only leaf nodes

30 Create a binary tree from an array of ints such that a left child has value less than its root's value, and a right child has value greater than or equal to the value of its root. Such a tree is displayed in the following diagram:

A binary tree with ordered values

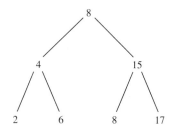

Insert a new element by comparing its value to the root and recurring down the proper subtree until NULL is reached.

31 For the tree of Exercise 30, write a function that uses inorder traversal to place the values of the nodes in sorted order in an array key[].

32 Write a program that deletes the root node of a binary tree and replaces the root with the rightmost leaf node.

Deleting the root node with replacement

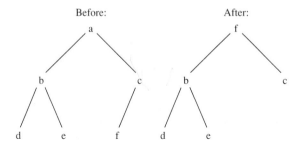

33 (Advanced) Write heapsort( ). This is a sorting routine based on an ordered binary tree. A heap is a binary tree in which a node has value smaller than any of its children. This property guarantees that the root is the smallest element in the tree. We wish to take an unordered array of values and create a heap with these values as data entries. Given a heap,

    1 Delete the root, placing it in an output array as the smallest element.
    2 Take the rightmost leaf node and make it the new root.
    3 Compare the root value to both children and exchange with the smaller of the two values.
    4 Continue to exchange values until the current node is smaller in value than its children.

Now the tree is once again a heap. Repeat these steps until the tree is empty and the array has the original tree values in sorted order. You must figure out how to get the tree into heap order to begin with; see Aho, Hopcroft, and Ullman, *Data Structures and Algorithms* (Reading, Mass.: Addison-Wesley, 1987).

34 Print out the nodes of a binary tree in level order. The root node is at level 0. On the next level of nodes are the children of the previous level. First, print the root node. Then print the left child and the right child that are at level 1. Continue printing the nodes from left to right, level by level. This is also called breadth-first traversal.

35 Write a routine that computes the maximum level leaf node of a general tree.

36 Write a function that converts a binary tree into a general tree representation.

37 Add a field called `weight` to our general tree structure. Write functions to
  (a) compute the sum of all node weights
  (b) compute the maximum weighted path, where the weighted path of node i is the weights of the nodes from the root to node i

It can be proved that the maximum weighted path occurs at a leaf, given that all weights are nonnegative.

38 Use a general linked list structure to program sparse matrix addition. A sparse matrix is one in which most of its values are zero. A nonzero element of a sparse matrix will be represented by the triple $(i, j, value)$. For each row i, the triples will be linked as a linear list headed by an array of pointers `row[i]`. Similarly, for each column j, the triples will be linked as a linear list headed by an array of pointers `col[j]`. To add matrix A to matrix B, we take each row and merge them into a matrix C. If both rows have a triple with the same column value, then in the output row c_{ij} is the sum $a_{ij} + b_{ij}$. Otherwise the element with the smallest column number becomes the next element of the output row.

39 (Advanced) The representation in Exercise 38 can also be used to do sparse matrix multiplication. Although addition can be performed with just row-linked lists, for multiplication, both row- and column-linked lists are used. Program sparse matrix multiplication.

40 (Project) Implement the sparse polynomial ADT. Use a linked list of elements to represent the nonzero terms of the polynomial. A term is a real coefficient and a power. Write a complete polynomial manipulation package. Your package should be able to input and output polynomials, and it should be able to add, subtract, multiply, and copy polynomials.

## CHAPTER 11

INPUT/OUTPUT AND THE OPERATING SYSTEM

In this chapter we explain how to use some of the input/output functions in the standard library, including the functions printf( ) and scanf( ). Although we have used these functions throughout this text, many details still need to be explained. We present extensive tables showing the effects of various formats. The standard library provides functions related to printf( ) and scanf( ) that can be used for dealing with files and strings. The use of these functions is explained.

General file input/output is important in applications where data reside in files on disks and tapes. We will show how to open files for processing and how to use a pointer to a file. Some applications need temporary files. Examples are given to illustrate their use.

The operating system provides utilities for the user, and some of these utilities can be used by the programmer to develop C software. A number of the more important tools for programmers will be discussed, including the compiler, *make*, *touch*, *grep*, beautifiers, and debuggers.

11.1 THE OUTPUT FUNCTION printf( )

The printf( ) function has two nice properties that allow flexible use at a high level. First, a list of arguments of arbitrary length can be printed, and second, the printing is controlled by simple conversion specifications, or formats. The function printf( ) delivers its character stream to the standard output file stdout, which is normally connected to the screen. The argument list to printf( ) has two parts:

    control_string   and   *other_arguments*

In the example

```
printf("she sells %d %s for $%f", 99, "sea shells", 3.77);
```

we have

      control_string: "she sells %d %s for $%f"
      other_arguments: 99, "sea shells", 3.77

The expressions in *other_arguments* are evaluated and converted according to the formats in the control string and then placed in the output stream. Characters in the control string that are not part of a format are placed directly in the output stream. The % symbol introduces a conversion specification, or format. A single conversion specification is a string that begins with % and ends with a conversion character.

`printf()`

Conversion character	How the corresponding argument is printed
c	as a character
d, i	as a decimal integer
u	as an unsigned decimal integer
o	as an unsigned octal integer
x, X	as an unsigned hexadecimal integer
e	as a floating-point number; example: `7.123000e+00`
E	as a floating-point number; example: `7.123000E+00`
f	as a floating-point number; example: `7.123000`
g	in the e-format or f-format, whichever is shorter
G	in the E-format or f-format, whichever is shorter
s	as a string
p	the corresponding argument is a pointer to `void`; its value gets printed as a hexadecimal number
n	the corresponding argument is a pointer to an integer into which gets printed the number of characters written so far; the argument is not converted
%	with the format %% a single % is written to the output stream; there is no corresponding argument to be converted

The function `printf()` returns as an `int` the number of characters printed. In the example

```
printf("she sells %d %s for $%f", 99, "sea shells", 3.77);
```

we can match the formats in the control string with their corresponding arguments in the argument list.

Format	Corresponding argument
%d	99
%s	"sea shells"
%f	3.77

Explicit formatting information may be included in a conversion specification. If it is not included, then defaults are used. For example, the format %f with corresponding argument 3.77 will result in 3.770000 being printed. The number is printed with six digits to the right of the decimal point by default.

Between the % that starts a conversion specification and the conversion character that ends it, there may appear in order

- zero or more flag characters that modify the meaning of the conversion specification. These flag characters are discussed below.

- an optional positive integer that specifies the minimum *field width* of the converted argument. The place where an argument is printed is called its *field*, and the number of spaces used to print an argument is called its *field width*. If the converted argument has fewer characters than the specified field width, then it will be padded with spaces on the left or right, depending on whether the converted argument is right- or left-adjusted. If the converted argument has more characters than the specified field width, then the field width will be extended to whatever is required. If the integer defining the field width begins with a zero and the argument being printed is right-adjusted in its field, then zeros rather than spaces will be used for padding.

- an optional *precision*, which is specified by a period followed by a nonnegative integer. For d, i, o, u, x, and X conversions, it specifies the minimum number of digits to be printed. For e, E, and f conversions, it specifies the number of digits to the right of the decimal point. For g and G conversions, it specifies the maximum number of significant digits. For an s conversion it specifies the maximum number of characters to be printed from a string.

- an optional h or l, which is a "short" or "long" modifier, respectively. If an h is followed by a d, i, o, u, x, or X conversion character, the conversion specification applies to a short int or unsigned short int argument. If an h is followed by an n conversion character, the corresponding argument is a pointer to a short int or unsigned short int. If an l is followed by a d, i, o, u, x, or X conversion character, the conversion specification applies to a long int or unsigned long int argument. If an l is followed by an n conversion character, the corresponding argument is a pointer to a long int or unsigned long int.

- an optional L, which is a "long" modifier. If an L is followed by an e, E, f, g, or G conversion character, the conversion specification applies to a long double argument.

The flag characters are

- a minus sign, which means that the converted argument is to be *left-adjusted* in its field. If there is no minus sign, then the converted argument is to be *right-adjusted* in its field.

- a plus sign, which means that a nonnegative number that comes from a signed conversion is to have a + prepended. This works with the conversion characters d, i, e, E, f, g, and G. All negative numbers start with a minus sign.

- a space, which means that a nonnegative number that comes from a signed conversion is to have a space prepended. This works with the conversion characters d, i, e, E, f, g, and G. If both a space and a + flag are present, the space flag is ignored.

- a #, which means that the result is to be converted to an "alternate form" that depends on the conversion character. With conversion character o, the # causes a zero to be prepended to the octal number being printed. In an x or X conversion, the # causes 0x or 0X to be prepended to the hexadecimal number being printed. In a g or G conversion, it causes trailing zeros to be printed. In an e, E, f, g, or G conversion, it causes a decimal point to be printed, even with precision 0. The behavior is undefined for other conversions.

- a zero, which means that zeros instead of spaces are used to pad the field. With d, i, o, u, x, X, e, E, f, g, and G conversion characters, this can result in numbers with leading zeros. Any sign and any 0x or 0X that gets printed with a number will precede the leading zeros.

In a format, the field width or precision or both may be specified by a ＊ instead of an integer, which indicates that a value is to be obtained from the argument list. Here is an example of how the facility can be used:

```
int      m, n;
double   x = 333.7777777;

.....                              /＊ get m and n from somewhere ＊/
printf("x = %＊.＊f\n", m, n, x);
```

If the argument corresponding to the field width has a negative value, then it is taken as a – flag followed by a positive field width. If the argument corresponding to the precision has a negative value, then it is taken as if it were missing.

The conversion specification %% can be used to print a single percent symbol in the output stream. It is a special case because there is no corresponding argument to be converted. For all the other formats, there should be a corresponding argument. If there are too many arguments, the extra ones are evaluated but otherwise ignored.

The field width is the number of spaces used to print the argument. The default is whatever is required to properly display the value of the argument. Thus the integer value 255 (decimal) requires three spaces for decimal conversion d or octal conversion o, but only two spaces for hexadecimal conversion x.

When an argument is printed, characters appropriate to the conversion specification are placed in a field. The characters appear right-adjusted unless a minus sign is present as a flag. If the specified field width is too short to properly display the value of the corresponding argument, the field width will be increased to the default. If the entire field is not needed to display the converted argument, then the remaining part of the field is padded with blanks on the left or right, depending on whether the converted argument is right- or left-adjusted. The padding character on the left can be made a zero by specifying the field width with a leading zero.

The precision is specified by a nonnegative number that occurs to the right of the period. For string conversions, this is the maximum number of characters to be printed from the string. For e, E, and f conversions, it specifies the number of digits to appear to the right of the decimal point.

Examples of character and string formats are given in the next table. We use double quote characters to visually delimit the field. They do not get printed.

Declarations and initializations

`char   c = 'A', s[] = "Blue moon!";`

Format	Corresponding argument	How it is printed in its field	Remarks
%c	c	"A"	field width 1 by default
%2c	c	" A"	field width 2, right adjusted
%-3c	c	"A "	field width 3, left adjusted
%s	s	"Blue moon!"	field width 10 by default
%3s	s	"Blue moon!"	more space needed
%.6s	s	"Blue m"	precision 6
%-11.8s	s	"Blue moo "	precision 8, left adjusted

Examples of formats used to print numbers are given in the next table. Again, we use double quote characters to visually delimit the field. They do not get printed.

Declarations and initializations

`int     i = 123;`
`double  x = 0.123456789;`

Format	Corresponding argument	How it is printed in its field	Remarks
%d	i	"123"	field width 3 by default
%05d	i	"00123"	padded with zeros
%7o	i	" 173"	right adjusted, octal
%-9x	i	"7b "	left adjusted, hexadecimal
%-#9x	i	"0x7b "	left adjusted, hexadecimal
%10.5f	x	" 0.12346"	field width 10, precision 5
%-12.5e	x	"1.23457e-01 "	left adjusted, e-format

11.2   THE INPUT FUNCTION scanf( )

The function scanf( ) has two nice properties that allow flexible use at a high level. The first is that a list of arguments of arbitrary length can be scanned, and the second is that the input is controlled by simple conversion specifications, or formats. The function scanf( ) reads characters from the standard input file stdin. The argument list to scanf( ) has two parts:

> *control_string*   and   *other_arguments*

In the example

```
char      a, b, c, s[100];
int       n;
double    x;

scanf("%c%c%c%d%s%lf", &a, &b, &c, &n, s, &x);
```

we have

> *control_string*:   "%c%c%c%d%s%lf"
> *other_arguments*:   &a, &b, &c, &n, s, &x

The other arguments following the control string consist of a comma-separated list of pointer expressions, or addresses. Note that in the preceding example, writing &s would be wrong; the expression s by itself is an address.

scanf( )

Conversion character	Characters in the input stream that are matched	Corresponding argument is a pointer to
c	any character, including white space	char
d, i	an optionally signed decimal	integer
u	an optionally signed decimal integer	unsigned integer
o	an optionally signed octal integer	unsigned integer
x, X	an optionally signed hexadecimal integer	unsigned integer
e, E, f, g, G	an optionally signed floating-point number	a floating type
s	a sequence of nonwhite space characters	char
p	what is produced by %p in printf( ), usually an unsigned hexadecimal integer	void *
n, %, [...]	see the next table	

Three conversion characters are of a special nature, and one of these, [...], is not even a character, although the construct is treated as such.

scanf()

Conversion character	Remarks
n	No characters in the input stream are matched. The corresponding argument is a pointer to an integer, into which gets printed the number of characters read so far.
%	A single % character in the input stream is matched. There is no corresponding argument.
[...]	The set of characters inside the brackets [ ] is called the *scan set*. It determines what gets matched. (See the explanation given below.) The corresponding argument is a pointer to the base of an array of characters that is large enough to hold the characters that are matched, including a terminating null character that is appended automatically.

The control string may contain

- white space, which matches optional white space in the input stream.

- ordinary nonwhite space characters, other than %. Each ordinary character must match the next character in the input stream.

- conversion specifications that begin with a % and end with a conversion character. Between the % and the conversion character there may be an optional * that indicates assignment suppression, followed by an optional integer that defines a maximum scan width, followed by an optional h, l, or L that modifies the specification character.

- the modifier h, which can precede a d, i, o, u, x, X conversion character. It indicates that the converted value is to be stored in a short int or in an unsigned short int.

- the modifier l, which can precede either a d, i, o, u, x, X conversion character or an e, E, f, g, G conversion character. In the first case, it indicates that the converted value is to be stored in a long int or in an unsigned long int. In the second case, it indicates that the converted value is to be stored in a double.

- the modifier L, which can precede an e, E, f, g, G conversion character. It indicates that the converted value is to be stored in a long double.

The characters in the input stream are converted to values according to the conversion specifications in the control string and placed at the address given by the corresponding pointer expression in the argument list. Except for character input, a scan field consists of contiguous nonwhite characters that are appropriate to the specified conversion. The scan field ends when a nonappropriate character is reached, or the scan width, if specified, is exhausted, whichever comes first. When a string is read in, it is presumed that enough space has been allocated in memory to hold the string and an end-of-string sentinel \0, which will be appended. The format %1s can be used to read in the next nonwhite character. It should be stored in a character array of size at least 2. The format %nc can be used to read in the next n characters, including white space characters. When one or more characters are read in, white space is not skipped. As with strings, it is the programmer's responsibility to allocate enough space to store these characters. In this case a null character is not appended. A format such as %1f can be used to read in a double. Floating numbers in the input stream are formatted as an optional sign followed by a digit string with an optional decimal point, followed by an optional exponent part. The exponential part consists of e or E, followed by an optional sign followed by a digit string.

A conversion specification of the form %[*string*] indicates that a special string is to be read in. If the first character in *string* is not a circumflex character, then the string is to be made up only of the characters in *string*. However, if the first character in *string* is a circumflex, then the string is to be made up of all characters other than those in *string*. Thus the format %[abc] will input a string containing only the letters *a*, *b*, and *c*, and will stop if any other character appears in the input stream, including a blank. The format %[abc] will input a string terminated by any of *a*, *b*, or *c*, but not by white space. The statement

```
scanf("%[AB \n\t]", s);
```

will read into the character array s a string containing A's, B's, and the white space characters blank, newline, and tab.

These conversion specifications interact in a predictable way. The scan width is the number of characters scanned to retrieve the argument value. The default is whatever is in the input stream. The specification %s skips white space and then reads in nonwhite space characters until a white space character is encountered or the end-of-file mark is encountered, whichever comes first. In contrast to this, the specification %5s skips white space and then reads in nonwhite characters, stopping when a white space character is encountered or an end-of-file mark is encountered or five characters have been read in, whichever comes first.

The function scanf() returns the number of successful conversions performed. The value EOF is returned when the end-of-file mark is reached. Typically this value is –1. The value 0 is returned when no successful conversions are performed, and this value is always different from EOF. An inappropriate character in the input stream can frustrate expected conversions, causing the value 0 to be returned. As long as the input stream can be matched to the control string, the input stream is scanned and values are converted and assigned. The process stops if the input is inappropriate for the next conversion specification. The value returned by scanf() can be used to test that input occurred as expected, or to test that the end of the file was reached.

An example illustrating the use of scanf() is

```
int    i;
char   c;
char   string[15];

scanf("%d , %*s %% %c %5s %s", &i, &c, string, &string[5]);
```

With the following characters in the input stream

```
45 , ignore_this  %  C  read_in_this**
```

the value 45 is placed in i, the comma is matched, the string "ignore_this" is ignored, the % is matched, the character C is placed in the variable c, the string "read_" is placed in string[0] through string[4] with the terminating \0 in string[5], and finally the string "in_this**" is placed in string[5] through string[14], with string[14] containing \0. Because four conversions were successfully made, the value 4 is returned by scanf().

11.3 THE FUNCTIONS fprintf(), fscanf(), sprintf(), AND sscanf()

The functions fprintf() and fscanf() are file versions of the functions printf() and scanf(), respectively. Before we discuss their use, we need to know how C deals with files.

The identifier FILE is defined in *stdio.h* as a particular structure, with members that describe the current state of a file. To use files, a programmer need not know any details concerning this structure. Also defined in *stdio.h* are the three file pointers stdin, stdout, and stderr. Even though they are pointers, we sometimes refer to them as files.

Written in C	Name	Remark
stdin	standard input file	connected to the keyboard
stdout	standard output file	connected to the screen
stderr	standard error file	connected to the screen

The function prototypes for file-handling functions are given in *stdio.h*. Here are the prototypes for `fprintf()` and `fscanf()`:

```
int    fprintf(FILE *fp, const char *format, ...);
int    fscanf(FILE *fp, const char *format, ...);
```

A statement of the form

```
fprintf(file_ptr, control_string, other_arguments);
```

writes to the file pointed to by *file_ptr*. The conventions for *control_string* and *other_arguments* conform to those of `printf()`. In particular,

```
fprintf(stdout, ...);
```
         is equivalent to   `printf(... );`

In a similar fashion, a statement of the form

```
fscanf(file_ptr, control_string, other_arguments);
```

reads from the file pointed to by *file_ptr*. In particular,

```
fscanf(stdin, ...);
```
         is equivalent to   `scanf(... );`

In the next section we will show how to use `fopen()` to open files and how to use `fprintf()` and `fscanf()` to access them.

The functions `sprintf()` and `sscanf()` are string versions of the functions `printf()` and `scanf()`, respectively. Their function prototypes, found in *stdio.h*, are

```
int    sprintf(char *s, const char *format, ...);
int    sscanf(const char *s, const char *format, ...);
```

The function `sprintf()` writes to its first argument, a pointer to `char` (string), instead of to the screen. Its remaining arguments conform to those for `printf()`. The function `sscanf()` reads from its first argument instead of from the keyboard. Its remaining arguments conform to those for `scanf()`. Consider the code

```
char    str1[] = "1 2 3 go", str2[100], tmp[100];
int     a, b, c;

sscanf(str1, "%d%d%d%s", &a, &b, &c, tmp);
sprintf(str2, "%s %s %d %d %d\n", tmp, tmp, a, b, c);
printf("%s", str2);
```

The function sscanf() takes its input from str1. It reads three decimal integers and a string, putting them into a, b, c, and tmp, respectively. The function sprintf() writes to str2. More precisely, it writes characters in memory, beginning at the address str2. Its output is two strings and three decimal integers. To see what is in str2, we invoke printf(). It prints the following on the screen:

```
go go 1 2 3
```

Caution: It is the programmer's responsibility to provide adequate space in memory for the output of sprintf().

Reading from a string is unlike reading from a file in the following sense: If we use sscanf() to read from str1 again, then the input starts at the beginning of the string, not where we left off before.

11.4 THE FUNCTIONS fopen() AND fclose()

Abstractly, a file can be thought of as a stream of characters. After a file has been opened, the stream can be accessed with file-handling functions in the standard library. In this section we want to explain the use of fopen() and fclose().

Files have several important properties: They have a name. They must be opened and closed. They can be written to, or read from, or appended to. Conceptually, until a file is opened nothing can be done to it. It is like a closed book. When it is opened, we can have access to it at its beginning or end. To prevent accidental misuse, we must tell the system which of the three activities—reading, writing, or appending—we will be performing on it. When we are finished using the file, we close it. Consider the following code:

```
#include <stdio.h>

int main(void)
{
    int     a, sum = 0;
    FILE    *ifp, *ofp;

    ifp = fopen("my_file", "r");     /* open for reading */
    ofp = fopen("outfile", "w");     /* open for writing */
    .....
```

This opens two files in the current directory: *my_file* for reading and *outfile* for writing. (The identifier ifp is mnemonic for "infile pointer," and the identifier ofp is mnemonic for "outfile pointer.") After a file has been opened, the file pointer is used exclusively in all references to the file. Suppose that *my_file* contains integers. If we want to sum them and put the result in *outfile*, we can write

```
while (fscanf(ifp, "%d", &a) == 1)
    sum += a;
fprintf(ofp, "The sum is %d.\n", sum);
```

Note that fscanf(), like scanf(), returns the number of successful conversions. After we have finished using a file, we can write

```
fclose(ifp);
```

This closes the file pointed to by ifp.

A function call of the form fopen(*filename*, *mode*) opens the named file in a particular mode and returns a file pointer. There are a number of possibilities for the mode.

Mode	Meaning
"r"	open text file for reading
"w"	open text file for writing
"a"	open text file for appending
"rb"	open binary file for reading
"wb"	open binary file for writing
"ab"	open binary file for appending

Each of these modes can end with a + character. This means that the file is to be opened for both reading and writing.

Mode	Meaning
"r+"	open text file for reading and writing
"w+"	open text file for writing and reading
. . . . .	

Opening for reading a file that cannot be read, or does not exist, will fail. In this case fopen() returns a NULL pointer. Opening a file for writing causes the file to be created if it does not exist and causes it to be overwritten if it does. Opening a file in append mode causes the file to be created if it does not exist and causes writing to occur at the end of the file if it does.

A file is opened for updating (both reading and writing) by using a + in the mode. However, between a read and a write or a write and a read there must be an intervening call to fflush() to flush the buffer, or a call to one of the file positioning function calls fseek(), fsetpos(), or rewind().

In some operating systems, including UNIX, there is no distinction between binary and text files, except in their contents. The file mechanism is the same for both types of files. In MS-DOS and other operating systems, there are different file mechanisms for each of the two types of files (see Exercise 22 for further discussion).

A detailed description of file handling functions such as fopen() and fclose() can be found in Appendix A, "The Standard Library." Consult the appendix as necessary to understand how the various functions are used.

11.5 AN EXAMPLE: DOUBLE SPACING A FILE

Let us illustrate the use of some file handling functions by writing a program to double space a file. In main(), we open files for reading and writing that are passed as command line arguments. After the files have been opened, we invoke double_space() to accomplish the task of double spacing.

```c
/* Double spacing a file. */

#include <stdio.h>
#include <stdlib.h>

void    double_space(FILE *, FILE *);
void    prn_info(char *);

int main(int argc, char **argv)
{
    FILE    *ifp, *ofp;

    if (argc != 3) {
        prn_info(argv[0]);
        exit(1);
    }
    ifp = fopen(argv[1], "r");      /* open for reading */
    ofp = fopen(argv[2], "w");      /* open for writing */
    double_space(ifp, ofp);
    fclose(ifp);
    fclose(ofp);
    return 0;
}

void double_space(FILE *ifp, FILE *ofp)
{
    int   c;

    while ((c = getc(ifp)) != EOF) {
        putc(c, ofp);
        if (c == '\n')
            putc('\n', ofp);    /* found a newline - duplicate it */
    }
}

void prn_info(char *pgm_name)
{
    printf("\n%s%s%s\n\n%s%s\n\n",
        "Usage: ", pgm_name, "  infile  outfile",
        "The contents of infile will be double-spaced ",
        "and written to outfile.");
}
```

Suppose we have compiled this program and put the executable code in the file *dbl_space*. When we give the command

    dbl_space file1 file2

the program will read from *file1* and write to *file2*. The contents of *file2* will be the same as *file1*, except that every newline character will have been duplicated.

DISSECTION OF THE *dbl_space* PROGRAM

■
```
#include <stdio.h>
#include <stdlib.h>

void    double_space(FILE *, FILE *);
void    prn_info(char *);
```
We have included *stdlib.h* because it contains the function prototype for exit(), which gets used in prn_info(). The identifier FILE is a structure defined in *stdio.h*. To make use of files, we do not need to know system-implementation details of how the file mechanism works. The function prototype for double_space() shows that it takes two file pointers as arguments.

■
```
int main(int argc, char **argv)
{
    FILE    *ifp, *ofp;

    if (argc != 3) {
        prn_info(argv[0]);
        exit(1);
    }
```
The identifiers ifp and ofp are file pointers. More explicitly, they are of type pointer to FILE. The program is designed to access two files entered as command line arguments. If there are too few or too many command line arguments, prn_info() is invoked to print information about the program and exit() is invoked to exit the program. By convention, exit() returns a nonzero value when something has gone wrong.

■
```
ifp = fopen(argv[1], "r");      /* open for reading */
ofp = fopen(argv[2], "w");      /* open for writing */
```
We can think of argv as an array of strings. The function fopen() is used to open the file named in argv[1] for reading. The pointer value returned by the function is assigned to ifp. In a similar fashion, the file named in argv[2] is opened for writing.

- `double_space(ifp, ofp);`
  The two file pointers are passed as arguments to `double_space()`, which then does the work of double spacing. One can see that other functions of this form could be written to perform whatever useful work on files was needed.

- `fclose(ifp);`
  `fclose(ofp);`
  The function `fclose()` from the standard library is used to close the files pointed to by `ifp` and `ofp`. It is good programming style to close files explicitly in the same function in which they were opened. Any files not explicitly closed by the programmer are closed automatically by the system on program exit.

- `void double_space(FILE *ifp, FILE *ofp)`
  `{`
  `    int  c;`
  The identifier `c` is an `int`. Although it will be used to store characters obtained from a file, eventually it will be assigned the value EOF, which is not a character.

- ```
  while ((c = getc(ifp)) != EOF) {
      putc(c, ofp);
      if (c == '\n')
          putc('\n', ofp);   /* found a newline - duplicate it */
  }
  ```
  The macro `getc()` reads a character from the file pointed to by `ifp` and assigns the value to `c`. If the value of `c` is not EOF, then `putc()` is used to write `c` into the file pointed to by `ofp`. If `c` is a newline character, another newline character is written into the file as well. This has the effect of double spacing the output file. This process continues repeatedly until an EOF is encountered. The macros `getc()` and `putc()` are defined in *stdio.h*.

11.6   USING TEMPORARY FILES AND GRACEFUL FUNCTIONS

In ANSI C, the programmer can invoke the library function `tmpfile()` to create a temporary binary file that will be removed when it is closed or on program exit. The file is opened for updating with the mode "wb+". In MS-DOS, a binary file can also be used as a text file. In UNIX, binary and text files are the same. In this section we write an elementary program that illustrates the use of `tmpfile()` and a graceful version of `fopen()`.
  ```

The name of our program is *replicate_with_caps*. First it reads the contents of a
file into a temporary file, capitalizing any letters as it does so. Then the program
adds the contents of the temporary file to the bottom of the first file.

```
/* Replicate a file with caps. */

#include <ctype.h>
#include <stdio.h>
#include <stdlib.h>

FILE    *gfopen(char *filename, char *mode);

int main(int argc, char **argv)
{
    int    c;
    FILE   *fp, *tmp_fp;

    if (argc != 2) {
        fprintf(stderr, "\n%s%s%s\n\n%s\n\n",
            "Usage: ", argv[0], "  filename",
            "The file will be replicated with some capital letters.");
        exit(1);
    }
    fp = gfopen(argv[1], "r+");
    tmp_fp = tmpfile();
    while ((c = getc(fp)) != EOF)
        putc(toupper(c), tmp_fp);
    rewind(tmp_fp);
    fprintf(fp, "---\n");
    while ((c = getc(tmp_fp)) != EOF)
        putc(c, fp);
    return 0;
}

FILE *gfopen(char *filename, char *mode)
{
    FILE    *fp;

    if ((fp = fopen(filename, mode)) == NULL) {
        fprintf(stderr, "Cannot open %s - bye!\n", filename);
        exit(1);
    }
    return fp;
}
```

Before we explain the program, let us see its effects. Suppose that in file *apple* we have the line

```
A is for apple and alphabet pie.
```

After we give the command

replicate_with_caps apple

the contents of the file will be

```
A is for apple and alphabet pie.
---
A IS FOR APPLE AND ALPHABET PIE.
```

DISSECTION OF THE *replicate_with_caps* PROGRAM

- ```
  fp = gfopen(argv[1], "r+");
  ```
  We are using a graceful version of fopen( ) to open a file for both reading and writing. If for some reason the file cannot be opened, a message will be printed and the program exited.

- ```
  tmp_fp = tmpfile();
  ```
  ANSI C provides the function tmpfile( ) to open a temporary file. The file mode is "wb+". On program exit, the file will be removed by the system. Consult Appendix A, "The Standard Library," for the function prototype and other details.

- ```
  while ((c = getc(fp)) != EOF)
      putc(toupper(c), tmp_fp);
  ```
  The macros getc( ) and putc( ) are defined in *stdio.h*. They are being used to read from one file and to write to another. The function prototype for toupper( ) is given in *ctype.h*. If c is a lowercase letter, toupper(c) returns the corresponding uppercase letter; otherwise, it returns c. *Caution:* Some ANSI C compilers do not get this right. (Hopefully, they will improve with time.) You may have to write

  ```
  while ((c = getc(fp)) != EOF)
      if (islower(c))
          putc(toupper(c), tmp_fp);
      else
          putc(c, tmp_fp);
  ```

  See Exercise 12 in Chapter 8 for further discussion.
  ```

■ `rewind(tmp_fp);`

This causes the file position indicator for the stream pointed to by `tmp_fp` to be set to the beginning of the file. This statement is equivalent to

```
fseek(tmp_fp, 0, 0);
```

See Appendix A, "The Standard Library," for the function prototypes and for an explanation of `fseek()`.

■ `fprintf(fp, "---\n");`
`while ((c = getc(tmp_fp)) != EOF)`
`    putc(c, fp);`

Now we are reading from the stream pointed to by `tmp_fp` and writing to the stream pointed to by `fp`. Note that a call to `rewind()` occurred before the switch from writing to reading on the stream pointed to by `tmp_fp`.

■ `FILE *gfopen(char *filename, char *mode)`
`{`
`    .....`

This is a graceful version of `fopen()`. If something goes wrong, a message is printed on the screen and we exit the program. Note that we wrote to `stderr`. In this program, we could just as well have written to `stdout`. However, in other programs that use this function, there is an advantage to writing to `stderr` (see Exercise 1).

11.7 ACCESSING A FILE RANDOMLY

The library functions `fseek()` and `ftell()` are used to access a file randomly. An expression of the form

`ftell(`*file_ptr*`)`

returns the current value of the file position indicator. The value represents the number of bytes from the beginning of the file, counting from zero. Whenever a character is read from the file, the system increments the position indicator by 1. Technically, the file position indicator is a member of the structure pointed to by *file_ptr*. *Caution:* The file pointer itself does not point to individual characters in the stream. This is a conceptual mistake that many beginning programmers make.

The function `fseek()` takes three arguments: a file pointer, an integer offset, and an integer that indicates the place in the file from which the offset should be computed. A statement of the form

`fseek(`*file_ptr*, *offset*, *place*`);`

sets the file position indicator to a value that represents *offset* bytes from *place*. The value for *place* can be 0, 1, or 2, meaning the beginning of the file, the current position, or the end of the file, respectively. *Caution:* The function fseek() and ftell() are guaranteed to work properly only on binary files. In MS-DOS, if we want to use these functions, the file should be opened with a binary mode. In UNIX, any file mode will work.

A common exercise is to write a file backwards. Here is a program that does this:

```
/* Write a file backwards. */

#include <stdio.h>

#define    MAXSTRING    100

int main(void)
{
    char    fname[MAXSTRING];
    int     c;
    FILE    *ifp;

    fprintf(stderr, "\nInput a filename:   ");
    scanf("%s", fname);
    ifp = fopen(fname, "rb");          /* binary mode for ms-dos */
    fseek(ifp, 0, SEEK_END);           /* move to end of the file */
    fseek(ifp, -1, SEEK_CUR);          /* back up one character */
    while (ftell(ifp) > 0) {
        c = getc(ifp);                 /* move ahead one character */
        putchar(c);
        fseek(ifp, -2, SEEK_CUR);      /* back up two characters */
    }
    return 0;
}
```

The prompt to the user is written to stderr so the program will work with redirection (see Exercise 1). We opened the file with mode "rb" so the program will work in both MS-DOS and UNIX.

11.8   FILE DESCRIPTOR INPUT/OUTPUT

A file descriptor is a nonnegative integer associated with a file. In this section we describe a set of library functions that are used with file descriptors. Although these functions are not part of ANSI C, they are available on most C systems in both

MS-DOS and UNIX. Because of minor differences, care is needed when porting code from UNIX to MS-DOS or vice versa.

File name	Associated file descriptor
standard input	0
standard output	1
standard error	2

Functions in the standard library that use a pointer to FILE are usually buffered. In contrast, functions that use file descriptors may require programmer-specified buffers. Let us illustrate the use of file descriptors with a program that reads from one file and writes to another, changing the case of each letter.

```
/* Change the case of letters in a file. */

#include <ctype.h>
#include <fcntl.h>
#include <unistd.h>             /* use io.h in ms-dos */

#define    BUFSIZE    1024

int main(int argc, char **argv)
{
    char    mybuf[BUFSIZE], *p;
    int     in_fd, out_fd, n;

    in_fd = open(argv[1], O_RDONLY);
    out_fd = open(argv[2], O_WRONLY | O_EXCL | O_CREAT, 0600);
    while ((n = read(in_fd, mybuf, BUFSIZE)) > 0) {
        for (p = mybuf; p - mybuf < n; ++p)
            if (islower(*p))
                *p = toupper(*p);
            else if (isupper(*p))
                *p = tolower(*p);
        write(out_fd, mybuf, n);
    }
    close(in_fd);
    close(out_fd);
    return 0;
}
```

DISSECTION OF THE *change_case* PROGRAM

■ ```
  #include <ctype.h>
  #include <fcntl.h>
  #include <unistd.h>   /* use io.h in ms-dos */
  ```
The header file *fcntl.h* contains symbolic constants that we are going to use. The header file *unistd.h* contains the function prototypes for open( ) and read( ). In MS-DOS we would include *io.h* instead.

■ ```
  in_fd = open(argv[1], O_RDONLY);
  ```
The first argument to open( ) is a file name; the second argument specifies how the file is to be opened. If there are no errors, the function returns a file descriptor; otherwise, the value –1 is returned. The identifier in_fd is mnemonic for "in file descriptor." On both MS-DOS and UNIX systems, the symbolic constant O_RDONLY is given in *fcntl.h*. It is mnemonic for "open for reading only."

■ ```
  out_fd = open(argv[2], O_WRONLY | O_EXCL | O_CREAT, 0600);
  ```
The symbolic constants in *fcntl.h* that are used to open a file can be combined with the bitwise OR operator. Here, we are specifying that the file is to be opened for writing only, that the file is to be opened exclusively (meaning that it is an error if the file already exists), and that the file is to be created if it does not exist. O_EXCL gets used only with O_CREAT. If the file is created, then the third argument sets the file permissions; otherwise, the argument has no effect. We will explain about file permissions below.

■ ```
  while ((n = read(in_fd, mybuf, BUFSIZE)) > 0) {
        .....
  ```
A maximum of BUFSIZE characters are read from the stream associated with in_fd and put into mybuf. The number of characters read is returned. The body of the while loop is executed as long as read( ) is able to get characters from the stream. In the body of the loop the letters in mybuf are changed to the opposite case.

■ ```
  write(out_fd, mybuf, n);
  ```
n characters in mybuf are written to the stream indicated by out_fd.

■ ```
  close(in_fd);
  close(out_fd);
  ```
This closes the two files. If the files are not explicitly closed by the programmer, the system will close them on program exit.

Caution: This program is not user-friendly. If you give the command

   change_case file1 file2

and *file2* already exists, then the file does not get overwritten, which is the behavior we wanted. A better-designed program would say something to the user in this case.

11.9 FILE ACCESS PERMISSIONS

In UNIX, a file is created with associated access permissions. The permissions determine access to the file for the owner, the group, and for others. The access can be read, write, execute, or any combination of these, including none. When a file is created by invoking open(), a 3-digit octal integer can be used as the third argument to set the permissions. Each octal digit controls read, write, and execute permissions. The first octal digit controls permissions for the user, the second octal digit controls permissions for the group, and the third octal digit controls permissions for others. ("Others" includes everybody.)

Meaning of each octal digit in the file permissions		
Mnemonic	Bit representation	Octal representation
r--	100	04
-w-	010	02
--x	001	01
rw-	110	06
r-x	101	05
-wx	011	03
rwx	111	07

Now, if we pack three octal digits together into one number, we get the file access permissions. The mnemonic representation is the easiest to remember. The first, second, and third group of three letters refers to the user, the group, and others, respectively.

Examples of file access permissions	
Mnemonic	Octal representation
rw-------	0600
rw----r--	0604
rwxr-xr-x	0755
rwxrwxrwx	0777

The permissions rwxr-xr-x mean that the owner can read, write, and execute the file; that the group can read and execute the file; and that others can read and execute the file. In UNIX, the mnemonic file access permissions are displayed with the *ls –l* command. In MS-DOS, file permissions exist, but only for everybody.

11.10   EXECUTING COMMANDS FROM WITHIN A C PROGRAM

The library function system( ) provides access to operating system commands. In both MS-DOS and UNIX, the command *date* causes the current date to be printed on the screen. If we want this information printed on the screen from within a program, we can write

```
system("date");
```

The string passed to system( ) is treated as an operating system command. When the statement is executed, control is passed to the operating system, the command is executed, and then control is passed back to the program.

In UNIX, *vi* is a commonly used text editor. Suppose that from inside a program we want to use *vi* to edit a file that has been given as a command line argument. We can write

```
char    command[MAXSTRING];

sprintf(command, "vi %s", argv[1]);
printf("vi on the file %s is coming up ...\n", argv[1]);
system(command);
```

A similar example works in MS-DOS, provided we replace *vi* by an editor that is available on that system.

As a final example, let us suppose we are tired of looking at all those capital letters produced by the *dir* command on our MS-DOS system. We can write a program that interfaces with this command and writes only lowercase letters on the screen.

```c
/* Write only lowercase on the screen. */

#include <ctype.h>
#include <stdio.h>
#include <stdlib.h>

#define    MAXSTRING    100

int main(void)
{
    char    command[MAXSTRING], *tmp_filename;
    int     c;
    FILE    *ifp;

    tmp_filename = tmpnam(NULL);
    sprintf(command, "dir > %s", tmp_filename);
    system(command);
    ifp = fopen(tmp_filename, "r");
    while ((c = getc(ifp)) != EOF)
        putchar(tolower(c));
    remove(tmp_filename);
    return 0;
}
```

First, we use the library function tmpnam() to create a temporary file name. Then we invoke system() to redirect the output of the *dir* command into the temporary file. Then we print on the screen the contents of the file, changing each uppercase letter to lowercase. Finally, when we are finished using the temporary file, we invoke the library function remove() to remove it. Consult Appendix A, "The Standard Library," for details about these functions.

11.11   USING PIPES FROM WITHIN A C PROGRAM

UNIX systems provide popen( ) and pclose( ) to communicate with the operating system. These functions are not available in MS-DOS systems. Suppose we are tired of looking at all those lowercase letters produced by the *ls* command on our UNIX system.

```
#include <ctype.h>
#include <stdio.h>

int main(void)
{
   int    c;
   FILE   *ifp;

   ifp = popen("ls", "r");
   while ((c = getc(ifp)) != EOF)
      putchar(toupper(c));
   pclose(ifp);
   return 0;
}
```

The first argument to popen( ) is a string that is interpreted as a command to the operating system; the second argument is a file mode, either "r" or "w". When the function is invoked, it creates a pipe (hence the name popen) between the calling environment and the system command that is executed. Here, we get access to whatever is produced by the *ls* command. Because access to the stream pointed to by ifp is via a pipe, we cannot use file-positioning functions. For example, rewind(ifp) will not work. We can only access the characters sequentially. A stream opened by popen( ) should be closed by pclose( ). If the stream is not closed explicitly, then it will be closed by the system on program exit.

11.12 ENVIRONMENT VARIABLES

Environment variables are available in both UNIX and MS-DOS. The following program can be used to print them on the screen:

```
#include <stdio.h>

int main(int argc, char *argv[], char *env[])
{
    int   i;

    for (i = 0; env[i] != NULL; ++i)
        printf("%s\n", env[i]);
    return 0;
}
```

The third argument to main() is a pointer to pointer to char, which we can think of as an array of pointers to char, or as an array of strings. The system provides the strings, including the space for them. The last element in the array env is a NULL pointer. On our UNIX system, this program prints

```
HOME=/c/c/blufox/center_manifold
SHELL=/bin/csh
TERM=vt102
USER=blufox
.....
```

To the left of the equal sign is the environment variable; to the right of the equal sign is its value, which should be thought of as a string. On our MS-DOS system, this program prints

```
COMSPEC=C:\COMMAND.COM
BASE=d:\base
INCLUDE=d:\msc\include
.....
```

The UNIX system provides a command to display the environment variables, but the command depends on which shell you are running. In the C shell the command is *printenv*, whereas in the Bourne shell and in MS-DOS the command is *set*. The output of the command is the same as the output of our program.

By convention, environment variables are usually capitalized. In a C program, we can use the library function getenv() to access the value of an environment variable passed as an argument. Here is an example of how getenv() can be used:

```
printf("%s%s\n%s%s\n%s%s\n%s%s\n",
    "           Name: ", getenv("NAME"),
    "           User: ", getenv("USER"),
    "          Shell: ", getenv("SHELL"),
    "Home directory: ", getenv("HOME"));
```

The function prototype is provided in *stdlib.h*. If the string passed as an argument is not an environment variable, the NULL pointer is returned.

11.13   THE C COMPILER

There are many C compilers, and an operating system may provide any number of them. Here are just a few of the possibilities:

Command	The C compiler that gets invoked
cc	The system-supplied native C compiler
acc	An early version of an ANSI C compiler from Sun Microsystems
bc	Borland C/C++ compiler, integrated environment
bcc	Borland C/C++ compiler, command line version
gcc	GNU C compiler from the Free Software Foundation
hc	High C compiler from Metaware
occ	Oregon C compiler from Oregon Software
qc	Quick C compiler from Microsoft
tc	Turbo C compiler, integrated environment, from Borland
tcc	Turbo C compiler, command line version, from Borland

In this section we discuss some of the options that can be used with the *cc* command on UNIX systems. Other compilers provide similar options.

If a complete program is contained in a single file, say *pgm.c*, then the command

  cc pgm.c

translates the C code in *pgm.c* into executable object code and writes it in the file *a.out*. (In MS-DOS, the executable file is *pgm.exe*.) The command *a.out* executes the program. The next *cc* command will overwrite whatever is in *a.out*. If we give the command

cc −o pgm pgm.c

then the executable code will, instead, be written directly into the file *pgm*; whatever is in *a.out* will not be disturbed.

The *cc* command actually does its work in three stages: First the preprocessor is invoked, then the compiler, and finally the loader. The loader, or linker, is what puts all the pieces together to make the final executable file. The −c option can be used to compile only—that is, to invoke the preprocessor and the compiler, but not the loader. This option is useful if we have a program written in more than one file. Consider the command

cc −c main.c file1.c file2.c

If there are no errors, corresponding object files ending in .o will be created. To create an executable file, we can compile a mixture of .c and .o files. Suppose, for example, that we have an error in *main.c*. We can correct the error in *main.c* and then give the command

cc −o pgm main.c file1.o file2.o

The use of .o files in place of .c files reduces compilation time.

Some useful options to the compiler

-c	Compile only, generate corresponding .o files.
-g	Generate code suitable for the debugger.
-o *name*	Put executable output code in *name*.
-p	Generate code suitable for the profiler.
-v	Verbose option, generates a lot of information.
-D *name=def*	Place at the top of each .c file the line #define *name def*.
-E	Invoke the preprocessor but not the compiler.
-I *dir*	Look for #include files in the directory *dir*.
-M	Make a makefile.
-O	Attempt code optimization.
-S	Generate assembler code in corresponding .s files.

Your compiler may not support all of these options, and it may provide others. Or it may use different flag characters. Compilers in MS-DOS usually support different memory models. Consult the documentation for your compiler for a detailed list of options. *Suggestion:* If you have never tried the −v option, do so. Some compilers produce a ton of information, and this information can be very useful when you are trying to understand all the details about the compilation process.

11.14 USING THE PROFILER

In UNIX, the *–p* option used with *cc* causes the compiler to produce code that counts the number of times each routine is called. If the compiler creates an executable file, then it is arranged so that the library function `monitor()` is automatically invoked and a file *mon.out* is created. The file *mon.out* is then used by the *prof* command to generate an execution profile.

As an example of how this all works, suppose we want an execution profile of the *quicksort* routine that we wrote in Chapter 8. Here is our function `main()`:

In file main.c:

```
#include <stdio.h>
#include <stdlib.h>
#include <time.h>

#define    N    50000

void   quicksort(int *, int *);

int main(void)
{
   int     a[N], i;

   srand(time(NULL));
   for (i = 0; i < N; ++i)
      a[i] = rand() % 10000;
   quicksort(a, a + N - 1);
   for (i = 0; i < N - 1; ++i)
      if (a[i] > a[i + 1]) {
         printf("SORTING ERROR - bye!\n");
         exit(1);
      }
   return 0;
}
```

To obtain an execution profile of our program, we first compile it with the *–p* option:

cc –p –o quicksort main.c quicksort.c

Next, we give the command

quicksort

This causes the file *mon.out* to be created. Finally, to get an execution profile, we give the command

  prof quicksort

This causes the following to be printed on the screen:

%time	cumsecs	#call	ms/call	name
46.9	7.18	9931	0.72	_partition
16.1	9.64	1	2460.83	_main
11.7	11.43	19863	0.09	_find_pivot
10.8	13.08			mcount
6.9	14.13	50000	0.02	_rand
6.4	15.12	19863	0.05	_quicksort
1.4	15.33			_monstartup
0.0	15.33	1	0.00	_gettimeofday
0.0	15.33	1	0.00	_profil
0.0	15.33	1	0.00	_srand
0.0	15.33	1	0.00	_time

Not all of the named functions are user-defined; some of them, such as _gettime-ofday, are system routines. An execution profile such as this can be very useful when working to improve execution time efficiency.

11.15 LIBRARIES

Many operating systems provide a utility to create and manage libraries. In UNIX, the utility is called the archiver, and it is invoked with the *ar* command. In the MS-DOS world, this utility is called the librarian, and it is an add-on feature. The Microsoft librarian, for example, is *lib*, whereas the Turbo C librarian is *tlib*. By convention, library files end in *.a* in UNIX, and end in *.lib* in MS-DOS. We will discuss the situation as it pertains to UNIX, but the general ideas apply to any librarian.

In UNIX, the standard C library is usually in the file */usr/lib/libc.a*, but the standard library can exist wholly or in part in other files as well. If UNIX is available to you, try the command

  ar t /usr/lib/libc.a

The key *t* is used to display titles, or names, of files in the library. There are more titles than you care to look at. To count them, you can give the command

  ar t /usr/lib/libc.a | wc

This pipes the output of the *ar* command to the input of the *wc* command, causing lines, words, and characters to be counted. (The name *wc* stands for "word count.")

It is not too surprising that the standard library grows with time. On a DEC VAX 11/780 from the 1980s, the standard library contained 311 object files. On a Sun machine that was relatively new in 1990, the standard library contained 498 object files. On the Sun machine that we happen to be using today, the number of object files is 563.

Let us illustrate how programmers can create and use libraries of their own. We will do this in the context of creating a "graceful library." In Section 11.6 we presented gfopen(), a graceful version of fopen(). In a directory named *g_lib*, we have 11 such graceful functions, and we continue to add more from time to time. These are functions such as gfclose(), gcalloc(), gmalloc(), and so forth. Each is written in a separate file, but for the purpose of building a library, they could just as well be in one file. To reinforce the idea of these functions, we give the code for gcalloc():

```
#include <stdio.h>
#include <stdlib.h>

void *gcalloc(int n, unsigned sizeof_something)
{
    void    *p;

    if ((p = calloc(n, sizeof_something)) == NULL) {
        fprintf(stderr, "\nERROR:  calloc() failed - bye.\n\n");
        exit(1);
    }
    return p;
}
```

To create our library, we must first compile the *.c* files to obtain corresponding *.o* files. After we have done this, we give the two commands

ar ruv g_lib.a gfopen.o gfclose.o gcalloc.o ...
ranlib g_lib.a

The keys *ruv* in the first command stand for replace, update, and verbose, respectively. This command causes the library *g_lib.a* to be created if it does not already exist. If it does exist, then the named *.o* files replace those of the same name already in the library. If any of the named *.o* files are not in the library, they are added to it. The *ranlib* command is used to randomize the library in a form that is useful for the loader.

Now suppose we are writing a program that consists of *main.c* and two other *.c* files. If our program invokes gfopen(), we need to make our library available to the compiler. The following command does this:

cc −o pgm main.c file1.c file2.c g_lib.a

If our program invokes a function and does not supply its function definition, then it will be searched for, first in *g_lib.a* and then in the standard library. Only those functions that are needed will be loaded into the final executable file.

If we write lots of programs, each consisting of many files, then each of the programs should be written in its own directory. Also, we should have a separate directory for our libraries such as *g_lib.a*, and another directory for associated header files such as *g_lib.h*. For each function in *g_lib.a*, we put its prototype in *g_lib.h*. This header file then gets included where needed. To manage all of this, we use the *make* utility. We discuss this in Section 11.17, "The Use of *make*."

11.16 HOW TO TIME C CODE

Most operating systems provide access to the underlying machine's internal clock. In this section we show how to use some timing functions. Because our functions are meant to be used in many programs, we put them into the library *u_lib.a*, our utility library. In Section 11.17 we will discuss a program that uses functions from both of our libraries *g_lib.a* and *u_lib.a*.

Access to the machine's clock is made available in ANSI C through a number of functions whose prototypes are in *time.h*. This header file also contains a number of other constructs, including the type definitions for clock_t and time_t, which are useful for dealing with time. Typically, the two type definitions are given by

```
typedef    long    clock_t;
typedef    long    time_t;
```

and in turn, these types are used in the function prototypes. Here are the prototypes for the three functions we will use in our timing routines:

```
clock_t    clock(void);
time_t     time(time_t *p);
double     difftime(time_t time1, time_t time0);
```

When a program is executed, the operating system keeps track of the processor time that is being used. When clock() is invoked, the value returned is the system's best approximation to the time used by the program up to that point. The clock units can vary from one machine to another. The macro

```
#define   CLOCKS_PER_SEC   60              /* machine-dependent */
```

is provided in *time.h*. It can be used to convert the value returned by clock() to seconds. *Caution:* In preliminary versions of ANSI C, this macro was called CLK_TCK.

The function time() returns the number of seconds that have elapsed since 1 January 1970. Other units and other starting dates are possible, but these are the ones typically used. If the pointer argument passed to time() is not NULL, then the value returned gets assigned to the variable pointed to as well. One typical use of the function is

```
srand(time(NULL));
```

This seeds the random number generator. If two values produced by time() are passed to difftime(), the difference expressed in seconds is returned as a double.

We want to present a set of timing routines that can be used for many purposes, including the development of efficient code. We keep these functions in the file *time_keeper.c*.

```
#include <stdio.h>
#include <stdlib.h>
#include <time.h>

#define    MAXSTRING    100

typedef struct {
    clock_t    begin_clock, save_clock;
    time_t     begin_time, save_time;
} time_keeper;

static time_keeper    tk;                /* known only to this file */

void start_time(void)
{
    tk.begin_clock = tk.save_clock = clock();
    tk.begin_time = tk.save_time = time(NULL);
}

double prn_time(void)
{
    char      s1[MAXSTRING], s2[MAXSTRING];
    int       field_width, n1, n2;
    double    clocks_per_second = (double) CLOCKS_PER_SEC,
              user_time, real_time;

    user_time = (clock() - tk.save_clock) / clocks_per_second;
    real_time = difftime(time(NULL), tk.save_time);
    tk.save_clock = clock();
    tk.save_time = time(NULL);

    /* print the values found, and do it neatly */

    n1 = sprintf(s1, "%.1f", user_time);
    n2 = sprintf(s2, "%.1f", real_time);
    field_width = (n1 > n2) ? n1 : n2;
    printf("%s%*.1f%s\n%s%*.1f%s\n\n",
        "User time: ", field_width, user_time, " seconds",
        "Real time: ", field_width, real_time, " seconds");
    return user_time;
}
```

Note that the structure tk is external to the functions and is known only in this file. It is used for communication between the functions. When start_time() is invoked, the values returned from clock() and time() are stored in tk. When prn_time() is invoked, new values from clock() and time() are used to compute and print the elapsed user time and the elapsed real time, and new values are stored in tk. User time is whatever the system allocates to the running of the program; real time is wall-clock time. In a time-shared system they need not be the same.

The function prn_total_time() is also in the file, but we have not shown it. It is similar to prn_time(), except that the elapsed times are computed relative to the last invocation of start_time() rather than the last invocation of any of the three functions.

Because our timing routines are meant to be used in a variety of programs, we put them into *u_lib.a*, our utility library. The following commands do this:

   cc −c time_keeper.c;   *ar ruv u_lib.a time_keeper.o*;   *ranlib u_lib.a*

In the header file *u_lib.h* we put the prototypes of the functions in *u_lib.a*. The header file then gets included elsewhere as needed.

Now we demonstrate how our timing routines can be used. In certain applications, fast floating-point multiplication is desired. Should we use variables of type float or double? The following program can be used to test this:

```
/* Compare float and double multiplication times. */

#include <stdio.h>
#include "u_lib.h"

#define    N    100000000        /* one hundred million */

int main(void)
{
    long      i;
    float     a, b = 3.333, c = 5.555;    /* arbitrary values */
    double    x, y = 3.333, z = 5.555;

    printf("Number of multiplies: %d\n\n", N);
    printf("Type float:\n\n");
    start_time();
    for (i = 0; i < N; ++i)
        a = b * c;
    prn_time();
    printf("Type double:\n\n");
    for (i = 0; i < N; ++i)
        x = y * z;
    prn_time();
    return 0;
}
```

On an older machine with a traditional C compiler, we find, much to our surprise, that single precision multiplication is *slower* than double precision multiplication! In traditional C, any `float` is automatically promoted to a `double`. Perhaps the results are due to the time it takes the machine to do the conversion. On another machine with an ANSI C compiler, we find that single precision multiplication is about 30% faster. This is in line with what we expected. When we tried the program on a Sun Sparcstation 10, we obtained the following results:

```
Number of multiplies: 100000000

Type float:

User time: 33.6 seconds
Real time: 34.0 seconds

Type double:

User time: 33.5 seconds
Real time: 33.0 seconds
```

Once again we are surprised! We expected that multiplication with `float`s would yield a 30% saving in time, but that is not the case. Note that the real time listed for `double`s is less than the user time. This happens because the clocking mechanism as a whole is only approximate. *Caution:* To get an accurate measure of machine multiplication time, the overhead of the `for` loops themselves, as well as general program overhead (relatively negligible), has to be taken into account.

11.17 THE USE OF *make*

For both the programmer and the machine, it is inefficient and costly to keep entirely in one file a moderate or large size program that has to be recompiled repeatedly. A much better strategy is to write the program in multiple *.c* files, compiling them separately as needed. The *make* utility can be used to keep track of source files and to provide convenient access to libraries and their associated header files. This powerful utility is always available in UNIX and often available in MS-DOS, where it is an add-on feature. Its use greatly facilitates both the construction and the maintenance of programs.

Let us suppose we are writing a program that consists of a number of *.h* and *.c* files. Typically, we would place all these files in a separate directory. The *make* command reads a file whose default name is *makefile*. This file contains the dependencies of the various modules, or files, making up the program, along with appropriate actions to be taken. In particular, it contains the instructions for compiling, or recompiling, the program. Such a file is called a *makefile*.

For simplicity, let us imagine that we have a program contained in two files, say *main.c* and *sum.c*, and that a header file, say *sum.h*, is included in each of the *.c* files. We want the executable code for this program to be in the file *sum*. Here is a simple makefile that can be used for program development and maintenance:

```
sum: main.o sum.o
        cc -o sum main.o sum.o

main.o: main.c sum.h
        cc -c main.c

sum.o: sum.c sum.h
        cc -c sum.c
```

The first line indicates that the file *sum* depends on the two object files *main.o* and *sum.o*. It is an example of a *dependency* line; it must start in column 1. The second line indicates how the program is to be compiled if one or more of the *.o* files have been changed. It is called an *action* line or a *command*. There can be more than one action following a dependency line. A dependency line and the action lines that follow it make up what is called a *rule*. *Caution:* Each action line must begin with a tab character. On the screen, a tab character looks like a sequence of blanks.

By default, the *make* command will make the first rule that it finds in the makefile. But dependent files in that rule may themselves be dependent on other files as specified in other rules, causing the other rules to be made first. These files, in turn, may cause yet other rules to be made.

The second rule in our makefile states that *main.o* depends on the two files *main.c* and *sum.h*. If either of these two files is changed, then the action line shows what must be done to update *main.o*. After this makefile has been created, the programmer can compile or recompile the program *sum* by giving the command

   make

With this command, *make* reads the file *makefile*, creates for itself a dependency tree, and takes whatever action is necessary.

The dependency tree used internally by make

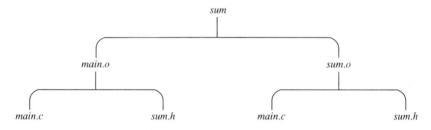

Certain rules are built into *make*, including the rule that a *.o* file depends on the corresponding *.c* file. Because of this, an equivalent makefile is given by

```
sum: main.o sum.o
        cc -o sum main.o sum.o

main.o: sum.h
        cc -c main.c

sum.o: sum.h
        cc -c sum.c
```

The *make* utility recognizes a number of built-in macros. Using one of them, we get yet another equivalent makefile:

```
sum: main.o sum.o
        cc -o sum main.o sum.o

main.o sum.o: sum.h
        cc -c $*.c
```

Here, the second rule states that the two *.o* files depend on *sum.h*. If we edit *sum.h*, then both *main.o* and *sum.o* must be remade. The macro `$*.c` expands to `main.c` when *main.o* is being made, and it expands to `sum.c` when *sum.o* is being made.

A makefile consists of a series of entries called *rules* that specify dependencies and actions. A rule begins in column 1 with a series of blank-separated target files, followed by a colon, followed by a blank-separated series of prerequisite files, also called *source* files. All the lines beginning with a tab that follow this are the actions—such as compilation—to be taken by the system to update the target files. The target files are dependent in some way on the prerequisite files and must be updated when the prerequisite files are modified.

In Exercise 33 in Chapter 8 we suggested that a serious comparison of `qsort()` and `quicksort()` be undertaken. We wrote a program to do this that compared the running times for three sorting routines: our own `quicksort()`, the system-supplied `qsort()`, and a `qsort()` from another system for which we were able to borrow the code. The borrowed `qsort()` consisted of some 200 lines of code in a single

file. Including this file, our program consisted of approximately 400 lines written in
five files. Here is the makefile that we used:

In file makefile:

```
# Makefile to compare sorting routines.

BASE     =  /home/blufox/base
CC       =  gcc
CFLAGS   =  -O -Wall
EFILE    =  $(BASE)/bin/compare_sorts
INCLS    =  -I$(LOC)/include
LIBS     =  $(LOC)/lib/g_lib.a  \
            $(LOC)/lib/u_lib.a
LOC      =  /usr/local

OBJS  =  main.o       another_qsort.o    chk_order.o  \
         compare.o    quicksort.o

$(EFILE): $(OBJS)
        @echo "linking ..."
        @$(CC)  $(CFLAGS)  -o $(EFILE)  $(OBJS)  $(LIBS)

$(OBJS): compare_sorts.h
         $(CC)  $(CFLAGS)  $(INCLS)  -c  $*.c
```

DISSECTION OF THE MAKEFILE FOR THE *compare_sorts* PROGRAM

■ `# Makefile to compare sorting routines.`
Comments can be put in a makefile. A comment begins with a # and extends
to the end of the line.

■ `BASE    =  /home/blufox/base`
This is an example of a macro definition. The general form of a macro definition
is

> *macro_name = replacement_string*

By convention, macro names are usually capitalized, but they do not have to
be. The replacement string can contain white space. If a backslash \ occurs at
the end of the line, then the replacement string continues to the next line. Our
home directory on this particular machine is `/home/blufox`. We created the
subdirectory `base` to hold all our other major subdirectories. We think of it as
our "base of operation." The macro BASE refers to this subdirectory.

■ CC   = gcc
CFLAGS = -O -Wall

The first macro specifies the C compiler that we are using, in this case the GNU C compiler. The second macro specifies the options, or "C flags," that will be used when *gcc* gets invoked. The *–O* option turns on the optimizer; the *–Wall* option asks for all warnings. If we had written

```
CC      = gcc
CFLAGS  =
```

instead, then the replacement string for CFLAGS would be empty.

■ EFILE   = $(BASE)/bin/compare_sorts

The macro EFILE specifies where we want to put our executable file. Macro evaluation, or invocation, occurs with a construct of the form $(*macro_name*). This produces the string value (possibly empty) of *macro_name*. The string value of the macro is also called its *replacement string*. Thus

```
EFILE   = $(BASE)/bin/compare_sorts
```

is equivalent to

```
EFILE   = /home/blufox/base/bin/compare_sorts
```

■ INCLS   = -I$(LOC)/include
LIBS   = $(LOC)/lib/g_lib.a \
          $(LOC)/lib/u_lib.a
LOC   = /usr/local

The first macro specifies the -I option followed directly by the name of a directory that contains include files. The second macro specifies two libraries. The third macro specifies another directory. Note that a backslash is used to continue to the next line. The first library, *g_lib.a*, is the graceful library, which we discussed in Section 11.15. The second library, *u_lib.a*, is the utility library, which we discussed in Section 11.16. Because our program invokes functions from these libraries, the libraries must be made available to the compiler. We keep the associated header files *g_lib.h* and *u_lib.h* in the directory $(LOC)/include. The compiler will have to be told to look in this directory for header files. Note that a macro can be evaluated before it has been defined.

■ OBJS = main.o   another_qsort.o   chk_order.o \
         compare.o   quicksort.o

The macro OBJS is defined to be the list of object files that occurs on the right side of the equal sign. Note that we used a backslash to continue the line. Although we put *main.o* first and then list the other *.o* files alphabetically, order is unimportant.

■
```
$(EFILE): $(OBJS)
        @echo "linking ..."
        @$(CC)  $(CFLAGS)  -o $(EFILE)  $(OBJS)  $(LIBS)
```
The first line is a dependency line. The second and third lines specify the actions to be taken. Note carefully that action lines begin with a single tab character. (It looks like eight blank spaces on the screen.) The @ symbol means that the action line itself is not to be echoed on the screen (see Exercise 28). Because macro invocation has the form

$(*macro_name*)

the construct $(EFILE) is replaced by

```
$(BASE)/bin/compare_sorts
```

which in turn is replaced by

```
/home/blufox/base/bin/compare_sorts
```

Similarly, $(OBJS) is replaced by the list of object files, and so forth. Thus the dependency line states that the executable file depends on the object files. If one or more of the object files has been updated, then the specified actions occur. The second action line is expanded to

```
@gcc  -O -Wall  -o /home/blufox/base/bin/compare_sorts  \
    main.o  another_qsort.o  chk_order.o  compare.o       \
    quicksort.o  /home/blufox/base/lib/g_lib.a            \
    /home/blufox/base/lib/u_lib.a
```

Although we have written it on four lines because of space limitations on the printed page, this is actually generated as a single line. *Suggestion:* If *make* is new to you, build your makefiles without the @ symbol at first. Later, after you understand its effects, you can use the @ symbol to prevent echoing.

■ $(OBJS): compare_sorts.h
              $(CC) $(CFLAGS) $(INCLS) -c $*.c

The first line is a dependency line; it says that all the object files depend on the header file *compare_sorts.h*. If the header file has been updated, then all the object files have to be updated, too. This is done through the action line. In UNIX, action lines *must* begin with a tab. In MS-DOS, they can start with a tab or with one or more blanks. The construct $* that occurs in the action line is a predefined macro called the *base filename macro*. It expands to the filename being built, excluding any extension. For example, if *main.o* is being built, then $*.c expands to main.c, and the action line becomes

```
gcc  -O -Wall  -I/usr/local/include  -c  main.c
```

Certain dependencies are built into the *make* utility. For example, each *.o* file depends on its corresponding *.c* file: This means that if a *.c* file is changed, then it will be recompiled to produce a new *.o* file, and this in turn will cause all the object files to be relinked.

■ -I/usr/local/include

An option of the form -I*dir* means "look in the directory *dir* for #include files." This option complements our use of libraries. At the top of the *.c* files making up this program, we have the line

```
#include "compare_sorts.h"
```

and at the top of *compare_sorts.h* we have the lines

```
#include "g_lib.h"
#include "u_lib.h"
```

These header files contain the function prototypes for the functions in our libraries. The -I option tells the compiler where to find these header files.

The make utility can be used to maintain programs in any language, not just C and C++. More generally, make can be used in any kind of project that consists of files with dependencies and associated actions.

11.18   THE USE OF *touch*

The *touch* utility is always available in UNIX and is often available in MS-DOS. It puts a new time on a file. The *make* utility decides which actions to take by comparing file times, and *touch* can be used to direct what *make* does.

To illustrate the use of *touch*, let us assume we have the makefile discussed in the previous section, along with the relevant *.h*, *.c*, and *.o* files. To put the current date on the file *compare_sorts.h*, we can give the command

　　touch compare_sorts.h

This causes the file to have a more recent time than all the object files that depend on it. Now, if we give the command

　　make

all the *.c* files will be recompiled and linked to create a new executable file.

11.19   OTHER USEFUL TOOLS

Operating systems provide many useful tools for the programmer. Here we will list a few of the tools found on UNIX systems, along with some remarks. Comparable utilities are sometimes available in MS-DOS.

Command	Remarks
cb	The C beautifier; it can be used to "pretty print" C code.
dbx	A source-level debugger; code must be compiled with the -g option.
diff	Prints the lines that differ in two files.
gdb	The GNU debugger; code must be compiled with the -g option.
grep	Searches for a pattern in one or more files; a major tool for programmers.
indent	A C code "pretty printer" with lots of options.
wc	Counts lines, words, and characters in one or more files.

The *cb* utility reads from stdin and writes to stdout. It is not very powerful. To see what it can do, try the command

　　cb < pgm.c

where *pgm.c* is poorly formatted. The utility *indent* is more powerful, but unlike *cb*, it is not universally available. To make serious use of *indent*, you will need to read the online manual.

A debugger allows the programmer to step through the code a line at a time and to see the values of variables and expressions at each step. This can be extremely helpful in discovering why a program is not acting as the programmer expected. The programming world is full of debuggers, and *dbx* is not a particularly good one. It just happens to be one that is generally available on UNIX systems. In the MS-DOS world, debuggers are an add-on product. Borland, Microsoft, and others provide excellent products.

Tools such as *diff*, *grep*, and *wc* are of a general nature. They get used by everyone, not just programmers. Although these are UNIX tools, they are often available in MS-DOS as well, especially *grep*, which is very useful to programmers.

Finally, let us mention that C can be used in conjunction with other high-level tools, some of which are languages in their own right.

Utility	Remarks
awk	A pattern scanning and processing language
bison	GNU's version of *yacc*
csh	The C shell, which is programmable
flex	GNU's version of *lex*
lex	Generates C code for lexical analysis
nawk	A newer, more powerful, version of *awk*
perl	Practical extraction and report language
sed	A stream editor that takes its commands from a file
yacc	"Yet another compiler-compiler," used to generate C code

Of particular importance to programmers are *lex* and *yacc*, or the corresponding GNU utilities, *flex* and *bison*; see Chapter 8 in *The UNIX Programming Environment* by Brian Kernighan and Rob Pike (Englewood Cliffs, N.J.: Prentice-Hall, 1984). The Free Software Foundation produces GNU tools. These tools run on many platforms, and they can be obtained via the Internet. (The Internet provides access to other tools from other places as well.) If you have an Internet connection, the command

> *ftp prep.ai.mit.edu*

will connect you to a machine from which you can download GNU tools. (First time *ftp* users will need assistance.)

11.20 SUMMARY

1 The functions `printf()` and `scanf()`, and the related file and string versions of these functions, all use conversion specifications in a control string to deal with a list of arguments of variable length.

2 The standard header file *stdio.h* is included if files are used. It contains the definitions of the identifier `FILE` (a structure) and the file pointers `stdin`, `stdout`, and `stderr`. It also contains prototypes of many file-handling functions and

definitions for the macros `getc()` and `putc()`. The function call `getc(ifp)` reads the next character from the file pointed to by `ifp`.

3 To open and close files, we use `fopen()` and `fclose()`, respectively. After a file has been opened, the file pointer is used to refer to the file.

4 A file can be thought of as a stream of characters. The stream can be accessed either sequentially or randomly. When a character is read from a file, the operating system increments the file position indicator by 1.

5 The system opens the three standard files `stdin`, `stdout`, and `stderr` at the beginning of each program. The function `printf()` writes to `stdout`. The function `scanf()` reads from `stdin`. The files `stdout` and `stderr` are usually connected to the screen. The file `stdin` is usually connected to the keyboard. Redirection causes the operating system to make other connections.

6 Files are a scarce resource. The maximum number of files that can be open simultaneously is given by the symbolic constant `FOPEN_MAX` in *stdio.h*. This number is system-dependent; typically, it is in the range from 20 to 100. It is the programmer's responsibility to keep track of which files are open. On program exit, any open files are closed by the system automatically.

7 A set of functions that use file descriptors is available in most systems, even though these functions are not part of ANSI C. They require user-defined buffers. The file descriptors of `stdin`, `stdout`, and `stderr` are 0, 1, and 2, respectively.

8 An operating system command can be executed from within a program by invoking `system()`. In MS-DOS, the statement

```
system("dir");
```

will cause a list of directories and files to be listed on the screen.

9 In UNIX, the function `popen()` can be used to communicate with the operating system. Consider the command

*wc *.c*

It prints on the screen the word count of all the *.c* files in the current directory. To get access to this stream of characters from within a program, the programmer can write

```
FILE    *ifp;

ifp = popen("wc *.c", "r");
```

Streams that are opened with `popen()` should be closed with `pclose()`.

10 Many operating systems provide a utility to create and manage libraries. In UNIX, the utility is called the archiver, and it is invoked with the *ar* command. In the MS-DOS world, this utility is called the librarian, and it is an add-on feature.

11 The *make* utility can be used to keep track of source files and to provide convenient access to libraries and associated header files.

11.21 EXERCISES

1 Rewrite the *dbl_space* program so it gets the name of the input file as a command line argument and writes to `stdout`. After this has been done, the command

   dbl_sp infile > outfile

can be used to double-space whatever is in *infile*, with the output being written into *outfile*. Because the program is intended to be used with redirection, it now makes sense to invoke `fprintf(stderr,...)` rather than `printf(...)` in `prn_info()`. If the error message is written to `stdout`, it will be redirected; the user will not see the message on the screen. The symbol > is used to redirect whatever is written to `stdout`. It does not affect whatever is written to `stderr`. Try writing the program two ways: with the error message being written first to `stderr` and then to `stdout`. Experiment with the two versions of the program so you understand the different effects.

2 Rewrite the *dbl_space* program so it uses a command line option of the form –*n*, where *n* can be 1, 2, or 3. If *n* is 1, then the output should be single-spaced. That is, two or more contiguous newline characters in the input file should be written as a single newline character in the output file. If *n* is 2, then the output file should be strictly double-spaced. That is, one or more contiguous newline characters in the input file should be rewritten as a pair of newline characters in the output file. If *n* is 3, the output file should be strictly triple-spaced.

3 Write `getstring()` and `putstring()` functions. The first function should use a file pointer, say `ifp`, and the macro `getc()` to read a string from the file pointed to by `ifp`. The second function should use a file pointer, say `ofp`, and the macro `putc()` to write a string to the file pointed to by `ofp`. Write a program to test your functions.

4 Write a program to number the lines in a file. The input file name should be passed to the program as a command line argument. The program should write to `stdout`. Each line in the input file should be written to the output file with the line number and a space prepended.

5 Read about the `ungetc()` function in Appendix A. After three characters have been read from a file, can `ungetc()` be used to push three characters back onto the file? Write a program to test this.

6 Write a program that displays a file on the screen 20 lines at a time. The input file should be given as a command line argument. The program should display the next 20 lines after a carriage return has been typed. (This is an elementary version of the *more* utility in UNIX.)

7 Modify the program you wrote in Exercise 6 to display one or more files given as command line arguments. Also, allow a command line option of the form *–n* to be used, where *n* is a positive integer specifying the number of lines that are to be displayed at one time. In MS-DOS, the command to clear the screen is *cls*; in UNIX it is *clear*. Try either one or the other of these commands on your system so you understand its effects. Use either system("cls") or system("clear") in your program just before you write each set of lines to the screen.

8 The library function fgets() can be used to read from a file a line at a time. Read about fgets() in Appendix A. Write a program called *search* that searches for patterns. If the command

   search hello my_file

is given, then the string pattern *hello* is searched for in the file *my_file*. Any line that contains the pattern is printed. (This program is an elementary version of *grep*.) *Hint:* Use the following code:

```
char    line[MAXLINE], *pattern;
FILE    *ifp;

if (argc != 3) {
   .....
}
if ((ifp = fopen(argv[2], "r")) == NULL) {
   fprintf(stderr, "\nCannot open %s\n\n", argv[2]);
   exit(1);
}
pattern = argv[1];
while (fgets(line, MAXLINE, ifp) != NULL) {
   if (strstr(line, pattern) != NULL)
      .....
```

9 Modify the function you wrote in Exercise 8. If the command line option *–n* is present, then the line number should be printed as well.

10 Compile the following program and put the executable code into a file, say *try_me*:

```
#include <stdio.h>

int main(void)
{
    fprintf(stdout, "She sells sea shells\n");
    fprintf(stderr, "by the seashore.\n");
    return 0;
}
```

Execute the program so you understand its effects. What happens when you redirect the output? Try the command

try_me > tmp

Make sure you read the file *tmp* after you do this. In UNIX, you should also try the command

try_me > & tmp

This causes the output that is written to stderr to be redirected, too. Make sure that you look at what is in *tmp*. You may be surprised!

11 Write a program called *wrt_rand* that creates a file of randomly distributed numbers. The filename is to be entered interactively. Your program should use three functions. Here is the first function:

```
void get_info(char *fname, int *n_ptr)
{
    printf("\n%s\n\n%s",
        "This program creates a file of random numbers.",
        "How many random numbers would you like?  ");
    scanf("%d", n_ptr);
    printf("\nIn what file would you like them?  ");
    scanf("%s", fname);
}
```

After this function has been invoked in `main()`, you could write

```
ofp = fopen(fname, "w");
```

However, the named file may already exist, and if it does, then overwriting it will destroy whatever is in the file currently. In this exercise we want to write cautious code. If the file already exists, report this fact to the user and ask permission to overwrite the file. Use for the second function in your program the following "careful" version of `fopen()`:

```
FILE *cfopen(char *fname, char *mode)
{
   char    reply[2];
   FILE    *fp;

   if (strcmp(mode, "w") == 0 && (access(fname, F_OK) == 0) {
      printf("\nFile exists.  Overwrite it?  ");
      scanf("%1s", reply);
      if (*reply != 'y' && *reply != 'Y') {
         printf("\nBye!\n\n");
         exit(1);
      }
   }
   fp = gfopen(fname, mode);
   return fp;
}
```

(Read about `access()` in Appendix A.) The third function is `gfopen()`, the graceful version of `fopen()` that was presented in Section 11.6. *Hint:* To write your randomly distributed numbers neatly, use the following code:

```
for (i = 1; i <= n; ++i) {
   fprintf(ofp, "%12d", rand());
   if (i % 6 == 0 || i == n)
      fprintf(ofp, "\n");
}
```

12 Accessing a string is not like accessing a file. When a file is opened, the file position indicator keeps track of where you are in the file. There is no comparable mechanism for a string. Write a program that contains the following lines:

```
char    c, s[] = "abc", *p = s;
int     i;
FILE    *ofp1, *ofp2;

ofp1 = fopen("tmp1", "w");
ofp2 = fopen("tmp2", "w");
for (i = 0; i < 3; ++i) {
    sscanf(s, "%c", &c);
    fprintf(ofp1, "%c", c);
}
for (i = 0; i < 3; ++i) {
    sscanf(p++, "%c", &c);
    fprintf(ofp2, "%c", c);
}
```

What gets written in tmp1 and tmp2? Explain.

13 In this exercise we examine a typical use of sscanf(). Suppose we are writing a serious interactive program that asks the user to input a positive integer. To guard against errors, we can pick up as a string the line typed by the user. The following is one way to process the string:

```
char    line[MAXLINE];
int     error, n;

do {
    printf("Input a positive integer:   ");
    fgets(line, MAXLINE, stdin);
    error = sscanf(line, "%d", &n) != 1 || n <= 0;
    if (error)
        printf("\nERROR: Do it again.\n");
} while (error);
```

This will catch some typing errors, but not all. If, for example, 23e is typed instead of 233, the error will not be caught. Modify the code so that if anything other than a digit string surrounded by optional white space is typed, the input is considered to be in error. Use these ideas to rewrite the *wrt_rand* program that you wrote in Exercise 11.

14 The two conversion characters x and X can be used to print an expression as a
    hexadecimal number. Are the two conversion characters equivalent? *Hint:* Try

```
printf("11259375 = %#lx\n", 11259375);
printf("11259375 = %#lX\n", 11259375);
```

(In case you are wondering, the number 11259375 was carefully chosen.)

15 Can your compiler handle the conversion character n correctly? (All the ones
    we tried could not.) Try the following:

```
int    a, b, c;

printf("a%nb%nc%n %d %d %d\n", &a, &b, &c, a, b, c);
```

16 Can we give flag characters in a conversion specification in any order? The
    ANSI C document is not too specific about this point, but it seems that the
    intent is for any order to be acceptable. See what happens with your compiler
    when you try the following code:

```
printf("%0+17d\n", 1);
printf("%+017d\n", 1);
```

17 Will the following code get a hexadecimal number from a string? What happens
    if 0x is deleted in the string?

```
char    s[] = "0xabc";
int    n;

sscanf(s, "%x", &n);
printf("Value of n: %d\n", n);
```

18 Did you read the table of conversion characters for scanf() carefully? Does
    the following code make sense? Explain.

```
char        s[] = "-1";
unsigned    n;

sscanf(s, "%u", &n);
printf("Value of n: %u\n", n);
```

19 Investigate how `tmpnam()` makes its names. Try executing, for example, the
following program:

```
#include <stdio.h>

int main(void)
{
    char      tfn[100];      /* tfn = tmp filename */

    tmpnam(tfn);
    printf("1: tfn = %s\n", tfn);
    tmpnam(tfn);
    printf("2: tfn = %s\n", tfn);
    tmpnam(tfn);
    printf("3: tfn = %s\n", tfn);
    return 0;
}
```

Execute the program repeatedly so you understand its effects. Notice that `tfn`
changes one way within the program, and it changes another way with each
execution of the program. On our system, the following line occurs in *stdio.h*:

```
#define   TMP_MAX   17576      /* 26 * 26 * 26 */
```

In ANSI C, repeated calls to `tmpnam()` are supposed to generate at least `TMP_MAX`
unique names. On our system, exactly `TMP_MAX` unique names are generated.
What happens on your system?

20 Is the Borland C/C++ compiler available to you? If so, try the command

> *bcc*

When no files are given with the command, then a list of all the options is
printed on the screen. This is a very nice feature. Try it.

21 Our program that double-spaces a file can be invoked with the command

> *dbl_space infile outfile*

If *outfile* exists, then it will be overwritten. This is potentially dangerous.
Rewrite the program so it writes to `stdout` instead. Then the program can
be invoked with the command

> *dbl_space infile > outfile*

This program design is much safer. Of all the system commands, only a few are
designed to overwrite a file. After all, nobody likes to lose a file by accident.

22 In the early days of MS-DOS, a control-z character within the file was used as
    an end-of-file mark. Although this is not done now, if a file has a control-z in it,
    and it is opened as a text file for reading, characters beyond the control-z may
    be inaccessible. Write a program with the following lines in it:

```
char    cntrl_z = '\032';     /* octal escape for control-z */
int     c;
FILE    *ifp, *ofp;

ofp = fopen("tmp", "w");
fprintf(ofp, "%s%c%s\n",
   "A is for apple", cntrl_z, " and alphabet pie.");
fclose(ofp);
ifp = fopen("tmp", "r");         /* open as a text file */
while ((c = getc(ifp)) != EOF)   /* print the file */
   putchar(c);
fclose(ifp);
printf("\n---\n");               /* serves as a marker */
ifp = fopen("tmp", "rb");        /* open as a binary file */
while ((c = getc(ifp)) != EOF)   /* print the file */
   putchar(c);
```

What gets printed? (Does the program act differently on a UNIX system?) In
MS-DOS, try the command

   type tmp

Only the characters before the control-z are printed. How do you know that
there are more characters in the file? *Hint:* Try the *dir* command. Normally,
control-z characters are not found in text files, but they certainly can occur in
binary files. Subtle problems can occur if you open a binary file for processing
with mode "r" instead of "rb".

23 If UNIX is available to you, experiment to see what the following program does:

```
#include <stdio.h>
#include <stdlib.h>

#define    MAXSTRING    100

int main(int argc, char **argv)
{
    char    command[MAXSTRING];

    sprintf(command, "sort -r %s", argv[1]);
    system(command);
    return 0;
}
```

Actually, the program needs improvement. Rewrite it so it prints a prompt to the user. Give the command

man sort

to read about the *sort* utility.

24 If you are a C programmer, should you care about assembler code? Surprisingly, the answer is yes. The –S option causes your compiler to produce a .s file, and that file can be useful to you, even if you cannot read a line of assembler code. Write a simple program that contains the following lines:

```
int   i = 10;

while (--i != 0)                    /* inefficient? */
    printf("i = %d\n", i);
```

The value of the expression --i != 0 controls the execution of the while loop. Is the control mechanism inefficient? Write another program that contains the lines

```
int   i = 10;

while (--i)                          /* better? */
    printf("i = %d\n", i);
```

Compile both of your programs with the −S option. Then look at the difference between the two .s files. In UNIX this can be done with the command

>   *diff pgm1.s pgm2.s*

Is your second program more efficient than your first?

25 Is Turbo C available to you? If so, make the following modifications to the *change_case* program we presented in Section 11.8. Include the standard header files *io.h* and *sys\stat.h*. Replace the octal constant 0600 by

```
S_IREAD | S_IWRITE
```

(These symbolic constants are discussed in the Turbo C manual.) With these changes the program should compile and execute. Does it?

26 If UNIX is available to you, give the command

>   *ls −l*

This provides a long listing of all the files and subdirectories in the current directory. Note that file modes are displayed. Read about the *chmod* utility in the online manual. To further your understanding about file modes, try commands similar to the following:

>   *date > tmp; ls −l tmp*
>   *chmod a+rwx tmp; ls −l tmp*
>   *chmod 0660 tmp; ls −l tmp*
>   *chmod 0707 tmp; ls −l tmp*

The numbers are octal. Are the leading zeros necessary?

27 Look carefully at the execution profile we presented in Section 11.14. You can see that rand() was called 50,000 times. This is correct because the size of the array is 50,000. Note that the number of function calls to find_pivot() equals the number of calls to quicksort(). By looking at the code, we easily convince ourselves that this, too, is correct. But what about the relationship between the number of calls to partition() and the number of calls to quicksort()? Can you give a precise explanation?

28 The last makefile that we presented in this chapter is a real one. Even though we dissected it, anyone who has not had experience with *make* will find the concepts difficult to grasp. If this utility is new to you, try the *make* command

after you have created the following file:

In file makefile:

```
# Experiment with the make command.

go: hello date list
        @echo Goodbye!
hello:
        @echo Hello!
date:
        @date; date; date
list:
        @pwd; ls
```

What happens if you remove the @ characters? What happens if a file named *hello* or *date* exists?

29 Create the following file, and then give the command *make*. What gets printed? Write your answer first; then experiment to check it.

In file makefile:

```
# Experiment with the make command!

Start: A1 A2
        @echo Start
A1: A3
        @echo A1
A2: A3
        @echo A2
A3:
        @echo A3
```

30 What gets printed?

```
#include <stdio.h>

int main(void)
{
    printf("Hello!\n");
    fclose(stdout);
    printf("Goodbye!\n");
    return 0;
}
```

CHAPTER **12**

ADVANCED APPLICATIONS

C has the ability to be close to the machine. It was originally used to implement UNIX, and building systems is still one of its important uses. In this chapter we describe some advanced applications, including material useful for systems programmers. We also discuss the use of matrices for engineers and scientists.

12.1   CREATING A CONCURRENT PROCESS WITH fork( )

UNIX is a multiuser, multiprocessing operating system. Each process has a unique process identification number. The following command will show you what your machine is currently doing:

ps −aux

Here is an example of its output:

```
USER       PID %CPU %MEM  SZ RSS TT STAT START   TIME   COMMAND
blufox   17725 34.0  1.6 146 105 i2 R    15:13   0:00 ps -aux
amber    17662  1.4  7.0 636 469 j5 S    15:10   0:08 vi find_it.c
root       143  0.5  0.1   5   3 ?  S    Jul 31 10:17 /etc/update
.....
```

The first line contains headings. The remaining lines supply information about each process: the user's login name, the process identification number, and so forth. (Read the online manual to find out more about the *ps* command.) The operating system runs many processes concurrently by time-sharing the machine resources.

In UNIX, the programmer can use fork( ) to create a new process, called the *child process*, that runs concurrently with the *parent process*. (It is not part of ANSI C.) The function fork( ) takes no arguments and returns an int. The following is a simple program illustrating its use:

504

```
#include <stdio.h>

int main(void)
{
    int    fork(void), value;

    value = fork();                                /* new process */
    printf("In main: value = %d\n", value);
    return 0;
}
```

The output of this program changes each time we run it. Here is an example of its
output:

```
In main: value = 17219
In main: value = 0
```

As noted, when fork() is invoked, it creates a new process, the child process. This
new process is an exact copy of the calling process, except that it has its own process
identification number. The function call fork() returns 0 to the child, and it returns
the child's process ID to the parent. In the output of our program, the first line was
printed by the parent, the second line by the child.

Let us modify this program by adding to the code a second copy of the statement

```
value = fork();
```

Here is what gets printed:

```
In main: value = 17394
In main: value = 0
In main: value = 0
In main: value = 17395
```

Note that the children have unique process identification numbers. The program
created four concurrent versions of main(). The order of execution of these processes is system-dependent and *nondeterministic*—that is, the order is not necessarily
the same for each execution of the program (see Exercise 1). *Caution:* Invoking
fork() too many times can cause the system to fail by exhausting all available
processes.

When fork() is invoked, it creates two processes, each with its own set of
variables. If a file pointer is used, however, care must be taken because the file
pointer in each of the processes will refer to the same underlying file.

The value returned by fork() can be used in an if-else statement to discriminate
between the actions of the child and the parent. In our next program we compute

Fibonacci numbers in the child process and print elapsed time in the parent process. We use `sleep()` to suspend execution of the parent process for 2-second intervals.

```
/* Compute Fibonacci numbers and print time asynchronously. */

#include <stdio.h>
#include <time.h>

int     fib(int);
int     fork(void);
void    sleep(unsigned);

int main(void)
{
    int    begin = time(NULL), i;

    if (fork() == 0)                              /* child */
        for (i = 0; i < 30; ++i)
            printf("fib(%2d) = %d\n", i, fib(i));
    else                                          /* parent */
        for (i = 0; i < 30; ++i) {
            sleep(2);
            printf("elapsed time = %d\n", time(NULL) - begin);
        }
    return 0;
}

int fib(int n)
{
    if (n <= 1)
        return n;
    else
        return (fib(n - 1) + fib(n - 2));
}
```

When this program is executed, the outputs of the two processes are intermixed in a nondeterministic fashion.

12.2   OVERLAYING A PROCESS: THE exec...() FAMILY

From within a program, the current process, meaning the program itself, can be overlaid with another process. To do this, the programmer calls a member of the exec...() family. (See Appendix A, "The Standard Library," for a list of all members.) These functions are not part of ANSI C, but, typically, they are available in both MS-DOS and UNIX.

We want to use the `execl()` function to illustrate how one process can be overlaid with another. The function prototype is

```
int    execl(char *path, char *arg0, ...);
```

In MS-DOS, this prototype is provided typically in the header file *process.h*. In UNIX, it can be in this header file or in some other. The first argument is the path of the executable file—that is, the new process. The remaining arguments correspond to the command line arguments expected by the new process. The argument list ends with the null pointer 0. The value –1 is returned if the executable file cannot be found or is nonexecutable.

Before we use `execl()` in a program, let us write two other small programs. We will use the compiled code to overlay another process.

In file pgm1.c:

```
#include <stdio.h>

int main(int argc, char **argv)
{
    int    i;

    printf("%s: ", argv[0]);
    for (i = 1; i < argc; ++i)        /* print the arg list */
        printf("%s ", argv[i]);
    putchar('\n');
    return 0;
}
```

In file pgm2.c:

```
#include <stdio.h>

int main(int argc, char **argv)
{
    int    i, sum = 0, value;

    for (i = 0; i < argc; ++i)        /* sum the arguments */
        if (sscanf(argv[i], "%d", &value) == 1)
            sum += value;
    printf("%s: sum of command line args = %d\n", argv[0], sum);
    return 0;
}
```

Next, we compile the two programs:

cc –o pgm1 pgm1.c;   cc –o pgm2 pgm2.c

Observe that *pgm1* and *pgm2* are executable files in the current directory. In our next program, we will overlay the parent process with one of these two processes.

```c
#include <stdio.h>
#include <process.h>

int main(void)
{
   int   choice = 0;

   printf("%s\n%s\n%s",
       "The parent process will be overlaid.",
       "You have a choice.",
       "Input 1 or 2: ");
   scanf("%d", &choice);
   putchar('\n');
   if (choice == 1)
       execl("pgm1", "pgm1", "a", "b", "c", 0);
   if (choice == 2)
       execl("pgm2", "pgm2", "1", "2", "3", "go", 0);
   printf("ERROR: You did not input 1 or 2.\n");
   return 0;
}
```

If we run this program under MS-DOS and enter 1 when prompted, here is what appears on the screen:

```
The parent process will be overlaid.
You have a choice.
Input 1 or 2: 1

C:\CENTER\PGM1.EXE: a b c
```

When a process is successfully overlaid, there is no return to the parent. The new process takes over completely.

In UNIX, fork( ) is often used when overlaying one process with another.

```c
if (fork() == 0)
    execl("/c/c/bf/bin/mmf", "mmf", "-f", 0);    /* execute mmf */
else
    .....                                        /* do something else */
```

Using the spawn...() Family

Most C systems in MS-DOS provide the spawn...() family of functions. This family is similar to the exec...() family, except that the first argument is an integer mode.

Modes for the spawn...() family	Meaning
0	Parent process waits until child process completes execution.
1	Concurrent execution—not yet implemented.
2	Child process overlays the parent process; same as equivalent exec...() call.

MS-DOS is not a multiprocessing operating system. Where a programmer might use fork() and execl() in UNIX, spawnl(0, ...) could be used instead in MS-DOS. Here is a call to spawnl() that invokes *chkdsk*:

```
spawnl(0, "c:\chkdsk", "chkdsk", "c:", "/f", 0);
```

Since the mode is 0, the parent process will wait until the child process *c:\chkdsk* completes execution before continuing with its work.

12.3   INTERPROCESS COMMUNICATION USING pipe()

In UNIX, the programmer can use pipe() to communicate between concurrent processes. The function prototype is given by

```
int    pipe(int pd[2]);
```

The function call pipe(pd) creates an input/output mechanism called a pipe. Associated file descriptors, or pipe descriptors, are assigned to the array elements pd[0] and pd[1]. The function call returns 0 if the pipe is created, and returns –1 if there is an error.

After a pipe has been created, the system assumes that two or more cooperating processes created by subsequent calls to fork() will use read() and write() to pass data through the pipe. One descriptor, pd[0], is read from, and the other, pd[1], is written to. The pipe capacity is implementation-dependent, but is at least 4096 bytes. If a write fills the pipe, the pipe is blocked until data is read out of it. As with other file descriptors, close() can be used to explicitly close pd[0] and pd[1].

To illustrate the use of pipe(), we will write a program that computes the sum of
the elements of an array. We compute the sum of each row concurrently in a child
process and write the values on a pipe. In the parent process, we read the values
from the pipe.

```
/*  Use pipes to sum N rows concurrently. */

#include <stdio.h>
#include <stdlib.h>

#define   N    3

int     add_vector(int v[]);
void    error_exit(char *s);
int     fork(void);
int     pipe(int pd[2]);
int     read(int fd, void *buf, unsigned len);
int     write(int fd, void *buf, unsigned len);

int main(void)
{
    int    a[N][N] = {{1, 1, 1}, {2, 2, 2}, {3, 3, 3}},
           i, row_sum, sum = 0,
           pd[2];                           /* pipe descriptors */

    if (pipe(pd) == -1)                      /* create a pipe */
        error_exit("pipe() failed");
    for (i = 0; i < N; ++i)
        if (fork() == 0) {                    /* child process */
            row_sum = add_vector(a[i]);
            if (write(pd[1], &row_sum, sizeof(int)) == -1)
                error_exit("write() failed");
            return;                           /* return from child */
        }
    for (i = 0; i < N; ++i) {
        if (read(pd[0], &row_sum, sizeof(int)) == -1)
            error_exit("read() failed");
        sum += row_sum;
    }
    printf("Sum of the array = %d\n", sum);
    return 0;
}
```

```
int add_vector(int v[])
{
    int i, vector_sum = 0;

    for (i = 0; i < N; ++i)
        vector_sum += v[i];
    return vector_sum;
}

void error_exit(char *s)
{
    fprintf(stderr, "\nERROR: %s - bye!\n", s);
    exit(1);
}
```

DISSECTION OF THE *concurrent_sum* PROGRAM

■
```
if (pipe(pd) == -1)                          /* create a pipe */
    error_exit("pipe() failed");
```
A pipe is created before other processes are forked. If the call to `pipe()` fails, we invoke `error_exit()` to write a message to the user and exit the program.

■
```
for (i = 0; i < N; ++i)
    if (fork() == 0) {                       /* child process */
        row_sum = add_vector(a[i]);
        if (write(pd[1], &row_sum, sizeof(int)) == -1)
            error_exit("write() failed");
        return;                              /* return from child */
    }
```
Each time through the loop, we use `fork()` to create a child process. After `row_sum` has been computed, we write it on the pipe with the function call

```
write(pd[1], &row_sum, sizeof(int))
```

If the call to `write()` fails, we invoke `error_exit()` to write a message to the user and exit the program. Note carefully that we explicitly `return` from the child after the call to `write()`. If we do not do this, then the children will themselves create children each time through the loop.

```
■  for (i = 0; i < N; ++i) {
      if (read(pd[0], &row_sum, sizeof(int)) == -1)
         error_exit("read() failed");
      sum += row_sum;
   }
```

In the parent process, we invoke `read()` to read `row_sum` from the pipe. If the call to `read()` fails, we invoke `error_exit()` to write a message to the user and exit the program.

12.4   SIGNALS

An exceptional condition, or signal, is generated by an abnormal event. For example, the user may type a control-c to effect an interrupt, or a program error may cause a bus error or a segmentation fault. A floating-point exception occurs when two very large floating numbers are multiplied, or when division by zero is attempted. ANSI C provides the function `signal()` in the standard library. Its function prototype and some macros are in *signal.h*. The material in this section applies to both MS-DOS and UNIX.

The exceptional conditions that can be handled by the operating system are defined as symbolic constants in *signal.h*. Some examples are

```
#define   SIGINT    2     /* interrupt */
#define   SIGILL    4     /* illegal instruction */
#define   SIGFPE    8     /* floating-point exception */
#define   SIGSEGV   11    /* segment violation */
```

Although the signals that can be handled are system-dependent, the ones that we have listed are common to most C systems.

If an exceptional condition is raised in a process, then the typical default action of the operating system is to terminate the process. The programmer can use `signal()` to invoke a signal handler that replaces the default system action. The function prototype is

```
   void   (*signal(int sig, void (*func)(int)))(int);
```

This function takes two arguments, an `int` and a pointer to a function that takes an `int`, and returns nothing. The function returns a pointer to a function that takes an `int` and returns nothing.

The function call `signal(sig, func)` associates the signal `sig` with the signal handler `func()`. This causes the system to pass `sig` as an argument to `func()` and invoke it when the signal `sig` is raised.

Some special signal handlers are defined as macros in *signal.h*. We will use two of them:

```
#define    SIG_DFL    ((void (*)(int)) 0)        /* default */
#define    SIG_IGN    ((void (*)(int)) 1)        /* ignore */
```

The casts cause the constants to have a type that matches the second argument to `signal()`. Here is an example of how the second macro gets used:

```
signal(SIGFPE, SIG_IGN);      /* ignore floating-point exceptions */
```

This causes floating-point exceptions to be ignored by the system. If at some later point we want to resume the default action, we can write

```
signal(SIGFPE, SIG_DFL);      /* take default action */
```

If a standard signal handler is inappropriate in a given application, the programmer can use `signal()` to catch a signal and handle it as desired. Imagine wanting to use an interrupt to get the attention of a program without terminating it. The following program illustrates this:

```
/* Using a signal handler to catch a control-c. */

#include <stdio.h>
#include <signal.h>
#include <stdlib.h>

#define    MAXSTRING    100

void    cntrl_c_handler(int sig);
int     fib(int n);

int main(void)
{
   int    i;

   signal(SIGINT, cntrl_c_handler);
   for (i = 0; i < 46; ++i)
      printf("fib(%2d) = %d\n", i, fib(i));
      return 0;
}

void cntrl_c_handler(int sig)
{
   char    answer[MAXSTRING];

   printf("\n\n%s%d\n\n%s",
      "Interrupt received!  Signal = ", sig,
      "Do you wish to continue or quit? ");
   scanf("%s", answer);
   if (*answer == 'c')
      signal(SIGINT, cntrl_c_handler);
   else
      exit(1);
}
```

The function `fib()` is not shown. It is the same function that we used in Section 12.1.

DISSECTION OF THE *fib_signal* PROGRAM

■ `signal(SIGINT, cntrl_c_handler);`
If the `SIGINT` signal is raised, the system catches it and passes control to the function `cntrl_c_handler()`.

■ `void cntrl_c_handler(int sig)`
```
    {
        char    answer[MAXSTRING];

        printf("\n\n%s%d\n\n%s",
            "Interrupt received!  Signal = ", sig,
            "Do you wish to continue or quit? ");
```
When `signal()` passes control to this function, a message is printed on the screen.

■ `if (*answer == 'c')`
```
        signal(SIGINT, cntrl_c_handler);
    else
        exit(1);
```
Depending on the answer typed by the user, we either reset our signal handling mechanism or we exit the program. The interrupt signal is special. On some systems, after an interrupt has occurred, the system reverts to default action. The statement

```
    signal(SIGINT, cntrl_c_handler);
```

allows us to catch another interrupt.

12.5 AN EXAMPLE: THE DINING PHILOSOPHERS

The dining philosophers problem is a standard model for synchronizing concurrent processes that share resources. Five philosophers are seated around a circular table. Each philosopher has one chopstick at his side and a bowl of rice in front of him. Eating rice requires two chopsticks. There are only five chopsticks, so at most two philosophers can be eating at any one time. Indeed, if each philosopher picked up one chopstick, none could have two and they would all be *deadlocked*. A philosopher may acquire only the chopsticks to his or her immediate left or right. The problem is to write a program with concurrent processes representing the philosophers, where each philosopher gets to eat fairly often.

In our program each philosopher will be an identically forked process. The solution will require the use of semaphores implemented as pipes. A *semaphore* is a special variable allowing *wait* and *signal* operations. (The `signal()` function that we use here has nothing to do with `signal()` in the standard library, which we discussed in the previous section.) The variable is a special location for storing unspecified values. The wait operation expects one item and removes it. The signal operation adds one item. The wait operation blocks a process until it can accomplish its removal operation. The signal operation can start up a blocked process.

```
/* The dining philosopher program. */

#include <stdio.h>
#include <stdlib.h>              /* for calloc() and exit() */

#define    N                5      /* number of philosophers */
#define    Busy_Eating      1
#define    Busy_Thinking    1
#define    Left(p)          (p)            /* chopstick macros */
#define    Right(p)         (((p) + 1) % N)

typedef    int *    semaphore;

semaphore    chopstick[N];                      /* global array */

int            fork(void);
semaphore      make_semaphore(void);
void           philosopher(int me);
void           pick_up(int me);
int            pipe(int pd[2]);
void           put_down(int me);
int            read(int fd, void *buf, unsigned len);
void           signal(semaphore s);
void           sleep(unsigned seconds);
void           wait(semaphore s);
int            write(int fd, void *buf, unsigned len);

int main(void)
{
   int    i;

   for (i = 0; i < N; ++i) {      /* put chopsticks on the table */
      chopstick[i] = make_semaphore();
      signal(chopstick[i]);
   }
   for (i = 0; i < N - 1; ++i)    /* create philosophers */
      if (fork() == 0)
         break;
   philosopher(i);                /* all executing concurrently */
   return 0;
}
```

The function main() creates each chopstick as a semaphore. Each chopstick starts out as an available resource. Then each philosopher is created as a concurrent forked process. Each philosopher executes philosopher(i), the routine that attempts to alternately eat and think.

```
/* Acquire chopsticks, input is philosopher number. */

void pick_up(int me)
{
   if (me == 0) {
      wait(chopstick[Right(me)]);
      printf("Philosopher %d picks up right chopstick\n", me);
      sleep(1); /* simulate slow pick up to encourage deadlock */
      wait(chopstick[Left(me)]);
      printf("Philosopher %d picks up left chopstick\n", me);
   }
   else {
      wait(chopstick[Left(me)]);
      printf("Philosopher %d picks up left chopstick\n", me);
      sleep(1); /* simulate slow pick up to encourage deadlock */
      wait(chopstick[Right(me)]);
      printf("Philosopher %d picks up right chopstick\n", me);
   }
}

/* Relinquish chopsticks, input is the philosopher number. */

void put_down(int me)
{
   signal(chopstick[Left(me)]);
   signal(chopstick[Right(me)]);
}

/* Philosopher process, input is the philosopher number. */

void philosopher(int me)
{
   char    *s;
   int     i = 1;

   for ( ; ; ++i) {      /* forever */
      pick_up(me);
      s = i == 1 ? "st" : i == 2 ? "nd" : i == 3 ? "rd" : "th";
      printf("%s%d%s%d%s%s\n",
         "Philosopher ", me, " eating for the ", i, s, " time");
      sleep(Busy_Eating);
      put_down(me);
      printf("Philosopher %d thinking\n", me);
      sleep(Busy_Thinking);
   }
}
```

The philosopher() routine attempts to acquire a left and right chopstick. If successful, it eats and returns the chopsticks and resumes thinking. It acquires the chopsticks by using the semaphore operation wait() on its left and right chopsticks. The function pick_up() is blocked until both chopsticks are acquired. It releases the chopsticks by using the semaphore operation signal() on its left and right chopsticks. The function put_down() is terminated when both chopsticks are released.

```
semaphore make_semaphore(void)
{
    int    *sema;

    sema = calloc(2, sizeof(int));        /* permanent storage */
    pipe(sema);
    return sema;
}

void wait(semaphore s)
{
    int    junk;

    if (read(s[0], &junk, 1) <= 0) {
        printf("ERROR: wait() failed, check semaphore creation.\n");
        exit(1);
    }
}

void signal(semaphore s)
{
    if (write(s[1], "x", 1) <= 0) {
        printf("ERROR: write() failed, check semaphore creation.\n");
        exit(1);
    }
}
```

The semaphore is constructed by a call to pipe(sema). The semaphore function wait() is blocked until an item of input can be read into junk. The semaphore function signal() produces an item of output.

This example is a standard one for operating system resource allocation in a multiprocessing environment. A detailed discussion of algorithms for these problems can be found in *The Logical Design of Operating Systems* by Lubomir Bic and Alan Shaw (Englewood Cliffs, N.J.: Prentice-Hall, 1988).

12.6   DYNAMIC ALLOCATION OF MATRICES

Engineers and scientists use matrices extensively. In this section we explain how a matrix can be created dynamically as an array of pointers so it can be passed to functions that are designed to work on matrices of different sizes.

Why Arrays of Arrays Are Inadequate

In Chapter 6 we discussed the simplest way of implementing matrices. Let us briefly review how this is done, and explain why this is unacceptable for lots of applications. If we want a 3×3 matrix, for example, we can declare

```
double    a[3][3];
```

This allocates space for a as an array of arrays. If we want to work with a locally, there is no problem. However, lots of operations on matrices, such as finding determinants or computing eigenvalues, are best done by calling a function. For the purpose of discussion, suppose we want to find the determinant of a. After the matrix a has been filled, we want to be able to write something like

```
det = determinant(a);
```

The function definition for determinant() will look like

```
double determinant(double a[][3])
{
    .....
```

Because the compiler needs the 3 to build the correct storage mapping function, our determinant function can be used only on 3×3 matrices. If we want to compute the determinant of a 4×4 matrix, we need to write a new function definition. This is unacceptable. We want to be able to write a determinant function that can be used for square matrices of any size.

Building Matrices with Arrays of Pointers

By starting with the type pointer to pointer to double, we can build a matrix of whatever size we want, and we can pass it to functions that are designed to work on matrices of any size. Let us start with the code we need to create the space for a matrix:

```
int       i, j, n;
double    **a, det, tr;

.....                              /* get n from somewhere */
a = calloc(n, sizeof(double *));
for (i = 0; i < n; ++i)
   a[i] = calloc(n, sizeof(double));
```

The size of the matrix does not have to be known a priori. We can get n from the user or read it from a file or compute it. It does not have to be coded as a constant in the program. Once we know the desired size, we use the standard library function calloc() to create the space for the matrix dynamically. The function prototype is given in *stdlib.h* as

```
void   *calloc(size_t nitems, size_t size);
```

Typically, the type definition for size_t is given by

```
typedef   unsigned   size_t
```

This type definition can be found in *stddef.h* and sometimes in *stdlib.h*, too. If size_t is not defined directly in *stdlib.h*, then *stddef.h* will be included there. A function call of the form

```
calloc(n, sizeof(type))
```

allocates space in memory for an array of n elements of the specified type. The base address of the array is returned. Thus the statement

```
a = calloc(n, sizeof(double *));
```

allocates space for a, which we can now think of as an array of pointers to double of
size n. In the for loop, each element of a is assigned the base address of space allocated in memory for an array of doubles of size n. We can think of a in memory as

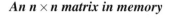

An $n \times n$ matrix in memory

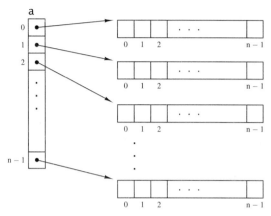

Now that space has been created for the matrix, we want to fill it. Let us assign
to the elements of a integer values that are randomly distributed in the range from
−9 to +9.

```
for (i = 0; i < n; ++i)
    for (j = 0; j < n; ++j)
        a[i][j] = rand() % 19 - 9;      /* from -9 to +9 */
```

Note that even though our matrix a is stored in memory as an array of pointers, the
usual matrix expression a[i][j] is used to access the element in the ith row, jth
column (counting from zero). Because a is of type double **, it follows that a[i]
is of type double *. It can be thought of as the ith row (counting from zero) of
the matrix. Because a[i] is of type double *, it follows that a[i][j] is of type
double. It is the jth element (counting from zero) in the ith row.

Now that we have assigned values to the elements of the matrix, we can pass the
matrix as an argument to various functions. Suppose we want to print it, compute
its determinant, and compute its trace. In the calling environment we can write

```
print_matrix(a, n);
det = determinant(a, n);
tr = trace(a, n);
```

The function definition for `print_matrix()` is given by

```c
void print_matrix(double **a, int n)
{
    int    i, j;

    for (i = 0; i < n; ++i) {
        for (j = 0; j < n; ++j)
            printf("%7.1f", a[i][j]);
        putchar('\n');
    }
    putchar('\n');
}
```

The function definition for `determinant()` begins as

```c
double determinant(double **a, int n)
{
    .....
```

Because the determinant function is complicated, we postpone further discussion until the exercises. The trace, however, is easy. By definition, the trace of a matrix is the sum of its diagonal elements:

```c
double trace(double **a, int n)
{
    int       i;
    double    sum = 0.0;

    for (i = 0; i < n; ++i)
        sum += a[i][i];
    return sum;
}
```

Adjusting the Subscript Range

In mathematics, the subscripts for vectors and matrices usually start at 1, not 0. We can arrange for our C code to do this, too. The following function can be used to create space for an n-vector:

```
double *get_vector_space(int n)
{
    int      i;
    double   *v;

    v = calloc(n, sizeof(double));
    return (v - 1);                        /* offset the pointer */
}
```

Because the pointer value that is returned has been offset to the left, subscripts in the calling environment will run from 1 to n rather than from 0 to $n - 1$.

An n-vector indexed from 1, not 0

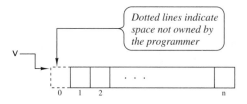

Note that in the picture, we drew dotted lines to indicate that the programmer does not own element 0. Now we can write code like the following:

```
int      n;
double   *v;

.....                                  /* get n from somewhere */
v = get_vector_space(n);
for (i = 1; i <= n; ++i)
    v[i] = rand() % 19 - 9;            /* from -9 to +9 */
.....
```

Instead of offsetting a pointer, we always have the option of allocating more space, and then not using it all.

```
v = calloc(n + 1, sizeof(double));     /* allocate extra space */
for (i = 1; i <= n; ++i)
    v[i] = ...
```

The technique of offsetting the pointer is better in the sense that no space is wasted. Let us use the technique to write a function that creates space for an $m \times n$ matrix with subscripts that start at 1 rather than 0.

```
double **get_matrix_space(int m, int n)
{
    int      i;
    double   **a;

    a = calloc(m, sizeof(double *));
    --a;                                  /* offset the pointer */
    for (i = 1; i <= m; ++i) {
        a[i] = calloc(n, sizeof(double));
        --a[i];                           /* offset the pointer */
    }
    return a;
}
```

We can think of the matrix a in memory as

An $m \times n$ matrix indexed from **1**, *not* **0**

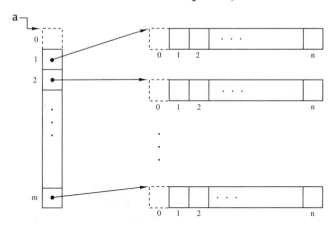

Note that once again we have used dotted lines to indicate space not owned by the programmer.

If a programmer wants space previously allocated by `calloc()` to be made available to the system again, then the function `free()` must be used. Let us suppose that in `main()` we write

```
int       i, j, n;
double    **a;

for ( ; ; ) {                          /* do it forever */
    .....                              /* get n from somewhere */
    a = get_matrix_space(n, n);
    for (i = 1; i <= m; ++i)
        for (j = 1; j <= n; ++j)
            a[i][j] = ...              /* assign values */
    .....                              /* do something */
    release_matrix_space(a, m);
}
```

Here is the function definition for `release_matrix_space()`. We have to be careful to undo the pointer offsets that occurred in `get_matrix_space()`.

```
void release_matrix_space(double **a, int m)
{
    int    i;

    for (i = 1; i <= m; ++i)
        free(a[i] + 1);
    free(a + 1);
}
```

Allocating All the Memory at Once

In certain applications, especially if the matrices are large, it may be important to allocate all the matrix space at once. At the same time, we want our matrices to be indexed from 1, not 0. Here is code that we can use to allocate space for our matrices:

In file matrix.h:

```
#include <stdio.h>
#include <stdlib.h>

typedef    double **    matrix;
typedef    double *     row;
typedef    double       elem;

.....

matrix    get_matrix_space(int m, int n);
void      release_matrix_space(matrix a);
void      fill_matrix(matrix a, int m, int n);
void      prn_matrix(const char *s, matrix a, int m, int n);
```

Note that we can get different kinds of matrices just by changing the typedef
appropriately.

In file space.c:

```
#include "matrix.h"

matrix get_matrix_space(int m, int n)
{
    int       i;
    elem *    p;
    matrix    a;

    p = malloc(m * n * sizeof(elem));    /* get space all at once */
    a = malloc(m * sizeof(row));
    --a;                          .       /* offset the pointer */
    for (i = 1; i <= m; ++i)
       a[i] = p + ((i - 1) * n) - 1;
    return a;
}

void release_matrix_space(matrix a)
{
    elem *    p;

    p = (elem *) a[1] + 1;               /* base address of the array */
    free(p);
}
```

Suppose that in some other function we write

```
int      m, n;
matrix   a;
```

```
.....                            /* get m and n from somewhere */
a = get_matrix_space(m, n);
```

Here is how we can think of a in memory:

Space for an m × n matrix allocated
*all at once and indexed from **1**, not **0***

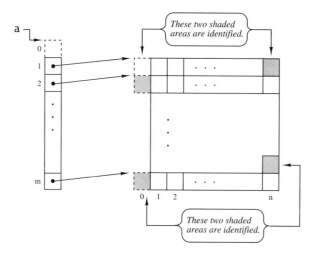

Caution: If we use algorithms that swap rows and we want to deallocate our matrix space, then we have to be careful not to lose the base address of the array in memory. We may want to redesign our abstract data type (ADT) matrix.

12.7   RETURNING THE STATUS

Throughout this text, at the end of every function definition for main(), we have written the line

```
return 0;
```

In this section we want to explain how the value returned from main() can be used by the operating system. From the viewpoint of the operating system, the value returned by a process is called its *status*. Processes include both programs and shell scripts. The operating system does not necessarily have to use the status that gets returned from a process.

In most operating systems, you communicate with the machine by clicking the mouse or typing commands on the keyboard. When you give commands such as

> *cc pgm.c*
> *date*
> *echo Beautiful!*

you are communicating via the shell. The shell (which is itself a program) interprets what you write and tries to execute your commands. There are three shells commonly found on UNIX systems: the Bourne shell *sh*, the C shell *csh*, and the Korn shell *ksh*.

To show how the value returned from main() (the program status) can be used, we are going to write a small program and then write a shell script that invokes our program. Here is our program:

In file try_me.c:

```
#include <stdio.h>

#define   MARKER    ">> "

int main(int argc, char **argv)
{
   int    val;

   printf("\n");
   printf(MARKER "    Input an integer: ");
   scanf("%d", &val);
   printf(MARKER "Value being returned: %d\n\n", val);
   return val;
}
```

Note that main() can return any integer value, not just zero. Note also that we are using a marker to clearly indicate the lines that are written to the screen by this program.

Next, we compile this program, putting the executable file in a directory that is in on our path.

> *gcc −o $base/bin/try_me try_me.c*

Now we are ready to write our shell script.

In file go_try:

```
#!/usr/bin/csh

##
## Experiment with the status.
##

echo ---
echo At the top: status = $status
try_me
echo ---
echo After try_me: status = $status
try_me
set val = $status
echo ---
echo After try_me again: val = $val
echo ""
echo ---
echo To exit from the while loop, input 0.
while ($val)
    try_me
    set val = $status
    echo In the loop: val = $val
end
```

DISSECTION OF THE *go_try* SHELL SCRIPT

- ■ `#!/usr/bin/csh`
  A comment starts with a # and continues to the end of the line. This line is special, however, because it begins with #! in column 1 at the top of the file. Lines such as this are read by the operating system. This line tells the operating system to use the C shell, which is /usr/bin/csh, to execute this file.

- ■ `## Experiment with the status.`
  Comments begin with a # and continue to the end of the line.

- ■ `echo ---`
  `echo At the top: status = $status`
  The echo command takes the remainder of the line and writes it to the screen. The symbol $, however, is special. The value of a shell variable is obtained by writing

  $shell_variable_name

  The shell variable `status` is a built-in variable.

■   ```
try_me
echo ---
echo After try_me: status = $status
```
At this point we invoke our program *try_me*. After we have done this, we want to examine the program status. (As we will see, our attempt fails.)

■     ```
try_me
set val = $status
echo ---
echo After try_me again: val = $val
```
After we invoke *try_me* again, we use the *set* command to create a shell variable named val that has, as its value, the current value of $status. (As we shall see, val has the value returned by main() in the program *try_me*.) We use the *echo* command to display $val on the screen.

■   ```
echo To exit from the while loop, input 0.
while ($val)
    try_me
    set val = $status
    echo In the loop: val = $val
end
```
Finally, we enter a loop so we can experiment and see the results printed on the screen.

Our shell script *go_try* is not very informative by itself. When we execute it, however, a lot of new ideas start to fall into place. To make the file executable, we give the command

    *chmod  u+x  go_try*
```

Finally, we give the command

go_try

and enter some numbers when prompted. Here is what appears on the screen:

```
---
At the top: status = 0

>>      Input an integer: 3
>> Value being returned: 3

---
After try_me: status = 0

>>      Input an integer: 7
>> Value being returned: 7

---
After try_me again: val = 7

. . . . .
```

DISSECTION OF THE OUTPUT FROM *go_try*

■   `---`
`At the top: status = 0`
The lines that begin with >> were written by the *try_me* program. The nonblank lines were written by *echo* commands in the shell script *go_try*. Every process resets the value of status upon exiting, and by convention 0 is used to signify normal termination of a process. An *echo* command is itself a process. The very first one we did was

```
echo ---
```

When this process terminated, it set the value of status to 0. This is reflected in the output line

```
At the top: status = 0
```

■   `>>      Input an integer: 3`
`>> Value being returned: 3`
These are lines generated by the *try_me* program. When prompted, we typed a 3 at the keyboard. The second line reports this.

■ ---
   After try_me: status = 0
   At first, this report surprised us, but then we remembered that status is ephemeral. The *echo* command that generated --- reset the status after *try_me*. Hence the value that gets reported is 0, not 3.

■ >>   Input an integer: 7
   >> Value being returned: 7

   After try_me again: val = 7
   After *try_me* is invoked again, we enter 7 when prompted. Immediately after *try_me* exits, we use the shell variable val to capture the current value of $status. In the shell script, the relevant lines are

```
try_me
set val = $status
echo ---
echo After try_me again: val = $val
```

The while loop in the shell script *go_try* allows the user to experiment. We observe that when we enter an integer *n*, the value that gets printed is *n* mod 256. In particular, –1 yields 255. Thus the program status is a nonnegative number between 0 and 255. When main() returns a value to the shell, the shell can use it for its own purposes, if this is desirable.

Although we used the UNIX C shell in our discussion in this section, the story is similar with respect to the other UNIX shells and with respect to MS-DOS.

12.8 SUMMARY

1 A concurrent process is code that executes simultaneously with the code that invoked it. In UNIX, fork() can be used to create a child process that is a copy of the parent process, except that the child has its own unique process identification number. If a call to fork() is successful, it returns 0 to the child and the child's process identification number to the parent; if unsuccessful, it returns –1.

2 In both MS-DOS and UNIX, a member of the exec...() family can be used
   to overlay one process with another. There is no return to the parent. Another
   family, spawn...(), is available in MS-DOS. With this family, it is possible to
   return to the parent. This use, in a certain sense, is comparable to the combined
   use of fork() and exec...() in UNIX.

3 In UNIX, the system call pipe(pd), where pd is a two-dimensional array of
   ints, creates a mechanism for interprocess communications called a pipe. After
   a pipe is open, calls to fork() are used to create processes that communicate
   via the pipe. The functions read() and write() are used.

4 The function signal() is available in the standard library. It can be used to
   associate a signal with a signal handler. The signal handler can be a function
   the programmer writes to replace the default system action. When the signal is
   raised, program control passes to the signal handler. The set of signals that are
   handled by the operating system is defined as macros in *signal.h*. This set is
   system-dependent, but some of the signals are common to both MS-DOS and
   UNIX.

5 The dining philosophers problem is a standard model for synchronizing concurrent processes that share resources. The problem is to write a program with
   concurrent processes representing the philosophers, where each philosopher gets
   to eat (share resources) fairly often.

6 A *semaphore* is a special variable allowing *wait* and *signal* operations. The
   variable is a special location for storing unspecified values. The wait operation
   expects one item and removes it. The signal operation adds one item. The wait
   operation blocks a process until it can accomplish its removal operation. The
   signal operation can start up a blocked process.

7 By starting with the type pointer to pointer to double, we can build a matrix of
   whatever size we want, and we can pass it to functions that are designed to work
   on matrices of any size. This is an important idea for engineers and scientists.

12.9   EXERCISES

1 Modify the simple forking program given in Section 12.1 so that it has three
   copies of the line

   ```
   value = fork();
   ```

   The output of the program is nondeterministic. Explain what this means. *Hint:*
   Execute your program repeatedly.

2 If fork() fails, no child process is created and −1 is returned. Write a program that contains the following code:

```
#define   N   3

for (i = 1; i <= N; ++i) {
    pid = fork();
    if (pid == 0)
        printf("%2d: Hello from child\n", i);
    else if (pid > 0)
        printf("%2d: Hello from parent\n", i);
    else
        printf("%2d: ERROR: Fork did not occur\n", i);
}
```

How large must N be on your system to get an error message printed?

3 In Section 12.2 we presented a program that illustrates how one process gets overlaid with another. Modify that program. Begin by creating another executable file, say *pgm3*, which prints the current date. Provide that as another choice for overlaying the parent process in the program you are modifying.

4 Does the *fortune* command work on your system? If so, find out where the executable code is. Then take one of your working programs and insert code similar to

```
if (fork == 0)
    execl("/usr/games/fortune", "fortune", 0);
```

What is the effect of doing this?

5 Write a program that uses n concurrent processes to multiply two $n \times n$ matrices.

6 Compile two programs into executables named *prog1* and *prog2*. Write a program that executes both concurrently by forking twice and using execl() to overlay the two executables.

7 When a pipe is filled to capacity on your system, how many characters does it hold? Write a program to find out. *Hint:* Write characters into the pipe until it blocks.

8 Change the dining philosophers program so that upon receiving an interrupt it prints out how many times each philosopher has eaten. Also, experiment to see what happens if the pick_up() function is changed so that philosopher number 3 picks up the right chopstick first and everyone else picks up the left chopstick first.

9 How signals are handled is system-dependent. Try the following program on different systems to see what happens:

```
#include <stdio.h>
#include <signal.h>
#include <math.h>            /* HUGE_VAL defined here */

int main(void)
{
    double   x = HUGE_VAL, y = HUGE_VAL;

    signal(SIGFPE, SIG_IGN);
    printf("Ignore signal: x * y = %e\n", x * y);
    signal(SIGFPE, SIG_DFL);
    printf("Default signal: x * y = %e\n", x * y);
    return 0;
}
```

10 Starting with a variable of type double **, we showed how a matrix can be built dynamically and then passed to functions. Do we really have to do it all dynamically? Consider the code

```
int      i;
double   *a[3], det;
double   trace(double **, int);        /* function prototype */

for (i = 0; i < 3; ++i)
    a[i] = calloc(3, sizeof(double));
.....                                   /* fill the matrix a */
tr = trace(a, 3);
```

The array a is being passed as an argument, but from the function prototype we see that an argument of type double ** is needed. Will your compiler complain? Explain.

11 In the 1970s, before C was available to us, we had occasion to use PL/1, a language that is commonly found on IBM mainframes. In the PL/1 manuals it was always stressed that the compiler could create vectors and matrices that started at any desired index. For example, a declaration of the form

```
int    automobiles[1989 : 1999];   /* a PL/1 style declaration */
```

would create an array of size 11, with its index starting at 1989. This array could be used to store the number of automobiles sold, or projected to be sold, in the years 1989 to 1999. Perhaps one reason this concept was stressed was that FORTRAN and other languages were not able to create such arrays. In C, of course, such an array can be created. Explain how this is done.

12 Filling matrices with integers that are randomly distributed in the range from $-N$ to $+N$ is convenient for testing purposes. If you are checking machine computations by hand, then a reasonable value for N is 2 or 3. Write a function that fills matrices.

```
void fill_matrix(double **a, int m, int n, int N)
{
    . . . . .
```

13 Let $A = (a_{ij})$ be an $n \times n$ matrix. The determinant of A can be computed using Gaussian elimination. This algorithm requires that for $k = 1$ to $n - 1$ we do the following: Start with a_{kk} and examine all the elements in its column that are below a_{kk}, including a_{kk} itself. Among those elements find the one that is the largest in absolute value. This element is called the *pivot*. If the pivot is in the ith row, and i is not equal to k, then interchange the ith and kth rows. (Keep track of the number of interchanges that are performed.) After this has been done, a_{kk} will be the pivot. If this value is zero, then the value of the determinant is zero and the algorithm is finished. Otherwise, for $i = k + 1$ to n add a multiple of the kth row to the ith row, where the multiple is given by $(-1/a_{kk}) \times a_{ik}$. The final step is to take the product of the diagonal elements of the matrix. If the number of row interchanges in the algorithm is even, then this product is the determinant. Otherwise, the negative of this product is the determinant. In this exercise you are to write a program that computes the determinant of $n \times n$ matrices. Use the function get_matrix_space() so that subscripts start at 1 rather than 0. *Hint:* Use hand simulation of the algorithm on a small matrix first so you understand the details of the algorithm.

```
for (k = 1; k <= n; ++k) {
   find the pivot element
   if the pivot is zero, return zero
   if the pivot is in the ith row, and i != k,
       then interchange the ith row with the kth row
       and increment the interchange counter i_cnt
   pivot = a[k][k];
   for (i = k + 1; i <= n; ++i) {
      multiplier = -a[i][k] * (1.0 / pivot);
      for (j = k; j <= n; ++j)
        a[i][j] += multiplier * a[k][j];
   }
}
if (i_cnt % 2 == 0)
   det = 1.0;
else
   det = -1.0;
for (i = 1; i <= n; ++i)
   det *= a[i][i];
return det;
```

14 One way to get a three-dimensional array is to make a declaration such as

```
double    a[9][2][7];
```

Suppose we want to pass this array to a function, and we want the function to work on three-dimensional arrays of various sizes. Because the function definition will require the 2 and the 7 to build the correct storage mapping function, implementing a as an array of arrays will not work. Instead, we can write

```
int      i, j, n1, n2, n3;
double   ***a;

.....                              /* get sizes from somewhere */
a = calloc(n1, sizeof(int **));
for (i = 0; i < n1: ++i) {
   a[i] = calloc(n2, sizeof(double *));
   for (j = 0; j < n2; ++j)
      a[i][j] = calloc(n3, sizeof(double));
}
```

Draw a picture of how a can be thought of in memory. Write a program that implements this scheme. Your program should get the sizes from the user interactively, allocate space for the three-dimensional array, and fill the array with randomly distributed integers from a small range. Note that each a[i] can be thought of as a matrix. Print the array on the screen by first printing a[0], then a[1], and so forth. Finally, print the sum of all the elements of the array. Use a function to compute this sum.

15 Consider the following program:

```
#include <stdio.h>

#define   N   3

double    trace(double *a[]);

int main(void)
{
  double    a[N][N] = {1, 2, 3, 4, 5, 6, 7, 8, 9};

  printf("The trace of a is %.3f\n", trace(a));
  return 0;
}

double trace(double **a)
{
    int       i, j;
    double    sum = 0.0;;

    for (i = 0; i < N; ++i)      /* N is hardwired in the body */
       for (j = 0; j < N; ++j)
           sum += a[i][j];
    return sum;
}
```

The compiler complains about the call trace(a). If we change this to

```
trace((double [N][N]) a)
```

will the compiler be happy? Will the code work? Explain.

16 Remote procedure call (RPC) is used in distributed systems to execute code on
    other machines on a network. First, the program running on the local machine,
    called a *client*, sends a request to the second machine, called a *server*. The server
    calls a routine to perform the requested service. Finally, the results of the request
    are returned to the client. The following code is based on Sun Microsystems
    RPC and was written by Darrell Long:

```
/*
// SUN MICROSYSTEMS RPC code.
// compile with acc rpc.c -lrpcsvc
*/

#include <stdio.h>
#include <rpc/rpc.h>
#include <rpcsvc/rstat.h>

/*
// Poll the host.
*/
void do_poll(char *host) {
    int      stat;
    struct   statstime result_stats;

    stat = callrpc(host, RSTATPROG, RSTATVERS_TIME,
                   RSTATPROC_STATS, xdr_void, 0,
                   xdr_statstime, &result_stats);
    if (stat == RPC_SUCCESS)
       fprintf(stdout, "DATA %s %ld %ld\n", host,
           result_stats.boottime.tv_sec,
           result_stats.curtime.tv_sec);
}

int main(void)
{
    do_poll("machine..school.edu"); /*polled machine*/
    return 0;
}
```

Run this code across your local network. Look in the file

/usr/include/rpcsvc/rstat.h

to figure out what these statistics mean.

CHAPTER **13**

MOVING FROM C TO C++

This chapter gives an overview of the C++ programming language. It also provides an introduction to C++'s use as an object-oriented programming language. In the chapter a series of programs is presented, and the elements of each program are carefully explained. The programs increase in complexity, and the examples in the later sections illustrate some of the concepts of object-oriented programming.

The examples in this chapter give simple, immediate, hands-on experience with key features of the C++ language. The chapter introduces the reader to stream I/O, operator and function overloading, reference parameters, classes, constructors, destructors, and inheritance. Mastery of the individual topics requires a thorough reading of a companion book such as either Pohl, *C++ for C Programmers*, 2d Ed. (Redwood City, Ca.: Benjamin/Cummings, 1993) or Pohl, *Object-Oriented Programming Using C++* (Redwood City, Ca.: Benjamin/Cummings, 1993).

Object-oriented programming is implemented by the `class` construct. The `class` construct in C++ is an extension of `struct` in C. The later examples in this chapter illustrate how C++ implements OOP (object-oriented programming) concepts, such as data hiding, ADTs, inheritance, and type hierarchies.

13.1 OUTPUT

Programs must communicate to be useful. Our first example is a program that prints on the screen the phrase "C++ is an improved C." The complete program is

```
// A first C++ program illustrating output.
//    Title:  Improved
//    Author: Richmond Q. Programmer

#include <iostream.h>

int main()
{
    cout << "C++ is an improved C.\n";
    return 0;
}
```

The program prints on the screen

```
C++ is an improved C.
```

DISSECTION OF THE *improved* PROGRAM

- ■ `// A first C++ program illustrating output.`
  The double slash `//` is a new comment symbol. The comment runs to the end of the line. The old C bracketing comment symbols `/* */` are still available for multiline comments.

- ■ `#include <iostream.h>`
  The *iostream.h* header introduces I/O facilities for C++.

- ■ `int main()`
  In C++ the empty parentheses always mean `main(void)`, never `main(...)`. C++ style is not to use the redundant `void` for declaring the empty argument list.

- ■ `cout << "C++ is an improved C.\n";`
  This statement prints to the screen. The identifier `cout` is the name of the standard output stream. The operator `<<` passes the string `"C++ is an improved C.\n"` to standard out. Used in this way the *output operator* `<<` is referred to as the *put to* or *insertion* operator.

- ■ `return 0;`
  A value of zero is returned to the system, indicating the successful completion of the program. Most systems allow you to ignore this requirement, or will give you a warning if you fail to return a value from `main()`.

We can rewrite our first program as follows:

```
// A first C++ program illustrating output.

#include <iostream.h>

main()
{
    cout << "C++ is an improved C." << endl;
    return 0;
}
```

Although it is different from the first version, it produces the same output. This version drops the explicit declaration of `main()` as returning an `int` and uses the fact that this `return` type is implicit. Here we use the output operator `<<` *put to* twice. Each time the `<<` is used with `cout`, printing continues from the position where it previously left off. In this case, the identifier `endl` forces a new line followed by a *flush*. The `endl` is called a *manipulator*.

13.2 INPUT

We will write a program to convert to kilometers the distance in miles from the **Earth** to the moon. In miles this distance is, on average, 238,857 miles. This number is an integer. To convert miles to kilometers, we multiply by the conversion factor 1.609, a real number.

Our conversion program will use variables capable of storing integer values and real values. In C++ all variables must be declared before their use, but unlike in C, they need not be at the head of a block. Declarations may be mixed in with executable statements. Their scope is from the point of the declaration to the end of the block within which they are declared. Identifiers should be chosen to reflect their use in the program. In this way, they serve as documentation, making the program more readable.

These programs assume a 4-byte `int`, but on some machines these variables should be declared `long`. You can check the constant INT_MAX in *limits.h*.

```
// The distance to the moon converted to kilometers.
//    Title: moon

#include <iostream.h>

int main()
{
    const int moon = 238857;

    cout << "The moon's distance from Earth is " << moon;
    cout << " miles." << endl;

    int moon_kilo = moon * 1.609;

    cout << "In kilometers this is " << moon_kilo;
    cout << " km." << endl;
    return 0;
}
```

The output of the program is

```
The moon's distance from Earth is 238857 miles.
In kilometers this is 384320 km.
```

DISSECTION OF THE *moon* PROGRAM

■ `const int moon = 238857;`
The keyword `const` is new in C++. It replaces some uses of the preprocessor command `define` to create named literals. Using this type modifier informs the compiler that the initialized value of `moon` cannot be changed. Thus it makes `moon` a symbolic constant.

■ `cout << "The moon's distance from Earth is " << moon;`
The stream I/O in C++ can discriminate among a variety of simple values without needing additional formatting information. Here the value of `moon` will be printed as an integer.

■ `int moon_kilo = moon * 1.609;`
Declarations can occur after executable statements. This allows declarations of variables to be nearer to their use.

Let us write a program that will convert a series of values from miles to kilometers. The program will be interactive. The user will type in a value in miles, and the program will convert this value to kilometers and print it out.

```
// Miles are converted to kilometers.
//   Title: mi_km

#include <iostream.h>
const double m_to_k = 1.609;
inline int convert(int mi) { return (mi * m_to_k); }

int main()
{
    int miles;

    do {
        cout << "Input distance in miles: ";
        cin >> miles;
        cout << "\nDistance is " << convert(miles) << " km." << endl;
    } while (miles > 0);
    return 0;
}
```

This program uses the input stream variable cin, which is normally standard input. The *input operator* >> is called the *get from* or *extraction* operator, which assigns values from the input stream to a variable. This program illustrates both input and output.

DISSECTION OF THE *mi_km* PROGRAM

■ const double m_to_k = 1.609;
C++ reduces C's traditional reliance on the preprocessor. For example, instead of having to use define, special constants, such as the conversion factor 1.609, are simply assigned to variables specified as constants.

■ inline int convert(int mi) { return (mi * m_to_k); }
The new keyword inline specifies that a function is to be compiled, if possible as inline code. This avoids function call overhead and is better practice than C's use of define macros. As a rule, inline should be done sparingly and only on short functions. Also note how the parameter mi is declared within the function parentheses. C++ uses *function prototypes* to define and declare functions. This will be explained in the next section.

■ do {
    cout << "Input distance in miles: ";
    cin >> miles;
    cout << "\nDistance is " << convert(miles) << " km." << endl;
} while (miles > 0);
The program repeatedly prompts the user for a distance in miles. The program is terminated by a zero or negative value. The value placed in the standard input stream is automatically converted to an integer value assigned to miles.

13.3 FUNCTIONS

The syntax of functions in C++ inspired the new function prototype syntax found in Standard C compilers. Basically, the types of parameters are listed inside the header parentheses. By explicitly listing the type and number of arguments, strong type checking and assignment-compatible conversions are possible in C++.

C++ allows functions to have arguments directly called by reference. Call-by-reference parameters are declared using the syntax

type& identifier

Also C++ function parameters can have default values. These are given in the function declaration inside the parameter list by

   = *expression*

added after the parameter.

The following example illustrates these points:

```
// Title: add3

#include <iostream.h>

// Use of a default value
inline void add3(int& s, int a, int b, int c = 0)
{
    s = a + b + c;
}

inline double average(int s) { return (s / 3.0); }

int main()
{
    int    score_1, score_2, score_3, sum, wtd_sum;

    cout << "\nEnter 3 scores: ";
    cin >> score_1 >> score_2 >> score_3;
    add3(sum, score_1, score_2, score_3);
    add3(wtd_sum, 2 * score_1, score_2);       // use default value 0
    cout << "            sum = " << sum << endl;
    cout << "            avg = " << average(sum) << endl;
    cout << "weighted sum = " << wtd_sum << endl;
    cout << "weighted avg = " << average(wtd_sum) << endl;
    return 0;
}
```

DISSECTION OF THE *add3* PROGRAM

- ```
  inline void add3(int& s, int a, int b, int c = 0)
  {
      s = a + b + c;
  }
  ```
  The variable s is call-by-reference. An actual argument passed in must be an lvalue, because that will be the actual address used when the procedure is called.
  ```

- add3(sum, score_1, score_2, score_3);
  The variable sum is passed by reference. Therefore it is directly manipulated and can be used to obtain a result from the function's computation.

- add3(wtd_sum, 2 * score_1, score_2); // use default value 0
  Here only three actual arguments are used in calling add3(). The fourth argument defaults to value zero.

13.4 CLASSES AND ABSTRACT DATA TYPES

What is novel about C++ is its aggregate type class. A class is an extension of the idea of struct in traditional C. A class provides the means for implementing a user-defined data type and associated functions and operators. Therefore a class can be used to implement an ADT. Let us write a class called string that will implement a restricted form of string.

```
// An elementary implementation of type string.

#include <string.h>
#include <iostream.h>

const int max_len = 255;

class string {
public:          // universal access
   void assign(const char* st) { strcpy(s, st); len = strlen(st); }
   int  length() { return len; }
   void print() { cout << s << "\nLength: " << len << "\n"; }
private:         // restricted access to member functions
   char s[max_len];    // implementation by character array
   int  len;
};
```

Two important additions to the structure concept of traditional C are found in this example: (1) It has members that are functions, such as assign, and (2) it has both public and private members. The keyword public indicates the visibility of the members that follow it. Without this keyword the members are private to the class. Private members are available for use only by other member functions of the class. Public members are available to any function within the scope of the class declaration. Privacy allows part of the implementation of a class type to be "hidden." This restriction prevents unanticipated modifications to the data structure. Restricted access, or *data hiding*, is a feature of object-oriented programming.

The declaration of member functions allows the ADT to have particular functions act on its private representation. For example, the member function `length` returns the length of the string defined to be the number of characters up to but excluding the first zero value character. The member function `print` outputs both the string and its length. The member function `assign` stores a character string into the hidden variable `s` and computes and stores its length in the hidden variable `len`.

We can now use this data type `string` as if it were a basic type of the language. It obeys the standard block structure scope rules of C. Other code that uses this type is a *client*. The client can use only the public members to act on variables of type `string`.

```
// Test of the class string.

int main()
{
    string  one, two;
    char    three[40] = {"My name is Charles Babbage."};

    one.assign("My name is Alan Turing.");
    two.assign(three);
    cout << three;
    cout << "\nLength: " << strlen(three) << endl;
    // Print shorter of one and two.
    if (one.length() <= two.length())
        one.print();
    else
        two.print();
    return 0;
}
```

The variables `one` and `two` are of type `string`. The variable `three` is of type pointer to `char` and is not compatible with `string`. The member functions are called using the dot operator or "structure member operator." As is seen from their definitions, these member functions act on the hidden private member fields of the named variables. One cannot write inside `main` the expression `one.len` expecting to access this member. The output of this example program is

```
My name is Charles Babbage.
Length: 27
My name is Alan Turing.
Length: 23
```

13.5 OVERLOADING

The term *overloading* refers to the practice of giving several meanings to an operator or a function. The meaning selected depends on the types of the arguments used by the operator or function. Let us overload the function `print` in the previous example. This will be a second definition of the `print` function.

```
class string {
public:            // universal access
   .....
   void print() { cout << s << "\nLength: " << len << "\n"; }
   void print(int n)
   {
      for(int i = 0; i < n; ++i)
         cout << s << endl;
   }
   .....
}
```

This version of `print` takes a single argument of type `int`. It will print the string n times.

```
three.print(2);    // print string three twice
three.print(-1);   // string three is not printed
```

It is also possible to overload most of the C operators. For example, let us overload + to mean concatenate two strings. To do this we need two new keywords: `friend` and `operator`. The keyword `operator` precedes the operator token and replaces what would otherwise be a function name in a function declaration. The keyword `friend` gives a function access to the private members of a class variable. A `friend` function is not a member of the class but has the privileges of a member function in the class in which it is declared.

```
// Overloading the operator + .

#include <string.h>
#include <iostream.h>

const int max_len = 255;

class string {
public:
    void assign(const char* st) { strcpy(s, st); len = strlen(st); }
    int  length() { return len; }
    void print() { cout << s << "\nLength: " << len << endl; }
    friend string operator+(const string& a, const string& b);
private:
    char s[max_len];
    int  len;
};

string operator+(const string& a, const string& b)    // overload +
{
    string temp;

    temp.assign(a.s);
    temp.len = a.len + b.len;
    if (temp.len < max_len)
        strcat(temp.s, b.s);
    else
        cerr << "Max length exceeded in concatenation.\n";
    return temp;
}

void print(const char* c)    // file scope print definition
{
    cout << c << "\nLength: " << strlen(c) << "\n";
}
```

```
int main()
{
    string    one, two, both;
    char      three[40] = {"My name is Charles Babbage."};

    one.assign("My name is Alan Turing.");
    two.assign(three);
    print(three);              // file scope print called
    // Print shorter of one and two.
    if (one.length() <= two.length())
        one.print();           // member function print called
    else
        two.print();
    both = one + two;          // plus overloaded to be concatenate
    both.print();
    return 0;
}
```

DISSECTION OF THE *operator+* FUNCTION

■ string operator+(const string& a, const string& b)
   Plus is overloaded. The two arguments it will take are both strings. The arguments are call-by-reference. Use of **const** indicates that the arguments cannot be modified.

■ string temp;
   The function needs to return a value of type **string**. This local variable will be used to store and return the concatenated string value.

■ temp.assign(a.s);
   temp.len = a.len + b.len;
   if (temp.len < max_len)
       strcat(temp.s, b.s);
   The string a.s is copied into temp.s by calling the strcpy library function. The length of the resulting concatenated string is tested to see that it does not exceed the maximum length for strings. If the length is acceptable, the standard library function strcat is called with the hidden string members temp.s and b.s. The references to temp.s, a.s, and b.s are allowed because this function is a friend of class string.

■ cerr << "Max length exceeded in concatenation.\n";
   The standard error stream cerr is used to print an error message, and no concatenation takes place. Only the first string will be returned.

■   `return temp;`

The operator was given a return type of `string`, and `temp` has been assigned the appropriate concatenated string.

13.6   CONSTRUCTORS AND DESTRUCTORS

A *constructor* is a member function whose job is to *initialize* a variable of its class. In OOP terms, such a variable is an *object*. In many cases this involves dynamic storage allocation. Constructors are invoked any time an object of its associated class is created. A *destructor* is a member function whose job is to deallocate, or *finalize*, a variable of its class. The destructor is called implicitly when an automatic object goes out of scope.

Let us change our `string` example by dynamically allocating storage for each `string` variable. We will replace the private array variable by a pointer. The remodeled class will use a constructor to allocate an appropriate amount of storage dynamically using the `new` operator.

```
// An implementation of dynamically allocated strings.

class string {
public:
    string(int n) { s = new char[n + 1]; len = n; }  // constructor
    void assign(const char* st) { strcpy(s, st); len = strlen(t); }
    int   length() { return len; }
    void print() { cout << s << "\nLength: " << len << "\n"; }
    friend string operator+(const string& a, const string& b);
private:
    char* s;
    int   len;
};
```

A constructor is a member function whose name is the same as the class name. The keyword `new` is an addition to the C language. It is a unary operator that takes as an argument a data type that can include an array size. It allocates the appropriate amount of memory from free store to store this type, and returns the pointer value that addresses this memory. In the preceding example, n + 1 bytes would be allocated from free store. Thus the declaration

```
string a(40), b(100);
```

would allocate 41 bytes for the variable a, pointed at by a.s , and 101 bytes for the variable b, pointed at by b.s. We add 1 byte for the end-of-string value 0. Storage obtained by new is persistent and is not automatically returned on block exit. When storage return is desired, a destructor function must be included in the class. A destructor is written as an ordinary member function whose name is the same as the class name preceded by the tilde symbol ~. Typically, a destructor uses the unary operator delete, another addition to the language, to automatically deallocate storage associated with a pointer expression.

```
// Add as a member function to class string.
~string() { delete []s; }    // destructor
```

It is usual to overload the constructor, writing a variety of such functions to accommodate more than one style of initialization. Consider initializing a string with a pointer to char value. Such a constructor is

```
string(const char* p)
{
    len = strlen(p);
    s = new char[len + 1];
    strcpy(s, p);
}
```

A typical declaration invoking this version of the constructor is

```
char*    str = "I came on foot.";
string   a("I came by bus."), b(str);
```

It would also be desirable to have a constructor of no arguments:

```
string() { len = 255; s = new char[255]; }
```

This would be invoked by declarations without parenthesized arguments and would, by default, allocate 255 bytes of memory. Now all three constructors would be invoked in the following declaration:

```
string   a, b(10), c("I came by horse.");
```

The overloaded constructor is selected by the form of each declaration. The variable a has no parameters and so is allocated 255 bytes. The variable b has an integer parameter and so is allocated 11 bytes. The variable c has a pointer parameter to the literal string "I came by horse." and so is allocated 17 bytes, with this literal string copied into its private s member.

13.7   OBJECT-ORIENTED PROGRAMMING AND INHERITANCE

A novel concept in OOP is the *inheritance* mechanism. This is the mechanism of *deriving* a new class from an existing one called the *base class*. The derived class adds to or alters the inherited base class members. This is used to share code and interface, and to create a hierarchy of related types.

Hierarchy is a method for coping with complexity. It imposes classifications on objects. For example, the periodic table of elements has elements that are gasses. These have properties that are shared by all elements in that classification. Inert gasses are an important special class of gasses. The hierarchy here is: An inert gas, such as argon, is a gas, which, in turn, is an element. This hierarchy provides a convenient way to understand the behavior of inert gasses. We know they are composed of protons and electrons, as this is shared description with all elements. We know they are in a gaseous state at room temperature, as this behavior is shared with all gasses. We know they do not combine in ordinary chemical reactions with other elements, as this is shared behavior with all inert gasses.

Consider designing a data base for a college. The registrar must track different types of students. The base class we need to develop captures a description of "student." Two main categories of student are graduate and undergraduate.

The OOP design methodology becomes:

1 Decide on an appropriate set of types.
2 Design in their relatedness, and use inheritance to share code.

An example of deriving a class is:

```
enum support {ta, ra, fellowship, other};
enum year {fresh, soph, junior, senior, grad};

class student {
public:
   student(char* nm, int id, double g, year x);
   void  print();
private:
   int        student_id;
   double     gpa;
   year       y;
   char       name[30];
};

class grad_student: public student {
public:
   grad_student (char* nm, int id, double g,
       year x, support t, char* d, char* th);
   void print();
private:
   support    s;
   char       dept[10];
   char       thesis[80];
};
```

In this example, grad_student is the derived class, and student is the base class. The use of the keyword public following the colon in the derived class header means that the public members of student are to be inherited as public members of grad_student. Private members of the base class cannot be accessed in the derived class. Public inheritance also means that the derived class grad_student is a subtype of student.

An inheritance structure provides a design for the overall system. For example, a data base that contained all the people at a college could be derived from the base class person. The student-grad_student relation could be extended to extension students, as a further significant category of objects. Similarly, person could be the base class for a variety of employee categories.

13.8   POLYMORPHISM

A *polymorphic* function has many forms. An example in Standard C is the division operator. If the arguments to the division operator are integral, then integer division is used. However, if one or both arguments are floating-point, then floating-point division is used.

In C++, a function name or operator is overloadable. A function is called based on its *signature*, defined as the list of argument types in its parameter list.

```
a / b          // divide behavior determined by native coercions

cout << a    // ad-hoc polymorphism through function overloading
```

In the division expression, the result depends on the arguments being automatically coerced to the widest type. So if both arguments are integer, the result is an integer division. If one or both arguments are floating-point, the result is floating-point. In the output statement, the shift operator << is invoking a function that is able to output an object of type a.

Polymorphism localizes responsibility for behavior. The client code frequently requires no revision when additional functionality is added to the system through ADT-provided code improvements.

In C, the technique for implementing a package of routines to provide an ADT shape would rely on a comprehensive structural description of any shape.

```
struct shape{ enum{CIRCLE, ...} e_val; double center, radius; ...};
```

would have all the members necessary for any shape currently drawable in our system, plus an enumerator value so that it can be identified. The area routine would then be written as

```
double area(shape* s)
{
  switch(s -> e_val) {
  case CIRCLE:  return (PI * s -> radius * s -> radius);
  case RECTANGLE: return (s -> height * s -> width);
  .....
}
```

Question: What is involved in revising this C code to include a new shape? *Answer*: An additional case in the code body and additional members in the structure. Unfortunately, these would have ripple effects throughout our entire code body. Each routine so structured has to have an additional case, even when that case is just adding a label to a preexisting case. Thus what is conceptually a local improvement requires global changes.

OOP coding techniques in C++ for the same problem uses a shape hierarchy. The hierarchy is the obvious one where circle and rectangle are derived from shape. The revision process is one in which code improvements are provided in a new derived class, so additional description is localized. The programmer overrides the meaning of any changed routines—in this case, the new area calculation. Client code that does not use the new type is unaffected. Client code that is improved by the new type is typically minimally changed.

C++ code following this design uses shape as an *abstract base class*. This is a class containing one or more pure virtual functions.

```cpp
// shape is an abstract base class
class shape {
public:
    virtual double area() = 0; // pure virtual function
};

class rectangle: public shape {
public:
    rectangle(double h, double w): height(h), width(w) {}
    double area() { return (height * width); }    // overridden fct
private:
    double height, width;
};

class circle: public shape {
public:
    circle(double r): radius(r) {}
    double area() { return ( 3.14159 * radius * radius); }
private:
    double radius;
};
```

Client code for computing an arbitrary area is polymorphic. The appropriate `area()` function is selected at run-time.

```
shape*  ptr_shape;

    . . . . .
    cout << " area = " << ptr_shape -> area();
    . . . . .
```

Now imagine improving our hierarchy of types by developing a `square` class.

```
class square: public rectangle {
public:
    square(double h): rectangle(h,h) {}
    double area() { return rectangle::area(); }
};
```

The client code remains unchanged. This would not have been the case with the non-OOP code.

13.9 TEMPLATES

C++ uses the keyword `template` to provide *parametric polymorphism*. Parametric polymorphism allows the same code to be used with respect to different types, where the type is a parameter of the code body. The code is written generically to act on `class T`. The template is used to generate different actual classes when `class T` is substituted for with an actual type.

An especially important use for this technique is in writing generic *container classes*. A container class is used to contain data of a particular type. Stacks, vectors, trees, and lists are all examples of standard container classes. We shall develop a stack *container* class as a parameterized type.

```
typedef boolean int;
const boolean true = 1;
const boolean false = 0;

// template stack implementation
template <class TYPE>
class stack {
public:
    stack(int size = 1000) :max_len(size)
        { s = new TYPE[size]; top = EMPTY; }
    ~stack() { delete []s; }
    void reset() { top = EMPTY; }
    void push(TYPE c) { s[++top] = c; }
    TYPE pop() { return s[top--]; }
    TYPE top_of() { return s[top]; }
    boolean empty() { return top == EMPTY; }
    boolean full() { return top == max_len - 1; }
private:
    enum   {EMPTY = -1};
    TYPE* s;
    int    max_len;
    int    top;
};
```

The syntax of the class declaration is prefaced by

template <class *identifier* >

This identifier is a template argument that essentially stands for an arbitrary type. Throughout the class definition, the template argument can be used as a type name. This argument is instantiated in the actual declarations. An example of a stack declaration using this is

```
stack<char> stk_ch;            // 1000 element char stack
stack<char*>  stk_str(200);    // 200 element char* stack
stack<complex> stk_cmplx(100); // 100 element complex stack
```

This mechanism saves us rewriting class declarations where the only variation would be type declarations.

When processing such a type, the code must always use the angle brackets as part of the declaration. Here are two functions using the stack template:

```
// Reversing a series of char* represented strings
void reverse(char* str[], int n)
{
    stack<char*> stk(n);    // this stack holds char*

    for (int i = 0; i < n; ++i)
        stk.push(str[i]);
    for (i = 0; i < n; ++i)
        str[i] = stk.pop();
}
```

In function reverse() a stack<char*> is used to insert n strings and then pops them in reverse order.

```
// Initializing a stack of complex numbers from an array
void init(complex c[], stack<complex>& stk, n)
{
    for (int i = 0; i < n; ++i)
        stk.push(c[i]);
}
```

In function init(), a stack<complex> variable is passed by reference, and n complex numbers are pushed onto this stack.

13.10   C++ EXCEPTIONS

C++ introduces an exception-handling mechanism that is sensitive to context. The context for raising an exception will be a try block. Handlers declared using the keyword catch are found at the end of a try block.

An exception is raised by using the throw expression. The exception will be handled by invoking an appropriate *handler* selected from a list of handlers found immediately after the handler's `try` block. A simple example of all this is

```
// stack constructor with exceptions
stack::stack(int n)
{
    if (n < 1)
        throw (n);          // want a positive value
    p = new char[n];        // create a stack of characters
    if (p == 0)             // new returns 0 when it fails
        throw ("FREE STORE EXHAUSTED");
}

void g()
{
    try {
        stack   a(n), b(n);
        .....

    }
    catch (int n) { ... }                // an incorrect size
    catch (char* error) { ... }          // free store exhaustion
}
```

The first `throw()` has an integer argument and matches the `catch(int n)` signature. This handler is expected to perform an appropriate action where an incorrect array size has been passed as an argument to the constructor. For example, an error message and abort are normal. The second `throw()` has a pointer to `char` argument and matches the `catch(char* error)` signature.

13.11 BENEFITS OF OBJECT-ORIENTED PROGRAMMING

The central element of OOP is the encapsulation of an appropriate set of data types and their operations. The class construct, with its member functions and data members, provides an appropriate coding tool. Class variables are the *objects* to be manipulated.

Classes also provide data hiding. Access privileges can be managed and limited to whatever group of functions needs access to implementation details. This promotes modularity and robustness.

Another important concept in OOP is the promotion of code reuse through the *inheritance* mechanism. This is the mechanism of *deriving* a new class from an existing one called the *base class*. The base class can be added to or altered to create the derived class. In this way a hierarchy of related data types can be created that share code.

Many useful data structures are variants of one another, and it is frequently tedious to produce the same code for each. A derived class inherits the description of the base class. It can then be altered by adding additional members, overloading existing member functions, and modifying access privileges. Without this reuse mechanism, each minor variation would require code replication.

The OOP programming task is frequently more difficult than normal procedural programming as found in C. There is at least one extra design step before one gets to the coding of algorithms. This involves the hierarchy of types that is useful for the problem at hand. Frequently, one is solving the problem more generally than is strictly necessary.

The belief is that OOP will pay dividends in several ways. The solution will be more encapsulated and thus more robust and easier to maintain and change. Also, the solution will be more reusable. For example, where the code needs a stack, that stack is easily borrowed from existing code. In an ordinary procedural language, such a data structure is frequently "wired into" the algorithm and cannot be exported.

All these benefits are especially important for large coding projects that require coordination among many programmers. Here the ability to have header files specify general interfaces for different classes allows each programmer to work on individual code segments with a high degree of independence and integrity.

OOP is many things to many people. Attempts at defining it are reminiscent of the story of the blind sages attempting to describe an elephant. We will offer one more equation:

$$OOP \ = \ type\text{-}extensibility \ + \ polymorphism$$

13.12   SUMMARY

1 The double slash // is a new comment symbol. The comment runs to the end of the line. The old C bracketing comment symbols /* */ are still available for multiline comments.

2 The *iostream.h* header introduces I/O facilities for C++. The identifier cout is the name of the standard output stream. The operator << passes its argument to standard out. Used in this way, the << is referred to as the *put to* operator. The identifier cin is the name of the standard input stream. The operator >> is the input operator, called *get from*, that assigns values from the input stream to a variable.

3 C++ reduces C's traditional reliance on the preprocessor. Instead of using define, special constants are assigned to variables specified as const. The new keyword inline specifies that a function is to be compiled inline to avoid function call overhead. As a rule, this should be done sparingly and only on short functions.

4 The syntax of functions in C++ inspired the new function prototype syntax found in Standard C compilers. Basically, the types of parameters are listed inside the header parentheses—for example, `void add3(int&, int, int, int)`. Call-by-reference is available as well as default parameter values. By explicitly listing the type and number of arguments, strong type checking and assignment-compatible conversions are possible in C++.

5 What is novel about C++ is the aggregate type `class`. A `class` is an extension of the idea of `struct` in traditional C. Its use is a way of implementing a data type and associated functions, and operators. Therefore a `class` is an implementation of an abstract data type (ADT). There are two important additions to the structure concept: (1) It includes members that are functions, and (2) it employs access keywords `public`, `private`, and `protected`. These keywords indicate the visibility of the members that follow. Public members are available to any function within the scope of the class declaration. Private members are available for use only by other member functions of the class. Protected members are available for use only by other member functions of the class and by derived classes. Privacy allows part of the implementation of a class type to be "hidden."

6 The term *overloading* refers to the practice of giving several meanings to an operator or a function. The meaning selected will depend on the types of the arguments used by the operator or function.

7 A constructor is a member function whose job is to initialize a variable of its class. In many cases this involves dynamic storage allocation. Constructors are invoked any time an object of its associated class is created. A destructor is a member function whose job is to finalize a variable of its class. The destructor is invoked implicitly when an automatic object goes out of scope.

8 The central element of object-oriented programming (OOP) is the encapsulation of an appropriate set of data types and their operations. These user-defined types are ADTs. The class construct, with its member functions and data members, provides an appropriate coding tool. Class variables are the *objects* to be manipulated.

9 Another important concept in OOP is the promotion of code reuse through the *inheritance* mechanism. This is the mechanism of *deriving* a new class from an existing one, called the *base class*. The base class can be added to or altered to create the derived class. In this way a hierarchy of related data types can be created that share code. This typing hierarchy can be used dynamically by `virtual` functions. Virtual member functions in a base class are overloaded in a derived class. These functions allow for dynamic or run-time typing. A pointer to the base class can also point at objects of the derived classes. When such a pointer is used to point at the overloaded virtual function, it dynamically selects which version of the member function to call.

10 A *polymorphic* function has many forms. A `virtual` function allows run-time selection from a group of functions overridden within a type hierarchy. An example in the text is the area calculation within the `shape` hierarchy. Client code for computing an arbitrary area is polymorphic. The appropriate `area()` function is selected at run-time.

11 C++ uses the keyword `template` to provide *parametric polymorphism*. Parametric polymorphism allows the same code to be used with respect to different types, where the type is a parameter of the code body. The code is written generically to act on `class T`. The template is used to generate different actual classes when `class T` is substituted for with an actual type.

12 C++ introduces an exception-handling mechanism that is sensitive to context. The context for raising an exception will be a `try` block. Handlers declared using the keyword `catch` are found at the end of a `try` block. An exception is raised by using the `throw` expression. The exception will be handled by invoking an appropriate *handler* selected from a list of handlers found immediately after the handler's `try` block.

13.13 EXERCISES

1 Using stream I/O, write on the screen the words

   `she sells sea shells by the seashore`

   (a) all on one line, (b) on three lines, (c) inside a box.

2 Write a program that will convert distances measured in yards to distances measured in meters. The relationship is 1 meter equals 1.0936 yards. Write the program to use `cin` to read in distances. The program should be a loop that does this calculation until it receives a zero or negative number for input.

3 Write a factorial program using the type `Big_Int`. This type or a variant—check your local C++ library—is an arbitrary size integer type. Note that the program looks like an ordinary C program, except that the include file imports the type `Big_Int`.

4 Take a working program, omit each line in turn, and run it through the compiler. Record the error messages each such deletion causes. For example, use the following code:

```
#include <iostream.h>

int main()
{
    int  m, n, k;
    cout << "\nEnter two integers: ";
    cin  >> m >> n;
    k = m + n;
    cout << "\nTheir sum is " << k << ".\n";
    return 0;
}
```

5 Write a program that asks interactively for your *name* and *age* and responds with

Hello *name*, next year you will be *next_age*.

where *next_age* is *age* + 1 .

6 Write a program that prints out a table of squares, square roots, and cubes. Use either tabbing or strings of blanks to get a neatly aligned table.

```
i        i * i       square root      i * i * i
-------------------------------------------------
1          1       1.00000              1
. . . . .
```

7 The C swapping function is

```
void swap(int *i, int *j)
{
    int  temp;

    temp = *i;
    *i = *j;
    *j = temp;
}
```

Rewrite this using reference parameters and test it.

```
void swap(int& i, int& j);
```

8   In traditional C, the following code causes an error:

```
#include <math.h>
#include <stdio.h>

int main()
{
    printf("%f is the square root of 2.\n", sqrt(2));
    return 0;
}
```

Explain the reason for this and why function prototypes in C++ avoid this problem. Rewrite using *iostream.h*.

9   Add to the class `string` a member function `reverse`. This function reverses
the underlying representation of the character sequence stored in the private
member s.

10   Add to the class `string` a member function `void print(int pos, int k)`.
This function overloads `print()` and is meant to print the k characters of the
string starting at position `pos`.

11   Overload the operator `*` in class `string`. Its member declaration will be

```
string string::operator*(int n);
```

The expression s * k will be a string that is *k* copies of the string s.   Check
that this does not overrun storage.

12   Write a `class person` that would contain basic information such as name,
birthdate, and address. Derive `class student` from `person`.

13   Write a `class triangle` that inherits from `shape`. It needs to have its own
`area()` member function.

14 The function reverse() can be written generically as follows:

```
// generic reversal
template <class T>
void reverse(T v[], int n)
{
    stack<T> stk(n);

    for (int i = 0; i < n; ++i)
        stk.push(v[i]);
    for (i = 0; i < n; ++i)
        v[i] = stk.pop();
}
```

Try this on your system, using it to reverse an array of characters and to reverse an array of char*.

15 (S. Clamage.) The following three programs behave differently:

```
// Function declarations at file scope
int f(int);
double f(double);    // overloads f(int)
double add_f()
{
    return (f(1) + f(1.0));    // f(int) + f(double)
}
```

Now we place one function declaration internally.

```
// Function declaration at local scope
int f(int);
double add_f()
{
    double f(double);             // hides f(int)
    return (f(1) + f(1.0));       // f(double) + f(double)
}
```

Now we place the other function declaration internally.

```
double f(double);
double add_f()
{
    int f(int);
    return (f(1) + f(1.0));       // What is called here?
}
```

Write some test programs that clearly show the different behaviors.

THE STANDARD LIBRARY

The standard library provides functions that are available for use by the programmer. Associated with the library are standard header files provided by the system. These header files contain prototypes of functions in the standard library, macro definitions, and other programming elements. If programmers want to use a particular function from the library, they should also include the corresponding header file. Here is a complete list of the header files:

<assert.h>	<limits.h>	<signal.h>	<stdlib.h>
<ctype.h>	<locale.h>	<stdarg.h>	<string.h>
<errno.h>	<math.h>	<stddef.h>	<time.h>
<float.h>	<setjmp.h>	<stdio.h>	

These files may be included in any order. Also, they may be included more than once, with the effect being the same as if they were included only once. In this appendix we organize our discussion by the header files.

A.1 DIAGNOSTICS: <assert.h>

The <assert.h> header file defines the assert() macro. If the macro NDEBUG is defined at the point where <assert.h> is included, then all assertions are effectively discarded. See Section 8.14 for an example and further discussion.

■ void assert(int expr);

If expr is zero (*false*), then diagnostics are printed and the program is aborted. The diagnostics include the expression, the filename, and the line number in the file.

A.2 CHARACTER HANDLING: <ctype.h>

The <ctype.h> header defines several macros that are used to test a character argument. In addition, two function prototypes of two functions are used to map a character argument.

Testing a character

■
```
int isalnum(int c);     /* is alphanumeric */
int isalpha(int c);     /* is alphabetic */
int iscntrl(int c);     /* is control */
int isdigit(int c);     /* is digit: 0-9 */
int isgraph(int c);     /* is graphic */
int islower(int c);     /* is lowercase */
int isprint(int c);     /* is printable */
int ispunct(int c);     /* is punctuation */
int isspace(int c);     /* is white space */
int isupper(int c);     /* is uppercase */
int isxdigit(int c);    /* is hexadecimal digit: 0-9, a-f, A-F */
```

These are typically implemented as macros; see *ctype.h* in your installation for details. If the argument c satisfies the test, then a nonzero value (*true*) is returned; otherwise zero (*false*) is returned. These macros should also be available as functions (see Section 8.14).

The printing characters are implementation-defined, but each occupies one printing position on the screen. A graphic character is any printing character, except for a space (' '). Thus a graphic character puts a visible mark on a single printing position on the screen. A punctuation character is any printing character other than a space (' ') or a character c for which isalnum(c) is true. The standard white space characters are space (' '), form feed ('\f'), newline ('\n'), carriage return ('\r'), horizontal tab ('\t'), and vertical tab ('\v'). The control characters are the audible bell ('\a'), backspace ('\b'), any character c for which isspace(c) is true other than space (' '), and control-c, control-h, and so on.

Mapping a character

The two functions tolower() and toupper() are used to map a character argument. *Caution:* Early versions of many ANSI C compilers did not implement these functions correctly.

■
```
int tolower(int c);
```

If c is an uppercase letter, the corresponding lowercase letter is returned; otherwise c is returned.

■   `int toupper(int c);`

If `c` is a lowercase letter, the corresponding uppercase letter is returned; otherwise `c` is returned. The next three macros often occur on ASCII machines. The first two are related to, but not the same as, `tolower()` and `toupper()`.

```
#define   _tolower(c)   ((c) + 'a' - 'A')
#define   _toupper(c)   ((c) + 'A' - 'a')
#define   toascii(c)    ((c) & 0x7f)
```

The hexadecimal constant `0x7f` is a mask for the low-order 7 bits.

A.3 ERRORS: `<errno.h>`

The identifier `errno` is defined here, along with several macros that are used to report error conditions.

```
extern int   errno;
```

Typically, there are lots of macros in *errno.h*. Which macros occur is system-dependent, but all names must begin with E. Various library functions use these macros for error reporting.

Two macros are common to all systems. These are used by the mathematical functions in the library:

```
#define   EDOM    33      /* domain error */
#define   ERANG   34      /* range error */
```

Values other than 33 and 34 could be used here, but these values are typical.

The *domain* of a mathematical function is the set of argument values for which it is defined. For example, the domain of the square root function is the set of all nonnegative numbers. A *domain error* occurs when a mathematical function is called with an argument not in its domain. When this happens, the system assigns the value EDOM to `errno`. The programmer can use `perror()` and `strerror()` to print a message associated with the value stored in `errno`.

A *range error* occurs when the value to be returned by the function is defined mathematically but cannot be represented in a `double`. When this happens, the system assigns the value ERANGE to `errno`.

A.4 FLOATING LIMITS: `<float.h>`

Macros that define various floating characteristics and limits are defined here. There are many of them. Some examples are

```
#define   FLT_MAX        3.402823466E+38F
#define   DBL_MAX        1.7976931348623157E+308
#define   LDBL_MAX       1.1897314953572317650857593266280070016E+4932L

#define   FLT_MIN        1.175494351E-38F
#define   DBL_MIN        2.2250738585072014E-308
#define   LDBL_MIN       3.3621031431120935062626778173217526030E-4932L

#define   FLT_EPSILON    1.192092896E-07F
#define   DBL_EPSILON    2.2204460492503131E-16
#define   LDBL_EPSILON   1.925929944387235853055977942584927319E-34L
```

The constants are system-dependent. Note that our system provides more precision and range for a long double than for a double. Not all systems do this; see *float.h* on your system.

A.5 INTEGRAL LIMITS: `<limits.h>`

Macros that define various integral characteristics and limits are defined here. There are many of them. Some examples are

```
#define   CHAR_BIT    8        /* number of bits in a byte */

#define   CHAR_MAX    127
#define   CHAR_MIN    (-128)
#define   SHRT_MAX    32767
#define   SHRT_MIN    (-32768)
#define   INT_MAX     2147483647
#define   INT_MIN     (-2147483648)
```

The constants are system-dependent.

A.6 LOCALIZATION: <locale.h>

The header <locale.h> contains programming constructs that can be used to set
or access properties suitable for the current locale. The following structure type is
defined:

```
struct lconv {
    char    *decimal_point;
    char    *thousands_sep;
    char    *currency_symbol;
    .....
};
```

The members allow for local variations, such as using a comma instead of a period
for a decimal point. At least six symbolic constants are defined.

```
#define   LC_ALL      1  /* affects all categories */
#define   LC_COLLATE 2   /* affects strcoll() and strxfrm() */
#define   LC_CTYPE    3  /* affects character handling functions */
#define   LC_MONETARY4   /* affects monetary info in localeconv() */
#define   LC_NUMERIC 5   /* affects decimal point used in lib fcts */
#define   LC_TIME     6  /* affects strftime() */
```

The values of the symbolic constants are system-dependent. Other macros beginning with LC_ can be specified. These macros can be used as the first argument to
the setlocale() function.

■   char *setlocale(int category, const char *locale);

The first argument is typically one of the symbolic constants. The second argument
is "C", "", or some other string. The function returns a pointer to a string of static
duration, supplied by the system, that describes the new locale, if it is available;
otherwise the NULL pointer is returned. At program startup, the system behaves as if

```
setlocale(LC_ALL, "C");
```

has been executed. This specifies a minimal environment for C translation. The
statement

```
setlocale(LC_ALL, "");
```

specifies the native environment, which is system-dependent. Using a macro other
than LC_ALL affects only part of the locale. For example, LC_MONETARY affects only
that part of the locale dealing with monetary information.

- ```
  struct lconv *localeconv(void);
  ```

A pointer to a structure provided by the system is returned. It is of static duration and contains numeric information about the current locale. Further calls to setlocale() can change the values stored in the structure.

A.7 MATHEMATICS: <math.h>

The <math.h> header file contains prototypes for the mathematical functions in the library. It also contains one macro definition:

```
#define   HUGE_VAL   1.7976931348623157e+308
```

The value of the macro is system-dependent.

The *domain* of a mathematical function is the set of argument values for which it is defined. A *domain error* occurs when a mathematical function is called with an argument not in its domain. When this happens, the function returns a system-dependent value, and the system assigns the value EDOM to errno.

A *range error* occurs when the value to be returned by the function is defined mathematically but cannot be represented in a double. If the value is too large in magnitude (overflow), then either HUGE_VAL or -HUGE_VAL is returned. If the value is too small in magnitude (underflow), zero is returned. On overflow, the value of the macro ERANGE is stored in errno. What happens on underflow is system-dependent. Some systems store ERANGE in errno; others do not.

- ```
  double cos(double x);
  double sin(double x);
  double tan(double x);
  ```

These are the cosine, sine, and tangent functions, respectively.

- ```
  double acos(double x);              /* arccosine of x */
  double asin(double x);              /* arcsine of x */
  double atan(double x);              /* arctangent of x */
  double atan2(double y, double x);   /* arctangent of y/x */
  ```

These are inverse trigonometric functions. The angle θ returned by each of them is in radians. The range of the acos() function is $[0, \pi]$. The range of the asin() and atan() functions is $[-\pi/2, \pi/2]$. The range of the atan2() function is $[-\pi, \pi]$. Its principal use is to assist in changing rectangular coordinates into polar coordinates. For the functions acos() and asin(), a domain error occurs if the argument is not in the range $[-1, 1]$. For the function atan2() a domain error occurs if both arguments are zero and y/x cannot be represented.
  ```

■   `double cosh(double x);`
       `double sinh(double x);`
       `double tanh(double x);`

These are the hyperbolic cosine, hyperbolic sine, and hyperbolic tangent functions, respectively.

■   `double exp(double x);`
       `double log(double x);`
       `double log10(double x);`

The `exp()` function returns e^x. The `log()` function returns the natural logarithm (base e) of x. The `log10()` function returns the base 10 logarithm of x. For both log functions, a domain error occurs if x is negative. A range error occurs if x is zero and the logarithm of zero cannot be represented. (Some systems can represent infinity.)

■   `double ceil(double x);`
       `double floor(double x);`

The ceiling function returns the smallest integer not less than x. The floor function returns the largest integer not greater than x.

■   `double fabs(double x);`   `/* floating absolute value */`

Returns the absolute value of x. *Caution:* The related function `abs()` is designed for integer values, not floating values. Do not confuse `abs()` with `fabs()`.

■   `double fmod(double x, double y);`   `/* floating modulus */`

Returns the value x (mod y). More explicitly, if y is nonzero, the value x - i * y is returned, where i is an integer such that the result is zero or has the same sign as x and magnitude less than the magnitude of y. If y is zero, what gets returned is system-dependent, but zero is typical. In this case a domain error occurs on some systems.

■   `double pow(double x, double y);`   `/* power function */`

Returns x raised to the y power. A domain error occurs if x is negative and y is not an integer.

■   `double sqrt(double x);`   `/* square root */`

Returns the square root of x, provided x is nonnegative. A domain error occurs if x is negative.

■ `double frexp(double value, int exp_ptr); /* free the exponent */`

This is a primitive used by other functions in the library. It splits `value` into mantissa and exponent. The statement

    x = frexp(value, &exp);

causes the relationship

   value = x $* 2^{exp}$

to hold, where the magnitude of x is in the interval [1/2, 1) or x is zero.

■ `double ldexp(double x, int exp);     /* load the exponent */`

The value $x * 2^{exp}$ is returned.

■ `double modf(double value, double i_ptr);`

Breaks `value` into integer and fractional parts. The function call

    modf(value, &i)

returns the value f, and indirectly the value `i`, so that

   value = i + f

A.8 NONLOCAL JUMPS: `<setjmp.h>`

The `<setjmp.h>` header provides one type definition and two prototypes. These declarations allow the programmer to make nonlocal jumps. A nonlocal jump is like a `goto`, but with the flow of control leaving the function in which it occurs. The type definition is system-dependent. The following is an example:

    typedef   long   jmp_buf[16];

An array of type `jmp_buf` is used to hold system information that will be used to restore the calling environment.

■ `int setjmp(jmp_buf env);`

Saves the current calling environment in the array `env` for later use by `longjmp()` and returns zero. Although on many systems this is implemented as a function, in ANSI C it is supposed to be implemented as a macro.

■   void longjmp(jmp_buf env, int value);

The function call longjmp(env, value) restores the environment saved by the most recent invocation of setjmp(env). If setjmp(env) was not invoked, or if the function in which it was invoked is no longer active, the behavior is undefined. A successful call causes program control to jump to the place following the previous call to setjmp(env). If value is nonzero, the effect is as if setjmp(env) were called again with value being returned. If value is zero, the effect is as if setjmp(env) were called again with 1 being returned.

A.9   SIGNAL HANDLING: <signal.h>

The <signal.h> header contains constructs used by the programmer to handle exceptional conditions, or signals. See Section 12.4 for an example. The following macros are defined in this header:

```
#define   SIGINT    2      /* interrupt */
#define   SIGILL    4      /* illegal instruction */
#define   SIGFPE    8      /* floating-point exception */
#define   SIGSEGV   11     /* segment violation */
#define   SIGTERM   15     /* asynchronous termination */
#define   SIGABRT   22     /* abort */
```

The constants are system-dependent, but these are commonly used. Other signals are usually supported; see the file *signal.h* on your system.

The macros in the next set may be used as the second argument of the function signal().

```
#define   SIG_DFL   ((void (*)(int)) 0)      /* default */
#define   SIG_ERR   ((void (*)(int)) -1)     /* error */
#define   SIG_IGN   ((void (*)(int)) 1)      /* ignore */
```

A system may supply other such macros. The names must begin with SIG_ followed by a capital letter.

■ void (signal(int sig, void (*func)(int)))(int);

The function call signal(sig, func) associates the signal sig with the signal handler func(). If the call is successful, the pointer value func of the previous call with first argument sig is returned, or NULL is returned if there was no previous call. If the call is unsuccessful, the pointer value SIG_ERR is returned.

The function call signal(sig, func) instructs the system to invoke func(sig) when the signal sig is raised. If the second argument to signal() is SIG_DFL, default action occurs; if it is SIG_IGN, the signal is ignored. When program control returns from func(), it returns to the place where sig was raised.

■ int raise(int sig);

Causes the signal sig to be raised. If the call is successful, zero is returned; otherwise a nonzero value is returned. This function can be used by the programmer for testing purposes.

A.10 VARIABLE ARGUMENTS: <stdarg.h>

The <stdarg.h> header file provides the programmer with a portable means of writing functions such as printf() that have a variable number of arguments. The header file contains one typedef and three macros. How these are implemented is system-dependent, but here is one way it can be done:

```
typedef   char *   va_list;

#define   va_start(ap, v)    ((void) (ap=(va_list)&v+sizeof(v)))
#define   va_arg(ap, type)   (*((type *)(ap))++)
#define   va_end(ap)         ((void) (ap = 0))
```

In the macro va_start(), the variable v is the last argument that gets declared in the header to your variable argument function definition. This variable cannot be of storage class register, and it cannot be an array type, or a type such as char that gets widened by automatic conversions. The macro va_start() initializes the argument pointer ap. The macro va_arg() accesses the next argument in the list.

The macro va_end( ) performs any cleanup that may be required before function exit. The following program illustrates the use of these constructs:

```
#include <stdio.h>
#include <stdarg.h>

int    va_sum(int cnt, ...);

int main(void)
{
    int      a = 1, b = 2, c = 3;

    printf("First call:  sum = %d\n", va_sum(2, a, b));
    printf("Second call: sum = %d\n", va_sum(3, a, b, c));
    return 0;
}

int va_sum(int cnt, ...)              /* sum the arguments */
{
    int      i, sum = 0;
    va_list  ap;

    va_start(ap, cnt);                /* startup */
    for (i = 0; i < cnt; ++i)
        sum += va_arg(ap, int);       /* get the next argument */
    va_end(ap);                       /* cleanup */
    return sum;
}
```

A.11   COMMON DEFINITIONS: <stddef.h>

The <stddef.h> header file contains some type definitions and macros that are commonly used in other places. How they are implemented is system-dependent, but here is one way of doing it:

```
typedef   char       wchar_t;
typedef   int        ptrdiff_t;
typedef   unsigned   size_t;

#define   NULL              ((void *) 0)
#define   offsetof(s_type, m)   ((size_t) &(((s_type *) 0) -> m))
```

Here, we defined the wide character type wchar_t as a plain char. A system can define it to be any integral type. It must be able to hold the largest extended character set of all the locales that are supported. The type ptrdiff_t is the type obtained when two pointers are subtracted. The type size_t is the type obtained with use of the sizeof operator. A macro call of the form offsetof(*s_type*, m) computes the offset in bytes of the member m from the beginning of the structure *s_type*. The following program illustrates its use:

```
#include <stdio.h>
#include <stddef.h>

typedef struct {
    double   a, b, c;
} data;

int main(void)
{
    printf("%d %d\n", offsetof(data, a), offsetof(data, b));
    return 0;
}
```

On most systems this program causes 0 and 8 to be printed.

A.12 INPUT/OUTPUT: <stdio.h>

The <stdio.h> header file contains macros, type definitions, and prototypes of functions used by the programmer to access files. Here are some example macros and type definitions:

```
#define    BUFSIZ          1024  /* buf size for all I/O buffers */
#define    EOF             (-1)  /* value returned on end-of-file */
#define    FILENAME_MAX    1024  /* max chars in filename */
#define    FOPEN_MAX       20    /* max number of open files */
#define    L_tmpnam        25    /* array size for tmp filename */
#define    NULL            0     /* null pointer value */
#define    TMP_MAX         17576 /* # of unique names
                                    generated by tmpnam() */
typedef    long      pos_t;      /* used with fsetpos() */
typedef    unsigned  size_t;     /* type from sizeof operator */
typedef    char *    va_list;    /* used with vfprintf() family */
```

The structure type FILE has members that describe the current state of a file. The name and number of its members are system-dependent. Here is an example:

```
typedef struct {
    int           cnt;      /* size of unused part of buffer */
    unsigned char *b_ptr;   /* next buffer location to access */
    unsigned char *base;    /* start of buffer */
    int           bufsize;  /* buffer size */
    short         flag;     /* info stored bitwise */
    char          fd;       /* file descriptor */
} FILE;

extern FILE  _iob[];
```

An object of type FILE should be capable of recording all the information needed to control a stream, including a file position indicator, a pointer to its associated buffer, an *error indicator* that records whether a read/write error has occurred, and an *end-of-file indicator* that records whether the end-of-file mark has been reached. How this is implemented is system-dependent. For example, the error indicator and the end-of-file indicator might be encoded bitwise in the structure member flag.

Typically, the type fpos_t is given by

```
typedef  long  fpos_t;
```

An object of this type is supposed to be capable of recording all the information needed to uniquely specify every position in a file.

Macros are used to define stdin, stdout, and stderr. Although we think of them as files, they are actually pointers.

```
#define  stdin   (&_iob[0])
#define  stdout  (&_iob[1])
#define  stderr  (&_iob[2])
```

Unlike other files, stdin, stdout, and stderr do not have to be opened explicitly by the programmer.

A few macros are intended for use with functions:

```
#define  _IOFBF    0    /* setvbuf(): full buffering */
#define  _IOLBF    0x80 /* setvbuf(): line buffering */
#define  _IONBF    0x04 /* setvbuf(): no buffering */
#define  SEEK_SET  0    /* fseek(): beginning of file */
#define  SEEK_CUR  1    /* fseek(): current position in file */
#define  SEEK_END  2    /* fseek(): end of file */
```

When a file is opened, the operating system associates it with a *stream* and keeps information about the stream in an object of type FILE. A pointer to FILE can be thought of as being associated with the file or the stream or both.

Opening, closing, and conditioning a file

■   FILE *fopen(const char *filename, const char *mode);

Performs the necessary housekeeping to open a buffered file. A successful call creates a stream and returns a pointer to FILE that is associated with the stream. If filename cannot be accessed, NULL is returned. The basic file modes are "r", "w", and "a", corresponding to read, write, and append, respectively. The file position indicator is set at the beginning of the file if the file mode is "r" or "w", and it is set at the end of the file if the file mode is "a". If the file mode is "w" or "a" and the file does not exist, it is created. An update mode (both reading and writing) is indicated with a +. A binary file is indicated with a b. For example, the mode "r+" is used to open a text file for both reading and writing. The mode "rb" is used to open a binary file for reading. The mode "rb+" or "r+b" is used to open a binary file for reading and writing. Similar conventions apply to "w" and "a" (see Section 11.4). In update mode, input may not be directly followed by output unless the end-of-file mark has been reached, or an intervening call to one of the file positioning functions fseek(), fsetpos(), or rewind() has occurred. In a similar fashion, output may not be directly followed by input unless an intervening call to fflush() has occurred or an intervening call to one of the file positioning functions fseek(), fsetpos(), or rewind() has occurred.

■   int fclose(FILE *fp);

Performs the necessary housekeeping to empty buffers and break all connections to the file associated with fp. If the file is successfully closed, zero is returned. If an error occurs or the file was already closed, EOF is returned. Open files are a limited resource. At most FOPEN_MAX files can be open simultaneously. System efficiency is improved by keeping only needed files open.

■   int fflush(FILE *fp);

If fp points to an output stream or points to an update stream for which the most recent operation was not input, then any unwritten data in the buffers for that stream get delivered to the file; If the call is successful, zero is returned; otherwise EOF is returned.

■   FILE *freopen(const char *filename, const char *mode, FILE *fp);

Closes the file associated with fp, opens filename as specified by mode, and associates fp with the new file. If the function call is successful, fp is returned; otherwise NULL is returned. This function is useful for changing the file associated with stdin, stdout, or stderr.

■   `void setbuf(FILE *fp, char *buf);`

If fp is not NULL, the function call `setbuf(fp, buf)` is equivalent to

    `setvbuf(fp, buf, _IOFBF, BUFSIZ)`

except that nothing is returned. If fp is NULL, the mode is _IONBF.

■   `int setvbuf(FILE *fp, char *buf, int mode, size_t n);`

Determines how the file associated with fp is to be buffered. The function must
be invoked after the file has been opened but before it is accessed. The modes
_IOFBF, _IOLBF, and _IONBF cause the file to be fully buffered, line buffered, and
unbuffered, respectively. If buf is not NULL, the array of size n pointed to by buf
is used as a buffer. If buf is NULL, the system provides the buffer. A successful
call returns zero. *Caution:* If an array of storage class automatic is used as a buffer,
then the file should be closed before the function is exited.

■   `FILE *tmpfile(void);`

Opens a temporary file with mode "wb+" and returns a pointer associated with the
file. If the request cannot be honored, NULL is returned. The system removes the
file after it is closed, or on program exit.

■   `char *tmpnam(char *s);`

Creates a unique temporary name that is typically used as a filename. If s is not
NULL, the name is stored in s, which must be of size L_tmpnam or larger. If s is
NULL, the system provides an array of static duration to store the name. Further calls
to tmpnam() can overwrite this space. In all cases the base address of the array in
which the name is stored is returned. Repeated calls to tmpnam() will generate at
least TMP_MAX unique names.

■   `char *tmpnam_r(char *s);`

This function has been specified by POSIX, an international committee concerned
with setting software standards. It is not an ANSI C function, but it can be found on
many UNIX systems. To write efficient programs for machines with more than one
CPU, the programmer needs access to library functions that are multithread-safe, or
reentrant. The function tmpnam_r() is designed to be a multithread safe version of
tmpnam(). (The letter *r* in tmpnam_r() stands for reentrant.) Most library functions
are already multithread-safe, or have been rewritten to be so. However, the function
tmpnam() cannot be made multithread safe because the call tmpnam(NULL) causes
the system to provide an array of static duration to store a name. This array cannot be
shared by two or more processes running simultaneously. The function tmpnam_r()
has the same functionality as tmpnam() except that if s is NULL, then the function
returns NULL. Thus with this function the programmer must provide the space for
the name.

Accessing the file position indicator

Functions in this section are used by the programmer to access a file randomly. The traditional functions for this purpose are fseek(), ftell(), and rewind(). ANSI C has added fgetpos() and fsetpos(). An implementation can design these functions to access files that are too large to be handled by the traditional functions. However, early versions of many ANSI C compilers have not taken advantage of this opportunity.

■   int fseek(FILE *fp, long offset, int place);

Sets the file position indicator for the next input or output operation for the file associated with fp. For a binary file, the position is offset bytes from place. The value of place can be SEEK_SET, SEEK_CUR, or SEEK_END, which correspond to the beginning of the file, the current position in the file, or the end of the file, respectively. The value of offset can be negative, zero, or positive, provided the resulting position in the file makes sense. (Clearly, the call fseek(fp, -1L, SEEK_SET) will not succeed.) On some systems, a binary file cannot meaningfully support calls to fseek() if place has the value SEEK_END. For a text file, either offset should be zero or offset should be a value returned by a previous call to ftell() on the same file and place should be SEEK_SET. If a function call to fseek() is successful, the end-of-file indicator is cleared, any effects of ungetc() on the file are undone, and zero is returned. A nonzero value gets returned if the call is unsuccessful.

■   long ftell(FILE *fp);

Returns the current value of the file position indicator for the file associated with fp. The value can be used later by fseek() to set the file position indicator to its position when ftell() was called. For a binary file, the value returned is a count of the number of bytes from the beginning of the file. For a text file, the value returned is system-dependent. The difference of two values returned by ftell() on a text file is not necessarily a meaningful measure of the number of characters read or written. An unsuccessful call to ftell() returns -1L and stores a system-dependent value in errno.

■   void rewind(FILE *fp);

Sets the file position indicator to the beginning of the file and clears the end-of-file and error indicators. The function call rewind(fp) is equivalent to

    (void) fseek(fp, 0L, SEEK_SET)

except that fseek() clears only the end-of-file indicator.

■   `int fgetpos(FILE *fp, fpos_t *pos);`

Gets the current value of the file position indicator for the file associated with `fp` and stores it in the object pointed to by `pos`. The stored value can be used later by `fsetpos()` to reset the file position indicator. A successful call returns zero; otherwise a system-dependent value is stored in `errno` and a nonzero value is returned.

■   `int fsetpos(FILE *fp, const fpos_t *pos);`

Sets the file position indicator to the value pointed to by `pos`. A successful call clears the end-of-file indicator and returns zero; otherwise a system-dependent value is written to `errno` and a nonzero value is returned.

Error handling

■   `void clearerr(FILE *fp);`

Clears the error and end-of-file indicators for the file associated with `fp`.

■   `int feof(FILE *fp);`

Returns a nonzero value if the end-of-file indicator has been set for the file associated with `fp`.

■   `int ferror(FILE *fp);`

Returns a nonzero value if the error indicator has been set for the file associated with `fp`.

■   `void perror(const char *s);`

Prints an error message associated with `errno` on `stderr`. First the string `s` is printed, followed by a colon and a space. Then the associated error message is printed, followed by a newline. (The function call `strerror(errno)` prints only the associated error message.)

Character input/output

■   `int getc(FILE *fp);`

Equivalent to `fgetc()`, except that it is implemented as a macro. Because `fp` may be evaluated more than once in the macro definition, a call with an argument that has side effects, such as `fgetc(*p++)`, may not work correctly.

■   `int getchar(void);`

The call `getchar()` is equivalent to `getc(stdin)`.

- `char *gets(char *s);`

Reads characters from `stdin` and stores them in the array pointed to by `s` until a newline is read or the end-of-file is reached, whichever occurs first. At this point, any newline is discarded and a null character is written. (In contrast, `fgets()` preserves the newline.) If any characters are written, `s` is returned; otherwise `NULL` is returned.

- `int fgetc(FILE *fp);`

Gets the next character from the file associated with `fp` and returns the value of the character read. If the end-of-file is encountered, the end-of-file indicator is set and `EOF` is returned. If an error occurs, the error indicator is set and `EOF` is returned.

- `char *fgets(char *line, int n, FILE *fp);`

Reads at most `n` - 1 characters from the file associated with `fp` into the array pointed to by `line`. As soon as a newline is read into the array or an end-of-file is encountered, no additional characters are read from the file. A null character is written into the array to end the process. If an end-of-file is encountered right at the start, the contents of `line` are undisturbed and `NULL` is returned; otherwise `line` is returned.

- `int fputc(int c, FILE *fp);`

Converts the argument `c` to an `unsigned char` and writes it in the file associated with `fp`. If the call `fputc(c)` is successful, it returns

```
(int) (unsigned char) c
```

otherwise it sets the error indicator and returns `EOF`.

- `int fputs(const char *s, FILE *fp);`

Copies the null-terminated string `s` into the file associated with `fp`, except that the terminating null character itself is not copied. (The related function `puts()` appends a newline.) A successful call returns a nonnegative value; otherwise `EOF` is returned.

- `int putc(int c, FILE *fp);`

Equivalent to `fputc()`, except that it is implemented as a macro. Since `fp` may be evaluated more than once in the macro definition, a call with an argument that has side effects, such as `putc(*p++)`, may not work correctly.

- `int putchar(int c);`

The call `putchar(c)` is equivalent to `putc(c, stdout)`.

- `int puts(const char *s);`

Copies the null-terminated string s to the standard output file, except that the terminating null character itself is not copied. Then a newline is written. (The related function `fputs()` does not append a newline.) A successful call returns a nonnegative value; otherwise EOF is returned.

- `int ungetc(int c, FILE *fp);`

Pushes the value (`unsigned char`) c back onto the stream associated with fp, provided the value of c is not EOF. At least one character can be pushed back. (Most systems allow more.) Pushed-back characters will be read from the stream in the reverse order in which they were pushed back. Once they have been read, they are forgotten; they are not placed permanently in the file. *Caution:* An intervening call to one of the file-positioning functions `fseek()`, `fsetpos()`, or `rewind()` causes any pushed-back characters to be lost. Also, until the pushed-back characters have been read, `ftell()` may be unreliable.

Formatted input/output

- `int fprintf(FILE *fp, const char *cntrl_string, ...);`

Writes formatted text into the file associated with fp and returns the number of characters written. If an error occurs, the error indicator is set and a negative value is returned. Conversion specifications, or formats, can occur in `cntrl_string`. They begin with a % and end with a conversion character. The formats determine how the other arguments get printed. See Section 11.1 for details.

- `int printf(const char *cntrl_string, ...);`

A function call of the form `printf(cntrl_string,` *other_arguments*`)` is equivalent to

  `fprintf(stdout, cntrl_string,` *other_arguments*`)`

- `int sprintf(char *s, const char *cntrl_string, ...);`

This is the string version of `printf()`. Instead of writing to stdout, it writes to the string pointed to by s.

- `int vfprintf(FILE *fp, const char *cntrl_string, va_list ap);`
  `int vprintf(const char *cntrl_string, va_list ap);`
  `int vsprintf(char s*, const char *cntrl_string, va_list ap);`

These functions correspond to `fprintf()`, `printf()`, and `sprintf()`, resectively. Instead of a variable length argument list, they have a pointer to an array of arguments as defined in *stdarg.h*.

■ int fscanf(FILE *fp, const char *cntrl_string, ...);

Reads text from the file (stream) associated with fp and processes it according to the directives in the control string. There are three kinds of *directives*: ordinary characters, white space, and conversion specifications. Ordinary characters get matched, and white space gets matched with optional white space. A conversion specification begins with a % and ends with a conversion character; it causes characters to be read from the input stream, a corresponding value to be computed, and the value to be placed in memory at an address specified by one of the other arguments. If the function is invoked and the input stream is empty, EOF is returned; otherwise, the number of successful conversions is returned. See Section 11.2 for details.

■ int scanf(const char cntrl_string, ...);

A function call of the form scanf(cntrl_string, *other_arguments*) is equivalent to

    fscanf(stdin, cntrl_string, *other_arguments*)

■ int sscanf(const char s, const char cntrl_string, ...);

This is the string version of scanf(). Instead of reading from stdin, it reads from the string pointed to by s. Reading from a string is unlike reading from a file in the following sense. If we use sscanf() to read from s again, then the input starts at the beginning of the string, not where we left off before.

Direct input/output

The functions fread() and fwrite() are used to read and write binary files, respectively. No conversions are performed. In certain applications, the use of these functions can save considerable time.

■ size_t fread(void *a_ptr, size_t el_size, size_t n, FILE *fp);

Reads at most n * el_size bytes (characters) from the file associated with fp into the array pointed to by a_ptr. The number of array elements successfully written is returned. If an end-of-file is encountered, the end-of-file indicator is set and a short count is returned. If el_size or n is zero, the input stream is not read and zero is returned.

■ size_t fwrite(const void *a_ptr,
                 size_t el_size, size_t n, FILE *fp);

Reads n * el_size bytes (characters) from the array pointed to by a_ptr and writes them to the file associated with fp. The number of array elements successfully written is returned. If an error occurs, a short count is returned. If el_size or n is zero, the array is not accessed and zero is returned.

Removing or renaming a file

- `int remove(const char *filename);`

Removes the file with the name `filename` from the file system. If the call is successful, zero is returned; otherwise –1 is returned. (This is the `unlink()` function in traditional C.)

- `int rename(const char *from, const char *to);`

Changes the name of a file. The old name is in the string pointed to by `from`. The new name is in the string pointed to by `to`. If a file with the new name already exists, what happens is system-dependent, but typically in UNIX the file gets overwritten. On most systems, the old and new names can be either files or directories. If one of the arguments is a directory name, the other one must be, too. Zero is returned if the call is successful; otherwise –1 is returned and a system-dependent value is written to `errno`.

A.13   GENERAL UTILITIES: `<stdlib.h>`

The `<stdlib.h>` header file contains prototypes of functions for general use, along with related macros and type definitions. Here are some examples of the macros and type definitions:

```
#include <stddef.h>                   /* for size_t and wchar_t */

#define   EXIT_SUCCESS   0            /* for use with exit() */
#define   EXIT_FAILURE   1            /* for use with exit() */
#define   NULL           0            /* null pointer value */
#define   RAND_MAX       32767        /* 2^15 - 1 */

typedef struct {
    int    quot;       /* quotient */
    int    rem;        /* remainder */
} div_t;

typedef struct {
    long quot;         /* quotient */
    long rem;          /* remainder */
} ldiv_t;
```

Dynamic allocation of memory

- ■ void *calloc(size_t n, size_t el_size);

Allocates contiguous space in memory for an array of n elements, with each element requiring el_size bytes. The space is initialized with all bits set to zero. A successful call returns the base address of the allocated space; otherwise NULL is returned.

- ■ void *malloc(size_t size);

Allocates a block of space in memory consisting of size bytes. The space is not initialized. A successful call returns the base address of the allocated space; otherwise NULL is returned.

- ■ void *realloc(void *ptr, size_t size);

Changes the size of the block pointed to by ptr to size bytes. The contents of the space will be unchanged up to the lesser of the old and new sizes. Any new space is not initialized. The function attempts to keep the base address of the block the same, but if this is not possible, it allocates a new block of memory, copying the relevant portion of the old block and deallocating it. If ptr is NULL, the effect is the same as calling malloc(). If ptr is not NULL, it must be the base address of space previously allocated by a call to calloc(), malloc(), or realloc() that has not yet been deallocated by a call to free() or realloc(). A successful call returns the base address of the resized (or new) space; otherwise NULL is returned.

- ■ void free(void *ptr);

Causes the space in memory pointed to by ptr to be deallocated. If ptr is NULL, the function has no effect. If ptr is not NULL, it must be the base address of space previously allocated by a call to calloc(), malloc(), or realloc() that has not yet been deallocated by a call to free() or realloc(). Otherwise the call is in error. The effect of the error is system-dependent.

Searching and sorting

■   void *bsearch(const void *key_ptr,
                 const void *a_ptr, size_t n_els, size_t el_size,
                 int compare(const void *, const void *));

Searches the sorted array pointed to by a_ptr for an element that matches the object pointed to by key_ptr. If a match is found, the address of the element is returned; otherwise NULL is returned. The number of elements in the array is n_els, and each element is stored in memory in el_size bytes. The elements of the array must be in ascending sorted order with respect to the comparison function compare(). The comparison function takes two arguments, each one being an address of an element of the array. The comparison function returns an int that is less than, equal to, or greater than zero, depending on whether the element pointed to by its first argument is considered to be less than, equal to, or greater than the element pointed to by its second argument. (The function bsearch() uses a binary search algorithm, which explains its name.)

■   void qsort(void *a_ptr, size_t n_els, size_t el_size,
              int compare(const void *, const void *));

Sorts the array pointed to by a_ptr in ascending order with respect to the comparison function compare(). The number of elements in the array is n_els, and each element is stored in memory in el_size bytes. The comparison function takes two arguments, each one being an address of an element of the array. The comparison function returns an int that is less than, equal to, or greater than zero, depending on whether the element pointed to by its first argument is considered to be less than, equal to, or greater than the element pointed to by its second argument. (According to tradition, the function qsort() implements a "quicker-sort" algorithm, which explains its name.)

Pseudo random number generator

■   int rand(void);

Each call generates an integer and returns it. Repeated calls generate what appears to be a randomly distributed sequence of integers in the interval [0, RAND_MAX].

- `void srand(unsigned seed);`

Seeds the random number generator, causing the sequence generated by repeated calls to rand() to start in a different place. On program startup, the random number generator acts as if srand(1) had been called. The statement

```
srand(time(NULL));
```

can be used to seed the random number generator with a different value each time the program is invoked.

Communicating with the environment

- `char getenv(const char *name);`

Searches a list of environment variables provided by the operating system. If name is one of the variables in the list, the base address of its corresponding string value is returned; otherwise NULL is returned (see Section 11.12).

- `int system(const char *s);`

Passes the string s as a command to be executed by the command interpreter (the shell) provided by the operating system. If s is not NULL and a connection to the operating system exits, the function returns the exit status returned by the command. If s is NULL, the function returns a nonzero value if the command interpreter is available via this mechanism; otherwise zero is returned.

Integer arithmetic

- `int abs(int i);`
  `long labs(long i);`

Both functions return the absolute value of i.

- `div_t div(int numer, int denom);`
  `ldiv_t ldiv(long numer, long denom);`

Both functions divide numer by denom and return a structure that has the quotient and remainder as members. The following is an example:

```
div_t   d;

d = div(17, 5);
printf("quotient = %d, remainder = %d\n", d.quot, d.rem);
```

When executed, this code prints the line

```
quotient = 3, remainder = 2
```

String conversion

Members of the two families `ato...()` and `strto...()` are used to convert a string to a value. The conversion is conceptual; it interprets the characters in the string, but the string itself does not get changed. The string can begin with optional white space. The conversion stops with the first inappropriate character. For example, both of the function calls

```
strtod("123x456", NULL)        and        strtod("\n 123 456", NULL)
```

return the `double` value 123.0. The `strto...()` family provides more control over the conversion process and provides for error checking.

- `double atof(const char *s);`   `/* ascii to floating number */`

Converts the string `s` to a `double` and returns it. Except for error behavior, the function call

```
atof(s)        is equivalent to        strtod(s, NULL)
```

If no conversion takes place, the function returns zero.

- `int atoi(const char *s);`   `/* ascii to integer */`

Converts the string `s` to an `int` and returns it. Except for error behavior, the function call

```
atoi(s)        is equivalent to        (int) strtol(s, NULL, 10)
```

If no conversion takes place, the function returns zero.

- `long atol(const char *s);`   `/* ascii to long */`

Converts the string `s` to a `long` and returns it. Except for error behavior, the function call

```
atol(s)        is equivalent to        strtol(s, NULL, 10)
```

If no conversion takes place, the function returns zero.

- `double strtod(const char *s, char **end_ptr);`

Converts the string `s` to a `double` and returns it. If no conversion takes place, zero is returned. If `end_ptr` is not NULL and conversion takes place, the address of the character that stops the conversion process is stored in the object pointed to by `end_ptr`. If `end_ptr` is not NULL and no conversion takes place, the value `s` is stored in the object pointed to by `end_ptr`. On overflow, either HUGE_VAL or -HUGE_VAL is returned and ERANGE is stored in `errno`. On underflow, zero is returned and ERANGE is stored in `errno`.

■ long strtol(const char *s, char **end_ptr, int base);

Converts the string s to a long and returns it. If base has a value from 2 to 36, the digits and letters in s are interpreted in that base. In base 36, the letters a through z and A through Z are interpreted as 10 through 35, respectively. With a smaller base, only those digits and letters with corresponding values less than the base are interpreted. If end_ptr is not NULL and conversion takes place, the address of the character that stops the conversion process is stored in the object pointed to by end_ptr. Here is an example:

```
char    *p;
long    value;

value = strtol("12345", &p, 3);
printf("value = %ld, end string = \"%s\"\n", value, p);
```

When executed, this code prints the line

```
value = 5, end string = "345"
```

Because the base is 3, the character 3 in the string "12345" stops the conversion process. Only the first two characters in the string are converted. In base 3, the characters 12 get converted to decimal value 5. In a similar fashion, the code

```
value = strtol("abcde", &p, 12);
printf("value = %ld, end string = \"%s\"\n", value, p);
```

prints the line

```
value = 131, end string = "cde"
```

Because the base is 12, the character c in the string "abcde" stops the conversion process. Only the first two characters in the string are converted. In base 12, the characters ab get converted to decimal value 131.

If base is zero, s gets interpreted as either a hexadecimal, octal, or decimal integer, depending on the leading nonwhite characters in s. With an optional sign and 0x or 0X, the string is interpreted as a hexadecimal integer (base 16). With an optional sign and 0, but not 0x or 0X, the string is interpreted as an octal integer (base 8). Otherwise, it is interpreted as a decimal integer.

If no conversion takes place, zero is returned. If end_ptr is not NULL and no conversion takes place, the value s is stored in the object pointed to by end_ptr. On overflow, either LONG_MAX or -LONG_MAX is returned and ERANGE is stored in errno.

- `unsigned long strtoul(const char *s, char **end_ptr, int base);`

Similar to `strtol()`, but returns an `unsigned long`. On overflow, either `ULONG_MAX` or `-ULONG_MAX` is returned.

Multibyte character functions

Multibyte characters are used to represent members of an extended character set. How the members of an extended character set are defined is locale-dependent.

- `int mblen(const char *s, size_t n);`

If `s` is `NULL`, the function returns a nonzero or zero value, depending on whether multibyte characters do or do not have state-dependent encoding. If `s` is not `NULL`, the function examines at most `n` characters in `s` and returns the number of bytes that comprise the next multibyte character. If `s` points to the null character, zero is returned. If `s` does not point to a multibyte character, the value -1 is returned.

- `int mbtowc(wchar_t *p, const char *s, size_t n);`

Acts the same as `mblen()`, but with the following additional capability: If `p` is not `NULL`, the function converts the next multibyte character in `s` to its corresponding wide character type and stores it in the object pointed to by `p`.

- `int wctomb(char *s, wchar_t wc);`

If `s` is `NULL`, the function returns a nonzero or zero value, depending on whether multibyte characters do or do not have state-dependent encoding. If `s` is not `NULL` and `wc` is a wide character corresponding to a multibyte character, the function stores the multibyte character in `s` and returns the number of bytes required to represent it. If `s` is not `NULL` and `wc` does not correspond to a multibyte character, the value -1 is returned.

Multibyte string functions

- `size_t mbstowcs(wchar_t *wcs, const char *mbs, size_t n);`

Reads the multibyte string pointed to by `mbs` and writes the corresponding wide character string into `wcs`. At most `n` wide characters are written, followed by a wide null character. If the conversion is successful, the number of wide characters written is returned, not counting the final wide null character; otherwise -1 is returned.

- `int wcstombs(char *mbs, const wchar_t *wcs, size_t n);`

Reads the wide character string pointed to by `wcs` and writes the corresponding multibyte string into `mbs`. The conversion process stops after `n` wide characters have been written or a null character is written, whichever comes first. If the conversion is successful, the number of characters written is returned, not counting the null character (if any); otherwise -1 is returned.

Leaving the program

- `void abort(void);`

Causes abnormal program termination, unless a signal handler catches SIGABRT and does not return. It depends on the implementation whether any open files are properly closed and any temporary files are removed.

- `int atexit(void (*func)(void));`

Registers the function pointed to by `func` for execution upon normal program exit. A successful call returns zero; otherwise a nonzero value is returned. At least 32 such functions can be registered. Execution of registered functions occurs in the reverse order of registration. Only global variables are available to these functions.

- `void exit(int status);`

Causes normal program termination. The functions registered by `atexit()` are invoked in the reverse order in which they were registered, buffered streams are flushed, files are closed, and temporary files that were created by `tmpfile()` are removed. The value `status`, along with control, is returned to the host environment. If the value of `status` is zero or EXIT_SUCCESS, the host environment assumes that the program executed successfully; if the value is EXIT_FAILURE, it assumes that the program executed unsuccessfully. The host environment may recognize other values for `status`.

A.14 MEMORY AND STRING HANDLING: `<string.h>`

The `<string.h>` header file contains prototypes of functions in two families. The functions `mem...()` are used to manipulate blocks of memory of a specified size. These blocks can be thought of as arrays of bytes (characters). They are like strings, except that they are not null-terminated. The functions `str...()` are used to manipulate null-terminated strings. Typically, the following line is at the top of the header file:

```
#include <stddef.h>          /* for NULL and size_t */
```

Memory handling functions

- `void *memchr(const void *p, int c, size_t n);`

Starting in memory at the address p, a search is made for the first unsigned character (byte) that matches the value (`unsigned char`) c. At most n bytes are searched. If the search is successful, a pointer to the character is returned; otherwise NULL is returned.

■   `int memcmp(const void *p, const void *q, size_t n);`

Compares two blocks in memory of size n. The bytes are treated as unsigned characters. The function returns a value that is less than, equal to, or greater than zero, depending on whether the block pointed to by p is lexicographically less than, equal to, or greater than the block pointed to by q.

■   `void *memcpy(void *to, void *from, size_t n);`

Copies the block of n bytes pointed to by from to the block pointed to by to. The value to is returned.

■   `void *memmove(void *to, void *from, size_t n);`

Copies the block of n bytes pointed to by from to the block pointed to by to. The value to is returned. If the blocks overlap, each byte in the block pointed to by from is accessed before a new value is written in that byte. Thus a correct copy is made, even when the blocks overlap.

■   `void *memset(void *p, int c, size_t n);`

Sets each byte in the block of size n pointed to by p to the value (unsigned char) c. The value p is returned.

String handling functions

■   `char *strcat(char *s1, const char *s2);`

Concatenates the strings s1 and s2. That is, a copy of s2 is appended to the end of s1. The programmer must ensure that s1 points to enough space to hold the result. The string s1 is returned.

■   `char *strchr(const char *s, int c);`

Searches for the first character in s that matches the value (char) c. If the character is found, its address is returned; otherwise NULL is returned. The call strchr(s, '\0') returns a pointer to the terminating null character in s.

■   `int strcmp(const char *s1, const char *s2);`

Compares the two strings s1 and s2 lexicographically. The elements of the strings are treated as unsigned characters. The function returns a value that is less than, equal to, or greater than zero, depending on whether s1 is lexicographically less than, equal to, or greater than s2.

■   `int strcoll(const char *s1, const char *s2);`

Compares the two strings s1 and s2 using a comparison rule that depends on the current locale. The function returns a value that is less than, equal to, or greater than zero, depending on whether s1 is considered less than, equal to, or greater than s2.

- char *strcpy(char *s1, const char *s2);

Copies the string s2 into the string s1, including the terminating null character. Whatever exists in s1 is overwritten. The programmer must ensure that s1 points to enough space to hold the result. The value s1 is returned.

- size_t strcspn(const char *s1, const char *s2);

Computes the length of the maximal initial substring in s1 consisting entirely of characters *not* in s2. For example, the function call

    strcspn("April is the cruelest month", "abc")

returns the value 13, because "April is the " is the maximal initial substring of the first argument having no characters in common with "abc". (The character c in the name strcspn stands for "complement," and the letters spn stand for "span.")

- char *strdup(const char *s)

This is not an ANSI C function, but it can be found on most C systems. The function strdup() duplicates the string pointed to by s and returns a pointer to the new string, or returns NULL if space for the new string cannot be allocated. Because the space for the new string is obtained by a call to malloc(), the programmer can use free() to release the space if so desired.

- char *strerror(int error_number);

Returns a pointer to an error string provided by the system. The contents of the string must not be changed by the program. If an error causes the system to write a value in errno, the programmer can invoke strerror(errno) to print the associated error message. (The related function perror() can also be used to print the error message.)

- size_t strlen(const char *s);

Returns the length of the string s. The length is the number of characters in the string, not counting the terminating null character.

- char *strncat(char *s1, const char *s2, size_t n);

At most n characters in s2, not counting the null character, are appended to s1. Then a null character is written in s1. The programmer must ensure that s1 points to enough space to hold the result. The string s1 is returned.

- `int strncmp(const char *s1, const char *s2, size_t n);`

Compares at most n characters lexicographically in each of the two strings s1 and s2. The comparison stops with the *n*th character or a terminating null character, whichever comes first. The elements of the strings are treated as unsigned characters. The function returns a value that is less than, equal to, or greater than zero, depending on whether the compared portion of s1 is lexicographically less than, equal to, or greater than the compared portion of s2.

- `char *strncpy(char *s1, const char *s2, size_t n);`

Precisely n characters are written into s1, overwriting whatever is there. The characters are taken from s2 until n of them have been copied or a null character has been copied, whichever comes first. After a null character has been copied, any of the remaining first n characters in s1 are assigned the value '\0'. If the size of s1 is n and the string length of s2 is n or larger, then s1 will not be null-terminated. The programmer must ensure that s1 points to enough space to hold the result. The value s1 is returned.

- `char *strpbrk(const char *s1, const char *s2);`

Searches for the first character in s1 that matches any one of the characters in s2. If the search is successful, the address of the character found in s1 is returned; otherwise NULL is returned. For example, the function call

```
strpbrk("April is the cruelest month", "abc")
```

returns the address of c in cruelest. (The letters pbrk in the name strpbrk stand for "pointer to break.")

- `char *strrchr(const char *s, int c);`

Searches from the right for the first character in s that matches the value (char) c. If the character is found, its address is returned; otherwise NULL is returned. The call strchr(s, '\0') returns a pointer to the terminating null character in s.

- `size_t strspn(const char *s1, const char *s2);`

Computes the length of the maximal initial substring in s1 consisting entirely of characters in s2. For example, the function call

```
strspn("April is the cruelest month", "A is for apple")
```

returns the value 9, because all the characters in the first argument preceding the t in the occur in the second argument, but the letter t does not. (The letters spn in the name strspn stand for "span.")

- `char *strstr(const char *s1, const char *s2);`

Searches in s1 for the first occurrence of the substring s2. If the search is successful, a pointer to the base address of the substring in s1 is returned; otherwise NULL is returned.

- `char *strtok(char *s1, const char *s2);`

Searches for tokens in s1, using the characters in s2 as token separators. If s1 contains one or more tokens, the first token in s1 is found, the character immediately following the token is overwritten with a null character, the remainder of s1 is stored elsewhere by the system, and the address of the first character in the token is returned. Subsequent calls with s1 equal to NULL return the base address of a string supplied by the system that contains the next token. If no additional tokens are available, NULL is returned. The initial call strtok(s1, s2) returns NULL if s1 contains no tokens. The following is an example:

```
char    s1[] = " this is,an    example ; ";
char    s2[] = ",; ";
char    *p;

printf("\"%s\"", strtok(s1, s2));
while ((p = strtok(NULL, s2)) != NULL)
    printf(" \"%s\"", p);
putchar('\n');
```

When executed, this code prints the line

```
"this" "is" "an" "example"
```

- `char strtok_r(char *s1, const char *s2, char *wrk_space_ptr);`

This function was specified by POSIX, an international committee concerned with setting software standards. It is not an ANSI C function, but it can be found on many UNIX systems. To write efficient programs for machines with more than one CPU, the programmer needs access to library functions that are multithread safe, or reentrant. (The second letter *r* in strtok_r() stands for reentrant.) Most library functions have been modified as necessary to be multithread safe. The function strtok(), however, is not multithread safe, because the string supplied by the system that contains the next token cannot be shared by two or more processes running simultaneously. The function strtok_r() is designed to be a multithread safe version of strtok(). The two functions are similar, except that a pointer to some work space supplied by the programmer must be passed as the third argument to strtok_r(). Here is an example program:

```
/* Use strtok_r() to find tokens. */

#include <stdio.h>
#include <stdlib.h>
#include <string.h>

#define    SEPARATORS    ",:; \n"

void    prn_tokens(char *s1, const char *s2, char **wrk_ptr);
char    *strtok_r(char *s1, const char *s2, char **wrk_ptr);

int main(void)
{
   char    s1[] = "   try_me:this is;   an,example ;;; ";
   char    s2[] = "try it:: ::for,the,second,;time";
   char    s3[] = "this example contains\n"
                  "two newline characters\n";
   char    *wrk;

   wrk = malloc(100 * sizeof(char));      /* work space */
   prn_tokens(s1, SEPARATORS, &wrk);
   prn_tokens(s2, SEPARATORS, &wrk);
   prn_tokens(s3, SEPARATORS, &wrk);
   return 0;
}

void prn_tokens(char *s1, const char *s2, char **wrk_ptr)
{
   char    *p;

   printf("\"%s\"", strtok_r(s1, s2, wrk_ptr));
   while ((p = strtok_r(NULL, s2, wrk_ptr)) != NULL)
      printf(" \"%s\"", p);
   putchar('\n');
}
```

When we run this program, this is what appears on the screen:

```
"try_me" "this" "is" "an" "example"
"try" "it" "for" "the" "second" "time"
"this" "example" "contains" "two" "newline" "characters"
```

The work space should be able to hold whatever string is passed in as a first argument. On our system, we cannot get access to the function prototype of strtok_r( ) in *string.h* unless the symbolic constant _REENTRANT is defined. For this example program, we can get around this restriction by supplying the function prototype ourselves. When _REENTRANT is defined, our compiler will check to see that only multithread safe functions are used.

■   size_t strxfrm(char *s1, const char *s2, size_t n);

Transforms the string s2 and places the result in s1, overwriting whatever is there. At most n characters, including a terminating null character, are written in s1. The length of s1 is returned. The transformation is such that when two transformed strings are used as arguments to strcmp( ), the value returned is less than, equal to, or greater than zero, depending on whether strcoll( ) applied to the untransformed strings returns a value less than, equal to, or greater than zero. (The letters xfrm in the name strxfrm stand for "transform.")

A.15 DATE AND TIME: <time.h>

The <time.h> header file contains prototypes of functions that deal with date, time, and the internal clock. Here are examples of some macros and type definitions:

```
#include <stddef.h>              /* for NULL and size_t */

#define   CLOCKS_PER_SEC   60    /* machine-dependent */

typedef   long   clock_t;
typedef   long   time_t;
```

Objects of type struct tm are used to store the date and time.

```
struct tm {
    int    tm_sec;      /* seconds after the minute: [0, 60] */
    int    tm_min;      /* minutes after the hour: [0, 59]   */
    int    tm_hour;     /* hours since midnight: [0, 23]     */
    int    tm_mday;     /* day of the month: [1, 31]         */
    int    tm_mon;      /* months since January: [0, 11]     */
    int    tm_year;     /* years since 1900                  */
    int    tm_wday;     /* days since Sunday: [0, 6]         */
    int    tm_yday;     /* days since 1 January: [0, 365]    */
    int    tm_isdst;    /* Daylight Savings Time flag        */
};
```

Note that the range of values for tm_sec has to accommodate a "leap second," which occurs only sporadically. The flag tm_isdst is positive if Daylight Savings Time is in effect, zero if it is not, and negative if the information is not available.

Accessing the clock

On most systems, the clock() function provides access to the underlying machine clock. The rate at which the clock runs is machine-dependent.

- clock_t clock(void);

Returns an approximation to the number of CPU "clock ticks" used by the program up to the point of invocation. The value returned can be divided by CLOCKS_PER_SEC to convert it to seconds. If the CPU clock is not available, the value −1 is returned. See Section 11.16 for more discussion.

Accessing the time

In ANSI C, time comes in two principal versions: a "calendar time" expressed as an integer, which on most systems represents the number of seconds that have elapsed since 1 January 1970, and a "broken-down time" expressed as a structure of type struct tm. The calendar time is encoded with respect to Universal Time Coordinated (UTC; previously, Greenwich Mean Time). The programmer can use library functions to convert one version of time to the other. Also, functions are available to print the time as a string.

- time_t time(time_t *tp);

Returns the current calendar time, expressed as the number of seconds that have elapsed since 1 January 1970 (UTC). Other units and other starting dates are possible, but these are the ones typically used. If tp is not NULL, the value also gets stored in the object pointed to by tp. Consider the following code:

```
time_t    now;

now = time(NULL);
printf("\n%s%ld\n%s%s%s%s\n",
    "                        now = ", now,
    "              ctime(&now) = ", ctime(&now),
    "asctime(localtime(&now)) = ", asctime(localtime(&now)));
```

When executed on our system, this code printed the lines

```
                        now = 685136007
              ctime(&now) = Tue Sep 17 12:33:27 1991
asctime(localtime(&now)) = Tue Sep 17 12:33:27 1991
```

■ `char *asctime(const struct tm *tp);`

Converts the broken-down time pointed to by `tp` to a string provided by the system. The function returns the base address of the string. Later calls to `asctime()` and `ctime()` overwrite the string.

■ `char *ctime(const time_t *t_ptr);`

Converts the calendar time pointed to by `t_ptr` to a string provided by the system. The function returns the base address of the string. Later calls to `asctime()` and `ctime()` overwrite the string. The two function calls

ctime(&now)   and   asctime(localtime(&now))

are equivalent.

■ `double difftime(time_t t0, time_t t1);`

Computes the difference `t1` - `t0` and, if necessary, converts this value to the number of seconds that have elapsed between the calendar times `t0` and `t1`. The value is returned as a `double`.

■ `struct tm *gmtime(const time_t *t_ptr);`

Converts the calendar time pointed to by `t_ptr` to a broken-down time, and stores it in an object of type `struct tm` that is provided by the system. The address of the structure is returned. The function computes the broken-down time with respect to Universal Time Coordinated (UTC). [This used to be called Greenwich Mean Time (GMT); hence the name of the function.] Later calls to `gmtime()` and `localtime()` overwrite the structure.

■ `struct tm *localtime(const time_t *t_ptr);`

Converts the calendar time pointed to by `t_ptr` to a broken-down local time, and stores it in an object of type `struct tm` that is provided by the system. The address of the structure is returned. Later calls to `gmtime()` and `localtime()` overwrite the structure.

■   `time_t mktime(struct tm *tp);`

Converts the broken-down local time in the structure pointed to by `tp` to the corresponding calendar time. If the call is successful, the calendar time is returned;
otherwise −1 is returned. For the purpose of the computation, the `tm_wday` and
`tm_yday` members of the structure are disregarded. Before the computation, other
members can have values outside their usual range. After the computation, the members of the structure may be overwritten with an equivalent set of values in which
each member lies within its normal range. The values for `tm_wday` and `tm_yday`
are computed from those for the other members. As an example, the following code
can be used to find the date 1000 days from now:

```
struct tm    *tp;
time_t        now, later;

now = time(NULL);
tp = localtime(&now);
tp -> tm_mday += 1000;
later = mktime(tp);
printf("\n1000 days from now: %s\n", ctime(&later));
```

■   `size_t strftime(char *s, size_t n,`
              `const char *cntrl_str, const struct tm *tp);`

Writes characters into the string pointed to by `s` under the direction of the control
string pointed to by `cntrl_str`. At most, n characters are written, including the null
character. If more than n characters are required, the function returns zero and the
contents of `s` are indeterminate; otherwise the length of `s` is returned. The control
string consists of ordinary characters and conversion specifications, or formats, that
determine how values from the broken-down time in the structure pointed to by
`tp` are to be written. Each conversion specification consists of a % followed by a
conversion character.

strftime()

Conversion specification	What gets printed	Example
%a	abbreviated weekday name	Fri
%A	full weekday name	Friday
%b	abbreviated month name	Sep
%B	full month name	September
%c	date and time	Sep 01 02:17:23 1993
%d	day of the month	01
%H	hour of the 24-hour day	02
%h	hour of the 12-hour day	02
%j	day of the year	243
%m	month of the year	9
%M	minutes after the hour	17
%p	AM or PM	AM
%s	seconds after the hour	23
%U	week of the year (Sun–Sat)	34
%w	day of the week (0–6)	5
%x	date	Sep 01 1993
%X	time	02:17:23
%y	year of the century	93
%Y	year	1993
%Z	time zone	PDT
%%	percent character	%

Consider the following code:

```
char      s[100];
time_t    now;

now = time(NULL);
strftime(s, 100, "%H:%M:%S on %A, %d %B %Y", localtime(&now));
printf("%s\n\n", s);
```

When we executed a program containing these lines, the following line was printed:

```
13:01:15 on Tuesday, 17 September 1991
```

A.16 MISCELLANEOUS

In addition to the functions specified by ANSI C, the system may provide other functions in the library. In this section we describe the non-ANSI C functions that are widely available. Some functions, such as `execl()`, are common to most systems. Other functions, such as `fork()` or `spawnl()`, are generally available in one operating system, but not in another. The name of the associated header file is system-dependent.

File access

■   `int access(const char *path, int amode);`

Checks the file with the name `path` for accessibility according to the bit pattern contained in the access mode `amode`. The function prototype is in *unistd.h* on UNIX systems and in *io.h* on MS-DOS systems. The following symbolic constants are defined in the header file:

F_OK	Check for existence.
R_OK	Test for read permission.
W_OK	Test for write permission.
X_OK	Test for execute or search permission.

Typically, the desired access mode is constructed by an OR of these symbolic constants. For example, the function call

```
access(path, R_OK | W_OK)
```

could be used to check whether the file permits both read and write access to the file. The function returns 0 if the requested access is permitted; otherwise −1 is returned and `errno` is set to indicate the error.

Using file descriptors

■   `int open(const char filename, int flag, ...);`

Opens the named file for reading and/or writing as specified by the information stored bitwise in `flag`. If a file is being created, a third argument of type `unsigned` is needed. It sets the file permissions for the new file. If the call is successful, a nonnegative integer called the *file descriptor* is returned; otherwise `errno` is set and −1 is returned. Values that can be used for `flag` are given in the header file that contains the prototype for `open()`. These values are system-dependent.

■   `int close(int fd);`

Closes the file associated with the file descriptor `fd`. If the call is successful, zero is returned; otherwise `errno` is set and −1 is returned.

- `int read(int fd, char *buf, int n);`

Reads at most n bytes from the file associated with the file descriptor fd into the object pointed to by buf. If the call is successful, the number of bytes written in buf is returned; otherwise errno is set and −1 is returned. A short count is returned if the end-of-file is encountered.

- `int write(int fd, const char *buf, int n);`

Writes at most n bytes from the object pointed to by buf into the file associated with the file descriptor fd. If the call is successful, the number of bytes written in the file is returned; otherwise errno is set and −1 is returned. A short count can indicate that the disk is full.

Creating a concurrent process

- `int fork(void);`

Copies the current process and begins executing it concurrently. The child process has its own process identification number. When fork() is called, it returns zero to the child and the child's process ID to the parent. If the call fails, errno is set and −1 is returned. This function is not available in MS-DOS.

- `int vfork(void);`

Spawns a new process using virtual memory efficiently. The child process has its own process identification number. The address space of the parent process is not fully copied, which is very inefficient in a paged environment. The child borrows the parent's memory and thread of control until a call to exec...() occurs or the child exits. The parent process is suspended while the child is using its resources. When vfork() is called, it returns zero to the child and the child's process ID to the parent. If the call fails, errno is set and −1 is returned. This function is not available in MS-DOS.

Overlaying a process

In this section we describe the two families exec...() and spawn...(). The first is generally available on both MS-DOS and UNIX systems, the second only on MS-DOS systems. On UNIX systems, fork() can be used with exec...() to achieve the effect of spawn...().

■ `int execl(char *name, char *arg0, ..., char *argN);`
   `int execle(char *name, char *arg0, ..., char *argN, char **envp);`
   `int execlp(char *name, char *arg0, ..., char *argN);`
   `int execlpe(char *name, char *arg0, ..., char *argN, char **envp);`
   `int execv(char *name, char **argv);`
   `int execve(char *name, char **argv, char **envp);`
   `int execvp(char *name, char **argv);`
   `int execvpe(char *name, char **argv, char **envp);`

These functions overlay the current process with the named program. There is no return to the parent process. By default, the child process inherits the environment of the parent. Members of the family with names that begin with `execl` require a list of arguments that are taken as the command line arguments for the child process. The last argument in the list must be the `NULL` pointer. Members of the family with names that begin with `execv` use the array `argv` to supply command line arguments to the child process. The last element of `argv` must have the value `NULL`. Members of the family with names ending in `e` use the array `envp` to supply environment variables to the child process. The last element of `envp` must have the value `NULL`. Members of the family with `p` in their name use the path variable specified in the environment to determine which directories to search for the program.

■ `int spawnl(int mode, char *name, char *arg0, ..., char *argN);`
   `.....`

This family of functions corresponds to the `exec...()` family, except that each member has an initial integer argument. The values for `mode` are 0, 1, and 2. The value 0 causes the parent process to wait for the child process to finish before continuing. With value 1, the parent and child processes should execute concurrently, except that this has not been implemented yet. The use of this value will cause an error. The value 2 causes the child process to overlay the parent process.

Interprocess communication

■ `int pipe(int pd[2]);`

Creates an input/output mechanism called a *pipe*, and puts the associated file descriptors (pipe descriptors) in the array pd. If the call is successful, zero is returned; otherwise `errno` is set and −1 is returned. After a pipe has been created, the system assumes that two or more cooperating processes created by subsequent calls to `fork()` will use `read()` and `write()` to pass data through the pipe. One descriptor, `pd[0]`, is read from; the other, `pd[1]`, is written to. The pipe capacity is system-dependent, but is at least 4096 bytes. If a write fills the pipe, it blocks until data is read out of it. As with other file descriptors, `close()` can be used to explicitly close `pd[0]` and `pd[1]`. This function is not available in MS-DOS.

Suspending program execution

- `void sleep(unsigned seconds);`

Suspends the current process from execution for the number of seconds requested. The time is only approximate.

Get current working directory

- `char getcwd(char buf, size_t n);`

Returns a pointer to the current working directory pathname. The function prototype is in *unistd.h* on UNIX systems and in *dir.h* on MS-DOS systems. The value of n must be at least one more than the length of the pathname returned. If buf is NULL, malloc() is used to allocate a char array of size at most n for the pathname, and in this case the pointer returned can be used by the programmer to deallocate the space with free() at some later time. If buf is not NULL, the pathname gets stored in the string pointed to by buf, and buf gets returned. In this case, it is the programmer's responsibility to make sure that buf points to enough space in memory to hold the pathname. If the call to getcwd() fails, NULL gets returned. If the failure is due to n not being large enough, then errno is set as well.

Random number generators

- `double drand48(void);`
  `long   lrand48(void);`

These are members of a family of random number generators that are generally available on UNIX systems. Their function prototypes are in *stdlib.h*. They implement a linear congruential algorithm with 48-bit arithmetic. The function drand48() returns a double. Repeated calls produce values uniformly distributed in the interval $[0, 1)$. The function lrand48() returns a long. Repeated calls produce values uniformly distributed in the interval $[0, 2^{31}]$.

- `void srand48(long seed);`

Seeds the random number generator for the rand48 family.

C LANGUAGE SYNTAX

In this appendix we give an extended BNF syntax for the ANSI version of the C language (see Section 2.2). This syntax, although intended for the human reader, is concisely written. The C language is inherently context-sensitive; restrictions and special cases are left to the main text. The conceptual output of the preprocessor is called a *translation unit*. The syntax of the C language pertains to translation units. The syntax for preprocessing directives is independent of the rest of the C language. We present it at the end of this appendix.

B.1 PROGRAM

program ::= { *file* }$_{1+}$
file ::= *decls_and_fct_definitions*
decls_and_fct_definitions ::= { *declaration* }$_{1+}$ *decls_and_fct_definitions$_{opt}$*
$\qquad$ | { *function_definition* }$_{1+}$ *decls_and_fct_definitions$_{opt}$*

B.2 FUNCTION DEFINITION

function_definition ::= { extern | static }$_{opt}$ *type_specifier*
$\qquad$ *function_name* (*parameter_declaration_list$_{opt}$*)
$\qquad$ *compound_statement*
function_name ::= *identifier*
parameter_declaration_list ::= *parameter_declaration* { , *parameter_declaration* }$_{0+}$

B.3 DECLARATION

declaration ::= *declaration_specifiers init_declarator_list$_{opt}$*
declaration_specifiers ::= *storage_class_specifier_or_typedef declaration_specifiers$_{opt}$*
$\qquad$ | *type_specifier declaration_specifiers$_{opt}$*
$\qquad$ | *type_qualifier declaration_specifiers$_{opt}$*

$storage\_class\_specifier\_or\_typedef$ ::= auto | extern | register | static
| typedef
$type\_specifier$ ::= char | double | float | int | long | short | signed
| unsigned
| void | $enum\_specifier$ | $struct\_or\_union\_specifier$
| $typedef\_name$
$enum\_specifier$ ::= enum tag_{opt} { $enumerator\_list$ } | enum tag
tag ::= $identifier$
$enumerator\_list$ ::= $enumerator$ { , $enumerator$ }$_{opt}$
$enumerator$ ::= $enumeration\_constant$ { = $const\_integral\_expr$ }$_{opt}$
$enumeration\_constant$ ::= $identifier$
$struct\_or\_union\_specifier$ ::= $struct\_or\_union$ tag_{opt} { $struct\_declaration\_list$ }
| $struct\_or\_union$ tag
$struct\_or\_union$ ::= struct | union
$struct\_declaration\_list$ ::= { $struct\_declaration$ }$_{1+}$
$struct\_declaration$ ::= $type\_specifier\_qualifier\_list$ $struct\_declarator\_list$;
$type\_specifier\_qualifier\_list$ ::= $type\_specifier$ $type\_specifier\_qualifier\_list$ $_{opt}$
| $type\_qualifier$ $type\_specifier\_qualifier\_list_{opt}$
$struct\_declarator\_list$ ::= $struct\_declarator$ { , $struct\_declarator$ }$_{0+}$
$struct\_declarator$ ::= $declarator$ | $declarator_{opt}$: $const\_integral\_expr$
$type\_qualifier$ ::= const | volatile
$declarator$ ::= $pointer_{opt}$ $direct\_declarator$
$pointer$ ::= { * | $type\_qualifier\_list_{opt}$ }$_{1+}$
$type\_qualifier\_list$ ::= { $type\_qualifier$ }$_{1+}$
$direct\_declarator$ ::= $identifier$ | ($declarator$)
| $direct\_declarator$ [$const\_integral\_expr_{opt}$]
| $direct\_declarator$ ($parameter\_type\_list$)
| $direct\_declarator$ ($identifier\_list_{opt}$)
$parameter\_type\_list$ ::= $parameter\_list$ | $parameter\_list$, ...
$parameter\_list$ ::= $parameter\_declaration$ { , $parameter\_declaration$ }$_{0+}$
$parameter\_declaration$ ::= $declaration\_specifiers$ $declarator$
| $declaration\_specifiers$ $abstract\_declarator_{opt}$
$abstract\_declarator$ ::= $pointer$ | $pointer_{opt}$ $direct\_abstract\_declarator$
$direct\_abstract\_declarator$ ::= ($abstract\_declarator$)
| $direct\_abstract\_declarator_{opt}$ [$const\_integral\_expr_{opt}$]
| $direct\_abstract\_declarator_{opt}$ ($parameter\_type\_list_{opt}$)
$identifier\_list$ ::= $identifier$ { , $identifier$}$_{0+}$
$typedef\_name$ ::= $identifier$
$init\_declarator\_list$ ::= $init\_declarator$ { , $init\_declarator$ }$_{opt}$
$init\_declarator$ ::= $declarator$ | $declarator$ = $initializer$
$initializer$ ::= $assignment\_expr$ | { $initializer\_list$ } | { $initializer\_list$, }
$initializer\_list$ ::= $initializer$ { , $initializer$ }$_{0+}$

B.4   STATEMENT

statement ::= *compound_statement* | *expr_statement* | *iteration_statement*
                  | *jump_statement* | *labeled_statement* | *selection_statement*
compound_statement ::= { *declaration_list*$_{opt}$ *statement_list*$_{opt}$ }
declaration_list ::= { *declaration* }$_{1+}$
statement_list ::= { *statement* }$_{1+}$
expr_statement ::= *expr*$_{opt}$;
jump_statement ::= break ; | continue ; | goto *identifier* ;
                      | return *expr*$_{opt}$;
labeled_statement ::= *identifier* : *statement*
                         | case *const_integral_expr* : *statement*
                         | default : *statement*
selection_statement ::= if (*expr*) *statement*
                           | if (*expr*) *statement* else *statement*
                           | *switch_statement*
switch_statement ::= switch (*integral_expr*)
                         { *case_statement* | default : *statement* | *switch_block* }$_1$
case_statement ::= { case *const_integral_expr* : }$_{1+}$ *statement*
switch_block ::= { { *declaration_list* }$_{opt}$ *case_default_group* }
case_default_group ::= { *case_group* }$_{1+}$
                          | { *case_group* }$_{0+}$ *default_group* { *case_group* }$_{0+}$
case_group ::= { case *const_integral_expr* : }$_{1+}$ { *statement* }$_{1+}$
default_group ::= default : { *statement* }$_{1+}$

B.5   EXPRESSION

expr ::= *constant* | *string_literal* | (*expr*) | *lvalue*
          | *assignment_expr* | *expr* , *expr* | + *expr*
          | - *expr* | *function_expr* | *relational_expr*
          | *equality_expr* | *logical_expr*
          | *expr* *arithmetic_op* *expr* | *bitwise_expr*
          | *expr* ? *expr* : *expr* | sizeof *expr*
          | sizeof (*type_name*) | (*type_name*) *expr*
lvalue ::= & *lvalue* | ++ *lvalue* | *lvalue* ++ | -- *lvalue* | *lvalue* --
           | *identifier* | * *expr* | *lvalue* [*expr*] | (*lvalue*)
           | *lvalue* . *identifier* | *lvalue* -> *identifier*
assignment_expr ::= *lvalue* *assignment_op* *expr*
assignment_op ::= = | += | -= | *= | /= | %= | &= | ^= | |= | >>= | <<=
arithmetic_op ::= + | - | * | / | %
relational_expr ::= *expr* < *expr* | *expr* > *expr*
                       | *expr* <= *expr* | *expr* >= *expr*

equality_expr ::= *expr* **==** *expr* | *expr* **!=** *expr*
logical_expr ::= **!** *expr* | *expr* **||** *expr* | *expr* **&&** *expr*
bitwise_expr ::= **~** *expr* | **∧** *expr*
      | *expr* **&** *expr* | *expr* **|** *expr*
      | *expr* **<<** *expr* | *expr* **>>** *expr*
function_expr ::= *function_name*(*argument_list$_{opt}$*)
       | (***** *pointer*) (*argument_list$_{opt}$*)
argument_list ::= *expr* {**,** *expr*}$_{0+}$
type_name ::= *type_specifier declarator$_{opt}$*

B.6 CONSTANT

constant ::= *character_constant* | *enumeration_constant* | *floating_constant*
     | *integer_constant*
character_constant ::= **'** *c* **'** | **L'** *c* **'**
c ::= any character from the source character set except **'** or **** or *newline*
   | *escape_sequence*
escape_sequence ::= **\'** | **\"** | **\?** | **** | **\a** | **\b** | **\f** | **\n** | **\r** | **\t** | **\v**
        | **** *octal_digit octal_digit$_{opt}$ octal_digit$_{opt}$*
        | **\x** *hexadecimal_digit* { *hexadecimal_digit* }$_{0+}$
enumeration_constant ::= *identifier*
floating_constant ::= *fractional_constant exponential_part$_{opt}$ floating_suffix$_{opt}$*
         digit_sequence exponential_part floating_suffix$_{opt}$
fractional_constant ::= *digit_sequence$_{opt}$* **.** *digit_sequence* | *digit_sequence* **.**
digit_sequence ::= { *digit* }$_{1+}$
digit ::= **0** | **1** | **2** | **3** | **4** | **5** | **6** | **7** | **8** | **9**
exponential_part ::= { **e** | **E** }$_1$ { **+** | **-** }$_{opt}$ *digit_sequence*
floating_suffix ::= **f** | **F** | **l** | **L**
integer_constant ::= *decimal_constant integer_suffix$_{opt}$*
       | *octal_constant integer_suffix$_{opt}$*
       | *hexadecimal_constant integer_suffix$_{opt}$*
decimal_constant ::= **0** | *nonzero_digit digit_sequence*
nonzero_digit ::= **1** | **2** | **3** | **4** | **5** | **6** | **7** | **8** | **9**
octal_constant ::= **0** { *octal_digit* }$_{0+}$
octal_digit ::= **0** | **1** | **2** | **3** | **4** | **5** | **6** | **7**
hexadecimal_constant ::= { **0x** | **0X** }$_1$ { *hexadecimal_digit* }$_{1+}$
hexadecimal_digit ::= **0** | **1** | **2** | **3** | **4** | **5** | **6** | **7** | **8** | **9**
         | **a** | **b** | **c** | **d** | **e** | **f** | **A** | **B** | **C** | **D** | **E** | **F**
integer_suffix ::= *unsigned_suffix long_suffix$_{opt}$* | *long_suffix unsigned_suffix$_{opt}$*
unsigned_suffix ::= **u** | **U**
long_suffix ::= **l** | **L**

B.7   STRING LITERAL

string_literal ::= "*s_char_sequence*" | L"*s_char_sequence*"
s_char_sequence ::= { *sc* }$_{1+}$
sc ::= any character from the source character set except " or \ or *newline*
      | *escape_sequence*

B.8   PREPROCESSOR

preprocessing_directive ::= *control_line newline* | *if_section* | *pp_token newline*
control_line ::= # include { <*identifier*> | "*identifier*" }
               | # undef *identifier* | # line *pp_token* | # error *pp_token*
               | # pragma *pp_token*
               | # define *identifier* {(*identifier_list*)}$_{opt}$ { *pp_token* }$_{0+}$
pp_token ::= *identifier* | *constant* | *string_literal* | *operator* | *punctuator*
            | *pp_token* ## *pp_token* | # *identifier*
if_section ::= *if_group* { *elif_group* }$_{0+}$ { *else_group* }$_{opt}$ *end_if_line*
if_group ::= # if *const_integral_expr newline preprocessing_directive*$_{opt}$
            | # ifdef *identifier newline* { *preprocessing_directive* }$_{opt}$
            | # ifndef *identifier newline* { *preprocessing_directive* }$_{opt}$
elif_group ::= # elif *constant_expr newline* { *preprocessing_directive* }$_{opt}$
else_group ::= # else *newline* { *preprocessing_directive* }$_{opt}$
end_if_line ::= # endif *newline*
newline ::= the newline character

DIFFERENCES: ANSI C COMPARED TO TRADITIONAL C

In this appendix we list the major differences between ANSI C and traditional C. Where appropriate, we have included examples. The list is not complete. Only the major changes are noted.

C.1 TYPES

- The keyword `signed` has been added to the language.

- Three types of characters are specified: plain `char`, `signed char`, and `unsigned char`. An implementation may represent a plain `char` as either a `signed char` or an `unsigned char`.

- The keyword `signed` can be used in declarations of any of the signed integral types and in casts. Except with `char`, its use is always optional.

- In traditional C, the type `long float` is equivalent to `double`. Because `long float` was rarely used, it has been removed from ANSI C.

- The type `long double` has been added to ANSI C. Constants of this type are specified with the suffix L. A `long double` may provide more precision and range than a `double`, but it is not required to do so.

- The keyword `void` is used to indicate that a function takes no arguments, or that a function returns no value.

- The type `void *` is used for generic pointers. For example, the function prototype for `malloc()` is given by

```
void    *malloc(size_t size);
```

A generic pointer can be assigned a pointer value of any type, and a variable of any pointer type can be assigned a generic pointer value. Casts are not needed. In contrast, the "generic" pointer type in traditional C is `char *`. Here, casts are necessary.

■   Enumeration types are supported. An example is

```
enum day {sun, mon, tue, wed, thu, fri, sat};
```

The enumerators in this example are `sun`, `mon`, ... , `sat`. Enumerators are constants of type `int`. They can be used in `case` labels in `switch` statements.

■   The header files *float.h* and *limits.h* contain macro definitions describing implementation characteristics. ANSI C requires that certain minimum values and ranges must be supported for each arithmetic type.

C.2   CONSTANTS

■   String constants separated by white space are concatenated. Thus

```
"abc"
"def" "ghi"        is equivalent to        "abcdefghi"
```

■   String constants are not modifiable. (Not all compilers enforce this.)
■   The type of a numeric constant can be specified by letter suffixes. Some examples are

```
123L        /* long          */
123U        /* unsigned      */
123UL       /* unsigned long */
1.23F       /* float         */
1.23L       /* long double   */
```

Suffixes may be lower- or uppercase. A numeric constant without a suffix is a type big enough to contain the value.

■   The digits 8 and 9 are no longer considered octal digits. They may not be used in an octal constant.
■   Hexadecimal escape sequences beginning with \x have been introduced. As with octal escape sequences beginning with \0, they are used in character and string constants.

C.3   DECLARATIONS

■   The type qualifier `const` has been added. It means that variables so declared are not modifiable. (Compilers do not always enforce this.)

- The type qualifier `volatile` has been added. It means that variables so declared are modifiable by an agent external to the program. For example, some systems put the declaration

  ```
  extern volatile int   errno;
  ```

  in the header file *errno.h*.

C.4 INITIALIZATIONS

- In ANSI C, automatic aggregates such as arrays and structures can be initialized. In traditional C, they must be external or of storage class `static`.
- Unions can be initialized. An initialization refers to the first member of the union.
- Character arrays of size n can be initialized using a string literal of exactly n characters. The implied string terminator \0 is forgotten. An example is

  ```
  char   today[3] = "Tue";
  ```

C.5 EXPRESSIONS

- For reasons of symmetry, a unary plus operator has been added to the language.
- In traditional C, expressions involving one of the commutative binary operators such as + or * can be reordered at the convenience of the compiler, even though they have been parenthesized in the program. For example, in the statement

  ```
  x = (a + b) + c;
  ```

  the variables can be summed by the compiler in some unspecified order. In ANSI C, this is not true. The parentheses must be honored.
- A pointer to a function can be dereferenced either explicitly or implicitly. If, for example, f is a pointer to a function that takes three arguments, then the expression

  ```
  f(a, b, c)      is equivalent to      (*f)(a, b, c)
  ```

- The `sizeof` operator yields a value of type `size_t`. The type definition for `size_t` is given in *stddef.h*.
- A pointer of type `void *` cannot be dereferenced without first casting it to an appropriate type. However, it can be used in logical expressions, where it is compared to another pointer.

C.6 FUNCTIONS

■ ANSI C provides a new function definition syntax. A parameter declaration list occurs in the parentheses following the function name. An example is

```
int f(int a, float b)
{
    .....
```

In contrast, the traditional C style is

```
int f(a, b)
int    a;
float  b;
{
    .....
```

■ The function prototype, which is a new style of function declaration, is provided. A parameter type list occurs in the parentheses following the function name. Identifiers are optional. For example,

```
int f(int, float);      and      int f(int a, float b);
```

are equivalent function prototypes. In contrast, the traditional C style is

```
int    f();
```

If a function has a variable number of arguments, then ellipses are used as the right-most argument. If it takes no arguments, then void is used (see Chapter 5).

■ Redeclaring a parameter identifier in the outer block of a function definition is illegal. The following code illustrates the error:

```
void f(int a, int b, int c)
{
    int    a;      /* error: a cannot be redefined here */

    .....
```

■ Structures and unions can be passed as arguments to functions, and they can be returned from functions. The passing mechanism is "call by value," which means that a local copy is made.

C.7 CONVERSIONS

- An expression of type `float` is not automatically converted to a `double`.
- When arguments to functions are evaluated, the resulting value is converted to the type specified by the function prototype, provided the conversion is compatible. Otherwise, a syntax error occurs.
- Arithmetic conversions are more carefully specified (see Section 3.11).
- The resulting type of a shift operation is not dependent on the right operand. In ANSI C, the integral promotions are performed on each operand, and the type of the result is that of the promoted left operand.

C.8 STRUCTURES AND UNIONS

- Structures and unions can be used in assignments. If `s1` and `s2` are two structure variables of the same type, the expression `s1 = s2` is valid. Values of members in `s2` are copied into corresponding members of `s1`.
- Structures and unions can be passed as arguments to functions, and they can be returned from functions. All arguments to functions, including structures and unions, are passed "call by value."
- If `m` is a member of a structure or union and the function call `f()` returns a structure or union of the same type, then the expression `f().m` is valid.
- Structures and unions can be used with the comma operator and in conditional expressions. Some examples are

```
int        a, b;
struct s   s1, s2, s3;

. . . . .
(a, s1)            /* comma expr having structure type */
a < b ? s1 : s2    /* conditional expr having structure type */
```

- If *expr* is a structure or union expression and `m` is a member, then an expression of the form *expr*.`m` is valid. However, *expr*.`m` can be assigned a value only if *expr* can. Even though expressions such as

```
(s1 = s2).m     (a, s1).m     (a < b ? s1 : s2).m     f().m
```

are valid, they cannot occur on the left side of an assignment operator.

C.9 PREPROCESSOR

■ Preprocessing directives do not have to begin in column 1.

■ The following predefined macros have been added:

　　__DATE__　　　__FILE__　　　__LINE__　　　__STDC__　　　__TIME__

(see Section 8.9).

■ A macro may not be redefined without first undefining it. Multiple definitions are allowed, provided they are the same.

■ The preprocessor operators # and ## have been added. The unary operator # causes "stringization" of a formal parameter in a macro definition. The binary operator ## merges tokens (see Section 8.10).

■ The preprocessor operator defined has been added (see Section 8.8).

■ The preprocessing directives #elif, #error, and #pragma have been added (see Sections 8.8 and 8.12).

C.10 MISCELLANEOUS

■ In traditional C, the operators += and =+ are synonymous, although the use of =+ is considered old-fashioned. In ANSI C, the use of =+, =*, and so on is not allowed.

■ Each of the following has a distinct name space: label identifiers, variable identifiers, tag names, member names for each structure and union. All tags for enum, struct, and union comprise a single name space.

■ Two identifiers are considered distinct if they differ within the first n characters, where n must be at least 31.

■ The expression controlling a switch statement can be any integral type. Floating types are not allowed. The constant integral expression in a case label can be any integral type, including an enumerator.

■ Pointers and ints are not interchangeable. Only the integer 0 can be assigned to a pointer without a cast.

■ Pointer expressions may point to one element beyond an allocated array.

■ External declarations and linkage rules are more carefully defined.

■ Many changes have been made to the standard library and its associated header files.

ASCII CHARACTER CODES

ASCII: American Standard Code for Information Interchange Left\Right Digits	0	1	2	3	4	5	6	7	8	9
0	nul	soh	stx	etx	eot	enq	ack	bel	bs	ht
1	nl	vt	np	cr	so	si	dle	dcl	dc2	dc3
2	dc4	nak	syn	etb	can	em	sub	esc	fs	gs
3	rs	us	sp	!	"	#	$	%	&	'
4	(	)	*	+	,	-	.	/	0	1
5	2	3	4	5	6	7	8	9	:	;
6	<	=	>	?	@	A	B	C	D	E
7	F	G	H	I	J	K	L	M	N	O
8	P	Q	R	S	T	U	V	W	X	Y
9	Z	[	\	]	^	_	'	a	b	c
10	d	e	f	g	h	i	j	k	l	m
11	n	o	p	q	r	s	t	u	v	w
12	x	y	z	{	|	}	~	del		

Some observations

1   Character codes 0-31 and 127 are nonprinting.
2   Character code 32 prints a single space.
3   Character codes for digits 0 through 9 are contiguous.
4   Character codes for letters A through Z are contiguous.
5   Character codes for letters a through z are contiguous.
6   The difference between a capital letter and the corresponding lowercase letter is 32.

The meaning of some of the abbreviations

bel	audible bell	ht	horizontal tab
bs	backspace	nl	newline
cr	carriage return	nul	null
esc	escape	vt	vertical tab

OPERATOR PRECEDENCE AND ASSOCIATIVITY

Operators	Associativity
() [] . -> ++ (*postfix*) -- (*postfix*)	left to right
++ (*prefix*) -- (*prefix*) ! ~ sizeof (*type*) + (*unary*) - (*unary*) & (*address*) * (*dereference*)	right to left
* / %	left to right
+ -	left to right
<< >>	left to right
< <= > >=	left to right
== !=	left to right
&	left to right
^	left to right
|	left to right
&&	left to right
||	left to right
?:	right to left
= += -= *= /= %= >>= <<= &= ^= |=	right to left
, (*comma operator*)	left to right

INDEX